TWENTY LESSONS IN
ENVIRONMENTAL SOCIOLOGY

Kenneth A. Gould
Brooklyn College of the City University of New York

Tammy L. Lewis
Muhlenberg College

New York   Oxford

OXFORD UNIVERSITY PRESS

2009

Oxford University Press, Inc., publishes works that further Oxford University's objective of excellence in research, scholarship, and education.

Oxford   New York
Auckland   Cape Town   Dar es Salaam   Hong Kong   Karachi   Kuala Lumpur
Madrid   Melbourne   Mexico City   Nairobi   New Delhi   Shanghai   Taipei   Toronto

With offices in
Argentina   Austria   Brazil   Chile   Czech Republic   France   Greece   Guatemala
Hungary   Italy   Japan   Poland   Portugal   Singapore   South Korea   Switzerland
Thailand   Turkey   Ukraine   Vietnam

Published by Oxford University Press, Inc.
198 Madison Avenue, New York, New York 10016
http://www.oup.com

Oxford is a registered trademark of Oxford University Press

Library of Congress Cataloging-in-Publication Data

Gould, Kenneth Alan.
    Twenty lessons in environmental sociology / Kenneth A. Gould & Tammy
L. Lewis.-- 1st ed.
        p. cm.

    ISBN-13: 978-0-19-537112-3 (pbk. : alk. paper)   1. Environmentalism--
Social aspects. 2. Human ecology.   3. Nature--Effect of human beings
on.   I. Lewis, Tammy L.   II. Title.
    GE195.G68   2008
    304.2--dc22

                                                                    2008004252

To Anna and Isabel

Contents

Annotated Table of Contents

at the keyboard of a computer, making a fast connection on the Internet; and a person physically dismantling a computer that has been "thrown away" in the United States and exported to an "e-waste processing center" in another country. Although these snapshots are only three out of many possibilities, they offer an excellent opportunity to connect structures across time and space and to learn about the insights and creative uses of theory in environmental sociology.

3. Theories in Environmental Sociology   25

Luiz C. Barbosa

This lesson explains the development and content of major theoretical approaches in the field of environmental sociology. It begins by providing a working definition of theory and an explanation of the utility of theoretical models. It then addresses the lack of emphasis on the environment in early sociological theories. It traces the beginnings of environmental sociology to concerns about the state of the environment, developments in ecology, and the rise of environmentalism in the 1960s and 1970s. Sociologists responded to these with calls for adoption of a "new ecological paradigm" in the discipline. This led to attempts to revise existing theories and to the development of new ones based specifically on the relationship between human societies and the environment. This discussion deals with theories of opposing political or ideological persuasions in the field including the treadmill of production, world systems, ecological modernization, green capitalism, second modernity, and risk society.

Part 2   Systemic Causes of Environmental Disruption

4. The State and Policy: Imperialism, Exclusion, and Ecological Violence as State Policy   47

David Naguib Pellow

This lesson explores the role of the U.S. nation-state as an institution that embraces and advances the causes of imperialism, racism, and environmental harm. Drawing on theories of the state, environment, and social inequality, the lesson explores how this dynamic emerged in history and then applies it to several cases. The author therefore recasts or reconsiders state imperialist policy as environmental policy, rather than examining practices that are formally defined as environmental. In this way, we might locate the deeper institutional and cultural roots of the environmental state and, in turn, think through a different set of questions that might push for reform or transformation of those practices. For example, instead of seeking to simply strengthen regulation of polluting industries that are in poor neighborhoods and communities of color, one might push for a greater democratization of the state and industry through the activation of civil society and social movements.

Increasing labor productivity has come to be viewed by political, economic, and academic elites as a panacea for economic progress. Yet this perspective represents only one view of increasing production by workers. The mechanisms by which labor productivity is achieved typically include substantial labor reduction, involving downsizing and shifts of the benefits of productivity away from workers and consumers and toward investors and senior management. Moreover, because replacing human labor with mechanical, chemical, and electronic technologies often requires heightened use of energy and water and increased disposal of wastes into natural systems, ecological disruption is typically associated with growing productivity through changes in production technology.

Transnational corporations (TNCs) are the most dominant and powerful social actors in the global political economy. Their main goal is to access markets, cheap labor and resources in order to maximize their profit margin. They have been successful in eroding local, national, and regional environmental and labor protection mechanisms through powerful special interest groups that lobby governments and global institutions. In many cases TNCs have more political and economic power than developing countries in places like sub-Saharan Africa and South and East Asia. In the absence of strong state regulations, TNC power in the twenty-first century has served to undermine social welfare benefits, job security, and environmental standards. This has not been widely reported in the global news media since the media is increasingly controlled by these same TNCs. It is not in the interests of TNCs to critique the social and environmental consequences of their growing influence in the global economy. Corporate control over news and information strongly shapes what the public knows and does not know about key social and environmental issues.

Concerns about science are central to the field of environmental sociology because it relies on scientific knowledge of the natural world to identify and understand environmental problems and because science, particularly in its link to technological development, has generated and expanded many of the ecological crises of the modern world. Here, the author distinguishes between the logic of science, which is based on the combination of rationalist and empiricist philosophies of knowledge, and the establishment of science, the social institutions that actually carry out scientific work. Environmental sociology appropriately relies on the logic of science to understand the human–environment interaction, but it is critical of the establishment of science, which is in many ways controlled by the ruling class and has frequently contributed to social and environmental problems, rather than helping to alleviate them. Thus, environmental sociologists study how scientific claims about the environment are influenced by social forces and contested by various interests as well as how the risks associated with new technologies are assessed.

A key factor in the way that societies establish their interactions with ecosystems is the choice of technologies they use and the ways that they use them. Throughout human history, technological change has led to significant, sometimes dramatic, changes in the relationship between social systems and ecosystems. Because of the importance of technological change and technological choice in establishing patterns of social system–ecosystem relationships, we need to understand how technological innovation alters social systems and ecosystems and how and why societies develop and implement new technologies. This lesson looks back at major epochs in the technological transformation of society–environment dynamics and explores the interests of the social institutions that most affect the direction of technological change.

The connection between human population and environmental quality has interested social theorists since Malthus posited that unchecked population growth would lead to famine, disease, and warfare. Neo-Malthusians incorporate much of Malthus' model to describe a linear, negative relationship between human population growth and environmental quality that can be modified through increasing food supply, such as with green revolution technologies, or through lowering birth rates, as with the demographic transition. Ehrlich's Neo-Malthusian model ($I = PAT$) takes into account how the environmental impact (I) of population growth (P) is mediated by affluence (A) and technology (T). Other social theorists question whether population growth even has a linear relationship with environmental impact. How and where people live creates different patterns of environmental impact, as does control over the distribution of resources. Concerns about population growth may also mask political uneasiness over social difference and inequality. Both linear and nonlinear models can describe the relationship between population growth and deforestation in Ecuador; this case demonstrates how more complex analysis calls into question the universality of the relationship between human population growth and environmental quality.

Part 3 Some Social Consequences of Environmental Disruption

10. Environmental Inequality and Environmental Justice   127

Michael Mascarenhas

Over the past several decades, public health researchers, activists, and policymakers have devoted a great deal of attention to understanding the social dimensions of environmental injustice. More recently, some scholars and health researchers have begun to explore the role of neoliberalist policies as a major contributing factor in the production of environmental injustices. Using examples from the U.S. and Canada, this lesson explores the intersection between these two concepts. In this lesson the author argues that neoliberalism has contributed to the political and economic justifications for the siting and growth of dirty industries in minority, indigenous, and low-income communities. In fact, he asserts that neoliberalism and contemporary environmental and social injustices are now different sides of the same coin.

11. The Sociology of Environmental Health   142

Sabrina McCormick

This lesson presents the field of environmental health and the obstacles that impede better address of it. This includes conflicts between the biomedical model and broader public health paradigms. It reviews several landmark cases that have shaped our understanding of environmental illness and reviews how tragedies and chronic mishaps reveal the way that toxins in our environment cause illness. To exemplify some of the obstacles to understanding and dealing with environmental illness, this lesson describes illnesses caused by heat waves—a critical issue that exemplifies how environmental conditions affect human health. Ultimately, the cases discussed demonstrate how those who suffer environmental illness often first make connections between health and the environment. In order for them to gain compensation for their losses and to stop these exposures, public officials must also accept their claims. These instances reflect power differences based on race, class, and gender, as well as macro-level structures in society.

Farms do not leap to mind as significant polluters. Yet, non-point source pollution from agriculture and especially livestock operations may now be the largest contaminant of America's waterways. This lesson explores how agriculture has become such a source of pollution by examining the case of the pork industry in North Carolina. First, the authors describe recent changes in the pork industry, focusing on the implementation of confined animal feeding operations for pork production and "lagoon and sprayfield" technologies for waste disposal. The concept of "externalities of scale" is introduced, referring to a constellation of adverse economic, social, and environmental impacts resulting from contemporary pork production and waste disposal practices that did not exist in the past. Exploring this issue further, the authors discuss the social and environmental impacts of contemporary pork production. They explain the change in the structure and ownership of pork production, showing how one multinational corporation came to own or control over 90% of all pork production, slaughtering, and processing in North Carolina. The concluding section examines the different roles state government played and describes the diverse social movement that pushed for and won greater environmental protections.

Flood and hurricane vulnerability is not simply the result of "natural" forces. It is, rather, a complex combination of human activities and cultural beliefs that take place within dynamic pre-existing physical environments. Municipal "growth machines" tend to downplay or ignore their communities' disaster risks in order to encourage more "economic development," which serves to increase long-term disaster vulnerability. This is often accomplished via an overreliance on structural mitigation techniques such as levees and floodwalls and a refusal to seriously consider the environmental issues associated with development in floodplains and coastal areas. People with lower socioeconomic status, such as minorities, the poor, women, children, and the elderly, are more vulnerable to catastrophic disaster impacts than those with more resources for a variety of reasons. The impact of Hurricane Katrina on New Orleans provides a wealth of examples of how the interplay of these cultural, social, and physical dynamics can result in a widespread catastrophe.

Climate change appears to be a problem caused by all people and requiring all to act equally, but there has been extreme inequality in who caused it and who will suffer most its consequences. The Kyoto Protocol is limping along without commitments from major emitters like the United States, Australia, China, and India, so a workable solution to the problem has not yet been found. This lesson reviews some basics on climate change and efforts to address it and combines these with some key insights from environmental justice and environmental sociology that might help move us forward together in addressing the problem. The author argues that inequality and development must be addressed together with environmental issues. Also explored are the extent and types of inequality in the climate issue and how our failure to address the inequality in global income and development prospects is making it impossible for the negotiations on the issue to move ahead. Without an open discussion about who caused it and what addressing it fairly would entail, many people will resist movement on climate change. Informed citizens need to understand the complexity of the problem and possible solutions, and they need to be included in efforts at addressing it meaningfully and fairly.

The U.S. environmental movement is perhaps the largest, most long-lived, and complex social movement in the United States. To understand this movement from a sociological viewpoint requires an analysis of the different belief systems or "discursive frames" that define the different communities that make up this movement. This lesson starts with a description of these discursive frames. Using this perspective, it then describes the historical development of the different communities and their relative levels of economic resource mobilization.

environmental conditions. Whether or not people are "closer to nature" in their ideologies, the author argues that environmental practices that contribute to resilience and possibilities for replenishment are also dependent upon types of environmental knowledge that emphasize balance, connectedness, interdependence, responsibility, and continuity. Not only do many forms of environmental relationships found among contemporary indigenous peoples deserve greater respect and legal status, but the author contends that the forms of "ecological wisdom" they practice should become a commonplace element of Western environmental thought and practice for decision makers and public citizens.

This lesson begins with a discussion of the always multiple, sometimes vague, and oft-conflicting definitions of "sustainable development." The authors connect this profusion of viewpoints to the inevitable tensions between the three basic goals of such development: economic growth, environmental protection, and social equity. The lesson then uses two detailed examples of ecotourism in Belize to illustrate these trade-offs and highlight how and by whom decisions regarding the goals of sustainable development are made. Three primary critical perspectives on sustainable development—free market environmentalism, policy/reformist, and critical structural—are also described and applied to the state of ecotourism in Belize.

In the concluding lesson, interlinking themes from throughout the book are briefly highlighted and analyzed. The authors then suggest areas of research that need to be pursued by environmental sociologists in the future and address concerns about what can practically be accomplished in the present. The lesson concludes with 20 wide-ranging questions for students to contemplate as they continue both their study of environmental sociology and their participation in the contemporary social, political, and environmental worlds.

Acknowledgments

We thank the people of Akwesasne for grounding us in the reality of what it means to be engaged in the struggle for physical, social, cultural, and environmental health.

Thanks also to our colleagues Jeff Broadbent, Stella Čapek, and Mike Mascarenhas for convincing us of the need for a book such as this.

Over the years, our students at Muhlenberg College, St. Lawrence University, and Brooklyn College have inspired us to create effective means to communicate the importance of sociology in understanding environmental issues.

For encouragement, enthusiasm, and cheese, we thank our editor at Oxford University Press, Sherith Pankratz.

Finally, for their ongoing support, Tammy thanks Jane Schoeneck and Ken thanks Carole Mehlman.

About the Contributors

Luiz C. Barbosa is professor of sociology at San Francisco State University. He is also affiliated with the Environmental Studies Program at the same institution. He is the author of several journal articles on the Brazilian Amazon rain forest, focusing on the effects of globalization, development, ideology, and environmental mobilization on both preservation and deforestation. He is also the author of the book *The Brazilian Amazon Rainforest: Global Ecopolitics, Development, and Democracy.*

Diane C. Bates is associate professor of sociology at The College of New Jersey, where she teaches courses in environmental sociology, research methods, and social change in Latin America. Raised along the Mississippi River in central Minnesota, she completed her bachelor's degree in northern California at Humboldt State University. She earned her Ph.D. at Rutgers University, where she began to document social and environmental changes in the southern Amazonian region of Ecuador in 1996. Her research has since been published in a variety of journals, including *Society & Natural Resources, Latin American Research Review, Latin American Press, Rural Sociology,* and *Ecuador Debate.* She is currently compiling new data from Ecuador and completing investigations with undergraduate researchers of communities affected by the Delaware River floods and a contaminated elementary school site in Trenton, New Jersey. She is a volunteer for the Delaware RiverKeeper Network and Community in Action–the North Trenton Civic Association.

Robert J. Brulle is an associate professor of sociology and environmental science in the Department of Culture and Communications and an affiliate associate professor of public health in the School of Public Health at Drexel University in Philadelphia, Pennsylvania. His research focuses on the U.S. environmental movement, critical theory, and public participation in environmental policy making. He is the author of over two dozen articles in these areas and of *Agency, Democracy and the Environment: The U.S. Environmental Movement from the Perspective of Critical Theory,* as well as coeditor, with David Pellow, of *Power, Justice and the Environment.*

Elizabeth H. Campbell received her Ph.D. from Binghamton University. Her dissertation focused on urban refugee protection, livelihoods, and possibilities for local integration. She has published her findings in the *Journal of Refugee Studies*, in *Refugee Survey Quarterly*, and for the Global Commission on International Migration, as well as other edited book collections. Her second area of focus is environmental sociology. As a graduate student, she designed and developed several courses on political economy, development and ecology, and human rights. As a Fulbright Scholar, she was based at the office of the United Nations High Commissioner for Refugees in Nairobi. She also worked on two separate occasions in Kakuma Refugee Camp in Kenya. Prior to that she worked for a monthly news magazine at the Alternative Information Center in Jerusalem. She is currently the Director of Refugee Council USA, a coalition of 23 nongovernmental organizations focused on refugee policy that is based in Washington, D.C.

Stella M. Čapek is professor of sociology in the Department of Sociology/ Anthropology at Hendrix College. She has a B.A. from Boston University and an M.A. and Ph.D. in sociology from the University of Texas at Austin. She teaches courses on Environmental Sociology; Social Change/Social Movements; Medical Sociology; Urban/Community Sociology; Images of the City; Gender and Family; Food, Culture, and Nature; and Sociological Theory. She is especially interested in interdisciplinary environmental studies, environmental justice, ecological identity, social constructions of nature, and sustainable community design. She has published articles on environmental justice, tenants' rights, urban/community issues, local interactions with wildlife, and health and environment. She has taught about sustainability and ecotourism in Costa Rica and in the U.S. Southwest. She has coauthored two books, *Community Versus Commodity: Tenants and the American City* and *Come Lovely and Soothing Death: The Right to Die Movement in the United States*

Adam Driscoll is a doctoral student in the Department of Sociology and Anthropology at North Carolina State University in Raleigh. He received his M.A. in sociology from East Carolina University and his B.S. in biology from Drexel University. He is currently studying environmental, economic, and political sociology. His goals are to better understand the macrolevel structures and institutions that govern and influence the distribution of wealth and power on both a national and global scale. He is the coauthor, along with Bob Edwards, of the forthcoming article "Economic Efficiency Leads to Environmental Inequality: An Analysis of the North Carolina Swine Industry."

Bob Edwards is associate professor of sociology and coastal resources management at East Carolina University in Greenville, North Carolina. He received his Ph.D. in sociology in 1995 from The Catholic University of America. A desire to understand the social organization of inequality integrates his research on social movements, organizations, and civil society with his work on environmentalism, environmental inequality, and natural hazards, as well as an emerging agenda on the impacts of coastal development and gentrification. He has published over 40 refereed articles and chapters. His work has appeared in the *American Sociological Review, Social Forces, Annual Review of Sociology,* and *Journal of Democracy* and he is coeditor of *Beyond Tocqueville: Civil Society and the Social Capital Debate in Comparative Perspective.* His research has been funded by grants from the National Science Foundation, National Oceanic and Atmospheric Administration, International Research Exchange, Federal Emergency Management Agency, North Carolina Division of Emergency Management, Natural Hazards Research and Applications Information Center, and North Carolina Sea Grant.

Kenneth A. Gould is professor and chair of sociology at Brooklyn College of the City University of New York (CUNY) and professor of sociology and earth and environmental sciences at the CUNY Graduate Center. His work in the political economy of environment, technology, and development examines the responses of communities to environmental problems, environmental social movement coalitions, the role of socioeconomic inequality in environmental conflicts, and the impacts of economic globalization on efforts to achieve ecologically and socially sustainable development trajectories. He is coauthor of *Environment and Society: The Enduring Conflict, Local Environmental Struggles: Citizen Activism in the Treadmill of Production,* and *The Treadmill of Production: Injustice and Unsustainability in the Global Economy.*

Tammy L. Lewis is associate professor in the Department of Sociology and Anthropology at Muhlenberg College and currently holds the Carol Zicklin Chair in the Brooklyn College Honors Academy. She studies transnational social movements, with a focus on Latin America, most recently as a Fulbright Scholar in Ecuador. She is coauthor of *Environment, Energy, and Society* with Craig R. Humphrey and Frederick H. Buttel. Her work has appeared in *Social Science Quarterly, Mobilization, Teaching Sociology,* and *The Chronicle of Higher Education.* She has been a council member of the Environment and Technology section of the American Sociological Association and served as Reviews Editor for *Society and Natural Resources.* She currently serves on the board of the Society for Conservation Biology's Social Science Working Group.

Michael Mascarenhas is an assistant professor in the Science and Technology Studies Department at Rensselaer Polytechnic Institute. He earned his doctorate in sociology from Michigan State University in 2005. He also holds graduate degrees in forestry and environmental science. In over a dozen publications, he has written on water, wolves, seed saving, standards, supermarkets, family farms, and forests. In short, his work examines the social inequalities and environmental injustices embedded within the practices, policies, and discourses of technoscience and nature.

Sabrina McCormick is on leave from her position as assistant professor of sociology and environmental science and policy at Michigan State University in order to be a Robert Wood Johnson Health and Society Scholar at the

University of Pennsylvania. Her areas of expertise include environmental health, social movements, and science studies. Her first book, *No Family History*, describes the political economy of breast cancer prevention and cure campaigns. Her current research focus is the political, scientific, and economic factors that shape efforts to address public health impacts of climate change.

Brian K. Obach is an associate professor of sociology at the State University of New York at New Paltz. His areas of specialization include social movements, environmental sociology, and political economy. He is the author of *Labor and the Environmental Movement: The Quest for Common Ground*, in which he examines the promise and pitfalls of crossmovement alliance building. His current research focuses on the organic agriculture movement and on whether a grassroots effort to forge an alternative agriculture system can resist cooptation by corporate agribusiness. He is active with his faculty union and participates in local environmental struggles. He plays rhythm guitar and sings with the all-faculty rock band Questionable Authorities.

David Naguib Pellow is professor of sociology at the University of Minnesota. His teaching and research focus on environmental justice issues in communities of color in the United States and globally. His books include *The Treadmill of Production: Injustice and Unsustainability in the Global Economy* (with Kenneth Gould and Allan Schnaiberg), *Resisting Global Toxics: Transnational Movements for Environmental Justice*, *The Silicon Valley of Dreams: Environmental Injustice, Immigrant Workers, and the High-Tech Global Economy* (with Lisa Sun-Hee Park), *Garbage Wars: The Struggle for Environmental Justice in Chicago*, *Urban Recycling and the Search for Sustainable Community Development* (with Adam Weinberg and Allan Schnaiberg), *Power, Justice, the Environment: A Critical Appraisal of the Environmental Justice Movement* (editor, with Robert J. Brulle), and *Challenging the Chip: Labor Rights and Environmental Justice in the Global Electronics Industry* (editor, with Ted Smith, David Sonnenfeld, and Leslie Byster).

J. Timmons Roberts is professor of sociology at the College of William and Mary, where he teaches courses including Environmental Sociology, Globalization and the Environment, and Introduction to Environmental Studies. He wrote this lesson while a sabbatical fellow at the Environmental Change Institute at Oxford University (2006–2007). He is coauthor of six books, including *A Climate of Injustice: Global Inequality, North–South Politics, and Climate Policy* (with Bradley Parks) and *Chronicles from the Environmental Justice Frontline* (with Melissa Toffolon-Weiss). His current research focuses on the role of foreign aid in addressing and compensating for climate change.

Allan Schnaiberg is professor emeritus of sociology at Northwestern University, Evanston, Illinois. His work in what later became known as "environmental sociology" (and still later, "environmental justice") started in 1971. Trained as a demographer and earlier as a chemist and metallurgical engineer, he was able to mediate between the sociopolitical expressions by natural scientists in the 1970s and the later analyses by social scientists of the societal–environmental dialectic. This was greatly enhanced by his collaboration in later years with Kenneth Gould, Adam Weinberg, and David Pellow. The common thread in his research has been the ways in which both environmental problems and environmental protections have been infused with social inequalities. He has traced these inequalities through his analyses of sociology of science, energy crises, appropriate technology, sustainable development, recycling, and environmental impact assessment.

Bahram Tavakolian studied cultural ecology at UCLA with Dr. Walter Goldschmidt, and he has conducted field research on pastoral nomads in Afghanistan, urban migration in Turkey, women's labor force participation in Scotland, and Native American acculturation in the United States. He is presently visiting professor of anthropology at Willamette University in Salem, Oregon; and he is professor emeritus of sociology/anthropology and a former director of the Environmental Studies Program at Denison University in Granville, Ohio. His current writing projects include a manuscript on the relationships between gender and nomadism in the Middle East and central Asia and another on British India's impact on tribe–state relations in Afghanistan.

Richard York is an associate professor of sociology at the University of Oregon and coeditor of the Sage journal *Organization & Environment*. His research focuses on human interaction with the natural environment and the philosophy, history, and sociology of science. He has published articles in *American Sociological Review, Conservation Biology, Gender & Society, Rural Sociology, Social Problems, Social Science Research, Sociological Forum, The Sociological Quarterly, Theory & Society*, and other scholarly journals. He has twice (2004 and 2007) received the Outstanding Publication Award from the Environment and Technology Section of the American Sociological Association.

Nicole Youngman is visiting assistant professor of sociology at Loyola University in New Orleans, Louisiana, specializing in environmental sociology and the sociology of disaster. A long-time New Orleans resident, she is completing her dissertation at Tulane University on the history of development and flood control in the city.

An Introduction to Environmental Sociology

Kenneth A. Gould
Tammy L. Lewis

THE ORIGIN AND PURPOSE OF THIS BOOK

The idea for this reader emerged from a discussion among a small group of environmental sociology professors en route to visiting Akwesasne, the St. Regis Mohawk reservation, to learn more about their struggles with toxic contamination from nearby industrial plants. On the ride to Akwesasne we started to talk about our environmental sociology courses and how dissatisfied we were with the undergraduate, introductory-level readers (edited books with chapters from various authors) in our subfield. The point of a reader is to bring together exemplary works in a given subfield to expose students to the range of ideas, concepts, theoretical approaches, and empirical research, without requiring them to read a large number of individual books. For us, the problem with the traditional reader is that the chapters are usually drawn from professional journal articles, written by sociologists for sociologists. That is, the materials used to speak to undergraduate students, whom we don't expect to be familiar with the subfield, are the same materials that professional, trained sociologists use to speak to professional, trained sociologists, whom we rightly do expect to be quite familiar with the language, theories, data, and debates in the subfield. The result is that the audience for whom the initial materials were written is poorly matched to the audience for the collected reader. Granted, the versions of professional journal articles included in most readers have been edited to make them more accessible to the undergraduate. But still, the bulk of each chapter originates in professor-to-professor communication, rather than professor-to-student communication. And neither the professors nor the students are particularly happy with the outcomes.

As we drove in a university van to the Mohawk reservation, we were struck by how odd it was that sociology professors, who largely earn their living by finding ways to explain their field to undergraduate students, are stuck assigning readings that are clearly not designed for that purpose. Each of us in the van taught environmental sociology to undergraduates. We decided that it would be much more useful to have an undergraduate reader that was based on our most successful professor-to-student communications (our classes), rather than our most impressive professor-to-professor communications (our published professional journal articles).

It is at that point that two of us decided to launch the project that has resulted in this book. We made a list of what we thought were the most important topics to include in an undergraduate environmental sociology course. We then approached our environmental sociology colleagues who we knew were enthusiastic teachers and had successfully taught undergraduate-level courses in environmental sociology. We asked them to choose among the topics and match them with their favorite class lectures, the ones both they and their students seemed to enjoy and get the most out of. Then, rather than asking them to give us their best professional research paper on that topic, we instead asked them to grab their lesson notes and write up the lesson as closely as they could to the way they actually teach it in class. We told them that what we wanted was the best approximation of a favorite class lecture in environmental sociology in written form.

To our knowledge, this is a completely new approach to creating an undergraduate reader, one that starts with the classroom experience, rather than being forced to fit into that experience. As editors, a big part of our job was to remind our contributors that the audience for their writing is undergraduate students. After all, when professors write in their subfield, it is almost always for other professors. That is, we know how to talk to you about what we do and what we know, but we generally have less practice in writing to you about that.

Given our histories as U.S.-based professors, our network of colleagues tends to be U.S.-based, which resulted in a collection from a U.S. perspective. We discuss this more in the concluding lesson of the book.

Our hope is that you will find the lessons in this book accessible, interesting, and challenging and that the fact that each lesson was originally written specifically for undergraduate students will make the experience of taking a course in environmental sociology more enjoyable, engaging, and beneficial.

WHAT IS ENVIRONMENTAL SOCIOLOGY?

Put most succinctly, *environmental sociology* is the study of how social systems interact with ecosystems. Of course, since environmental sociology explores all of the ways that these two very complex systems impact each other, it is a very wide field of scientific investigation. Just trying to understand social systems or ecosystems alone is a daunting task. Trying to understand how the two affect each other is a monumental effort indeed. Ecosystems, their qualities and changing dynamics, impact social systems in many ways, from the way we organize language to the way we organize economic systems. Similarly, social systems and their qualities and shifting dynamics also impact ecosystems in numerous ways, from the organization of backyard gardens to the disorganization of global climate systems.

That social systems and ecosystems are deeply interconnected may seem obvious, but the intellectual history of sociology over the past 150 years or so provides little evidence that the depth and breadth of this dynamic interaction has been fully appreciated by sociologists. Similarly, the intellectual history of the science of ecology over roughly the same period also provides little evidence that the full scope of the impact of social systems on ecosystems had been well incorporated. Part of the reason for this lack of focus had to do with the need to first develop some fairly workable understandings of both social systems and ecosystems separately, before attempting to understand how they interact. However, since they do interact a lot, it is still surprising that our explanations of each developed with little reference to the other.

Another part of the explanation of this lack of synthesis has to do with the notion of bifurcation. That is, in Western tradition, nature and society tend to be thought of as separate domains. Society happens in some places and nature in others, and the two are examined separately by different groups of researchers. Yet another part of the reason for the failure to treat the two systems as dynamically intertwined has to do with the nature of academic organization. This is especially true for sociology, which emerged as a discipline much later than the natural sciences.

In seeking to carve out a distinct intellectual and organizational niche for itself within the academy, and thus establish itself as a legitimate field of scholarly pursuit, sociologists put much effort into defining sociology as something distinct from the natural sciences. That is, sociologists intentionally tried to separate their field of study from the already established fields that studied physical nature. As a result, any attempt at incorporating the natural world within sociology was seen as ceding intellectual ground to natural science, and thus undermining the effort to establish sociology as a distinct field of study with a separate area of investigation.

Despite the social barriers to fully integrating the study of social systems and ecosystems, over time the increasing confidence of sociology as a fully established and legitimate discipline and the increasing urgency of the negative impacts of social systems on ecosystems created both the social space and the social need for the emergence of environmental sociology.

All that said, it is important to note that environmental sociology is not equally rooted in sociology and ecology. Environmental sociology remains a subfield of sociology, one in which its practitioners are more open to including ecological variables within their analyses and who have chosen to apply and develop sociological analysis precisely where social systems and ecosystems intersect. Environmental sociologists bring the sociological lens and apply their sociological imaginations to the ways in which social systems generate and respond to ecological change. They are not ecologists and are not prepared to address the deep complexity of ecosystems. Instead, their training is in the study of the deeply complex ways that social systems are organized and change. Their special focus is on how social systems are organized and change in response to the natural world, just as the changes they produce in the natural world force them to further respond and change.

A BRIEF HISTORY OF ENVIRONMENTAL SOCIOLOGY

One social response to environmental change has been the institutionalization of the study of social system–ecosystem interactions. The brief history

we present here highlights the *institutional* trajectory of environmental sociology. We focus on the development of organizational structures intended
to sustain the subdiscipline. In elaborating this history, we touch upon the
key social forces that led to its emergence and how it fits into the broader
context of sociology. The institutions are clearly tied to key individuals in
the field. However, rather than focus on these individuals, we focus on the
"real-world" events and intellectual concerns embedded in the era in which
the subfield first emerged.

Environmental sociology has only been an officially recognized subfield
within sociology since around 1976, with its institutionalization as one of the
American Sociological Association's topical sections. Prior to that time, "the
environment" was not considered within the purview of sociology. Indeed, as
noted earlier, in developing sociology as a discipline, the "founding fathers"
sought to distance the study of "social facts" (Durkheim) from studies of the
biophysical world in order to legitimize the new "science of society," sociology
(see Lesson 2). In the late 1800s, the environment was not part of sociology.
When we consider that a key concern of classical sociology was to understand
the broad-scale social changes brought about by industrialization and modern
state bureaucracies, the omission of the "the environment" and examination
of "environmental inequalities" seem impossible from our contemporary perspective. Today, environmental sociologists study how social institutions interact with the environment and ask how industrial capitalism and modern state
bureaucracies affect social and environmental inequalities and vice versa.

If we revisit the "classics" in sociology, searching to discover to what degree
the founders may have looked at the environment, we do not see much in the
analyses of Max Weber or Emile Durkheim. For example, we could stretch
to see that Durkheim analyzed the effects of "cosmic factors"—season, temperature, etc.—on suicide rates (though he dismisses their causal relevance),
but there really is not much there. Contemporary research by John Bellamy
Foster and others suggests that Karl Marx was more attentive to the environment, though this was not a central focus and is certainly not Marx's legacy.
In the 1970s, bringing the environment into sociological analysis occurred
consciously and deliberately.

The institutional history of environmental sociology coincides with the
emergence of the modern "ecology movement." Both were born in the late
1960s and early 1970s. Within a relatively short span of time, the professional
organizations of sociologists incorporated formal niches for environmental sociology. The Rural Sociological Society's Natural Resources Research
Group formed in the mid-1960s (it has had numerous name changes). The
Society for the Study of Social Problems started a group on environmental
problems in 1973, and the American Sociological Association's Environment
and Technology section formed in 1976 (originally it was called the section
on "environmental sociology").

The institutionalization of environmental sociology reflected the growing
attention of society in general, and social scientists in particular, to issues of
the environment. Intellectuals working in the fields of human ecology, rural

sociology, and urban sociology, and researching topics such as social movements, found their intellectual interests intersecting with real-world events during this time period. This same era witnessed numerous environmental "crises," such as the energy crisis of the early 1970s, the Santa Barbara oil spill (1969), toxic wastes being discovered in the residential neighborhood of Love Canal (1978), and the accident at the nuclear power plant in Three Mile Island (1979).

Coupled with these crises was rising public concern regarding the environment and the resulting emergence of environmental organizations including the Environmental Defense Fund (1967), Friends of the Earth (1969), and Natural Resources Defense Council (NRDC, founded 1970). Political actions were also taking place. In 1969, Congress passed the National Environmental Policy Act, which President Nixon signed into law in 1970. The Environmental Protection Agency (EPA) was established in 1970, followed by the passage of key environmental laws: the Clean Air Act (1970), the Clean Water Act (1972), the Pesticide Control Act (1972), and the Resource Conservation and Recovery Act (1976). The year 1970 also marked the first Earth Day. Political attention was not just national but international, including the 1972 United Nations Conference on the Human Environment held in Stockholm. Environmental sociologists were not immune to their surroundings. They, too, responded to socioenvironmental changes and began researching the causes of environmental degradation, public opinion regarding the environment, and the social responses of the public and institutions to environmental changes.

Just as early sociology sought to distinguish itself from other sciences, early environmental sociology tried to distinguish itself from "mainstream sociology." Writing in the late 1970s, William Catton and Riley Dunlap, early environmental sociologists, wrote an oft-cited paper that argued that virtually all sociological theories were anthropocentric; i.e. they view human society as the center of the natural world, with humans controlling and using the environment without regard for the natural resource–based limits to social growth. They termed this sociological worldview the "human exemptionalism paradigm" (HEP). By contrast, they argued for a competing worldview that would critique mainstream sociology's HEP worldview. They called their alternative the "new ecological paradigm" (NEP). The NEP started from the assumptions that humans are one of many interdependent species in the global ecosystem and part of a large web of nature, that humans depend on a finite biophysical environment, and that humans cannot stand above ecological laws. The HEP–NEP distinction provided environmental sociology with a way to differentiate itself from mainstream sociology. However, we have yet to see sociology as a discipline fully embrace the NEP worldview, though "the environment" and "environmental issues" have drawn the attention of researchers working in various other sociological subfields with greater frequency over time.

Environmental sociology has by now established itself as a recognized subfield in sociology. The continuation of the environment as a social problem has reinforced this, giving environmental sociologists a relevant role to play in examining the potential paths toward environmental reform and synthesis of the social and ecological systems. On its website, the Environment and Technology section of the American Sociological Association explains the role of environmental sociology in this way:

> Many of society's most pressing problems are no longer just "social." From the maintenance of genetic diversity to the disposal of radioactive wastes, from toxics in the groundwater below us to global warming of the atmosphere above, the challenges of the 21st century are increasingly coming to involve society's relationships with the environment and technologies upon which we all depend. These interrelationships involve a range of complexities and implications that could not have been imagined in the early days of sociology. They are of sociological interest not just because of their significance to society, but also because of their significance to sociology.

Many of our environmental sociology colleagues in other nations are not organized in the same manner as American sociologists are. Because of this, the interactions between North American environmental sociologists and sociologists throughout the rest of the world have been facilitated by the International Sociological Association's Research Committee on Environment and Society (RC24), which was formed in 1971 and has seen continued growth (in international meetings) and increased significance among environmental sociologists over time.

Finally, in looking to institutions, there is every reason to believe that environmental sociology will continue to thrive as a subdiscipline. The structures for the continued production of knowledge and dissemination of knowledge and the education of professionals are well-established and growing. For instance, there are well-established journals in which environmental sociologists publish (*Capitalism, Nature, Socialism; Organization & Environment; Society and Natural Resources*). And, perhaps more important, recent institutional growth in the field is evidenced by the growth in graduate programs dedicated specifically to environmental sociology (students interested in this should explore the Environment and Technology section's website for the most up-to-date list). This book will introduce you to the work that environmental sociologists do.

THE LAYOUT OF THE BOOK

This book is divided into four parts as a way of broadly organizing your introduction to the ways in which environmental sociologists think about and study the relationships between social systems and ecosystems. The book begins with a brief introduction to socioenvironmental theory, followed by three sections addressing the social causes, consequences, and responses to environmental disruption. The book concludes by looking at where the sociological study of society–environment interactions might productively focus in coming years and suggests some important questions that remain incompletely answered.

Part 1 of the book introduces you to the variety of theoretical frameworks that environmental sociologists have developed to describe and explain the patterns they have uncovered in the ways that social systems and ecosystems interact. These patterns of interaction range from the micro-level, at which people as social beings encounter and comprehend the natural world, to the macro-level, at which the global economy shapes and is shaped by the constraints of the biosphere. By beginning with a broad overview of socioenvironmental theories, we hope to provide you with an opportunity to see how these theories both guide and emerge from the types of analyses you will read in the next three parts of the book.

Part 2 of the book explores the systemic causes of social disruption of ecosystems. The focus here is on the ways in which major social institutions such as governments, corporations, and labor generate and respond to environmental change and interact with each other in regard to environmental conditions. Since science and technology are primary mechanisms through which humans understand and mediate their relationships with ecosystems, an additional focus of Part 2 is the social institutions and processes that shape science and technological innovation. Finally, Part 2 concludes with an examination of population dynamics and the ways in which human population change and distribution intersect with ecosystemic processes. Throughout Part 2, you will be asked to think critically about the social dynamics of power as environmental sociologists recognize that the capacity to determine the nature of social system–ecosystem interactions is not distributed equally throughout society.

In Part 3 of the book, the focus is on the consequences of environmental disruption for social systems. That is, where Part 2 looks at how and why society changes the environment, this next part of the book looks at how the environment changes society. The disorganization of ecosystems produced by social systems impacts those social systems in a wide variety of ways. Those social impacts of human-induced environmental change do not affect all people equally or in the same ways. Therefore, you will find that a primary focus of Part 3 is on issues of social inequality in terms of who bears the costs of environmental disruption, from local through global levels of distribution. In particular, the concepts of "environmental justice" and "environmental health" are introduced and further explored through specific analyses of food production systems, "natural" disasters, and global climate change. Paralleling what you will have read in Part 2, your reading of Part 3 will help you to see that, just as the power to determine the ways in which social systems and ecosystems interact is unevenly distributed throughout society, so is the power to avoid or deal with the results of these interactions.

Part 4, the final part of the book, examines the ways in which society has responded to human-induced environmental disruption. Much of the focus here is on how and why communities, social movements, and nongovernmental organizations have mobilized to address a wide variety of environmental concerns. This type of citizen mobilization has emerged all over the world, at the local, regional, national, and transnational levels, with great variation in the environmental issues focused on and the strategies employed. Part 4 exposes you to this rich variety of social response to problems arising from the ways that social system–ecosystem relations are currently organized. Part 4 also introduces you to "sustainable development," a concept intended to guide efforts toward reorganizing the relationships between social systems and ecosystems in ways that produce fewer environmental disruptions and greater social benefits. We conclude with a brief discussion of the future of environmental sociology at the dawn of the twenty-first century; raise some questions that remain to be fully answered about the social causes, consequences, and responses to environmental problems; and suggest some areas of focus for the further sociological study of social system–ecosystem relations. In the spirit of engaging students in an area we find intellectually stimulating and vitally important to the future, we hope that you might take on researching and answering these questions to advance the state of the discipline and improve the prospects for our socioenvironmental future.

SOURCES

Buttel, Frederick H. 2003. "Environmental Sociology and the Explanation of Environmental Reform." *Organization & Environment* 16:306–44.

Catton, William R. and Riley E. Dunlap. 1978. "Environmental Sociology: A New Paradigm." *American Sociologist* 13:41–49.

Foster, John Bellamy. 1999. "Marx's Theory of Metabolic Rift: Classical Foundations for Environmental Sociology." *American Journal of Sociology* 105(2):366–405.

Schnaiberg, Allan. 1980. *The Environment: From Surplus to Scarcity*. New York: Oxford University Press.

Part 1

THEORY

The Social Construction of Nature
Of Computers, Butterflies, Dogs, and Trucks

Stella M. Čapek

Environmental sociology is wide-ranging field that includes a variety of theories and methodological approaches. If you did this for a living, you might find yourself studying topics as seemingly different as the environmental movement, public opinion, natural resource use, social impacts of technology, inequality and environmental justice, constructions of nature and gender, the economics and politics of environmental policy, sustainable community design, or particular issues such as global warming, deforestation, and population—and that is only a partial list. But regardless of the topic, the job of theory in environmental sociology is to make social structure visible—that is, to identify the stable, persistent, often hidden patterns of social relationships that become established over time. And social relationships are only the beginning of the story, since *environmental* sociology is about understanding the two-way relationship between society and the environment. Theory is like any other process that makes hidden things visible; just as ultraviolet light reveals striking color patterns that are there all along but invisible to the naked eye, sociological theories throw a certain kind of (analytical) light on society to illuminate social and environmental connections that are not immediately obvious.

One way to look at social structure is to see it as invisible "strings" that link individuals to social groups and to the environment in a patterned way. Why are these relationships so invisible in the first place? Some are taken for granted and are simply not thought about, while others are masked by power relationships. Still others are extremely complex, making it difficult to discern a pattern. Environmental sociology offers theoretical models that make key relationships more visible and allow us to understand better what holds them in place. By making structures visible, theories also offer us the opportunity to make more conscious choices about participating in or changing these patterns. Without understanding how they work, and who and what is attached to them (including ourselves), conscious choice is impossible.

In the following discussion, we will consider several snapshot images that will invite us to apply theories from environmental sociology. Because theory can often seem abstract, I want us to imagine actual bodies in actual places—our own bodies, or those of others. In fact, whether we are considering the globalization of environmental problems or the background levels of chemicals in our bloodstreams, our research questions and theories always connect to real people in specific situations. The three scenes that I will ask us to consider are these: a person throwing a can out of the window of a speeding truck; a person sitting at the keyboard of a computer, making a fast connection on the Internet; and a person physically dismantling a computer that has been "thrown away" in the United States and exported to an "e-waste processing center" in another country. Although these snapshots are only three out of many possibilities, they offer an excellent opportunity to connect structures across time and space and to learn about the insights and creative uses of environmental sociology.

I will draw on several theories from environmental sociology. They are all related, even though they address very different scales of human action, from individual and small group (micro) behavior to "big picture" (macro) patterns like globalization and shifting ideas about time and space. First, I will discuss a micro-level concept, "naturework," that comes out of symbolic interactionist theory. Symbolic interactionism focuses on how human beings and social groups symbolically communicate and acquire a sense of identity through social interaction. Naturework looks at how human beings construct ideas about nature and their relationship to it. Then, I will "zoom out" to theories of globalization and modernization that explore how space and time are being experienced in new ways by human beings. The context for these structures is a global capitalist system shaped by a "treadmill" logic, a social structure that continues to churn out ideas, material arrangements, and identities that have enormous implications for the environment. All of these theories shed light on the snapshot scenes we will consider—the truck, the computer, the people who have a relationship to these technologies, and even creatures like butterflies and dogs. They will show how small, cumulative actions ripple outward into the global ecosystems of the planet, and how important it is to keep nature "in the picture" as we make social decisions.

NATUREWORK AND ITS USES:
OF TRUCKS AND BUTTERFLIES

Scene One: A truck zooms down the freeway, the window rolls down, an arm appears, and fingers reach out to toss a can from the moving vehicle. The can sails through the air and lands along the edge of the highway with a small crash. Maybe it's a beer bottle or a cigarette butt. Or an entire ashtray full of cigarette butts. Whatever it is, it lands on the side of the road as the truck quickly disappears over the horizon. The object becomes part of a jagged mosaic of broken glass shards, cigarettes, cans, miscellaneous objects considered trash, and—as I once learned doing a highway cleanup— wings from migrating butterflies that can't compete with the cars speeding down the highway. The delicately beautiful but damaged butterfly wings are a small, well-kept secret in a roadside no-man's land that stretches for miles.

What can an environmental sociologist do with this scene, and how can she or he use theory to create new angles of vision on it? I choose this particular act—what we call in this society "littering"—because it seems to be a very simple, *unthinking* act. But of course, this unthinking act would be *unthinkable* under a different set of social circumstances, in another time or place. Sociology in general, and environmental sociology in particular, suggests that the simplest act is not simple at all and is rarely individual or private—it is part of a network of actions and social relationships that have consequences for other people and for the environment.

Gary Alan Fine has coined a useful term, *naturework*, that refers to how we constantly work to transform "nature" into culture, filtering it through the screen of social meanings that we have learned. To a social constructionist like Fine, there is no such thing as "raw" nature. For example, when we look at a tree, we notice some things about it and not others. While nature, or the tree, does in fact exist, what is more important, he would argue, is that we inevitably construct an image of what the tree is and behave toward it accordingly. Fine points out that "being 'in nature' implies being in culture" since culture influences how we see the tree. When we transform nature into culture, we create consequences for individuals as well as social policy.

Symbolic interactionists point out that human beings are constantly at work, negotiating meaning and constructing reality. For example, we invent (or someone else invents) terms like "wilderness," "Mother Nature," "desert," "human being," "freeway," and "global warming." Some of these terms are more contested than others, but all represent a human interpretation of what "nature" is "doing." Likewise, we invent words for what animals are "saying" and teach them to children; for example, in English, a dog says "bow wow!" while in Czech, the same dog (according to human translators) says "haf haf!" Language is part of a broader task of classifying and making sense of things, and in fact, much of naturework has to do with creating and maintaining borders between categories. For example, where is the line drawn between humans and (other) animals? (If we didn't care about this line, we wouldn't insult people by calling them "animals.") What kind of line exists between humans and the technologies that we invent? Between nature and "civilization"? What kind of nature is "good" or "bad," dangerous or safe? Do we include nature inside the boundaries of our skin, or do we see it as exclusively outside us?

These kinds of boundary questions generate others that are even more specific. For example, how do you (or I) feel about particular animals? Should they be hunted? Protected? Pets? Food? What about the human body? Should you shave the hair off of certain parts of your body? Should you mask the odors of nature? Should you apply cosmetics to distinguish yourself from or to signal your connection with nature? Do you think of nature as female (as in "Mother Nature")? Do you know the names of the trees, the birds, the rivers? Does the sight of a tree or a sunset make you glad? When you go camping (if you go camping), do you take many things with you? Do you carry a cell phone? When you walk or drive, are you plugged into your own private music system and personal theme music? Are you a "frequent flyer"? When you travel, do you take photographs? A few? Many? Do you have allergies and see nature as an attacker or a nuisance? Is your model of the "American Dream" a detached single-family home with a lawn? Do you know where your trash goes? All of these small, often unthinking decisions represent naturework and result in a particular relationship with the ecosystem and a specific set of outcomes. A symbolic interactionist would point out that although naturework might seem more obvious when we interpret big events like hurricanes, most naturework happens on a daily basis and is enacted through the seemingly insignificant details of our lives. It doesn't *feel* like work because the categories that we use to understand the world appear normal to us and, in many cases, emotionally and morally reassuring.

Let's go back to the truck, the highway, the arm, and the flying can. How might the concept of naturework help us to interpret this situation? In fact, many things have to be in place for the can to be tossed out the window. First, one has to feel separated from the place where the can will fall. If this piece of earth is considered just "dirt" or empty space at the edge of a highway, not an alive organic material that interacts with us at every moment, it is easy to see it as a kind of trash receptacle or sponge to absorb waste. This is also not likely to be a place where one's loved ones live. Second, one has to assume that he or she is not accountable for the act of "trashing." Speeding down the highway, it is easy to leave behind any thought of consequence or accountability and to assume that no one will care, or at least no one will know who threw the can (notice that this also implies that we are accountable at most to another human being—perhaps a police officer—rather than the ecosystem or the Earth's biosphere). Third, in not giving this action much thought, one has to assume it is fairly trivial (as the word "littering" suggests). No thought is given to cumulative impacts because "nature" will clean it up, there is plenty of space in the trash can, or there are better things to worry about on a given day. All of these assumptions add up to one conclusion: *It doesn't matter*.

The idea that it doesn't matter is supported by social patterns that encourage a certain kind of naturework. Let's look at this more closely. A person driving down the highway in a fast-moving vehicle is likely to feel quite (unrealistically) separated from what is outside, including nature in the form of landscape and weather. U.S. culture, or very specific groups in that culture, invented the idea that cars and trucks are a good way to get around, that their average replacement time should be about 3 years, that they are better than public transportation, that they are an important marker of status, that speed is to be valued, that the Earth is just material that we drive on and use for our own purposes, and that throwing a can out the window represents freedom. The common piece of naturework in all of these constructions is the view that we are separate from the natural world and have the power to control it or ignore it. William Catton and Riley Dunlap, in a classic article on the models, or paradigms, that we use to interpret our relationship to the ecosystem, call this view the "human exemptionalist paradigm" (HEP) (see Lesson 1). Instead of seeing ourselves as part of the ecological system of the planet (or what they called NEP, a "new ecological paradigm"), we see ourselves as apart from it, in a controlling position that is enhanced by our technology. A banner that I saw displayed recently at a local Toyota dealer could be a poster for the HEP worldview: Next to an image of a speeding car are the words "Hear the atmosphere scream as you tear it in half." The ad sells the idea that the domination of nature (especially through speed and technology) is an attractive and highly desirable experience. One need not look far to find many messages like this in contemporary societies like that of the United States.

But what if the Earth were considered sacred, or if, as scientist Donella Meadows and others have argued, we are in fact participants in a part-nered dance with nature? What if invisible strings linked the hand to the can that is thrown and the strings lingered in place, reminding us of con-sequences? What if ecological thinking were so prevalent that it would be impossible to "litter"? Sociologists Michael Bell and Michael Carolan point out that presently in the United States if a person does not consciously go out of his or her way to take environmentally beneficial actions, by default the status quo results in environmental harm. A different set of default arrangements, a different design, could support ecological sustainabil-ity. Under those conditions—and this is Bell and Carolan's point—even unthinking acts would be more likely to produce environmental benefits. For example, if more sustainable materials were designed into the front end of the manufacturing process, it would be far easier to recycle materi-als. "Green architect" William McDonough, for example, discusses a "cra-dle to cradle" concept, where a product reaches the end of its life cycle only to be "born" into a new use. Urban and environmental sociologist Harvey Molotch reminds us that "How we desire, produce, and discard the durables of existence helps form who we are, how we connect to one another, and what we do to the earth."

Let's explore the "desire" piece of the formula. A key point to remember is that while we are busy constructing the meaning of the world and our own identities through naturework, others are busily attempting to construct our identities for us. For example, the advertising industry, an essential feature of contemporary global capitalism, works around the clock to construct us primarily as "consumers" always in need of a newer, more "cutting-edge" product. The social psychology of capitalism depends on us experiencing a kind of "halo effect" around an item we desire, a halo that quickly begins to fade as soon as we possess the item and our attention moves to a new object (think about how this works in your own experience when you buy things). The social and economic (and political) relationships of capitalism depend on intense competition and a drive to increase profits. This pattern is built around a kind of "treadmill" logic, as Allan Schnaiberg and others have pointed out; individuals and corporations run in place faster and faster in an effort to keep up in the (now global) game of competition (see Lesson 3).

The treadmill creates a voracious appetite for natural resources as people are persuaded to "toss" older products. This may include tossing a can out of the window or getting rid of a truck or a computer after a few years, to replace it with the latest model. It is not considered too important to know where things go after they leave our hands. What is important is the desire for the new object.

The advertising industry fuels our desires by specializing in a particular kind of naturework: It attracts buyers by invoking a love of nature but sells products that often disconnect us from nature. In the multibillion-dollar cosmetics industry, for example, the "natural look" not only carries a large price tag but sells a fabricated image of perfection. "Natural skin" enhanced by cosmetics is billed as fresh and flawless, while nature itself includes many flaws and irregularities (and much more variety). Similarly, local organic apples are likely to contain many more blemishes but more freshness and diversity than their mass-produced relatives available at national grocery store chains and based on monoculture and industrialized agriculture. "Natural" cosmetics often contain unsafe products that arguably do some violence to the environment and to the body that wears them. From name-brand undergarments billed as the "natural woman's" look to cosmetics that disguise what nature has given, it is a simulacrum, or false imitation, of nature that is being sold, not nature itself. In fact, "real" nature is not considered particularly attractive. This should not be surprising since the advertising industry has to be interested only in what can be captured and converted into a commodity and sold, and nature "in the raw" eludes capture.

If we shift our attention from cosmetics to ads for vehicles, we also find nature in the picture. A desire for the pure, untouched, and wide open landscape is a staple feature of most television ads for cars, trucks, jeeps, sport-utility vehicles, and off-road vehicles. But in this case nature is seen as a place to "get away from it all" and/or a place that is waiting to be conquered by human technology. Nature is in fact a backdrop or a stage set for the enactment of key cultural fantasies about "freedom" and "domination" and "individualism." Since the vehicle conquers nature by representing the freedom to go anywhere and since, if the vehicle and others like it truly do go anywhere, there will soon be no pristine environment, the ad is selling pure paradox. Just as importantly, it sells the idea that the purchase of an expensive product is the admission ticket to this ego-enhancing performance.

But suppose that one's own naturework leans in the direction of ecological sustainability (see Lesson 19) and one wishes to step off the "treadmill" by becoming disinterested in consuming new products. Sociologist Zygmunt Bauman argues that this person is the true outsider, the deviant in a consumption-based society. To be socially accepted or even understandable to one's neighbors, a person needs to revel in the seduction of ever new and identity-expanding choices offered by consumer goods, whether these are the latest models of cars, adventure tourism "packages," cosmetics, or a multitude of other possibilities. How true is this? Bauman is right that this has been the mainstream script for many years in countries like the United States.

But the acceptance or rejection of this notion depends on time, place, situation, awareness, and socioeconomic position. The theories of environmental sociology can help us consider under what conditions ecologically sustainable actions become more or less possible. They can also teach us about what stands in the way of sustainable actions and solutions—from naturework to the treadmill logic of global capitalism to what Bell and Carolan call "technological somnambulism," the tendency to unquestioningly accept the use of and spread of new technologies.

Consider this example: Because of a history of strong labor unions, Sweden has had a law that supports the right of workers to discuss the implications of a new technology before it is introduced into the workplace. But at my college, such decisions are administratively made at the top. A new photocopying machine undercut previously successful efforts to use recycled paper because the paper tended to jam in the new machine, causing extra work for administrative assistants. The paper was phased out, and no one had a chance to talk about it at all. "Nature" became a threat to efficiency and was removed. But as more colleges and institutions become interested in how they contribute to a sustainable "ecological footprint," the possibility arises for more democratic discussions, better research into design, and a clearer grasp of cost–benefit balance that comes with any new technology.

Since technologies always have complex (and often unanticipated) impacts on society and the environment, environmental sociology can play a key role in identifying impacts that are not immediately obvious (see Lesson 8). For example, it can help us to identify the range of "stakeholders" who will be helped and/or harmed by a particular technology, and it can offer a systematic way to evaluate the "goods" and "bads" for social groups (and for nature, or the ecosystem, an often forgotten stakeholder). For example, I benefit from a feature on the new photocopier that allows me to be a "remote user," printing two-sided (good for the environment!) copies from my office. That new possibility represents a positive and exciting aspect of innovation. But the machine doesn't use recycled paper, and if it breaks down, my colleagues and I can't fix it ourselves by undoing a paper jam, as we could with the previous model—we have to call our Information Technology division and hope that someone is "home." So when we look at a new technology (cell phones, for example), we always need to ask for whom it is beneficial and why. The difficult challenge is to arrive at an overall picture of costs and benefits. That would require many groups with different kinds of knowledge and experience to be part of a democratic discussion. The theories of environmental sociology produce models and research findings that contribute to a "big-picture" understanding of any technology, as well as the naturework through which we see it.

Today, we have growing evidence that the mainstream script based on "conquering" nature is fraying around the edges, under pressure from the realities of global warming and impending oil scarcity, as well as movements for social and environmental justice. When I find myself looking at yet another advertising banner at the local car dealer with a picture of a truck and the words "It's a big, tough truck. What's not to like?" I think about how many of my students and colleagues would make a list of "what's not to like" quite different from what they thought even a year ago. Certainly, Ford and General Motors have discovered that suddenly there is much "not to like" about their large, fuel-inefficient vehicles. Many of my students now find the image of the lone vehicle presented as a powerful object of desire conquering an empty landscape (is it Alaska? Montana? New Mexico?) to be laughable, even ridiculous. Many of them would like bike paths, public transportation, and fuel efficiency. But to arrive at critique and to construct fresh choices, a person needs to have thought about it and to become aware of the many uses of naturework.

OF TIME, SPACE, AND COMPUTERS

Scene Two: Somebody sits with his or her fingers on a computer keyboard, looking at an electronic screen offering the promise of instant global communication. Time magazine, in December 2006, celebrated this hypothetical person by selecting her/him as "Person of the Year." The magazine's cover contained the image of a partially reflective metal-like computer screen that "you" are invited to look into. The accompanying message is that you, the person with fingers on the keyboard, are person of the year because, in a world democratized and decentralized by the Internet, you have tremendous power and influence. Like the truck's passenger in Scene One—but even more so—"you" have the freedom to go anywhere, fast. But unlike the passenger in the truck, you aren't tossing anything out of the window. Or are you?

Clearly, *Time* magazine's editors decided that in the United States use of the Internet was so widespread that the computer (and its imagined connection to "you") deserved a place on the cover, instead of the usual choice of one influential person. The accompanying article claims that the ability to use the Internet represents the end of top–down authority and the rise of democratic freedom to shape the world. It also celebrates "community and collaboration on a scale never seen before." A very empowered "you" sits in front of the screen, reveling in your historically new choices.

What would an environmental sociologist notice about this image and what it presupposes? First, he or she would notice that this is an image aimed only at those who have access to this technology. Second, the sociologist would take a hard look at the idea that access to the Internet makes you free from top–down authority and constraint. While there are significant opportunities to gather and share information in ways previously unavailable (and unimaginable), spyware on many websites and restricted access to information in the wake of 9–11 are only two examples that undermine the assumption that the Internet represents total freedom. And an *environmental* sociologist would inquire about connections to and disconnections from the environment that accompany the person sitting at the computer screen.

We could begin, once again, with the concept of "naturework." Where is nature in this picture? Unless "you" are looking at a virtual image of nature on the screen, the environment seems to be conspicuous by its absence. The computer is most likely indoors (although a new technological advantage is portability—you may have taken your laptop to a park). You are probably looking intently at the computer screen for extended periods of time, and you are probably in a sedentary posture. Nature is present in the form of your body, and your actions are shaping that body (your eyes, your posture, your health). Nature is also present in the materials that make up the room you are sitting in (the built environment) or in trees in the park—but if you are looking at the computer screen, you are less apt to notice your surrounding environment. Chances are that you are also ignoring your *internal* environment that is sending signals about eye strain, hunger, brain overload, and bad posture. All of this adds up to a separation from your immediate environment, a version of what sociologist Anthony Giddens calls "disembedding." Let's consider how the ideas of Giddens and some other scholars of modernity might help us analyze the relationship between the computer, the person, and the natural environment.

Social theorist Anthony Giddens claims that a new aspect of human experience in "late modern" societies is the way that time and space are rearranged to "connect presence and absence." Because of an increasingly globalized and interconnected world and because of the development of electronic communication and spaces (like cyberspace) that are not connected to actual places, human beings experience what Giddens calls "disembedding" and "distanciation." *Disembedding* refers to social relations being "lifted out" of their local contexts and restructured across time and space. In other words, global economies and electronic communication networks connect us to physically absent people in places that are geographically remote from us (China, perhaps, or a friend in another city). This way of relating to people and places at a distance, or *distanciation*, comes to be a normal and expected part of our social organization and interactions.

New technologies harness the wonder of new understandings of nature, including how to make space and time work differently (up to a point). The problem is that these technologies are offered as if there were no strings attached—like the car sitting in a pristine landscape, the computer or cell phone suggests limitless freedom and no drawbacks. But there are limits of a very real kind. Giddens points out that relationships at a distance depend entirely on trust—trust that unseen people are who they claim to be and trust in "expert systems," such as those who set up and maintain the electronic networks (or the Information Technology experts who maintain the photocopier for me, the "remote user"). And there are other kinds of limits that interfere with our ability to understand the bigger picture. Giddens argues, for example, that the new arrangement of space and time "tears space away from place." Notice the violence of the metaphor—this new development not only breaks the historical relationship between humans and physical places, but there is some roughness to the break. Giddens' metaphor suggests ragged edges and torn roots. And there is an additional twist—our local places are becoming harder to know and understand because they are, Giddens says, penetrated and reshaped by distant global influences. This makes it more difficult to clearly understand our relationship to the environment since what is visible locally may be deceptive. Radiation and invisible toxic pollution affect us whether we see them or not and can be disguised in the most beautiful landscape.

Time is also experienced in a radically new way in modern societies. Social relationships are increasingly separated from a natural calendar of seasons and cycles of day and night. We produce materials such as nuclear waste whose impact reaches far into a future whose time-scale we cannot even imagine. The expanding possibility of instantaneous global communication has reshaped expectations about how time "works." Speed is highly valued, from raising speed limits on highways to faster Internet connections and instant messaging. However, an environmental sociologist can easily make the argument that rising speeds make it more difficult to pay attention to one's local environment, whether a person is in a truck driving down a freeway or sitting at a computer keyboard, intently concentrating on the Internet "highway." Add a cell phone to this mix of speed and attention and the sense of absence from the local environment increases exponentially (as car accident statistics show quite clearly). Although many people pride themselves on their ability to multitask, studies show that it often doesn't work very well in terms of work quality, personal health, and consequences for social relationships. People report not having enough time to pay attention to everything from family to politics to their own mental health (think about how this works for you—do you have enough time?).

A feature of the new time–space structure described by Giddens and others is that it blurs the boundaries between many formerly separate categories of experience. Sociologist George Ritzer—best known for studying the global spread of "McDonaldization" and new forms of consumption—draws on Jean Baudrillard's concept of "implosion" to describe these new combinations of time and space. *Implosion* refers to one phenomenon collapsing, or contracting, into another. One example is the merging of the categories of home and shopping. In an electronically networked world, one does not need to leave one's home to go shopping and if one desires, one can shop in the middle of the night at an online "cyberstore." Who is minding the cyberstore, and where is he or she located? We usually don't know. Even money is not required, just a credit card (with a promise of payment or growing debt in the future). Thus, home/store, local/global, and future/present collapse into one ambiguous category.

As Ritzer and others point out, such implosions represent ever-new opportunities for selling goods and promoting consumption, a feature that goes hand in hand with the expanding treadmill of global capitalism. Speeded-up experiences of time and access to new, "disembedded" electronic spaces erase earlier limits around consumption. Ritzer calls this a "reenchantment of the world," a process that draws in new consumers through ever more "spectacular" opportunities to consume. Meanwhile, just as these implosions create new connections, they create disconnections, particularly from local people and natural environments. The fact that distant or virtual spaces appear more real and compelling than our immediate environment can create a disturbing gap in our understanding of the environmental consequences of our behavior. It is no accident that, although advertisements for computers and cell phones still sell fantasies related to freedom, power, and individualism, the theme of nature and desire for nature appears to have dropped out of the picture. The seductive magic of a computer or a cell phone permits its user to leap across space and time, a thrilling possibility. But this possibility is embedded in a system that persuades "consumers" to use up resources even faster, producing more waste as they pursue the latest upgrade. Although we may assume that our key relationships are no longer with the physical places that surround us (including nature, in a local and specific way), we still have a relationship with our local environment. Even if—especially if—that relationship is neglected, there are ecological consequences.

THE TRUCK AND THE COMPUTER REVISITED: TOSSING NATURE OUT THE WINDOW?

Putting together some ideas from the theories we have considered, we can look at the similarities and differences between the truck and the computer. Both are, we could say, fast-moving vehicles, although the computer is connected to fast motion in cyberspace. The truck speeding through the landscape is already altering the human experience of time and space, leaving places behind and focusing attention inside the vehicle or on the road ahead. But the computer screen is a gateway into a virtual world where time and space are compressed and recombined, making the disconnection from the natural environment even more striking. Both vehicles are attractive because they allow the "driver" to rush toward certain things (freedom?) and away from others (boredom? stultifying locations and relationships? limits?). Both involve the consumption of items that enhance the identity of the consumer. The truck is connected to a certain lifestyle that is linked to other consumption items (some of which are used up and tossed out of the window on the way). The computer is likewise connected to a lifestyle that is attractive to its "driver." Does he or she also use things up and toss them away while speeding through cyberspace? If so, what are they, and where do they land?

To answer such questions we need, once again, to look for nature and environment in the picture. Leaving aside the interesting debate about where nature ends and technology begins (a discussion well worth having but probably not now), we can see that the truck is driving through an actual place, even if the landscape is seen only through windows or through a rear-view mirror. The computer seems to have nothing to do with nature at all. But a closer look at both scenes will reveal naturework that creates separation and (illusory) control. The natural environment is as physically real as ever but has become less visible because of social organization and technology.

We said earlier that it is the job of social and environmental theory to make relationships visible. If we return to the image of the invisible strings connecting people to each other (and to their technological inventions) and if we follow the strings back to the hands that put together the computer and the hands that will someday dismantle it, it will be impossible to ignore the ecological impact of the production, distribution, consumption, and disposal of computers, especially when multiplied by the number of users. No matter how liberated from place or from nature a person feels, the reality is that the computer was manufactured from earth elements and goes back to the earth and that there are tangible material consequences at each end of the production process (see Lesson 8). These include components that are poisonous to human beings and other life forms. There is a real cost—medical, social, and political—to ignoring these matters. Yet, quite often no more thought is given to throwing away an older model of computer than is given to throwing the can out of the truck. With a growing mountain of obsolete equipment and the message that throwing things away is necessary and even pleasing, it is clear that something big is going out the window—the idea of nature as a visible or significant presence and an enormous amount of material that can do environmental harm. And so we arrive at our third and last snapshot.

Scene Three: A young boy (or girl) picks through a heap of discarded electronic equipment from the United States. The actual place may be southern China or Delhi, India (we know this because of research conducted by environmental sociologists). We can begin to imagine this girl or boy (or man or woman) at a low-tech "e-waste processing center," a place where people with few other choices manually harvest this highly toxic electronic waste for salvageable materials. The pay is low, and there are no protections in place for their bodies or for the surrounding environment.

We can only begin to imagine this scene because most computer users in the United States and in many other places have never seen it. It is disturbing to imagine it and to think that in some way we participate in it. Although from a distance the computer production process appears to be a clean and "high-tech" operation, at both the assembling and disassembling ends it is hazardous and farmed out to low-wage assembly line–style factories in developing nations. Instead of a can being thrown to the edge of a U.S. highway, electronic toxic waste is landing in places that are globally "at the edge of the highway" as Western nations (and even more so multinational corporations) speed by in pursuit of economic growth and political power. The "tearing away" from place first evident in the truck scene now has global dimensions. The difference is that globalization extends the arc of the object being disposed of and expands its geographical reach. Like the butterfly wings at the edge of the highway, the export of toxic components has been a well-kept secret. And that is the latest challenge for theorists in environmental sociology—to make these global structures plainly visible so that we can see and so that we can act.

CONCLUDING THOUGHTS: OF NATURE AND DOGS

Although this discussion has included only a small slice of what environmental sociologists do with theory, it reflects the wide range of interests and levels of analysis that are characteristic of the field. From naturework to shifting arrangements of time and space in the context of global capitalism, it offers tools for understanding the connection between our individual identities, nature, and broad patterns that are reshaping the context of our human experience and generating new kinds of relationships.

At the same time, we can notice that there is creative resistance to these patterns, some of which is also expressed through technology—for example, one might be using the computer to research social change and to connect with organizations working for ecological sustainability. There are many groups around the world working for environmental justice and for safeguards that would change Scene One, for example, by making it more visible to the people in Scene Three (see Lessons 10, 15, and 17). When environmental sociologists produce theories and research to document and analyze relationships between society and environment, they contribute to the possibility of real social change.

Here is a closing thought and one last image. My friend and colleague Elaine lives in a rural area over in the next town, in a self-designed house that reflects her fondness for stained glass art and large dogs. On her way to work, some of the dogs run alongside her truck for a little while, then turn around and go home before she hits the main road. But one morning, after an ice storm, the story line changed. She had to drive very slowly on the slippery unpaved road leading from her house. Because the truck couldn't "outrun" her most enthusiastic dog, he jumped in the back of her truck, rode to the university, and entertained himself by barking at passersby for much of the day. We don't know whether he *really* said "bow wow!" or "haf haf!" but we know that he attracted a lot of attention as an element of "nature" out of place.

I remember this story for several reasons. I like to think about how that dog insisted on connecting time and space and refused to be left behind in the "home" world while my friend went to "work" (he didn't appreciate distanciation). He brings to mind the many things we think we can outrun, including our impacts on the environment. Like the barking dog, fossil fuel scarcity and global warming are reminders of ecological actualities that we cannot continue to outrun. In our speeded-up world, you could say that our road is getting slippery and there are plenty of signs that we need to slow down and take an immediate, careful, and radical look at our actions and at our connections to the environment.

I propose that it would be even more appropriate to see social theory as the barking dog in this picture, shaking up our usual routines and reminding us that we are dialoguing with the environment, whether we want to see it or not. It is our social structures that are blocking our view of everything from tiny damaged butterfly wings to global flows of hazardous waste. If we accept the invitation from environmental sociology, we will be connecting the invisible strings that link our hands with the things that we throw away, looking to see where they land, questioning relationships of power and desire, and moving toward a better design for socioecological relationships.

SOURCES

Bauman, Zygmunt. 1997. *Postmodernity and Its Discontents*. New York: New York University Press.

Bell, Michael Mayerfeld and Michael S. Carolan. 2004. *An Invitation to Environmental Sociology*. Thousand Oaks, CA: Pine Forge.

Catton, William R., and Riley E. Dunlap. 1980. "A New Ecological Paradigm for Post-Exuberant Sociology." *American Behavioral Scientist* 24:15–47.

Fine, Gary Alan. 1998. *Morel Tales: The Culture of Mushrooming*. Cambridge, MA: Harvard University Press.

Giddens, Anthony. 1990. *The Consequences of Modernity*. Stanford, CA: Stanford University Press.

McDonough, William. 2002. *Cradle to Cradle: Remaking the Way We Make Things*. Minneapolis, MN: Sagebrush Educational Resources.

Meadows, Donella. 2004. "Dancing with Systems." *The Systems Thinker* 13(2):2–6.

Molotch, Harvey. 2003. *Where Stuff Comes From: How Toasters, Toilets, Cars, Computers, and Many Other Things Come to Be as They Are*. New York: Routledge.

Ritzer, George. 1999. *Enchanting a Disenchanted World: Revolutionizing the Means of Consumption*. Thousand Oaks, CA: Pine Forge.

Schnaiberg, Allan, and Kenneth Alan Gould. 1994. *Environment and Society: The Enduring Conflict*. New York: St. Martin's.

Smith, Ted, David A. Sonnenfeld, and David Naguib Pellow, eds. 2006. *Challenging the Chip: Labor Rights and Environmental Justice in the Global Electronics Industry*. Philadelphia, PA: Temple University Press.

Theories in Environmental Sociology

Luiz C. Barbosa

A good place to begin a discussion of sociological theories of the environment is by providing a definition of what theory is. There are several definitions in the literature. A definition that I use in my own courses is by sociologist Jonathan Turner. In his book *The Structure of Sociological Theory, Fifth Edition* (1991) he states that "Theory is a 'story' about how and why events in the universe occur." This is a simple but useful way of understanding what theories are. Theories are indeed stories or narratives about how things work. Turner also points out that sociologists do no agree on what kind of stories sociology as a discipline should develop; that is, they do not agree on what procedures should be used in developing explanations, the knowledge that can be developed, etc. Because of this lack of consensus, the discipline has some vastly different stories or narratives about how the social world is organized. However, this is not a feature unique to sociology. Competing explanations about phenomena are characteristic of intellectual pursuits, especially those under the banner of science.

There are a couple of ideas that could be added to Turner's notion of theory as a story. First, sociological theories differ from commonsensical interpretations of events in the sense that they are intellectually guided stories. This means sociologists use the tools of reason or logic and empirical evidence to build theories. This is different from assumptions people make about the world based on values, religion, and their own experiences or interpretations. These explanations often contradict themselves. This is not to claim that sociological theories lack imperfections. However, social scientists use logical reasoning in an attempt to make different parts of a theory fit together coherently. Each theory contains a web of logical statements about relationships among concepts or ideas. For example, Karl Marx (1818–1883) argued that changes in the substructure or the economic base of society lead to changes in the superstructure of society—its culture, politics, religion, etc. He also argued that there are links between ideology and political life and between these and religion. His theory contains a web of relationships in which one concept affects another and so on. Another example is the relationship between consumption and environmental degradation in the field of environmental sociology. One can connect the idea of consumption with many other variables or ideas, such as culture, advertising, ideology, wealth, boredom, etc. Theorizing assumes the world has order and that events do not happen randomly. It is about searching for cause-and-effect relationships.

Having a theory about whatever phenomenon one wants to explain can be beneficial for several reasons.

- A theory can provide guidance for investigation.
- A theory can make people think in broader terms than immediate relationships being investigated.
- One can build on an existing framework provided by a theory; that is, one can add new concepts or ideas to the general framework of the theory.
- A theory can help us generate hypotheses about relationships between concepts.

However, having a theory can also present problems. It can

- blind us to ideas or relationships not covered by the theory
- lead us to think at the wrong level of analysis for the problem(s) being investigated
- make us exclude possible causes

Theories are only good if empirical evidence mounts in their support. If they are not able to withstand empirical evidence, they should be either modified or entirely discarded. Unfortunately, this does not always happen. Once a community of scholars subscribes to a theory, they sometimes attempt to prevent it from falling—a phenomenon that happens in all sciences. For example, for a long time theories based on the skeleton of Piltdown man, or *Eoanthropus dawsoni*, discovered in 1912 prevailed in British archeology. Piltdown man was believed to be the missing link between human beings and other apes. British archeologists were reluctant to accept theories and evidence that contradicted prevailing explanations. Eventually, the skeleton of Piltdown man was proven to be a fake. Power relationships, prestige, time and effort spent in research, etc., influence a theory's survival; for example, the fact that Piltdown man was "British" certainly kept the theory alive. However, theories eventually fall when there is little or no evidence to support them, when better theories emerge, or when there is too much contradicting evidence against them, as was the case with Piltdown man.

One important issue to keep in mind when evaluating a theory is background information. Issues of race, ethnicity, class, gender, and sexual orientation can affect the composition of a theory and its acceptance. For example, discrimination in academic life meant sociological theories dealing with women and minorities were disregarded until the early twentieth century. Furthermore, the background of the theorist matters. For example, the first sociological theories dealing with African American communities were written by whites and depicted African American communities as pathological versions of the white community. They were written at a time when few African Americans found jobs in academia. Even though sociological works written by African Americans such as William E. B. DuBois (1868–1963) and Oliver Cox (1901–1974) existed, they were relegated to marginal status. Another issue to keep in mind is timing or time period. Sociologists do not exist in a vacuum. They are part of the social matrix of their time; that is, they are affected by history and the social institutions that surround them. As these change, arising issues lead sociologists to reflect and theorize about their world. As described below, environmental sociology itself is a product of a very specific period of time.

Whole courses are taught in sociological theory. The philosophical controversies alone make it a fascinating field of study. Keep in mind that the above explanation is an oversimplification for the sake of discussion. However, one can draw on these ideas when evaluating sociological theories in the field of environmental sociology. The theories below should be thought of as competing "stories" or "narratives" about the relationship between human societies and the environment.

THE ENVIRONMENT AND CLASSICAL SOCIOLOGY

The first theories in sociology were influenced by two main events in history: the Enlightenment and the Industrial Revolution. These events were associated with a great deal of optimism about human beings and human societies. Enlightenment scholars believed human beings were endowed with reason and could think for themselves; thus, they did not need the prescribed thinking and behaviors dictated by religious dogma. These scholars also believed human beings could be perfected given the right social conditions and institutions. They thought that, using reason and science, "natural laws" would be uncovered and this would lead to control of nature and to progress. They believed nature could be subdued. An exception to this optimistic view was the work of Thomas Robert Malthus (1766–1834) (see Lesson 9). In his 1798 *Essay on the Principle of Population,* he argued that while population grew geometrically (2, 4, 16, 32 . . .), the amount of land put under cultivation and food output grew arithmetically (1, 2, 3, 4 . . .); thus, people would eventually run out of food. According to Malthus, the future of the human species was one of devastation caused by famines, pestilence, wars, etc. Despite Malthus' views, the intellectual mood of the time remained one of great optimism. Innovations brought about through science during the Industrial Revolution further legitimized these ideas of progress. Indeed, in the course of a brief period of history human beings accomplished marvelous things. It seemed that, by understanding the laws of nature, human beings were no longer controlled by them.

Sociological theories that emerged in the nineteenth century were concerned with understanding the forces that held society together and the forces that led to its transformation, the questions of order and change. There was much concern with social problems brought about by industrialization and modernization in general. The environment was marginal in these theories, if included at all. The emphasis was on human exceptionalism; that is, on the uniqueness of human beings and human societies. For example, Karl Marx emphasized human beings' ability to think and transform the environment; he thought of our species as the only species capable of replicating the environment. He also believed raw materials are given to us gratis (for free) by nature and that it is human labor that gives it value. Thus, Marx failed to notice the intrinsic value of nature. Human exceptionalism was especially prevalent in the sociology of Émile Durkheim (1858–1917). Durkheim argued that social phenomena are social facts; they are real in their manifestations. In the same fashion as electricity, gravity, etc. are invisible to us but we are able to feel their manifestations, social phenomena such as morality and the collective consciousness, which are nonmaterial and invisible, affect us through their coercive powers—they affect the way we think and behave. For example, most Americans would feel embarrassed being naked in a public place such as a shopping mall, a feeling that is a by-product of socialization and a manifestation of the collective consciousness within us. In other societies the norm is just the opposite. In many Amazonian indigenous villages, people walk around with few or no clothes. Durkheim believed that social facts should be explained through other social facts. In his view, psychological, biological, environmental, and other factors do not satisfactorily explain sociological phenomena. For example, in his famous book *Suicide* (1897) he showed how a decision that appears so personal or "psychological" as taking one's own life has sociological antecedents or causes, for example, the attachments an individual has to social groups. Durkheim's methodology was very influential in establishing what contemporary sociologists call "social constructions," for example, institutions, culture, relationships, etc., as the focus of study in sociology. As described below, it was not until the 1970s that the environment became a topic of serious investigation in the discipline.

The lack of attention to the environment has had special consequences in the field of social change and development, which grew in importance in the discipline in the 1950s and 1960s. Theories in this field have been more than just theories. They are prescriptions for development, which are often adopted as policy by international organizations and governments—for example, to help poor countries rise from poverty. Theories in this field have disregarded environmental consequences in their prescriptions for development. They have often described the environment in terms of raw materials and resources. While Marxist and neoliberal (market-based) theories proposed different means to achieve development, socialism versus free markets, both intellectual camps had disregard for nature in common. The concern with sustainable development would not enter this field of study until the late 1980s, largely after the publication of the report by the Bruntland Commission titled *Our Common Future*, which brought the concept of sustainable development to the forefront (see Lesson 19).

THE BIRTH OF ENVIRONMENTAL SOCIOLOGY

The emergence of the field of environmental sociology reflects preoccupation with the state of the environment in the United States in the 1960s and early 1970s. The publication of Rachel Carson's *Silent Spring* in 1962 spearheaded the modern environmentalist movement by raising public awareness about the impact of pesticides on the environment. Issues such as nuclear energy, toxic waste, and pollution were also brought to the center of attention and stirred protest. The introduction of Earth Day in 1970 and the United Nations Conference on Environment and Development in Stockholm in 1972 largely reflected social concerns over these issues. However, the field of environmental sociology would not take off until the late 1970s. Prior to that, interest in environmental issues in the discipline was limited to the field of urban sociology and its attempt to apply ecological models to describe the layout of cities. This "human ecology" was especially prominent at the University of Chicago in the 1920s with the works of sociologists such as Robert E. Park (1864–1944). A series of journal articles by William Catton and Riley Dunlap in the late 1970s and early 1980s was essential in launching the new field of environmental sociology. In these articles, these scholars argued that all theories in sociology were alike in their shared assumption of human exceptionalism from the laws of nature. As noted in Lesson 1, they called this prevailing paradigm or model "human exceptionalism paradigm" (HEP)— which was later changed to "human exemptionalism paradigm" (also HEP). They argued that HEP was based on the assumption that due to culture, technology, language, and elaborate social organizations human beings are exempt from ecological principles and are able to bend environmental limitations. HEP places social and cultural factors as the main determinants of human affairs, a view which, as described above, was highly influenced by scholars such as Durkheim. Catton and Dunlap proposed a "new ecological paradigm" (NEP) for sociology, and the other social sciences for that matter. Even though they acknowledged some of the exceptional characteristics human beings possess, they argued that our species is one species among many others in the web of life. NEP posits that human affairs are affected by an intricate set of causal relationships within nature. Like all other species on Earth, ours also depends on a finite biosphere for survival. Human inventiveness can temporarily extend carrying capacity limits, but ecological laws cannot be repealed. While NEP was a step in the right direction, it should be kept in mind that it is largely a critique of lack of concern for the environment in sociology. While it suggests directions for the discipline, it is not a theory.

While the works of Catton and Dunlap were important in the development of environmental sociology, developments in ecology and in the environmentalist movement prior to the late 1970s were equally important. Efforts to make ecology "sociological" came before efforts to make sociology "environmental." In the early 1960s, Murray Bookchin (1921–2006) introduced "social ecology" as an alternative to views held by ecologists, who identified ecological problems solely with the preservation of wildlife and wilderness. Bookchin argued that present ecological problems arise from deep-seated social problems; unless these are solved, ecological problems will persist. That is, for him ecological problems cannot be separated from sociological problems. This observation makes a great deal of sense to me as I write this lesson in Rio de Janeiro, Brazil, during a research sabbatical. Slums in Rio often begin when squatters invade public lands or forests. As slums grow, the forests that surround the area begin to disappear. Bookchin viewed social inequality as the ultimate cause of ecological problems. He saw hierarchical mentality and class relationships prevalent in society as giving rise to the very idea of dominating the natural world. Social ecology calls for abolition of hierarchy and for the reconstruction of society along ecological lines. This would first entail the elimination of private property, which is the main cause of inequality in society. In the new society property would be held communally.

The rise of ecofeminism in the environmentalist movement of the early 1970s was also an important development in the rise of environmental sociology. It specifically associated one form of inequality with environmental destruction: patriarchy or male dominance. The publication of Rosemary Ruether's *New Woman, NewEarth* in 1975 established the foundations for this brand of environmentalism. In this book she argued there can be no liberation for women and no solution to the ecological crisis without elimination of all forms of exploitation. Ruether argues that eliminating hierarchy is the first step toward construction of an ecological society. This has become a raison d'être for ecofeminism.

Another influence in the development of environmental sociology was deep ecology. In 1972 at the Third World Futures conference in Bucharest, Norwegian philosopher Arne Naess presented a paper in which he laid out the differences between "shallow" and "deep" ecologies. According to him, the former is primarily concerned with resource depletion and usefulness of the Earth for human beings, while the latter is concerned with the intrinsic value of the Earth—its diversity and richness. Naess later developed some basic principles for deep ecology which are summarized below.

- Harmony with nature
- Biospherical egalitarianism or species equality: other species should be able not only to survive but to thrive
- Material objects should serve bigger objectives such as self-actualization, not consumption for the sake of consumption
- Awareness of the limits of our planet's resources
- Use of environmentally appropriate technologies
- Emphasis on recycling
- Emphasis on bioregions and recognition of human differences

Naess's ideas were popularized in the United States especially through the works of sociologist Bill Devall and philosopher George Sessions. Their book

Deep Ecology: Living as if Nature Mattered became a classic in the ecological literature. In addition to adopting Naess's basic principles, this book emphasizes spirituality. The authors argue in favor of Eastern and Native American religious philosophies, which they view as promoting harmony with nature relative to the beliefs in Judeo-Christian religions. For example, Native American cultures see elements of the environment as sacred, while Christianity preaches that humans were given domain over the entire Earth by God.

The rise of deep ecology has led to an enduring debate with social ecology, which was largely spearheaded by Murray Bookchin until his death in 2006. Bookchin argued against the "mysticism" of deep ecology. This is illustrated by an essay he wrote titled "Social Ecology Versus Deep Ecology: A Challenge for the Ecology Movement." In this essay he stated that "The greatest differences . . . within the so-called ecology movement are between a vague, formless, often self-contradictory, and invertebrate thing called deep ecology and a long-developing, coherent, and socially oriented body of ideas that can best be called social ecology." He called deep ecology a mixture of "Hollywood and Disneyland, spiced with homilies from Taoism, Buddhism, spiritualism, reborn Christianity, and in some cases eco-fascism."

Sociologists would respond to philosophical debates in ecology, developments in the environmentalist movement, and Catton and Dunlap's call for adoption of NEP with new theoretical insights that together created a new and exciting field of study within the discipline. It is ironic that while criticizing the "human exemptionalism" of the classical tradition in sociology, the new theories they developed share a background with the classical tradition, what environmental sociologist Frederick Buttel calls an "ontological kinship." That is, theories in environmental sociology largely built on basic concepts already in existence in the discipline. Below are some of these theories. The list is not comprehensive. It only includes those theories believed to be the most important in the field. They are grouped together into categories that broadly reflect their intellectual or ideological orientations. Be warned that not everyone will agree with this classification. You should think of the text below as a "story" or narrative about the theories being explained, a story about stories so to speak. One important issue that I would like you to keep in mind when reading my account is the philosophical debate about the sustainability of capitalism. Some of the theories, for example, treadmill of production and ecological modernization theory, have a definite stand on this issue, while others are more ambiguous. I think the question of system sustainability is of central importance for solutions to pressing problems such as climate change(see Lesson 14).

NEO-MARXIST POLITICAL-ECONOMY THEORIES

The emphasis of Marxist theory in sociology has been on the class conflict that originates out of competition for the economic spoils or resources of society. In capitalist society, the bourgeoisie, the capitalist class, owns the means of production—that is, the banks, factories, etc.—and the proletariat, the workers, sell their labor. For Karl Marx, those who have wealth have everything else in society: power, prestige, and influence. For him, capitalism benefits the elites and alienates the proletariat, who are paid low wages for hard, mechanical work that lacks creativity. He believed the bourgeoisie was able to maintain power and the status quo through control of the means of production, violence, and ideological indoctrination. Marx also saw capitalism as a system that needs to perpetually reproduce itself or expand in order to thrive. However, this systemic requirement leads to the crisis of overproduction. Saturation of the economy forces capitalists to look for new ways to invigorate it, for example, through the introduction of new technologies and products, through conquest of new markets, etc. Marx believed that capitalism, like all the previous modes of production, contained the seeds of its own destruction. Each successive crisis of overproduction would make future crises increasingly more difficult for the bourgeoisie to manage; for example, new markets would end, and eventually the system would collapse. Under the leadership of the proletariat, revolution would take place and eventually a new mode of production would arise, socialism. This would be an intermediary stage, which eventually would culminate in communism.

Neo-Marxist models build on Marx's notion of conflict in capitalist society while downplaying or rejecting other aspects of his theory. These models are not limited to class analysis, for example, bourgeoisie versus proletariat, but include a whole range of other conflicts such as gender, ethnic, racial, political, and so on. These approaches also tend to reject the notion that the proletariat is at the forefront of a socialist revolution that is about to happen.

Ecological Marxism

There are different varieties of ecological Marxism. We already described the work of Murray Bookchin on social ecology above. His work is very representative of the main premises of this theoretical perspective. His claim that in order to understand environmental problems we need to seek their source in the system of inequality human beings have created is a fundamental principle in ecological Marxism. In addition to inequality, the approach emphasizes the contradictions that exist in capitalism. For example, one of the most significant contributions in this area is James O'Connor's argument that capitalism undermines the factors that sustain it, such as human labor and the environment. He argues that in addition to the contradiction between capital and labor characteristic of the system, the first contradiction of capitalism, there is a second contradiction between these two factors and nature—both capital and labor depend on the exploitation of the environment. Similar to the first contradiction of the system, the second contradiction can also induce crisis. A good example of this is climate change and the costs associated with it. As the problem deepens, it will very likely adversely impact capitalism and may even affect its ability to function at all in some places. Hurricane Katrina exemplifies the potential seriousness of

~blem. Just imagine if more hurricanes of Katrina's magnitude would
'ed areas on a regular basis (see Lesson 13). The costs would be
most likely would shake the system. Other conditions
warming, such as rising sea levels, will also generate
rises throughout the world. Ecological Marx-
Nature, Socialism, which has been very influen-
ental sociology.

theory has its origins in the publication of Allan
ment: From Surplus to Scarcity in 1980. It is one of
es in the field of environmental sociology. In *The*
argues that human societies depend on flows of
thus are not exempt from the two basic laws of
t law is that of conservation of matter and energy,
nd energy cannot be created or destroyed; they can
second law is that of entropy, which states that all
re degradations that change energy from more to
fewer forms. Huma.   ial organization gives the impression that we are
above these laws; our economic, social, cultural, and other systems obfuscate
the fact that we ultimately depend on nature and that the laws of thermody-
namics cannot be repealed. Even though it is often ignored, human beings
exist within the environmental matrix of the biosphere like any other species
on Earth. Our ingenuity has given us more flexibility but has not exempted
us from the forces of nature.

Human beings have maintained an increasingly damaging relationship
with the environment since the times we were primarily "biological consumers," as hunters and gatherers. As the economies of human societies
became more complex, they began to exercise additional pressure on the
environment through processes of interchange involving withdrawals and
additions. *Withdrawals* are raw materials we take from nature in order to
transform them into objects either for "use value" (utility or function) or for
"exchange value" (market value), or both. *Additions* are what we return to
the environment, for example, pollution and garbage. These cycles of withdrawal and addition can disorganize biospheric systems. Industrialization
meant our environmental impact would increase. Machines could produce
faster, and new technologies were more energy- and chemical-intensive. This
meant that industry took more from the environment and returned more
toxic elements(see Lessons 5 and 12).

The aim of the treadmill of production is profit for capitalists and investors. The system has to continuously produce and grow in order to generate
profit. One way to maximize profit has been to invest in new technologies
capable of replacing human labor. To amortize the fixed and operating costs
of new technologies, industrial production had to be increased, which raised
the volume of production waste and the toxicity of wastes. What is ironic

about this process is that workers have helped sow the seeds of their own degradation. By generating profits with their work, they have allowed for higher investments in labor-saving technologies, which have replaced them. Influenced by the corporate-framed ideology of modernization, growing world competitiveness, and free trade, workers have been indoctrinated to accept automation and the transfer of jobs overseas. They had to acquiesce to a situation created by corporations that pushed for free trade and established subsidiaries abroad.

Following a neo-Marxist line of thinking, treadmill of production theory argues that the social institutions of modern industrial society are intertwined and supportive of the treadmill of production. These institutions help "lubricate" the treadmill. For example, the welfare state allocates a significant share of the surplus generated by economic expansion to safety-net mechanisms such as workers' compensation or disability, unemployment insurance, etc., which help maintain workers loyal to the system. The state promotes growth, which is viewed as necessary for the stability and health in general of society. When sectors of the economy such as housing stop growing, government officials usually take steps to stimulate them, for example, by lowering interests rates. Labor unions are also supportive of the treadmill since growth generally means jobs for workers—even though with globalization jobs may actually be created in different parts of the world. Education is another social institution that helps maintain the system, by educating future professionals. The family is another example. Its function as an agent of socialization has made it the target of marketers. Through television and other media, families are encouraged to shop. Our lives have become so intertwined with the treadmill of production that shopping sometimes is defined as a civic duty. For example, people were encouraged to shop after the tragic events of September 11, not only as a sign of defiance to terrorists but also to keep the economy moving.

Perhaps the most controversial claim made by scholars who subscribe to the treadmill of production concerns the environmentalist movement and environmental efforts such as recycling. Due to its reformist nature, the environmentalist movement is viewed as ineffective. Despite its efforts since the 1960s, environmental degradation continues. The leverage acquired by environmentalists does not begin to compare with the power of those in charge of the treadmill of production; the latter have vast amounts of economic resources they can use to direct the system, while environmentalists have to struggle to amass resources. Treadmill of production scholars argue that efforts such as recycling provide the illusion that people can maintain their consumption lifestyles if they do "their part" to compensate for their consumption patterns, when in reality their lifestyles—or the lifestyle of their societies—are unsustainable in the long run.

Critics of the treadmill of production theory argue against its materialist approach and point to the importance of other factors, such as culture, in creating and solving environmental problems. They believe that changes in cultural practices, such as changes in consumption habits, can lead to improved environmental conditions. Some are also uncomfortable with what they view as the "pessimism" or lack of "hope" in the approach. They argue that the theory disempowers those willing to take small steps to ameliorate environmental conditions, for instance, through recycling and other programs. They think these small steps are more appealing to the public than radical systemic changes. As we shall see below, some critics argue that what modern societies need is not a radical change of economic systems but more and better technologies.

World-System Theory

World-system theory is built on neo-Marxist ideas and thus has a heavy emphasis on economic relationships. It emerged largely as a reaction to neoliberal theories of development, especially modernization theory, in the debate about the causes of development and underdevelopment. Modernization theory argued that the "traditional" values of Third World societies were largely responsible for their underdevelopment. These societies were described as rigid, undemocratic, unscientific, uneducated, and in need of modernization, which meant capitalism, political reform, and Westernization of values. This theory became the darling of international organizations in the 1950s and 1960s. World-system theory emerged largely as a reaction to this blame-the-victim approach. It emphasized the history of colonialism as the main cause of the underdevelopment of the third world. Thus, like many of the theories discussed in this lesson, it was not originally devised as a theory about the environment. However, scholars have used it to explain environmental issues and have generated some very interesting insights, especially about global environmental issues. In my opinion, it has a great deal of potential in helping us understand the current global environmental crisis.

As proposed by sociologist Immanuel Wallerstein, world-system theory argues that the capitalist world economy has its roots in the period of time he termed "the long sixteenth century," from 1450 to 1640. With maritime voyages, the European economy began to expand and colonialism was set in motion. By the nineteenth century Europe had, with a few exceptions, engulfed all corners of the world. The nature of this emerging economy was capitalist since its main goal was trade and profit. Its spread would create a global division of labor with western Europe at its center or core and the colonies at its periphery—the United States and later Japan joined the core in the twentieth century. The relationship between the core and the periphery has been one of exploitation; the core has exploited the periphery for raw materials, labor, and as a market. In between these two zones lies the semi-periphery, a category consisting of countries that declined from the core or managed to rise from the periphery, for example, South Korea, Brazil, and Mexico. In addition to proposing this global stratification system, the theory argues that the capitalist world economy is characterized by economic and political cycles. Economic cycles can be of short duration, such as a short recession, or long-term trends, or *"longue durées,"* which can last decades or centuries. Political cycles are characterized by cycles of hegemony (dominance) in which one country leads the core and thus exerts an enormous amount of influence in shaping the system as a whole. Wallerstein argues that three countries have been hegemonic since the rise of this economy in the long sixteenth century: the United Provinces in the seventeenth century, the United Kingdom in the nineteenth century, and the United States in the twentieth century. Each shaped the system according to its needs.

An important feature of the theory is that capitalism has led to increasing rationalization and commodification. *Rationalization* is a complicated process of social change that involves the demystification of the world through the replacement of tradition, emotions, religious dogma, etc. by impersonal bureaucratic institutions and science. *Commodification* means the transformation of anything, including human beings, into goods or commodities that can be sold in the market; a market exchange value is attached to them. It involves economic as well as social mechanisms. A good example of this is land. Land for the native peoples of the Americas was held communally. The capitalism Europeans introduced to the region required land to be commodified; thus, it became private property that could be marketed. Rhinoceros horns are another example of the social–economic elements of commodification. Rhinoceros are threatened by extinction because people are willing to pay large sums of money for their horns, which are highly valued in some cultures as an aphrodisiac. Note that rhinoceros horns are made of the same substance as human fingernails, keratin. Another important feature of the theory is dominance. In his book *Historical Capitalism with Capitalist Civilization*, Wallerstein argues that capitalism is controlled by a new kind of human being in history, *Homo economicus*, who shapes the rules of the system in the pursuit of profit. The rest of us have to follow these rules. For example, we have to have an understanding of basic principles of economics in order to survive. To put this to a test, just try to obtain goods, including food, from a store without having money or some form of acceptable payment. The United States is a capitalist society, where one cannot survive very well without a job and access to currency. While this is basic knowledge, we do not think about it until we are confronted with unfortunate situations such as unemployment.

The pioneering work that applied world-system theory to the understanding of environmental issues was Stephen Bunker's *Underdeveloping the Amazon*. In this book Bunker argued that the sale of natural resources from the Third World to the first world, for example, minerals and forest resources, represented a permanent loss for the former. This loss of irreplaceable resources eventually created underdevelopment in the areas being exploited, not development. Once the resources were exhausted, these areas plunged into cycles of economic instability and poverty. For Bunker, this trade in natural resources meant irreplaceable transfers of assets from the periphery to the core.

Bunker's work made people think about the global links involved in deforestation and other environmental problems. For environmental world-system theorists like me interested in Amazonia, the message was clear: Some of the major environmental problems of our time need to be understood in relation to the dynamics of an evolving world-system. Global inequalities involving core, semiperipheral, and peripheral zones are directly linked to environmental degradation and should not be ignored. For example, many of the environmental problems in the periphery and semiperiphery are associated or intertwined with the populations of the core. Consumption in the core has been associated with deforestation, strip mining, and pollution in general. Every time someone buys furniture made of mahogany, there is a good chance that he or she is contributing to deforestation in places such as Amazonia. There is also the issue of excessive consumption in the core relative to its population size of less than 20% of the global population. Problems such as climate change are heavily associated with overconsumption by these countries. The semiperiphery is also implicated. In attempting to catch up with the core, some of these countries have literally razed their environments, for example, cutting their forests for timber, agriculture, and mining. Some of these countries have been guided by ideologies of predatory development, such as "Develop 50 years in 5." The intensity of development in the semiperiphery has led to high levels of environmental degradation. As a matter of fact, world-system researchers, such as Thomas Burns and his colleagues, have noticed that degradation is more intense in the semiperiphery than in the core and the periphery. Environmental degradation is limited in the periphery by lack of development, and intense environmentalism in the core has led to passage of strict environmental laws. On the other hand, semiperipheral countries sacrifice their environments for the sake of development. In countries such as Thailand people have to wear surgical masks due to heavy traffic pollution.

Despite its potential to help us understand the dynamics of the global environmental crisis, world-system theory remains largely underutilized. Some scholars find the categorization of countries into core, periphery, and semiperiphery limiting. Even though these have been extended to include new categories such as the semicore and several subcategories of periphery, this has failed to attract large numbers. It is difficult for a theory based on economic relationships and advocating radical change to compete with new theories based on cultural explanations and that are reformist. Contemporary sociologists tend to gravitate to explanations that are based on "the social construction of reality" rather than to what they view as "economic determinism." Unfortunately, one cannot understand some of the critical environmental issues of our time without a dispassionate examination of the economic bases of our society and our world.

NEOLIBERAL THEORIES

The underlying ideas of neoliberalism can be traced to classical economics, especially to the works of Adam Smith (1723–1790). Smith proposed that commercial society, what we now call "capitalist society," was fundamentally different from previous forms because commerce played such a fundamental role in its composition. He argued that, unlike previous societal forms, commercial society needed less government, not more. Government would be relegated few functions, such as protection against foreign enemies, utilities (sewage, water, etc.), and, above all, protection of private property. Government should also act to prevent monopolies, which thwart competition. Smith believed that instead of government interference these societies should be regulated by market forces, by the "invisible hand of the market." Competition in a market economy would benefit everyone and would keep the system in synchrony. Merchants who sold at high prices would be outcompeted by those who sold at lower prices, inefficient companies would be replaced by more efficient ones, and so on. Competition would also lead to creativity as individuals would search for new products to sell. For Smith, the pursuit of gain was the most basic of human drives and individuals should be left alone to satisfy it. In the end, the whole society would benefit from individual effort.

Smith was not the only classical economist. However, his ideas, more than those of any other scholar, established the foundations of (economic) liberal thought. In neoliberal thinking, the market continues to be viewed as the best mechanism to achieve important societal goals, such as development and eradication of poverty. Theories about the environment which follow this philosophical view also rely on market mechanisms. Their basic assumption is that consumers make rational choices and they will choose, if properly educated, environmentally friendly goods. They also argue that competition will lead corporations to adopt environmentally friendly technologies once a few of their competitors adopt them.

Ecological Modernization Theory

We can think of ecological modernization theory as an antithesis to treadmill of production theory. Its beginnings are associated with the works of European scholars such as Joseph Huber, Martin Jänicke, Arthur Mol, and Gert Spaargaren. The theory is based on the premise that capitalism is a system flexible enough to permit movement in the direction of "sustainable capitalism." In order to achieve this, the theory argues that solutions to the environmental problems of modern industrial societies require additional modernization and "superindustrialization." That is, instead of retreating to a world of simplicity, as suggested by radical environmentalists, what modern industrial societies need is to use better and environmentally friendly technologies as a means of dealing with environmental problems. The theory also relies on postmodern notions of "reflexive modernization." Reflexivity involves the individual and society constantly reexamining their own circumstances—beliefs, social practices, etc.—in light of new information or knowledge. At the institutional level, this means that institutions such as government and corporations would use knowledge and technologies about the environment to change social conduct and institutional arrangements.

Transformation of state environmental policy is central in this institutional development. However, while the stewardship of the process would start in government, it would be transferred to the market, which is viewed as a more efficient mechanism for solving problems than the state. This would advance and accelerate the ecological transformation process due to competition, availability of investment capital, and so on. The state would continue to play a vital role in managing the environment. It would provide the infrastructure and incentives for the adoption of environmentally sound policies and technologies and create the right conditions for self-regulation. *LOL*

Like its predecessor, modernization theory, ecological modernization theory has been embraced by international organizations. One way of looking at its acceptance by these organizations is that the theory provides "practical" or "realistic" solutions to current environmental problems. When better technologies are employed, they indeed produce results such as less pollution and more energy efficiency. However, acceptance also reflects the theory's neoliberal stance, which is in line with the capitalist ideology that prevails in many international organizations. Its emphasis is on reforming or modernizing the system rather than radically challenging it.

Ecological modernization theory has become a popular approach in environmental sociology, presenting the strongest challenge to the supremacy treadmill of production theory has maintained in the field since the 1980s. Some of its main arguments have also been reincarnated or have paralleled theoretical developments in the field of economics. *Natural Capitalism: Creating the Next Industrial Revolution* by economists Paul Hawken, Amory Lovins, and L. Hunter Lovins promotes a similar thesis about the role of technology, government, and the market in solving environmental problems. For these scholars, the next industrial revolution will be a response to changing patterns of scarcity, which will create tough conditions but also opportunities for adaptable companies. Their theory has four basic arguments, which are similar to those in ecological modernization theory:

- *Radically increase the productivity of resource use.* Fundamental changes in technology and design can lead to substantial savings.
- *Shift to biologically inspired production (biomimicry) with closed loops, no waste, and no toxicity.* Natural capitalism seeks to eliminate waste altogether.
- *Shift the business model away from the making and selling of "things" to providing the service that the "thing" delivers.* The natural capitalism model delivers value as a continuous flow of services.
- *Reinvest in natural and human capital.* Any good capitalist reinvests in productive capital.

The message of the above theories is clear: Capitalism is adaptable enough to be greened, and the market is the best mechanism to generate concrete environmental solutions. For their proponents, one does not throw the baby out with the bath water. Capitalism has generated high levels of prosperity and lifestyle sophistication for the developed countries, and it should not be substituted with systems based on less sophisticated technologies or with some form of ecosocialism. For critics, capitalism has created the major environmental problems of our time, and it cannot be tamed. In order for the system to thrive, it needs growth and expansion; in turn, this means utilization of natural resources and some form of waste. They also criticize the "techno-fix" solutions proposed by scholars who subscribe to modernization theory and similar theories. They argue that technology cannot fix all environmental problems and that it can also create new ones. They state that in the end these theories do not address overconsumption and the long-term environmental sustainability of the capitalist system.

SECOND MODERNITY THEORIES

Postmodern theories focus on the crisis of modern societies caused by a range of factors, such as declining faith in the political system, deindustrialization caused by globalization, shifts in labor markets, loss of trust in science, cultural changes, and too much individualism and rationalization in Western societies. Two sociologists have been prolific in addressing this societal transformation, German sociologist Ulrich Beck and British sociologist Anthony Giddens. Beck's work is heavily influenced by the sociology of Max Weber (1864–1920). Weber's emphasis was on the increasing rationalization of modern society and its contradictions or irrational consequences. He is famous for writing that modern societies were becoming "iron cages" of bureaucratic rules from which individuals could not escape. Beck's sociology captures transformations in modern society as people react to problems created by rational institutions. According to him, this new age, the beginning of "second modernity," is characterized by a high degree of uncertainty as people lost faith in rational institutions such as government and science; we have realized that these are part of the problem. Giddens' sociology has similar themes. For him, modern societies have entered a stage of "high" or "late" modernity, which is highly related to globalization. Giddens opposes the notion proposed by some scholars that modern societies have become "postmodern." He believes changes taking place in the West are part of the process of modernization itself, not "postmodernization." People's values and even self-identity in these societies are being transformed by globalization, which he views as a process of Westernization catapulted by the expansion of modernization from the West to other parts of the world. From his perspective, modern societies are undergoing a process of transformation caused by self-evaluation or "reflexivity." People in these societies are questioning the old order and establishing new social and institutional practices.

Risk Society

Ulrich Beck is credited with introducing the concept of "risk society." Anthony Giddens also has elaborated on related themes such as reflexivity. For Beck, risk is a systematic way of dealing with hazards and insecurities induced and introduced by modernization itself. Modern societies differ from other forms of society in the sense that risks are created by decisions, instead of naturally occurring hazards such as famines, floods, and so on, which plague other societies. Modern societies take deliberate risks. For people in these societies, risk is endemic. They rely on scientific knowledge, weighing the probabilities of risk. However, most people do not fully understand this type of knowledge. According to Beck, as knowledge and technology race ahead, people are left behind, panting in ignorance, increasingly unable to understand and control the machines on which they depend. People's lack of knowledge leads to the mystification of science, to which scientists also contribute with their robes, institutions, etc. People rely on scientists for interpretations of scientific information. This reliance is sometimes problematic. Beck argues that scientists have made errors and are often blind about risk. For him, science weighs the distribution of risks and errors, which are often created by science itself (see Lesson 7). A good illustration of this is nuclear power. It has been made accessible as a result of scientific investigation. Nuclear power plants are built and run with consideration of risks or the probability of accidents. Scientists have weighed the risks and have told the public it is a safe form of energy.

Beck suggests that a problem faced by modern societies is the loss of faith in the institutions of modernity such as science, business, and politics. These institutions were supposed to guarantee rationality and security, but they failed. People no longer trust them. However, they are forced to rely on these institutions' expert systems for vital information. Major accidents such as Three Mile Island and Chernobyl have made people realize the enormous power of destruction of modern technologies (see Lesson 8). They have become reluctant to accept new technologies even when told they are safe. They feel they cannot trust the information since public officials, scientists, and corporate leaders might make mistakes or lie. The case of genetically modified foods is also illustrative of this situation. People fear this type of food even though they have been assured that risks such as allergies have been studied and proven to be small. Whole societies are reluctant to accept these risks. For example, there are severe restrictions imposed on genetically modified foods in the European Union and Japan.

Beck also argues that modern societies have experienced the collapse of collective or group-specific sources of meaning. This simply means that people in these societies are not under intense pressure to conform to social norms as in the past or in other types of society. While this allows them the freedom to choose, it also creates problems. Choice means trying untested possibilities, which means taking risks. Since collective meanings are no longer strong in modern societies, individuals and institutions need to engage in constant evaluations of their choices, a process Beck calls "reflexive modernization." For him, Western modernization is in the process of destroying itself. In its place a "reflexive modern society" is emerging based on the constant reappraisal and reevaluation of values and priorities as technologies change. Risk society scholars generally argue that "reflexivity" is the key element in uncovering solutions to the problems faced by modern societies, including environmental ones. This requires people, social institutions, and society in general to apply existing knowledge to reevaluate personal and institutional practices as well as risk. They argue that science itself needs to undergo a process of "reflexive scientization"; that is, it must turn its skepticism toward evaluating and criticizing itself.

The risk society concept is quite useful in terms of making us understand the costs and benefits of risk taking and why people are reluctant to accept certain strategies or technologies due to fear of the consequences. The notion of reflexivity also directs us to using available knowledge to evaluate our actions and policies in the pursuit of an environmentally conscious and friendly society. This is good. However, we need to be cognizant that reflexivity also involves the inclusion of different points of view. In 2006, Anthony Giddens published an article in an online version of the British newspaper the *Guardian* in which he claims the environmentalist movement should be "ditched." In this article, he argued that climate change is finally at the center of public attention and the "debate should not be left in the hands of those hostile to science and technology." He also claimed that discussion of the issue should be guided by scientists, as if the environmentalist movement, which has faced the toughest battles for the preservation of the environment, has nothing to contribute. Hasn't science been criticized for being part of the problem? Don't we need different voices in finding solutions? Giddens' argument to ditch the movement appears to be a case of "reflexivity" relying solely on what is perceived as "rational," which according to Beck's argument was a main cause of the problem in the first place.

FINAL THOUGHTS

The above theories often provide competing explanations about the relationship between human societies and the environment. However, they also complement each other. It does not matter if one subscribes to treadmill of production theory or modernization theory; risk is an important problem that people in the contemporary world face. It should be an issue of major consideration in any theory dealing with industrialization and the environment. Also, one cannot fully understand environmental degradation without taking into account the global stratification system. Treadmill of production scholars, for example, would have much to gain by integrating elements of world-system theory into their own theory. In recent years they have addressed issues pertaining to the "Global South" versus the "Global North," but this, in my opinion, has not been enough. World-system theory offers a more developed explanation of stratification that would bring theoretical refinement on this issue to treadmill of production theory. World-systems theory would also benefit by borrowing ideas from treadmill of production theory since both production and consumption are major defining factors in the contemporary world.

As climate change becomes a reality, it will become necessary for environmental sociologists to improve their theoretical models, combine them, and/or develop new ones. Climate change will likely create social issues that current theories do not address (see Lesson 14). For example, what will happen to the populations of low-lying countries with rising sea levels? How will this add to already existing problems such as immigration and poverty? What will happen to political relationships between developing and developed countries with climate change? Will rich countries intervene when developing countries cut their forests or pollute the environment? We will need theories that address issues such as these. Unfortunately, the field of environmental sociology is likely to grow in importance by necessity as the global environmental situation is likely to get worse rather than better.

SOURCES

Beck, Ulrich. 1992. *Risk Society: Towards a New Modernity*. Thousand Oaks, CA: Sage.

Bookchin, Murray. 1985. "Social Ecology Versus Deep Ecology: A Challenge for the Ecology Movement." *Green Perspective* 4–5.

Bookchin, Murray. 1991. *The Ecology of Freedom: The Emergence and Dissolution of Hierarchy*, rev. ed. Montreal, Canada: Black Rose Books.

Bookchin, Murray. 1995. *The Philosophy of Ecology: Essays on Dialectical Naturalism*. Montreal, Canada: Black Rose Books.

Bunker, Stephen G. 1988. *Underdeveloping the Amazon*. University of Chicago Press: Chicago.

Burns, Thomas J., Eward L. Kick, and Byron L. Davis. 2003. "Theorizing and Rethinking Linkages Between the Natural Environment and the Modern World-System: Deforestation in the Late 20th Century." *Journal of World Systems Research* 9:357–90.

Buttel, Frederick. 1996. "Environmental and Resource Sociology: Theoretical Issues and Opportunities for Synthesis." *Rural Sociology* 61(1):56–75.

Buttel, Frederick. 2000. "Ecological Modernization as Social Theory." *Geoforum* 31:57–65.

Catton, William R., and Riley E. Dunlap. 1978. "Environmental Sociology: A New Paradigm." *American Sociologist* 13:41–49.

Devall, Bill, and George G. Sessions. 1985. *Deep Ecology*. Salt Lake City, UT: Peregrine Smith Books.

Giddens, Anthony. 2006. "We Should Ditch the Green Movement." *Guardian Unlimited*.

Gould, Kenneth A., David N. Pellow, and Allan Schnaiberg. 2004. "Interrogating the Treadmill of Production: Everything You Wanted to Know About the Treadmill but Were Afraid to Ask." *Organization & Environment* 17:296–316.

Hawken, Paul, Amory Lovins, and L. Hunter Lovins. 1999. *Natural Capitalism: Creating the Next Industrial Revolution*. Boston: Little, Brown and Co.

Malthus, Robert Thomas. 1798. *Essay on the Principle of Population as It Affects the Future Improvement of Society, with Remarks on the Speculations of Mr. Godwin, Mr. Condorcet, and Other Writers*, 1st ed. London: J. Johnson. Retrieved February 13, 2007 (http://www.econlib.org/library/Malthus/malPop.html).

Mol, Arthur P. J. 2001. *Globalization and Environmental Reform: The Ecological Modernization of the Global Economy*. Cambridge, MA: MIT Press.

Naess, Arne. 1973. "The Shallow and the Deep Long Range Ecology Movements: A Summary." *Inquiry* (Oslo), Volume 16.

O'Connor, James R. 1973. *The Fiscal Crisis of the State*. Palgrave Macmillan.

Ruether, Rosemary Radford. 1975. *New Woman, New Earth: Sexist Ideologies and Human Liberation*. New York: Seabury Press.

Schnaiberg, Allan. 1980. *The Environment: From Surplus to Scarcity*. New York: Oxford University Press.

Turner, Jonathan. 1991. *The Structure of Sociological Theory*. Belmont, CA: Wadsworth.

Wallerstein, Immanuel. 1996. *Historical Capitalism with Capitalist Civilization*. London, UK: Verso.

World Commission on Environment and Development. 1987. *Our Common Future*. New York: Oxford University Press.

Part 2

SYSTEMIC CAUSES OF ENVIRONMENTAL DISRUPTION

The State and Policy:
Imperialism, Exclusion, and Ecological Violence as State Policy

David Naguib Pellow

W hen most people think of the state and policy in relation to the environment they think of environmental policies such as the Clean Air Act or the Endangered Species Act. However, what I'd like to do in this lesson is to explore the role of the U.S. nation-state as an institution that embraces and advances the causes of imperialism, racism, and ecological violence. Drawing on theories of the state, environment, and social inequality, the lesson explores how this dynamic emerged in history and then applies it to several cases. We therefore recast or reconsider state imperialist policy as environmental policy, rather than examining practices that are formally defined as environmental.

THE NATION-STATE AS AN ENGINE OF PROFIT AND ENVIRONMENTAL HARM

Perhaps the most enduring academic view of the state (that is, the government and its various administrative arms, agencies, and structures) is that of pluralism. The concept of a pluralist state is closely associated with the writings of Alexis de Tocqueville and Robert Dahl. The pluralist idea is that politics in a democracy is a process in which various associations (for example, trade unions, business groups, churches, activist organizations) engage in a competition for access to state resources and governmental control. Rather than a situation in which the state is an autocratic authority, pluralism involves groups sharing power with the state, thus avoiding dominance by government or by any particular interest group. Interest groups and associations strive to influence state policy making through this process, thus allowing citizens multiple venues for voicing their concerns and gaining access to the political system. In practice, however, the political process in the United States is often less pluralist than many of us might imagine. The theoretical perspectives presented below reflect this more critical view of power and social change with a focus on environmental concerns.

The Treadmill of Production

Sociologists Allan Schnaiberg and Kenneth Gould developed a theoretical framework that captures the dynamics of how market forces and political institutions interact to produce ecological disorganization while creating wealth and power for a minority of persons and lower wages and less power for the majority. This "treadmill of production" is a system in which we can observe the increasing accumulation of wealth and investments into capital-intensive technologies, rising social inequalities, and greater ecological "withdrawals" (natural resource extraction) and "additions" (pollution), all of which are encouraged and facilitated by the nation-state. The treadmill is a model that describes and explains how capitalist societies have become deeply antiecological and antihumanist (see Lesson 3).

While the litany of ecologically destructive practices associated with the treadmill is familiar (polluted air, land, and watersheds, for example), the social costs are less apparent in the popular imagination. One of the best ways to increase profits is to not only ignore polluting processes but to reduce labor costs. Most businesses do this by introducing computer automation, cutting wages, downsizing employment rolls, and reducing workers' benefits. As a result, we witness increasing levels of economic inequality and instability nationally and globally. Some indicators include the following: the number of temporary workers has increased dramatically in the last two decades, the richest 2,500 people on the planet possess as much wealth (property, assets, stocks) as do the poorest 2.5 billion, 1% of the population of the United States possesses around 40% of the wealth in that country, 20% owns 80% of the wealth, and real wages have declined precipitously since the early 1970s. What all of this leads to is a workforce where a growing percentage of people are non-unionized, hold temporary jobs, receive low wages, and are at risk of experiencing high levels of under- and unemployment. By contrast, at the other end of the spectrum, we see a smaller elite class of white-collar "knowledge workers" with higher pay, higher education levels, higher social status, greater career mobility options, and safer jobs. Furthermore, we have greater pollution levels, social instability, social conflict, and pressures on the state to take up the slack for people who have been downsized and have no child-care or health-care benefits. The state has, of course, been offering billions of dollars in subsidies to corporations in hopes of keeping such organizations within the national borders and therefore has fewer funds to pay out to citizens/consumers/workers in social benefits. Furthermore, as the ideology of economic growth at all costs becomes a dominant theme in this nation, there is less political will or sympathy for downsized workers.

According to Schnaiberg and Gould, the modern treadmill of production really grew in scope beginning in the post-World War II era. This was a time when wages were rising for most workers and a new era of prosperity was ushered in by an alliance among industry, labor unions, and the state. The post-1945 political economy was largely held together by an implicit contract. Private capital's need for a reliable labor force aided in the development of strong trade unions that could collectively bargain for wage increases and safer working conditions. Workers' need for jobs and their general satisfaction with unprecedented material gains led to a "no strike" pledge with management. The state played its part by expanding public education in order to produce a higher-quality labor force, while also expanding consumer credit to make sure that domestic demand for goods kept pace with the increase in production. Overall, these were good economic times.

But as economic globalization intensified, the industrial and governmental belts began to tighten. As early as the 1960s in the United States, the treadmill had already begun to undergo significant changes from its post-1945 structure. With increasing international competition, investors and managers became concerned about the existing pact between management and labor, which ensured a relatively high wage for workers as employees accommodated the treadmill by maintaining the peace between unions and companies. As global economic competition heated up, industry felt the need to cut costs in order to remain solvent and/or to continue offering high rates of return to investors and shareholders. They did this by weakening the labor movement, reducing workers' wages, and downsizing many positions in firms. Those actions—combined with the movement of companies to lower-cost regions of the country or to other nations—created massive unemployment in urban areas and a national crisis in the form of chronic economic downturns during the 1970s–1990s (see Lesson 5). Before and during this time we also saw an exponential increase in the use of chemicals and toxins in industrial production (with a weak or nonexistent environmental regulatory system), producing urban and rural wastelands across the nation. So in many urban areas we now have extensive unemployment, hundreds of square miles of abandoned factories, and toxic hotspots. Ecological disruption and social disruption exist side by side and go hand in hand: These dynamics form the essence of the treadmill of production. The treadmill of production produces and reinforces social and economic inequalities locally, nationally, and globally.

Environmental Justice Studies

A related and growing field of scholarly inquiry—environmental justice studies—focuses on a subset of concerns associated with the impacts of the treadmill of production. Environmental justice studies emphasize the unequal outcomes of market-based and state economic and environmental policy making on people of color, indigenous populations, and the working class or poor. The major concern of scholars in this field is the problem of environmental inequality—that is, when a population suffers a high burden of environmental harm and is excluded from environmental decisions affecting its communities (see Lesson 10). More often than not, such populations include those groups on society's political, economic, and cultural margins. Research on environmental inequality dates back to the 1970s when scholars were reporting significant correlations between socioeconomic status and air pollution in U.S. urban centers. Hence, for more than three decades we have had quantitative and empirical evidence of social disparities in the distribution of pollution in the United States. Beginning in the 1980s, researchers focused more directly on the links between pollution and race via studies of the proximity of hazardous waste sites to communities of color. This research demonstrated that, in many cases, race was the best predictor of where hazardous waste sites would be located in the United States, prompting the use of the term *environmental racism* to characterize these disparities. Scholars and activists working on this problem generally embrace the idea of environmental justice, which is a goal or a vision in which no community is unfairly burdened with environmental harms and where social justice and ecological sustainability prevail. Unfortunately, society is deeply structured along intensely unequal social relations and fundamentally wedded to toxic technologies, so environmental justice will likely remain an elusive goal for some time.

The Risk Society

Another theoretical framework I would like you to consider is German social theorist Ulrich Beck's idea of the "risk society." The risk society is marked by a fundamental transformation in the relationship among industry, the state, civil society, and the environment. That is, at this point in history (which some scholars refer to as "late modernity"), we witness an exponential increase in the production and use of hazardous chemical substances. These practices emanate from the state and industry to civil society through production, consumption, and disposal practices, elevating the level of social and physical risk to scales never before imagined. For more than two decades, the United States has been the world's leading producer and exporter of toxic waste, with an estimated 500 million tons. In the late 1980s and 1990s the United States was producing more than one ton of hazardous waste for every child, woman, and man in the nation. What this means is that the very idea of the modern U.S. nation-state is made possible by the existence of toxins—chemical poisons—that permeate every social institution, human body, and the natural world itself. To be modern, then, is associated with a degree of manipulation of the natural and social worlds that puts them both at great risk. To be modern also requires the subjugation and control over certain populations designated as "others," those less than fully deserving of citizenship, as a way of ameliorating the worst impacts of such a system on the privileged. These two tendencies—the manipulation of the natural and social worlds—are linked through the benefits that toxic systems of production produce for the privileged and the imposition of the costs of that process on people and places deemed less valuable and therefore expendable. In a sense, then, Beck and Schnaiberg and Gould come together to offer a broader theory of environmental inequality from which we can more effectively analyze the role of the state as a contributor to ecological and social violence.

In his classic book *Imagined Communities: Reflections on the Origin and Spread of Nationalism*, Benedict Anderson proposes the following definition of a nation: "an imagined political community . . . and imagined as both inherently limited and sovereign." The nation is imagined because, while members of this community cannot know or meet everyone inside its borders, in our minds we each live in and share this community. The very idea of a nation-state is rooted in *sovereignty*—the ability of a nation's citizens to self-govern and to determine their own fate without interference from others. This is important because very often a powerful nation's practices prohibit another nation from self-governance, and this is frequently done in order to gain access to valuable ecological resources, in addition to consumer and labor markets.

While the U.S. nation-state clearly embraces the agenda and logic of capitalism, this also has broader social impacts and roots. Ultimately, this is because states—as nations—are inherently exclusionary constructions; they write certain people and social categories out of power and citizenship, while including others. For example, states reflect historic and ongoing gender ideologies and interests. Leading feminist legal theorist Catherine MacKinnon describes the state (for example, police, military, and legal institutions) as gendered in so far as it has a predominantly male orientation, meaning that not only do men constitute the majority of people in positions of authority within the state but the state works to protect men's interests. The state as a gendered institution is revealed in its relationship to nature as well. No doubt drawing from biblical roots that encourage humans to dominate the Earth and men to dominate women, the U.S. and European Union states engage nature through ideologies and practices of domination. In her groundbreaking book *The Sexual Contract*, Carole Pateman contends that western European nation-states were founded on a "sexual contract"—the exclusion of women from public spheres of power. Historian Carol Merchant links that exclusion to the ways in which Western cultures imagine and behave toward nature. Geographer David Harvey would agree. In his writings he argues that the idea that people were meant to dominate nature—emerging from the Enlightenment period—is only half right. He contends that the domination of nature thesis is not so much about dominating or controlling the environment or nature as it is a means through which the domination of humans by other humans is accomplished. Thus, historically, the rich rule the poor, men control women, and powerful nations rule over weaker nations; and this is accomplished through the resources and power ultimately derived from human exploitation of the environment.

My point here is to locate the state's treatment of people in the same ideological, discursive, and structural space as the state's relationship to nature. For example, the field of environmental justice studies maintains that the exploitation of people and the exploitation of the environment are linked. Thus, when the environmental integrity of working class neighborhoods, indigenous lands, and communities of color is harmed by state and corporate practices, this also results in harm done to public health and the social well-being of the persons living in these spaces (see Lesson 10).

Building on Carole Pateman's writings, Charles Mills argues that the U.S. nation-state constitutes a "racial contract" in that it reflects the fact that European Americans founded this nation, at least partially, through acts of excluding Africans and Native Americans. Drawing on Hobbes' notion of the body politic as a leviathan, Mills asks, if we take the nation as a body metaphor seriously, what about those parts of the national body that are viewed as surplus, as waste? The answer is that they can be discarded like any other form of waste. He argues that some populations—such as African Americans—constitute such waste, or "black trash," and are therefore viewed as socially and politically disposable. If these bodies and their communities are viewed as a form of social contamination, it would only make sense that society's physical waste would be colocated among these bodies, communities, and spaces. If the people themselves are viewed as dirty, filthy, and disposable, then environmental racism and injustice (via the location of polluting factories or waste dumps in these communities) are perfectly rational state practices. Thus, the state excludes certain populations from power and meaningful citizenship, and this practice intersects conveniently and reinforces the treadmill of production by placing the least desirable persons in the least desirable spaces. For example, sociologists Robert Bullard, Paul Mohai, Robin Saha, and Beverly Wright reported in a 2007 study titled *Toxic Wastes and Race at Twenty*:

- In 2000, the majority of persons in neighborhoods hosting hazardous facilities are people of color (host neighborhoods are defined as communities within 1.8 miles of a facility). People of color are 56% of the population in these neighborhoods, as compared to non-host areas, where people of color are 30%.
- Those neighborhoods hosting clusters of several hazardous facilities have higher percentages of people of color than communities without such clusters (69% versus 51%). Those areas containing clusters of facilities also contain populations experiencing high poverty rates.
- Not only do racial disparities in hazardous facility siting still exist, they have actually *intensified*, creating greater environmental inequalities today than reported in 1987. That is, in many parts of the nation, African Americans, Hispanics/Latinos, and Asian Americans/Pacific Islanders are more concentrated in neighborhoods hosting hazardous facilities than they were twenty years ago.

What much of this implies then is that the U.S. state is not operating based on pluralist principles. Rather, the U.S. state largely exists to further the interests of some groups over others. This practice extends beyond the U.S. border into other nations, producing unequal relations between the United States and peoples around the globe. Another way of thinking about this is to define it as imperialism. *Imperialism* is best characterized as a system of foreign power in which another culture, people, and way of life penetrate, transform, and come to define a colonized society. In the next sections, I discuss the role of U.S. imperialism in relation to other peoples of the Americas and the world and how it produced environmental harm. The point here is to frame these practices as a window into the de facto environmental policy regime of the U.S. state.

U.S. IMPERIALISM

The Monroe Doctrine is perhaps the single most important factor in the development of U.S. imperialism in the nineteenth century. On December 2, 1823, President James Monroe declared the Americas off-limits to any new European colonization. Latin American leaders initially hailed this new policy as a protective mechanism, until they realized that the United States would soon turn the doctrine into its opposite: Latin America, especially the Caribbean basin, was turned into a virtual U.S. sphere of influence. Politicians and media leaders used the doctrine to develop the idea of "America for the Americans." Simón Bolívar, the great liberator of many South American nations, would soon declare that the United States seemed destined to torment the Americas in the name of freedom. Many Latin American leaders and environmental activists (especially indigenous leaders) argue that the United States pursues a similar agenda to this day, with continued proclamations of bringing democracy and freedom to nations around the world. This underscores an unresolved tension in U.S. history and present-day politics: the contradiction between our ideals of freedom and our predilection for conquest. And that propensity for conquest is driven not only by a desire for consumer markets and cheap labor but also by a thirst for access to ecological wealth in the form of rich natural resources in the global South.

A short while later, a more powerful ideological proposition was put forth on the public agenda, which took the Monroe Doctrine much further. This was Manifest Destiny, the ideology of racial and cultural superiority that guided the United States westward across the continent into Mexican territory, south into Central America and the Caribbean, across the Pacific, and beyond. There was a strong religious component to this concept, which embraced the domination of allegedly inferior peoples and the United States' right to do what it wishes with their land and ecological resources. Writing in support of the annexation of Texas during July of 1845, politician John O'Sullivan coined the phrase "Manifest Destiny" to describe American expansionism:

> Yes, we are the nation of progress, of individual freedom, of universal enfranchisement. This is our high destiny, and in nature's eternal, inevitable decree of cause and effect we must accomplish it. All this will be our future history, to establish on earth the moral dignity and salvation of man—the immutable truth and beneficence of God. For this blessed mission to the nations of the world, which are shut out from the life-giving light of truth, has America been chosen; and her high example shall smite unto death the tyranny of kings, hierarchs, and oligarchs, and carry the glad tidings of peace and good will where myriads now endure an existence scarcely more enviable than that of beasts of the field.

O'Sullivan's phrase was adopted by Republican congressman Robert Winthrop and others in their work to mobilize for war against Mexico and the takeover of that nation's northern territories. Following O'Sullivan's ideas, God had entrusted the United States with "the development of the great experiment of liberty and federated self-government." Even the great poet Walt Whitman found the white man's burden appealing: "We want to see our country and its rule far-reaching only inasmuch as it will take off the shackles that prevent men the even chance of being happy and good." Before the decade ended, the United States had conquered the entire Southwest and forced Mexico to accede to the Treaty of Guadalupe Hidalgo signed in 1848.

The expansionist tendencies that we saw in the 1830s and 1840s continue through today with free-trade agreements and proxy wars the U.S. military and corporations are waging in the Americas. For two centuries we have seen a massive and intensified siphoning of natural resources and economic wealth from south of the border north to the United States, from what Uruguayan author Eduardo Galeano calls "the open veins of Latin America." The United States is the most economically privileged nation on the planet, in large part thanks to the extraction of copper from Chile; hardwoods from Brazil; oil from Mexico, Venezuela, and Ecuador; tin from Bolivia; bananas from Guatemala, Costa Rica, and Honduras; sugar from Cuba; and beef from Argentina. Not only has this imperial arrangement resulted in great poverty in Latin America but the ecological toll from this resource extraction is extraordinary, including deforestation, oil spills, air pollution, soil erosion, species extinction, and the violence associated with countless tons of herbicides and pesticides that U.S.-based agencies and corporations send to be sprayed on crops, watersheds, and agricultural workers' bodies in the region. Women, children, migrant farm workers, and poor populations suffer especially great burdens from pesticides (see Lesson 11). Not surprisingly, indigenous peoples do as well. For example, Plan Colombia's aerial spraying of tons of pesticides on coca and poppy plants in Colombia disproportionately impacts indigenous people's land and health in that nation, violating their right to a clean environment as is customary under international law. The Foundation for Advancements in Science and Education (FASE) recently concluded that U.S. chemical manufacturers regularly sell tons of pesticides that are banned in the United States because of their highly toxic nature to Latin American nations, where they are in widespread use in agriculture.

The process set into motion with the Monroe Doctrine and Manifest Destiny continued far beyond Latin America to Asia and elsewhere. At the same time the U.S. empire was going global, there was a domestic expansion into Native American territories as well.

U.S. Federal Policies and Treaty Making

The same year the Monroe Doctrine came into being another, much older ideology of domination was being refashioned. In 1823, Supreme Court Chief Justice John Marshall reinterpreted the "doctrine of discovery," an idea that European explorers and nations employed for centuries. The decision in the U.S. Supreme Court's *Johnson v. McIntosh* case resulted in what has been called the Marshall Doctrine, which concluded that the right of native peoples to their lands is diminished and that the sovereignty of the discoverers (read "Europeans") was inherently superior to that of indigenous peoples. Some scholars argue that this was a creative interpretation of the original doctrine of discovery laid out in a series of papal bulls begun by Pope Innocent IV in the thirteenth century and evolving over the years so that by the early seventeenth century it had become a core part of international law, or what is referred to as the "law of nations." These legal norms allowed Europeans to acquire land in foreign places only if it was uninhabited or if native peoples gave or sold the land by consent. This meant that Europeans were thus required to enter into treaty making with native peoples around the world, which recognized their sovereignty; and the British, for example, generally did so. So Justice Marshall's doctrine was important because it represented a major shift in policy that departed from what was considered international law at the time. Marshall pushed even further in what are called the "Cherokee opinions" of the early 1830s (the Supreme Court decisions in *Cherokee Nation v. Georgia*, 1831, and *Worcester v. Georgia*, 1832), seeking to strengthen the logic of the *McIntosh* decision, given that it was not likely to withstand international legal scrutiny. Thus, he developed the thesis that native peoples within North America constituted nations since they inhabited territories and were ruled by governments with the capacity to engage in commerce and treaty making. However, Marshall maintained—drawing on the ideas contained in the *McIntosh* decision—that native nations were a "peculiar type" of nation that were "domestic" to and "dependent upon" the United States. Hence, native nations enjoyed a subordinate sovereignty vis-à-vis the United States. In other words, this was nothing less than a relationship enjoyed by an empire with its colonies. The implication of these legal decisions was that natural resources such as land, minerals, timber, fish, water, and other ecological wealth in Native America were legally constructed as available for the taking if the U.S. government deemed it necessary. One example of this policy was the Dawes Severalty Act of 1887, through which the federal government began "registering" Indians and forcing them to live on lands that were subdivided into individual private property lots. The aim was to "civilize" Native Americans by encouraging them to embrace the notion of private property while drastically reducing their land base, liberating "surplus" lands for white settlers, private companies, and the federal government. While much of this land was dedicated to homesteading (for white families who settled in the West), much of it was ultimately used to create the first national parks and national forests in the United States, which Ansel Adams became famous for photographing, often excluding evidence of native peoples from such vistas. Some estimates are that the Dawes Act resulted in the removal of two-thirds of land (around 150 million acres) from native peoples. A 1928 congressional study—the Miriam Report—concluded that these policies left "an overwhelming majority of the Indians...poor, even extremely poor." Native peoples were relegated to lands that the federal government believed to be of little economic value, with few mineral and other natural resources.

Other native peoples challenged the Dawes Act in the courts, but in the 1903 *Lone Wolf v. Hitchcock* case, the Supreme Court extended federal power to argue that the U.S. government possessed a right to selectively abide by treaties it had made with native nations. This was the final consolidation of the Marshall Doctrine and led to a formal disempowerment of native nations.

One of the great ironies of the Dawes Act was that much of the land base to which Native Americans were relegated eventually was determined to be among the most well-endowed, natural resource-rich areas on the planet. It is estimated that two-thirds of all uranium deposits in the United States, one-fourth of the nation's sulfur coal, and one-fifth of oil and natural gas reserves are on (or beneath) Native American reservation lands. Moreover, reservation lands are also rich in metals and minerals such as gold, iron, molybdenum, copper, iron, zinc, nickel, and bauxite. Thus, the unequal relationship between the U.S. government and tribal governments—as developed in the *McIntosh, Cherokee,* and *Lone Wolf* cases—made possible the siphoning of such environmental wealth from Native America to the United States of America. The infamous Bureau of Indian Affairs was the agency that supervised this effort and, unfortunately, often failed to ensure the protection of ecosystems during and after extractive projects. One outcome of these state policies is that, particularly on reservations where uranium mining has occurred, the extent of radioactive contamination is considerable. Socially and economically, another more visible outcome of this history is that native communities are among the poorest in the hemisphere, with a range of public and mental health problems that have been at epidemic levels for many years. Native American Studies scholars such as Andrea Smith, Ward Churchill, Paula Gunn Allen, and others reveal that unemployment, alcoholism, domestic violence, rape, suicide, and numerous other social ills are abnormally high in many Native American communities.

The Struggle Goes On

This process of imperialism and ecological violence continues today, well beyond U.S. borders. At the turn of the twenty-first century the Colombian government and Los Angeles–based Occidental Petroleum were moving forward with plans to drill for oil on the traditional lands of the indigenous U'wa people. U.S.-based Fidelity Investments Corporation was a major financing entity in this effort and former Vice President Al Gore owned considerable stock in the Occidental Petroleum company. The U'wa opposition to the oil project was so strong that they vowed to commit collective suicide if the project went forward, believing that it would be better to die by their own hands than to watch the inevitable destruction of their culture and their homeland. Many environmental and human rights organizations in the United States and globally joined the U'wa in solidarity, placing considerable pressure on

Fidelity, Occidental, and Al Gore. Fortunately, the drilling project was halted because the company claimed there was insufficient oil in the area.

Native Hawaiians, or *Kanaka Maoli*, live in a state that hosts more federal hazardous waste sites than any other U.S. state. Many of these sites were created through polluting activities carried out by the U.S. military, which has compromised and, in some cases, destroyed native land and fisheries. Between 1964 and 1973, the U.S. Navy released 4.8 million gallons of radioactive waste into Pearl Harbor from its submarines. The Navy also dumped more than 2,000 55-gallon steel drums of solid radioactive waste off the shoreline, posing a major threat to ocean life. Similar dynamics characterize the Clark and Subic U.S. military bases in the Philippines and many others elsewhere. The U.S. military is one of the world's greatest sources of pollution and, with more than 700 bases around the planet, one of the leading purveyors of institutional violence. These cases also demonstrate that U.S. state practices often tend to steer clear of pluralism and remain steadfastly hegemonic.

CONCLUSION

This lesson considers the history and actions of the U.S. nation-state as an imperial institution that routinely produces environmental destruction and social inequality. Offering a sampling of theories of environment-society relationships, social inequality, and state formation, I argue that in order to fully understand how contemporary U.S. policies result in environmental racism and inequality, one must consider the historical, legal, economic, and cultural roots of the U.S. nation-state itself. Such an exploration reveals that the United States is an imperial presence in the Americas and globally, and this has dire consequences for any effort to produce social and environmental justice here or elsewhere. In this way, we might locate the deeper origins of the environmental state and, in turn, think through a different set of questions that might push for reform or transformation of those practices. For example, instead of seeking to simply strengthen regulation of polluting industries in poor neighborhoods and communities of color, one might push for a greater democratization of the state and industry. Indeed, if we truly wish to move toward sustainability and social justice, we must confront U.S. imperialism itself directly and imperialism more generally wherever it arises.

Today, environmental justice and human rights movements are merging together as a global force for social change and democratization. Activists in Europe, the Americas, Africa, and Asia are collaborating to challenge socially and ecologically harmful state and corporate policies around hydroelectric power, incineration, and mineral extraction, for example, while offering alternatives for sustainability and social justice (see Lesson 17). Articulating a vision of global justice and human rights, the Principles of Environmental Justice—drafted at the First National People of Color Environmental Leadership Summit in Washington, D.C., 1991—contained a number of key demands in this vein. For example, the first principle calls for the "right to be free from ecological destruction"; the second principle calls for the right to be "free from any form of discrimination or bias"; the fourth principle invokes the "fundamental right to clean air, land, water, and food"; the fifth principle affirms the "fundamental right to political, economic, cultural and environmental self-determination of all peoples"; the eighth principle cites the right "to a safe and healthy work environment"; the tenth principle argues that governmental acts of environmental injustice are violations of international law and of "the Universal Declaration On Human Rights, and the United Nations Convention on Genocide." Taken separately and together, these principles speak impressively to a body of international law and human rights that has been in development for six decades. More importantly, in order for these principles to become reality, states and corporations would have to undergo dramatic transformations that would embrace democracy as standard operating procedure. The work of activists in the environmental justice and human rights movements has become quite sophisticated at combating global environmental inequalities through the engagement of a range of institutions, thus developing an emerging form of global citizenship and, by extension, a burgeoning transnational public sphere that might ultimately lead to greater democratization of our global society.

SOURCES

Anderson, Benedict. 1991. *Imagined Communities: Reflections on the Origin and Spread of Nationalism*. New York: Verso.

Beck, Ulrich. 1992. *Risk Society: Towards a New Modernity*. Thousand Oaks, CA: Sage.

Bullard, Robert D., Paul Mohai, Robin Saha, and Beverly Wright. 2007. "Toxic Waste and Race at Twenty 1987–2007." United Church of Christ.

Churchill, Ward. 2003. *Perversions of Justice: Indigenous Peoples and Anglo-American Law*. San Francisco, CA: City Lights.

Dahl, Robert. 1961. *Who Governs? Democracy and Power in an American City*. New Haven, CT: Yale University Press.

Galeano, Eduardo. 1997. *Open Veins of Latin America: Five Centuries of the Pillage of a Continent*. New York: Monthly Review Press.

Harvey, David. 1997. *Justice, Nature and the Geography of Difference*. Cambridge, MA: Blackwell Publishers.

Hirst, Paul Q., ed. 1994. *The Pluralist Theory of the State: Selected Writings of G. D. H. Cole, J. N. Figgis, and H. J. Laski*. London, UK: Routledge.

MacKinnon, Catherine. 1982. "Feminism, Marxism, Method, and the State." *Signs* 7(Spring):515–44.

Merchant, Carolyn. 1980. *The Death of Nature: Women, Ecology and the Scientific Revolution*. San Francisco: Harper.

Mills, Charles W. 1999. *The Racial Contract*. Ithaca, NY: Cornell University Press.

O'Sullivan, John. 1845. "The Great Nation of Futurity." *The United States Democratic Review* 6(July):426–30.

Pateman, Carole. 1988. *The Sexual Contract*. Palo Alto, CA: Stanford University Press.

Schnaiberg, Allan, and Kenneth Gould. 2000. *Environment and Society: The Enduring Conflict*. Caldwell, NJ: Blackburn Press.

5

Labor Productivity and the Environment

Allan Schnaiberg

THE PROMISE VERSUS THE HISTORY OF PRODUCTIVITY

Conceptualizing Productivity

The essence of productivity is an increase in economic production for each worker employed.[1] In many industrial societies, the argument has increasingly been made that, with increased productivity, new social problems will be solved. In theory, it is argued that higher productivity and profitability *permit* more savings and investments in social and environmental programs. During the last quarter-century, even more economic policy has been mobilized to argue that companies and economies without growing productivity are doomed to be displaced by firms and countries where productivity is higher. As international trade has increased and manufacturing has shifted to lower-wage societies, productivity has become labeled as the key component of "competitiveness."

Yet in practice, the historical processes by which productivity gains have actually been achieved give the lie to this argument. Productivity tends to be a solution primarily for investors and some managers (many of them also become some of the downsized workers). For workers, their communities, and the natural world in which they are embedded, this has become one of the most egregious bait-and-switch social policies.

The Perspective of Corporate Investors and Managers

The greater the productivity of an organization, the greater its profitability, according to modern economics. If I am able to raise the amount of production accomplished by each of my workers each day, my costs of production are reduced. I am then able to sell this commodity at a somewhat lower price than my competitors and thereby increase my share of the market for this product.

When this happens over some time period, my profits tend to rise, for two reasons: (1) while I may lower my price somewhat, I generally do not lower it as much as my savings on wages, so I increase my profit on every item I sell; (2) as I compete more effectively over my competitors, I make additional profits because of the increased number of items I am selling. The first of these effects is often defined as my *profit margin* per item I sell (revenue minus costs), and the second is my *profit ratio* (total revenue divided by total cost). These processes vary within countries and across the global economy. For the productive company, they are uniformly desirable outcomes; for the less productive, they are often fatal. In modern economic analysis and journalism, as well as modern politics, though, the focus is on the "winners" and not the "losers," in what can be seen as a kind of economic Darwinism.

Yet this is a very selective view of "productivity." Productivity typically has negative effects on the social fabric of a society and the ecological sustainability of its natural environment. To understand this, let's first look more realistically at how productivity is increased. Measurement of actual worker productivity is complex since it requires holding constant a variety of efficiency components in production, to separate out the effects of the workers themselves.

Generally, managers fall back on a simplified calculus: If I can do the same job with fewer workers, then workers' productivity has increased. Some of this is achieved by reorganizing production technologies. But it often generates greater pressure on workers to work harder, longer, and with more workplace tension than they faced previously. Managers can unilaterally decide to "downsize" a workforce—that is, to lay off some significant portion of their workers—and have been doing so in Western economies for decades now.

Perspectives of Workers/Communities

In order for this to increase productivity, the remaining workers must be willing and/or able to compensate for the production of those who were downsized. Their *willingness* can be induced by coercive and/or seductive measures: "Work more or we'll fire you," and/or "Work harder and we'll pay you some additional bonus payments." The first is effective where workers have few other job opportunities. But the coercive strategy carries with it new potential threats of slowdowns, sabotage, and higher worker turnover in response to the rising stress of the workplace. The seductive is more effective when the firm has more control of its other costs than its competitors. Its effectiveness dwindles when the total of new worker payments begins to approximate the prior payroll levels.

In addition to their willingness to increase their labor efforts, though, workers must have the *capacity* to do so. Reducing the labor force by only a modest proportion of workers may be designed to increase the workload of the remaining workers. From a managerial perspective, this creates more efficiency and enhances both productivity and profits.

Perspectives on the Environment

Most of the changes in twentieth-century production systems after 1945 consisted of some combination of new energy applications and new chemical processes, generating much less labor-intensive forms of production. Corn production changes, as noted below, exemplify this process in agriculture. Rising chemical pollution emerged in both workplaces (including cornfields) and communities (rivers and streams near cornfields). Parallel changes occurred in much manufacturing, where the materials and processes by which products were formed moved away from the hands of workers and into mechanical and electronic machinery (see Lesson 8).

The modern environmental movement in the 1960s arose in great degree in response to new fears of chemical pollution, exemplified by Rachel Carson's *Silent Spring*, which presented the widespread reproductive effects of DDT, an early and powerful pesticide. In the 1970s, some environmental movement attention moved to shortages of fossil fuels, due to changes in the concentration of oil production overseas and the decline of U.S. production.

More recently, three decades of scientific research has affirmed that the use of fossil fuels has increased carbon dioxide and other "greenhouse gases." These have been correlated with rising atmospheric and oceanic temperatures, altering climate and water distribution and threatening even more disruptions of social and economic life, as well as of ecosystems (see Lesson 14). Although the modern environmental movement was initiated in the United States, the aggregate pollution and depletion (of both energy sources and natural habitats) actually rose in the United States during the period of organized environmental movements, and much greater movement resistance has become embedded within European Union societies.

I now outline two major paths by which investors and managers attempt to increase the productivity of their workers.

RAISING PRODUCTIVITY BY CHANGING PRODUCTION TECHNOLOGIES

One major approach is investment in new production technologies, frequently involving more electronic and mechanical equipment, within existing workplaces. This was the essential strategy used by corn growers.

The Case of Corn

One of the most detailed examples is Michael Pollan's history of corn production. Maize was a very old plant in America. It was generally harvested by hand, and even among early cultivators in Latin America, some manual pollination was done to create new varieties of corn. Corn became essentially an industrialized crop in the United States, especially after 1945. Ever-growing levels of fertilizers, pesticides, and herbicides were utilized to increase the yield of corn per acre.

Gradually, corn production has become essentially a plantation operation, with growing sizes of landholdings and replacement of the labor of planting, harvesting, and storing the grain with mechanized equipment. Likewise, with the large capital investments involved, planters wanted more predictable crops, to cover their loans for the new equipment. Additional equipment was purchased to irrigate cornfields. And the demand for high-yield hybrid corn seeds rose as planters sought to further reduce their risks of pests and water shortages.

The scale of capital investment in corn production rose substantially, and the successful planters bought out the land of smaller and "less productive" farmers. In addition, the debt burden for even large landholders became unsustainable, and many abandoned corn production. Overall, there were substantial increases in the levels of corn production. At first blush, this seemed to serve the economic interests of large landholders quite well. There were a number of social and ecological costs, however. As corn production was industrialized, rural labor forces were eliminated, communities contracted, and local enterprises collapsed because of a lack of wage income and consumer spending.

Moreover, agricultural wastes from cornfields increasingly became toxic, and with growing irrigation there was an increased runoff of chemical pesticides and herbicides into local streams and rivers. And the fossil fuel demands per bushel of corn produced rose substantially. From the standpoint of energy efficiency, the energy inputs involved in corn production vastly exceeded the caloric value of the corn produced.

Despite these social and ecological problems, corn production in the United States has increased substantially. While this seemed to reward "productive" corn planters, it also created new cross-pressures on them. The first problem with rising corn production was that there was too limited a market for all the corn produced. One of the hidden vulnerabilities of increased productivity is that more product must be sold. Productive organizations that lack sufficient markets will find their profits reduced eventually, and investors will move their capital elsewhere. Corn planters responded to this challenge in several ways. Paradoxically, as corn surpluses grew and prices fell, corn producers actually increased their acreage and planting, selling more corn at lower prices, to hold onto their equipment and land. This created still more corn surpluses, further dropping prices and threatening the revenues of corn planters.

Two additional strategies were developed. The first was to widen the use of corn, both in foodstuffs and as animal feed. Pollan outlines how grass-fed beef and other food animals became transformed into corn-fed animals. For livestock owners, this eventually led to enclosures for animals since there was no longer any necessity for grazing. The factory cornfield eventually led to the factory farm, with diminished freedom of movement for all livestock (see Lesson 12).

Because this enclosed corn-fed regimen raised the threat of communicable diseases among densely settled animals, corn feeds were reformulated to include antibiotics and other organic chemicals, designed to both reduce disease and hasten the growth of the animals. The end result of this has been an increase in the chemical levels of corn and meat of all kinds, eventually entering into the human food chain and the land and waters near both cornfields and factory farms.

As corn prices dropped further, research into the use of corn as a synthetic food component rose because the price of corn products was competitive with many other natural food sources. Yet even this expansion of the market did not sufficiently cushion the income of corn planters. They began an extensive and successful lobbying campaign to argue for federal price supports for corn. Part of the campaign was to portray corn producers as just "farmers" living in small towns, who needed protection from the vagaries of weather and markets.

In the current political climate, moreover, corn producers have scored yet another victory. After the crisis of U.S. terrorism on 9–11, a new drive to increase "energy security" in the United States was put on the national agenda. One of the most direct and least politicized strategies that emerged was federal support for a vastly expanded production of ethanol, produced from fermented corn. So successful has this been for corn planters over the past decade that the market for corn is no longer saturated and corn prices have begun to rise.[2] This means that corn, a "renewable" resource, has become a core element of both food and transportation. The fact that producing corn is energy-inefficient in both domains has been essentially ignored by most analysts.

Is Corn's History Representative of Other Productivity Processes?

The details of productivity changes for corn overlap to a considerable extent with those for other commodities. While it is true that agricultural production entails more uncertainties than factory production, many of the historical processes just outlined hold for many industries. Where the role of human labor has been reduced in the production process, the alternative technology is often a mixture of increased fossil fuel energy and increased application of synthetic chemicals. Waste has always been a by-product of all manufacturing processes. But when machines replace human labor, they offer new capacities for managers and investors, but also new challenges. Purchase of new equipment generally entails both capital outlays and debt, and the result is increased managerial pressure to recoup the investment with increased production and sales.

Just as water power replaced some human workers and steam replaced water power, fossil fuels and electricity replaced steam as a driving force of production. This was true not only in the actual production machinery but also in the materials used in products. Wood was replaced by metals and metals by plastics and other synthetic materials. Many of these new processes and products entail toxic chemicals in processing or products.

While some new forms of pollution control were added to production systems and some forms of energy efficiency were even achieved, aggregate production and its ecological externalities increased. Contemporary environmental regulation has required producers to negotiate some *qualitative* controls over their production systems. But almost no governments sought to place *quantitative* limits on the volume of production and profits.

Some of this involved direct political struggles between "shareholders" (investors and managers) and "stakeholders" (workers and community residents). But much of this economic expansion was built into the logic of a newly capitalized production apparatus. Once an enterprise laid out financial capital for a new set of production machinery, there was an increasing motive to recoup this investment and raise profits by increasing the volume of production and net revenues. Workers could be downsized—but it was less economically and politically acceptable for managers to downsize newer capital equipment. Indeed, in fields such as information technology, growing capital outlays were increasingly necessary to *sustain* profits, let alone increase them, in the face of growing technological competition.

In part because of this disparity between disinvesting in workers and investing in physical production equipment, ecological pressures on habitats were both directly and indirectly increased. The indirect pressures arose precisely because the ratio of physical capital to workers grew substantially and the capacity of managing physical capital to generate profits outstripped managerial controls of workers. In order for employment to remain stable, workers had to join in efforts to ensure that firms were encouraged to invest still more. This appeared to be the only way in which replacement jobs could be generated.

An earlier form of pressure involved mobilizing the firm's workers to reject the government's environmental regulation. This sometimes meant that workers in industrial communities accepted living in a highly toxic environment because their employment seemed dependent on maintaining existing production forces. And government agencies likewise avoided threatening these sources of jobs.

However, the contemporary alliance for new investments and jobs was even more powerful in aligning workers with investors' and managers' interests. Despite this "common front," growth of profits and wealth of the economic elite far outstripped the wages of workers—initially, blue-collar workers and then increasingly middle-class and professional workers. This often led to workers voting for tax reductions for corporations, as well as diminished environmental and public health protection, to help sustain "competitiveness" in the national and global markets.[3]

This coalition for productivity and competitiveness also leads to a disjuncture between rising social needs of displaced and reduced-wage workers, on the one hand, and workers' support for lower taxation of corporations and investors, on the other hand. Moreover, there seems to be diminished community support for mainstream environmental movements. Environmental enforcement can raise the costs of corporations and often requires larger regulatory expenditures by government agencies. In effect, then, one benefit of choreographing rising productivity by investors and managers is that it mutes the voices raised in opposition to the social and environmental outcomes.

RELOCATION AND "OUTSOURCING"

Domestic Relocation

The concept of relocation is deceptively simple: if local workers cost too much, firms should find cheaper workers elsewhere. Relocating plants domestically, to areas with cheaper workers, is one major strategy. For some decades after the 1960s, U.S. manufacturers shifted production out of "rustbelt" communities (eastern, northern and midwestern)—where workers were unionized. Plants were shifted to "sunbelt" communities (southern and western), where state law, work shortages, and managerial threats and inducements inhibited worker unions from forming. Industries such as textiles were shifted almost completely from rustbelt states.

Many of the sunbelt communities, in their quest for new employment and taxation, simultaneously offered little enforcement of environmental protection. This afforded higher rates of productivity for employers since corporate expenses for some raw materials (including water) and for much of their waste disposal were lower than they had been in somewhat more regulated rustbelt communities.

Outsourcing: International Relocation

Outsourcing, or moving production away from northern industrial economies and into less developed southern ones, is an extension and substitute for relocation within the country. This has been the most common U.S. pattern of recent decades. This shift has primarily been due to the search for higher productivity and profits, both for cheaper labor and for lowered waste disposal costs. Ironically, whereas some of the earlier movement of capital to less developed areas involved less sophisticated technologies, movement has been accelerated even in production (and servicing) of high-technology products, such as electronics. While the labor component of total production costs is not small, a large portion of the costs of production involves larger energy and chemical applications to production.

The most notable of these shifts has been in the production of silicon computer chips, the ultimate in high-value products. Part of the movement of "silicon" from Silicon Valley in California appears to have been the highly toxic production processes and the growing concerns of local environmental movement groups and worker organizations.

Much of the investment in underdeveloped countries—ranging from China to Mexico—involves heightened workplace pollution and local air and water pollution. In each case, the host government has colluded with foreign investors, trading these social and ecological costs to provide more job opportunities (often for displaced agricultural workers) and higher tax revenues. These interests coalesce with those of investors in countries like the United States who are seeking greater returns on their investments (directly tied in the modern economy to higher productivity and profits).

In the United States, domestic relocation meant moving away from unionized workers. As union membership declined in the United States, the very investment strategy that had lowered union resistance also permitted a global search for new production locations for investors. Historically, in addition to union resistance, this centrifugal tendency had been restrained by the friction of space, the complexities of communications, and the unpredictable systems of national control over foreign investors.

With the rise of electronic communications, rapid airplane travel, and the increasing global pressures to "free up markets," many of these frictions were reduced. A faster pace of technological research and development made previous investments depreciate much faster (and were often accelerated with depreciation allowances in taxes paid to the government). Indeed, the pace of increased capitalization of production and the rise of large profits and corporate mergers made many such costs relatively small in the face of new opportunities for investment and profits.

Ecologically, this search for cheaper workers and workplace locations expanded the range of habitats that were becoming disrupted to make room for factories, mines, and natural resource processing facilities. New workers often lived in the midst of corporate structures that seemed modern and communities that were among the most despoiled in modern human history.

Both China and Mexico exemplify such recent trends, although Mexico was far more directly pressured by foreign investors. The health and ecological costs are substantial in both countries. Acceptance of these conditions by both workers and their governments supports the productivity-based model of "competitiveness."

Among the most recent of these processes is the outsourcing of white-collar service work—built around the availability of both more powerful computers and advanced telecommunications systems. The direct effect of these new office systems on the environment is primarily in energy intensification of overseas service work. But the rising toxic problems of both computer chip production and computer scrapping may also predict other health hazards for humans and habitats.

CONCLUSION

Increased labor productivity has become a standard economic indicator for the U.S. economy. When productivity "falters," alarms are raised that the United States will no longer remain "competitive" with its trading partners.

The harsh reality is that manufacturing is basically no longer carried out in the United States, and agriculture offers a limited range of jobs (and many of those are reserved for cheap undocumented Mexican workers). Labor unions have been largely downsized, along with their previous members. Major unions today have grown in the service sector because U.S. investors have moved their capital abroad.

Yet communities and workers still fantasize about the return of the factory, and every domestic and foreign manufacturer is encouraged to relocate in a U.S. community. Communities and their populations seeking jobs are willing to subsidize private producers and often to ignore local ecological degradation to attract new investors.

Labor productivity has largely been achieved by investors and managers, and only a small group of workers has benefited from it. In the process, a substantial human and environmental toll has been paid.

NOTES

1. Other kinds of productivity goals are possible: for instance, an increase in production per dollar invested in technology or the increase in production generated by the application of energy. Neither of these is treated as a social goal in the way that labor productivity has been over the last quarter-century. Ironically, in an era focused on labor productivity, the ratio of financial packages offered for chief executive officers compared to the wages of the average workers has increased exponentially, regardless of whether the corporation itself has increased in profits.
2. Problems with ethanol production from corn have led some researchers to search for more energy-efficient (and cost-effective) feedstocks for ethanol, such as saw grasses.
3. Freudenburg (1991) has argued that, in reality, "good" business climate ratings actually correlate with worse economic outcomes; the states named as having "bad" business climates actually had better economic performance (growth in jobs and incomes) over subsequent 5- and 10-year periods.

SOURCES

Freudenburg, William R. 1991. "A 'Good Business Climate' as Bad Economic News?" *Society and Natural Resources* 3(Spring):313–31.

Gould, Kenneth A., David N. Pellow, and Allan Schnaiberg. 2008. *The Treadmill of Production: Injustice and Unsustainability in the Global Economy.* Boulder, CO.: Paradigm Publishers.

Pellow, David N. and Lisa Sun-Hee Park. 2002. *The Silicon Valley of Dreams: Environmental Injustice, Immigrant Workers, and the High-Tech Global Economy.* New York: New York University Press.

Pollan, Michael. 2006. *The Omnivore's Dilemma: A Natural History of Four Meals.* New York: Penguin.

Smith, Ted, David A. Sonnenfeld, and David N. Pellow, eds. 2006. *Challenging the Chip: Labor Rights and Environmental Justice in the Global Electronics Industry.* Philadelphia, PA: Temple University Press.

6

Corporate Power:
The Role of the Global Media in Shaping What We Know About the Environment

Elizabeth H. Campbell

I n pursuit of privileging corporate actors in the global market, TNC elites have been increasingly successful in lobbying international organizations, such as the World Trade Organization (WTO), for increased freedoms on the movement of capital, technology, and goods and services. The WTO, established in 1995, is the main governing organization of the multilateral trading system, staffed by unelected bureaucrats, whose proceedings are held in secret, thereby denying public participation. TNCs, with the consent of global organizations and through binding regional and global trade agreements, undermine the efforts of individual governments to regulate TNCs within their borders.

Take, for example, Chapter 11 of the 1994 North American Free Trade Agreement (NAFTA), negotiated to promote the free flow of goods and services among the United States, Canada, and Mexico. This provision was supposedly written to protect investors if foreign governments tried to seize their property, but corporations have stretched NAFTA's Chapter 11 to undermine environmental decisions and the decisions of local communities. In California a billion-dollar case was filed against the United States because of an effort by the state government to protect the health of its citizens through the enactment of an environmental protection law that banned the chemical methyl tertiary-butyl ether (MTBE). This gasoline additive, found to cause cancer in laboratory animals, infiltrated 30 public water systems and another 10,000 groundwater sites. University of California scientists were commissioned to assess the problem, and their study warned that the state was placing its water resources at risk. On March 25, 1999, California's governor ordered that MTBE be phased out of all gasoline sold in the state.

In response, Methanex, a Canadian company that is the world's largest producer of the key ingredient in MTBE, claimed under Chapter 11 of NAFTA that its market share, and therefore its future profits, were being expropriated by the governor's action. The company argued that it be allowed to sell the product in California or be paid $970 million dollars in compensation. While NAFTA may protect corporate investors like Methanex, it does not protect ordinary people who may became ill from the contaminated water or taxpayers who will pay the bill if the secret tribunal decides in favor of such companies. NAFTA makes no provisions for a full appeal to U.S. courts and sets no caps on the amount of damages that can be awarded a corporation. This is an example of a foreign corporation invoking regional trade agreements that trump state laws aimed at protecting the health and environment of its people.

Motivated largely by profit margin, TNCs increasingly operate with little public accountability. How did this happen? Why did the American public agree to a shift in power from local people and states to unaccountable, unelected international institutions and TNCs? How did the public endorse job insecurity and outsourcing, lower wages, downsizing of the welfare state, decline in social services, and a rollback of environmental protection standards? Like all industries, the media industry is now both global in scope and largely owned by a handful of TNCs. This lesson examines the rise and influence of corporate power in the global media industry and its impact in shaping what we know or don't know about social and environmental issues.

THE NEED FOR DIVERSITY OF VIEWS IN A DEMOCRACY

The country's largest media giants have achieved unprecedented success in writing the media laws and regulations in favor of their own corporations and against the interests of the public. Their concentrated power permits them to become one of the largest factors in socializing each generation about politics, the environment, and personal values. Today's media conglomerates have almost total power to set the agenda for what will and will not be discussed in mainstream newspapers and magazines and on TV and radio. Environmental issues are often debated in such ways to ensure that corporations are never pointed out as a cause or source of environmental degradation.

Debate around global warming is a classic example (see Lesson 14). For well over a decade the debate about global warming, driven by corporate interests and crafted by powerful think tanks and public relations (PR) firms, has largely centered on whether or not it is a problem. People generally do not favor action on issues when arguments appear to be "balanced" on both sides and there is clear doubt. Corporations and the institutions representing them play a key role in providing "credible experts" who are normally not atmospheric scientists but nonetheless confidently dispute scientific claims of global warming. By disproportionately saturating the global media with these so-called experts, they offer enough manufactured doubt to ensure that governments take no initiative to act.

Powerful think tanks in Washington, D.C., that have enormous influence in shaping the debate, such as the CATO Institute, the Heritage Foundation, and the Competitive Enterprise Institute, use scare tactics by asserting that cuts in energy consumption would hurt the world's workers, the struggling poor, and the elderly. Further, they argue that renewable energy sources like solar and wind are not only expensive but also environmentally damaging. These think tanks use emotive arguments and fear tactics to bash environmentalists and environmental issues, rather than engaging with them on a more reasoned, substantive basis. Moreover, such think tanks promote the views of a few scientists who disagree with the vast majority of atmospheric scientists that warming is a consequence of the increasing levels of greenhouse gases in the atmosphere, much of which stems from the burning of nonrenewable energy resources like coal, gas, and oil. Widespread public concern over this issue is not translating into government action, in part because the issue cannot be seriously debated and better understood in the mainstream media. The corporate media works hard to avoid larger questions of power and institutional reform by instead focusing on controversial scientific reports and discrediting individual advocates.

By reducing complex issues like global warming to simplistic special interest–driven sound bites about whether or not it really exists, citizens consuming the media become incapable of understanding and acting on real debate and questioning and instead prefer easy answers, quick fixes, and easy-to-grasp phrases. Audiences thus grow apathetic, cynical, and quiescent about media presentations of environmental issues, which has resulted in an increasingly widespread lack of interest in engaging in them. Democracy, however, demands an informed, active, and involved citizenry in order to best ensure that the majority of voices and interests are well represented. As seen from the above example with MTBE and Methanex, foreign corporations are primarily concerned with profit making and have little to no regard for the way in which their business activities disrupt local environments. It is only local citizens and governments—and not absentee corporate landlords—that know best when the air they breathe, the water they drink, and the food they consume is contaminated; thus, such persons are best situated to respond to the problem. A well-informed citizenry that is exposed to all angles and interests in a substantive issue is more motivated and better equipped to engage in the political decision-making process. The more citizens who engage in the democratic process to ensure their interests are protected through the enactment of environmental and labor laws, the stronger the democratic system becomes. A democracy beholden only to corporate interests will never pursue a path toward social and environmental sustainability.

THE RISE OF TRANSNATIONAL CORPORATIONS

Historically, the corporation was a public institution created by the government to serve public interests. Early American corporations could only be created through special charters granted by state legislatures. These charters limited what corporations could do, for how long, and how much they could accumulate. In legal theory, corporations were classified as concessions or grants of the government. They were political creations, over which the state had great regulation and control. The initial creation of private finance was to help aid in the expansion of state colonial and imperial interest as well as to help in war efforts between empires. As corporations increased their wealth and therefore their political power, laws that initially tried to manage them were further relaxed.

By the nineteenth century corporations became increasingly privatized in both law and ideology. That is, they were no longer beholden to public officials but rather to private citizens who invested in them. As a result, their power and influence in the public greatly expanded. Many legal and cultural justifications for public accountability were stripped away. Corporations were reinvented as natural manifestations of free exchange among individuals, separate from the state. The public charter system basically collapsed, and the right of state legislatures to regulate corporations was eliminated.

Relying on the Fourteenth Amendment, added to the Constitution in 1868 to protect the rights of freed slaves, the U.S. Supreme Court ruled that a private corporation is a "natural person" under the U.S. Constitution and consequently has the same rights and protection extended to persons by the Bill of Rights, including the right to free speech. Corporations were thus given the same "rights" to influence the government in their own interests as were extended to individual citizens, paving the way for corporations to use their wealth to dominate public thought and discourse. Corporations, as "persons," were thus free to lobby legislatures, use the mass media, and construct a public image that they believed would best serve their interests.

Prior to the 1868 ruling, only humans were "endowed by their creator with certain inalienable rights." Today, corporations can claim rights instead of just privileges. In terms of politics, it was once a felony for corporations to give money to politicians and political parties. By claiming the human right of free speech, corporations expanded that to mean the unlimited right to put corporate money into politics. Today, corporations largely control the U.S. political parties and individual politicians. In terms of business, state and local communities once had stronger laws that protected and encouraged entrepreneurs and local businesses. Today, by invoking "discrimination" under the Fourteenth Amendment, many of these laws have been abolished. Local and regional economies are less able to protect themselves from predatory TNCs that have no long-term investment in the local communities. The Fourteenth Amendment has also been invoked by corporations to defend their right to privacy. In doing so, TNCs have been successful in ensuring that federal regulatory agencies do not investigate them for crimes. Finally, as natural persons, corporations successfully lobbied states to change corporate charter laws to eliminate "public good" provisions from charters, to allow for multiple purposes, and to exist forever.

DEFINING CHARACTERISTICS OF CORPORATIONS

From this "right" of the corporation, corporate interests have been increasingly equated with the human interest: Consumption is happiness. Through advertising, marketing, and control of information, corporations are able to create desires, invent needs, and foster traditions that encourage unquestioned consumption. Product advertisement is a multi-billion-dollar industry. Corporations today spend over half as much per capita on advertising than the world spends on education. Those who control the mass media control the core culture.

Unlike that of other entities, corporate influence is better situated to penetrate all aspects of social, cultural, and political life through a wide variety of means. In addition to their power to influence the public through advertising and through the control and influence of the mainstream media, corporations have exceptional influence on public policy. This can range from financing large parts of elections to creating corporate-funded think tanks and "grassroots" front groups to represent industry interests in the name of concerned citizens. PR firms have become adept at creating the impression of grassroots support for corporate causes so as to convince politicians to oppose environmental reforms. The names of the corporate front groups are carefully chosen to mask the real interests behind them. For example, prior to disbanding in 2002, the Global Climate Coalition, a coalition of 50 U.S. trade associations and private companies representing oil, gas, coal, automobile, and chemical interests, aimed to cast doubt on the severity of the problems associated with global warming and instead created confusion by magnifying uncertainties.

Today, there is a common set of shared beliefs, values, and assumptions of how corporations operate. Corporations are largely understood to be private, sovereign enterprises. There is a fundamental belief in the separation between the public and the private and that to live in an undemocratic economy is irrelevant for governmental democracy. Sustained economic growth is viewed as the sole path toward human progress. In order to maximize this growth, the preferred environment is the "free" market economy. The assumption is that privatization—or a corporate-controlled economy—removes inefficiencies in the public sector, allowing more goods to be brought to more people faster.

The largest TNCs penetrate every single country. They exceed most governments in size and power and define the policy agendas of states and international bodies, such as the WTO and increasingly the United Nations (UN). All TNCs are motivated by profit above and beyond any other interest, such as environmental integrity or social equality. TNCs are extremely mobile. They are able to transcend state boundaries with little difficulty. Detached from people and place, TNC owners are easily able to hire and fire employees at will. Employees of TNCs are therefore expendable, a trend which contributes to rising job insecurity. There is no longer a commitment to the local since TNCs belong to the global marketplace. This is dangerous as it is the local that is best situated to detect and respond appropriately to environmental issues. Absentee ownership is a key defining feature of today's TNCs. Most are monopolistic and discourage competition. This is evidenced by the fact that 70% of world trade is controlled by just 500 corporations. A mere 1% of all TNCs own half the total stock of direct foreign investment. With unmatched political and economic resources, the main goal for corporations today continues to be their struggle to wholly liberate themselves from the burden of public social and environmental accountability yet, at the same time, lobby Congress for greater subsidies to pursue their interests.

CORPORATE WELFARE

Each year the U.S. Congress pays out tens of billions of dollars to American corporations in the form of direct subsidies and tax breaks. In fiscal year 2006 these subsidies totaled $92 billion. Corporate welfare costs more than four times as much as welfare to the poor. TNCs thus collect more government handouts than all of the nation's poor people combined. One of the largest recipients of corporate welfare is weapons contractors like General Electric (GE)—also a global media conglomerate which owns and operates NBC Universal. One way contractors get subsidies is by mandating that military aid given to foreign countries be used to buy American weapons. Each year this program results in the transfer of tens of billions of U.S. taxpayer dollars to U.S. weapons merchants. The most successful U.S. industries would not be competitive internationally if the federal government had not developed their basic technology with taxpayers' money through programs like the Advanced Technology Program and then given it away to private corporations (see Lesson 8).

In addition to providing jet engines for military aircraft, GE makes nuclear reactor missile propulsion systems and delivery vehicles for nuclear weapons. It has designed more than 90 nuclear power plants in over 10 countries. Between 1946 and 1965, GE made plutonium for the U.S. military at Hanford Nuclear Reservation, a massive 570 square mile facility in Washington. One of the worst incidents during GE's tenure at Hanford was a calculated experiment in which radioactive particles containing more than 500 times the radiation of the Three Mile Island accident, when nuclear reactors suffered a partial meltdown, were deliberately released into the air. The toxic and radioactive legacy left behind at Hanford is staggering. Thousands of citizens living downwind continue to suffer from cancer and other chronic illnesses. Today, GE continues to sell nuclear weapon technology abroad, with no acknowledgment of the complex and persistent environmental damage caused by radioactive material. In addition to penetrating the global ecosystem and food chain, nuclear waste is a global problem with no sustainable solutions.

In 2005 GE spent over $24 million lobbying the U.S. Congress to craft legislation that would benefit its company and garner contracts. In recent elections it has shelled out over $2 million in campaign contributions. This work paid off as it was awarded over $2,526,300,000 in federal contracts in fiscal year 2005. GE also featured in the top 10 corporate recipients of U.S. government subsidies, totaling tens of millions of dollars. GE garnered direct subsidies from the government in light of over 25 proven instances of fraud, waste, and abuse in handling government contracts. Some of this negligence includes violations of polychlorinated biphenyl (PCB) regulations, violations of California's pesticide registration requirements, emission violations, violations of Florida's and New York's hazardous waste laws, and violation of the Clean Air and Clean Water Acts. Indeed, GE is no friend of the environment. In recent years GE has lobbied hard to overturn the U.S. Superfund Law of 1980, which allows the government to hold polluters responsible for cleaning up their toxic chemicals. GE argued instead that it was unconstitutional for the Environmental Protection Agency (EPA) to force the company to pay for the cleanup of the Hudson River in New York, where GE dumped carcinogenic PCBs for over three decades. Given GE's history and its control over the global media, it should be no surprise that complex environmental issues are not presented or thoroughly debated on NBC or its countless subsidiaries.

In addition to foreign-policy spending and research and development that funds corporate technology, corporations benefit from other public projects. Corporations are able to use the public infrastructure, such as transportation and communication. They benefit greatly from the public investment in education: Today's students are tomorrow's workforce. Corporations also benefit from publicly funded environmental cleanups, such as the Hanford Nuclear Reservation. Up until the late twentieth century, corporations freely disposed of their toxic industrial waste into rivers, waterways, and neighborhoods. The multi-billion-dollar health-care and long-term environmental costs of this waste have largely been absorbed by the taxpayers since corporations use their influence in Congress to ensure they will not be held accountable and their influence in media to ensure the public is not informed.

In addition to benefiting from these public institutions, corporations are increasingly privatizing these historically public institutions as well. Education, health care, security, policing, detention, corrections facilities, public lands, public water, and public airways are increasingly being privatized. This means that TNCs are currently attempting to monopolize, for example, control of world water systems and supplies. Several years ago the World Bank, one of the world's largest lenders and sources of development assistance, adopted a policy of water privatization and full-cost water pricing in poor, developing countries (see Lesson 17). In the United States, city water systems have now been contracted to corporations like Bechtel Group, Inc., a corporation with a long history of environmental abuses, to upgrade. Privatization of public resources means that democratically elected governments sign away their control over domestic water supplies by participating in trade treaties like NAFTA and the WTO, where TNCs are granted unprecedented rights to public resources.

The powers to educate, jail, rehabilitate, care for the poor, and manage nature itself are all being entrusted to corporations, which have no accountability to the public. As these functions are sold off, the government itself is transformed, if not dismantled, into an institution of private enterprise, where ordinary citizens have no voice. TNCs are considered individual citizens under the law and are dependent upon public money for their own growth and expansion, but they are not accountable to the public. As more public lands and institutions are privatized by TNCs, as TNC profit margins trump all other interests, and as the public is increasingly squeezed out of the decision-making arena, there has been comparatively little media attention toward this seismic social change. The following sections thus examine more closely the role of the corporation in the global media and how it shapes our knowledge and decisions on a wide variety of issues.

THE HISTORY OF CORPORATE GLOBAL MEDIA

We are increasingly inundated with information, but what do we know? How do we know it? And what don't we know? We quickly tire of sound bites, sensationalized stories, and buzz words—but often before we even begin to understand the complexity behind the attention-grabbing headlines. Like all industries, media is also becoming increasingly global in the age of the connected international corporate system. It currently serves two main functions. First, global media plays a central economic role for nonmedia firms by facilitating their business interests. This is done by providing advertising outlets to facilitate corporate expansion into new markets, new countries, and new regions. Second, the global media's news and entertainment provide an informational and ideological environment that helps to sustain the political, economic, and moral basis for marketing goods and for having a dominant free-market agenda. The media is central to convincing us that American-style democracy and the free-market economy are the only paths toward "freedom."

The role of the media in our society can only be understood in a political and economic context. That is, who owns and controls the media, and for what purposes, has always been a political issue. Until the twentieth century, media were largely local and national. Today, in the same way that corporations have become increasingly global in nature, so too have the media. The owners and producers of media no longer have only their national interests in mind but rather the interests of profit making on a global scale. As the global capitalist system continued to develop, communication was central to expanding commercial interests.

The first form of global media was wire-based international news agencies such as Reuters and eventually the Associated Press. These entities produced news and then sold it to local and national newspaper publishers. By the 1850s there were about four main commercial news agencies that had established a cartel, dividing the entire world market for news production and distribution. These were European—Germans, French, British, and eventually Americans. Since the very beginning of global media, dating back to at least the mid-nineteenth century, global news services have been oriented to the needs and interests of the wealthy nations which provide their revenue. These news agencies sold news content to their own nations as well as colonized nations, which could not support their own global news services.

The emergence and ascension of the TNC laid the groundwork for the rise of the global media. The film industry and then radio broadcasting were two of the first forms of global media. By 1914, 85% of the world film audience was watching American films. The experience with these media elevated the importance of control of media and telecommunications systems in general as a powerful political tool. By the end of World War II, through the use of global media, the United States was able to assert its global dominance as a hegemonic power or world leader.

Along with its policies of opening markets throughout the world for trade, the United States also advocated for the "free flow of information." In theory, the idea that news, information, ideas, and opinions have unrestricted movement across political boundaries is largely positive. In practice, the "free flow of information" has instead meant that U.S. TNCs are able to operate globally, across borders, with minimal oversight, fewer checks and balances, and fewer contending voices. It was an attempt to establish a global media system in its own image. While the American-dominated global media wanted free access to news and information markets, they were not necessarily interested in freedom of information and diversity of opinions and perspectives, critical aspects of a flourishing and sustainable democracy. The post-World War II era was thus characterized by a shift away from public-owned national and local media toward commercially owned global media.

With the spread of English global news media came increased commercial marketing—that is, more commercials and advertising—and the consolidation of formerly distinct media industries such as film, music, publishing, and broadcasting. By the 1970s, the beginning of economic "free"-market rule on a global scale, the trajectory and nature of the global media system were clear: It was largely a profit-driven system dominated by TNCs based in highly industrialized capitalist nations, especially the United States. State deregulation of private industries, a decline in the social welfare state, and privatization of state-run companies and services—the defining characteristics of economic globalization—greatly facilitated the expansion of TNCs and hence the increasing growth and consolidation of global media.

An example of state deregulation of private industries includes the infamous 1994 Republican Party "Contract with America," heavily influenced by corporate-sponsored think tanks that encouraged measures aimed at repealing existing environmental regulations, preventing new ones, and disabling the authorities that enforce environmental regulations. Think tanks and congressional representatives alike argued that the cost of federal regulations to the economy totaled billions of dollars annually. These unsubstantiated concerns were manifested in several pieces of legislation that sought to override the mandates of the Clean Air Act, the Clean Water Act, the Safe Drinking Water Act, and the Endangered Species Act among others.

Contrary to the fact that TNC interests are outwardly anti-governmental regulation, the TNC-dominated system of economic globalization has been a political choice that has nonetheless been aided by governments. After all, it is states that are signatories to various international trade agreements that facilitate the growth and expansion of TNC interests. Today, the system of free-market liberalism rests upon the widespread acceptance of a global corporate ideology. This ideology has played an important role in rationalizing and sanctifying unequal relations of power. It helps explain why the Enron scandal—perhaps the largest corporate scandal in history—has largely disappeared, while Hollywood drama continues to receive ongoing prime-time coverage. The ideology that the free-market economy is actually free and that what is good for corporations is good for the people—acting through the global media—is today a powerful form of social control.

CORE ELEMENTS OF THE GLOBAL MEDIA CORPORATE IDEOLOGY

There are two core elements of the new global media corporate ideology. The first element is the idea that markets allocate resources efficiently and should provide the means of organizing economic and perhaps all human life. It is dominated by a strong belief in privatization—reducing public control and increasing corporate control, thereby increasing profit margins. The second element is that freedom is often equated with the absence of any state business regulations. Political freedom is something different, and it is often subservient to economic freedom. In other words, the idea is that economic freedom leads to and guarantees political freedom. Media is, however, not free at all. Instead, it tends to regard corporate domination as natural and benevolent. The media preach both overtly and covertly the virtues of commercialism and the market. Today's global media has no social, moral, or political obligations beyond the pursuit of profit.

Concentrated wealth and power, on the one hand, and dire poverty, hunger, famine, and landlessness, on the other, cannot exist outside of systemic propaganda in modern democracies. There are several essential ingredients or news filters that constitute the propaganda model. These elements interact with and reinforce one another. The raw material of news must pass through these filters in order to be printed. The elite domination of the media and the marginalization of competing voices which results from the operation of these filters occur so naturally that media newspeople believe they are interpreting the news "objectively."

SIZE, OWNERSHIP, AND PROFIT ORIENTATION

The United States' most widespread news, commentary, and daily entertainment are controlled by only six firms that are among the world's largest corporations. In comparison, 25 years ago in the mid-1980s there were some 50 corporate owners of the media. Today these corporate owners are AOL-Time Warner, Disney, Viacom, NewsCorp, Bertelsmann, and General Electric. These corporations have more annual revenue than the next 20 combined. Together these six corporations own newspapers, magazines, book publishing houses, and movie and TV production studios. Most recently, these corporations also own the national delivery systems for the programming they control or lease, such as broadcast networks and cable. Moreover, they increasingly own the delivery mechanisms into each American home or office as well, such as telephone company lines, cable systems, and satellite dishes.

The process of increased ownership over all aspects of media production and distribution is called *vertical integration*. Vertical integration is a defining characteristic of TNCs and is defined as the control over a total process—from the raw material (news) to fabrication (fashioning it into a newspaper or broadcast network) to sales. Vertical integration allows for price control and monopoly. If there are only six corporations controlling the bulk of the information and these corporations are largely interested in selling their specific agenda and self-interest (free-market ideology), it means that, despite more information, there is less and less diversity in its content; hence, it becomes less democratic.

These six corporations constitute a private ministry of information and culture. Through their ascendance to power, they have successfully implemented a system of tiers. At the top are leading news sources such as the *New York Times* and CNN, from which the local papers and broadcast networks, situated at the bottom, get their national and international news; therefore, there is a single perspective being portrayed from the global to the national to the local level. While it is expressed in different media and by different actors, the message stems from the same source. The directors of these companies are usually businesspeople interested less in the quality of the product and more in the size of the profit margin. If, for example, information about the personal lives of Hollywood film stars attracts a large audience base, this will be the sole determining factor in shifting media resources to cover this information. Profit-driven media is further entrenched by the fact that it is banks and other institutional investors who are large owners of media stock. Again, profit margin is the single most defining factor in what constitutes news, not moral, political, or social obligations to keep the public informed of key issues relating to their health and well-being.

Since these companies are extremely diverse and, in the example of GE, own everything from radio to newspapers and from weapons to nuclear power, the corporate media owners have huge stakes in political decisions. In other words, it is less likely for these corporate owners to encourage their news sources to investigate environmental problems linked to corporations. Take, for example, the story that the radioactive metal-processing industry, the Department of Energy (DOE), and the Nuclear Regulatory Commission (NRC) pushed for new regulations that dispensed with the need for special radioactive recycling licensing. Under new special government permits, "decontaminated" radioactive metal is being sold to manufacture everything from knives, forks, and belt buckles to zippers, eyeglasses, and dental fillings.

In addition, these same entities were able to raise the acceptable level of *millirems*, a unit of measure that estimates the damage radiation does to human tissue. By the NRC's own estimate, the proposed standards could cause 100,000 cancer fatalities in the United States alone. Moreover, the DOE has entered a precedent-setting contract at Oak Ridge, Tennessee, where atomic weapons were once developed, that could release over 100,000 tons of radioactively contaminated nickel, steel scrap, and copper. The metal is beginning to go to metal-processing facilities, then to product manufacturers with no warning labels, notification, or consent from the potentially exposed workers or consumers. Any items made from these metals could be contaminated. The mainstream media has failed to cover this issue due to the fact that radioactive metal recyclers in the United States, part and parcel of the global media owners, are looking toward hot metal as a big moneymaker. Those who hold alternative views on this subject have simply been suppressed.

THE ROLE OF ADVERTISING

The media is required to conform to advertisers' wishes. Political discrimination is therefore structured into advertising allocations. Only those with money can buy space. Those with the most money are TNCs, which also share the same ideology and agenda of the promotion of free-market capitalism. Advertisers choose selectively among programs on the basis of their own principles. Large corporate advertisers on television will rarely sponsor programs that engage in serious criticism of corporate activities. Other institutional voices, perspectives, and ideas are systemically denied opportunities to access the global media as they do not bring to bear the same resources or money needed to purchase space to sell their ideas. Such examples include local organic farming cooperatives, environmental sustainability projects, alternative energy sources, endangered species issues, conservation issues, and recycling initiatives.

In addition, the global media's attempt to attract larger audiences (in order to secure more profits) means that there is increased competition for advertising. Advertisers are also primarily interested in profit margins and thus wish to advertise their products in places where they can reach the largest audiences. Again, if the largest audiences can be formed most quickly and most easily through the tactics of shock value, crude vulgarity, sex, violence, and celebrity gossip, then there is an incentive for the global media to focus superficial attention on these stories rather than on in-depth coverage of complex social, economic, environmental, and political issues.

This has led to the phenomenon best described as "infotainment" and "advertorials." These terms depict how "news" has become mostly entertainment information and how editorial commentary is largely driven by the special interests of advertising companies. Morning and evening news programs today largely consist of analyses of the previous evening's television shows, particularly the so-called reality-based TV programs. Guests largely include celebrities, design and fashion experts, pop culture specialists, and musicians. This has led to the deterioration of the quality of news, which has now been reorganized largely to serve corporate ambitions and not independent, diverse public information on which democracy depends. Simply debating whether the news has a liberal or conservative bias is a distraction from corporate control and dominance of the global media.

GLOBAL MEDIA SOURCES

As the global media corporations continue to be concerned mostly with profit margin, there has been a dramatic reduction in the number of field reporters and overseas bureaus. Investing in sustained, in-depth, field-based investigation and reporting is expensive. Most of these positions and bureaus have been cut. Parts of American news production have been outsourced to countries like India with huge concentrations of cheap labor. Another cost-saving technique has been the increasing reliance on "official sources" for important political and economic information. The global media increasingly turns to information provided by the government, businesses, and other "experts" as the key source for important stories on a wide variety of issues. Institutions like the Pentagon, the U.S. State Department, and corporate entities like GE have the resources available to provide media organizations with information via press statements, speeches, forthcoming reports, scheduled press conferences, and photo opportunities.

These large bureaucracies of the powerful subsidize the mass media and gain special access by their contribution to reducing the media's costs of acquiring the raw materials necessary to produce the news. The large entities that provide this subsidy become "routine" and "authoritative" news sources with privileged access to the global media. Free speech is thus directly tied to one's wealth. Media power is political power, and only the wealthiest are able to fully access it. Those institutions or entities without entire departments dedicated to public relations are often unable to access the global media to express their concerns or offer their own reports on key issues. This has contributed to a political narrowness of the news, a lack of rich debate, and a general decline in the diversity of perspectives portrayed in the news. If most of the news turns to the same sources for authoritative positions on issues, there is thus little room for widespread debate; hence, it is easy to conclude that the news is objective. Moreover, as journalists increasingly rely on corporate and governmental entities for the sole source of their information, they often become more reluctant to challenge these sources so as not to damage their established relationship.

VIOLATING THE CORPORATE AGENDA

Since the media carries the free-market agenda, when it criticizes or diverges from the agenda, corporate-sponsored institutional monitors harass and put extreme pressure on the media to tow the line. Whenever the media does not adopt the official corporate or governmental position on an issue, these monitors will systemically attack the media for careless reporting, unfounded claims, and other violations. As mentioned above, the best example of this is the issue of global warming. Instead of engaging this issue thoroughly to examine different options of addressing the root causes, each new scientific report or global treaty was met by harsh, well-organized, PR-driven, corporate backlash that sought to discredit the individual authors and the reports themselves.

These tactics reach back to the beginning of the modern environmental movement with the 1962 publication of Rachel Carson's book *Silent Spring*, which detailed the environmental destruction of DDT and other dangerous toxins and subsequently helped to raise awareness about environmental destruction. In response, the agrichemical industry doubled its PR budget and distributed thousands of book reviews trashing *Silent Spring*. Monsanto chemical company published *The Desolate Year*, a parody in which failure to use pesticides causes an insect plaque to devastate crops across the United States. Today, entire PR firms exist in part to help corporations propagandize and lobby against environmental protection. U.S. businesses spend an estimated $1 billion a year on the services of antienvironmental PR professionals who help wage their battles in the global media.

The threat of these attacks serves to condition the media to expect trouble—and cost increases—for violating the corporate agenda. In return, the media respects these power holders and rarely questions their ulterior motives. Self-censorship thus occurs without the need of an officially stated policy to deter media from covering certain topics. Political variety in the media is thus absent. This is partially explained by the fact that the same companies that fund anti-environmental campaigns and movements also pour money into mainstream environmental organizations. This tactic helps ensure that the environmental organizations see corporations as partners and not as enemies. As the old saying goes, "Don't bite the hand that feeds you." It also allows corporations to buy a green image that is worth millions in the consumer marketplace. Moreover, by maintaining close relationships with environmental organizations, corporations are better able to understand environmental organizations' key critiques. In doing so, corporations can shape their PR campaigns directly around environmental organizations' agendas.

GLOBAL MEDIA EVASION

While it is clear that the global media focuses largely on pursuing a free-market agenda that encourages consumption and acceptance of official positions on a wide variety of political, economic, environmental, and social issues, equally important is what the media fails to focus upon. A great example is garbage, a key social and environmental issue of the twenty-first century. What happens to the household, corporate, chemical, restaurant, industrial, and toxic waste generated each and every day? Most of the public has absolutely no idea since it is largely omitted by the global media; yet, it is a defining feature of modern, industrial societies. Of course, the millions of metric tons of garbage and the long-term social and environmental impacts of landfills and incinerators are important issues currently impacting millions of people's lives—though not those of key power holders; thus, it becomes a nonissue.

By focusing on style and process over content, the media diverts its attention to things like one's wardrobe, word choice, and presentation skills rather than the content of one's argument or statement. Moreover, by offering "two sides of the story," the media fails to look at the multiple sides and angles to any story. In any given issue, there is not simply a "pro" and an "anti" position but rather a plethora of diverse views and opinions. These voices are all shored up into either the "for" or the "against" camp. This is certainly clear with environmental issues, where one must choose to be either an "environmentalist" or an "antienvironmentalist" when in fact some individuals and groups support some reforms and conservation efforts but have concerns about others.

For instance, the issue of oil drilling in the Artic wilderness is often simplified in the news media as those who are in favor or against it. A more complete examination might put the single issue into a broader framework that examines energy production and consumption and various priorities and goals of either reinforcing or changing these habits. By isolating complex issues such as energy into a single issue of support for or against oil drilling in a specific region, the public fails to understand the relationships and connections between global energy production and consumption. In other words, "both sides of the story" are never the complete story.

In addition, complex issues like energy, while often reported upon, are never explained by the media. Dependence on nonrenewable fossil fuels, corporate control over these resources, and the violence created by their withdrawal are rarely examined. News articles seek to "report" on real-time events but rarely provide a context in which the public might be better able to understand them. Extremely complex social, political, economic, and environmental processes are reduced to fragmented and unconnected factoids. This type of reporting fails to associate social and environmental problems with the socioeconomic forces that created them. Most of the public is thus left with the impression that energy consumption, corporate power, the war on terrorism, and toxic waste are completely distinct, unrelated issues. It is clear that the rise of global commercial media coincides with a decline in public-owned media and public affairs news stories.

CONCLUSION: CORPORATE MEDIA POWER IN THE WIRELESS FUTURE

Today, the single most valuable piece of property worth owning are the radio frequencies of the electromagnetic spectrum over which an increasing amount of communication and commercial activity will be broadcast in the era of wireless communications. Personal computers, palm pilots, wireless Internet, cellular phones, pagers, radios, and television all rely on the radio frequencies of the spectrum to send and receive messages, pictures, audio, and data. In an era where more and more of daily communications are in cyberspace, access to the airwaves is critical.

Those who can pay will, of course, be connected; but it is unclear about those millions of people who cannot afford access. If the flow of human communications is controlled by global media companies and governments increasingly have little influence, to whom will citizens turn to ensure that a diversity of social, political, environmental, and economic views are expressed—especially when they may differ from those of the corporate owners? Moreover, when companies like AOL-Time Warner and Disney own the channels of communication as well as much of the content that flows through them, what mechanisms will be put in place to ensure that a diversity of voices and perspectives is nourished?

In addition, when these companies control the channels of communication, who will ensure that they do not exploit the personal data of individuals floating through cyberspace? What safeguards will be put in place to protect citizens? When citizens' very right to communicate with one another is no longer assured or secured by the government but controlled by global media conglomerates, how will citizens access the important information, news, and analysis needed to make informed decisions about critical social and environmental issues?

SOURCES

Bagdikian, Ben. 2000. *The Media Monopoly*. Boston, MA: Beacon.

Beder, Sharon. 1998. *Global Spin*. White River Junction, VT: Chelsea Green.

Derber, Charles. 1998. *Corporation Nation*. New York: St. Martin's Griffin.

Herman, Edward, and Noam Chomsky. 1988. *Manufacturing Consent*. New York: Pantheon.

Herman, Edward, and Robert McChesney. 1997. *The Global Media*. New York: Continuum.

Korten, David. 2001. *When Corporations Rule the World*. Bloomfield, CT: Kumarian.

McMichael, Philip. 2000. *Development and Social Change*. Thousand Oaks, CA: Pine Forge.

Moyers, Bill. 2002. "Trading Democracy." *NOW*, PBS, February 1, 2002.

Stauber, John, and Sheldon Rampton. 1995. *Toxic Sludge Is Good for You*. Monroe, ME: Common Courage Press.

Zepezauer, Mark, and Arthur Naiman. 1996. *Take the Rich Off Welfare*. Tucson, AZ: Odonian.

7

The Science of Nature and the Nature of Science

Richard York

On July 16, 1945, the detonation of the first atomic bomb—Trinity—lighted the skies near Alamogordo, New Mexico. It was the product of the Manhattan Project, which had started with a small group of researchers in 1939 but by 1945 had become the greatest scientific undertaking in history. How large the explosion would be was not known with certainty beforehand. Of course, there was the concern that it would be a dud and produce no explosion at all. However, some of the scientists on the project thought it might be big enough to incinerate the entire state of New Mexico. In fact, there was some concern that the explosion could ignite the atmosphere, thereby destroying virtually all life on Earth. In the actual event, it produced a 20-kiloton explosion, far greater than any bomb had ever produced before but, fortunately, not sufficient to engulf the Earth. More than six decades later, we still live with the dark legacy of this explosion and the many thousands—most much bigger—that followed it. Science had unlocked the secrets of the atom, and those secrets gave humanity the power to destroy itself.

Some of the greatest minds in history, the architects of this marvel of science, including the enigmatic genius J. Robert Oppenheimer who had led the development of the mighty weapon, subsequently came to regret what they had unleashed on the world. In an interview two decades after the Trinity test, Oppenheimer recalled the following:

> We knew the world would not be the same. A few people laughed, a few people cried, most people were silent. I remembered the line from the Hindu scripture, the Bhagavad-Gita. Vishnu is trying to persuade the Prince that he should do his duty and to impress him takes on his multi-armed form and says, "Now, I am become Death, the destroyer of worlds." I suppose we all thought that, one way or another.

In their creation of the atomic bomb, the scientists of the Manhattan Project had demonstrated, more forcefully than ever had been done before, both the enlightening power of science to gain knowledge of the world and the horror that the scientific establishment could foist upon humanity and nature.

If we are to understand the world in which we live and to bring about a sustainable and just society, we must grapple with both of these aspects of science: its power and its horror. From its foundation, the field of environmental sociology has taken a realist stance about environmental problems—they are indeed real, not just a socially constructed perception—and, thus, has always had a commitment to learning from the natural sciences, which study the ecosystems and natural resources upon which all societies depend. However, environmental sociologists have also always recognized the role that science, particularly in its contribution to technological development, has played in generating the modern environmental crisis. Thus, questions about the role of science in society have been central to the field of environmental sociology.

Most environmental sociologists would probably agree to a large extent that we must be simultaneously appreciative and skeptical of science. If we are to understand the human interaction with the natural environment and to overcome the environmental problems which we face, we must follow a fine line between two extremes: on the one hand, the outright rejection of science and, on the other, the uncritical valorization of the scientific establishment. Here, I present an examination of the tension between these two extremes and discuss some of the various ways environmental sociology has engaged the science question.

Before going any further, however, we must first answer the following question: What is "science?" Unfortunately, there is no single widely accepted answer, which is in part due to the multifaceted meaning of the term. To help us gain some understanding of the topic, I will make a distinction between two different aspects of science. One I will call "the logic of science" and the other I will call "the establishment of science." The basic argument I will make is that we need to understand, appreciate, and have a commitment to the former, while being highly critical of the latter.

By "the logic of science" I mean the philosophy of knowledge that underlies the scientific enterprise, informing its methods and theories. Science developed from the fusion of empirical and rational philosophies of knowledge, with particular emphasis on the former. Both of these philosophies can be traced back to the ancient Greeks in the Western tradition (with parallels in other cultures), but their modern versions emerged in the seventeenth century. Francis Bacon (1561–1626) is often identified as a key figure who initiated the scientific revolution, with his argument that we should reject the long established medieval practice of looking for truth in texts and, rather, seek knowledge from an examination of the natural world. This is the fundamental claim of empiricism: All true knowledge comes from our senses—sight, hearing, taste, touch, and smell—not from ungrounded speculation or divine revelation. Thus, perhaps the most central feature of a scientific approach to knowledge is that it relies on observation of the world of our experiences. Furthermore, it seeks explanations of the features of the empirical world grounded in conditions of the world itself, not in realms inaccessible to our senses, such as those invoked by mysticism and religion.

The scientific project also incorporated insights from rationalism, an intellectual tradition dating back to some of the greatest scholars of antiquity, such as Pythagoras and Plato, which was revitalized in the early modern era by René Descartes (1596–1650). Descartes and other rationalists were interested in how knowledge could be gained without reliance on the senses since they considered the senses to be easily fooled. In a thought experiment, Descartes wondered what knowledge we could be certain of if our senses were systematically fooled by, for example, demons that wished to trick us. The modern version of this thought experiment is well presented in a movie with which perhaps many of you are familiar: *The Matrix*. In *The Matrix* the world that nearly all humans experience is an illusion generated in their minds by a computer. Although they perceive it as real, they are in fact kept in pods from birth to death, never actually experiencing the real world, which was largely destroyed in a war between humans and the machines they created. The key question for the rationalist, then, is this: If we live in such a world where our senses cannot be relied upon to give us accurate information, how can we have a sure foundation for knowledge?

Due to these types of concerns, rationalists prefer to base knowledge on what can be logically deduced from a parsimonious set of assumptions that is not based on sensory experience. This is best exemplified in the field of mathematics, where theorems are proven strictly by logical inference from a minimal number of axioms ("self-evident" propositions) without reliance on observational evidence. Rationalism is concerned with what the logical consequences are of a given set of propositions. In combining these two philosophies of knowledge, rationalism and empiricism, the logic of science can be described as an approach to gaining knowledge about the world based on the rational analysis of empirical evidence. Thus, empiricism grounds rationalism in the world of our senses, while rationalism tempers empiricism by teaching us to be skeptical of the reliability of the observational evidence available to us. Now, as I will discuss, this should not be taken to mean that scientific analysis in practice has always or even typically adhered to the strictures of rationalism and empiricism, but rational empiricism is at the core of science, at least in its ideal form.

All claims about the existence of environmental problems or an environmental crisis have embedded in them an assertion about the condition of an objective external world. If we are to understand this objective world, we need a methodological program that allows us to gain definite knowledge of it. The scientific philosophy outlined above provides the basis of a methodological program that can help us to understand the material world in which we live. Since efforts aimed at understanding the environmental crises of modernity and the role humans play in them are fundamentally concerned with the constituency of the natural world, the environmental social sciences cannot divorce themselves from the natural sciences. Following a scientific approach, if we want to have real knowledge of the natural environment, we must rely on empirical evidence about that environment, not ideological, spiritual, or other nonempirical arguments.

Now, it should be apparent to you that this discussion leaves out some very important issues. What does science have to tell us about ethical questions?

After all, many of our most pressing concerns about the environment, as well as in other realms, are about what is right or wrong, not what is true or false. For example, the question of whether we *ought* to allow the killing of whales is at base a value question: Do whales (and other creatures for that matter) have moral worth? This is not the same as the questions of what the current population sizes are of various species of whales (or other creatures) and whether certain practices (for example, industrial whaling vessels prowling the world's oceans) are likely to drive whales to extinction. Indeed, some people even profess indifference to the extinction of many species. Considered in this light, it is clear that many of the hottest environmental debates are founded on both factual and ethical questions: (1) What are the effects of human activities on the natural environment? (2) Are the consequences of human activity good or bad, desirable or undesirable? The simple fact of the matter is that the logic of science can help us to address the first question but is mute with regard to the second. Thus, we see that there is an important scope condition to scientific inquiry. Scientific analysis can address questions of fact—that is, empirical questions—but it can provide no particular guidance about questions of right and wrong—that is, ethical questions. This is not to say that science does not raise serious ethical issues—a point to which I will return shortly.

While there is considerable virtue in the logic of science, when we turn to the "establishment of science" we find much about which to be critical. By the "establishment of science" I mean the actual practice of science, the social, economic, political, and cultural institutions which support it; the research centers (universities, transnational corporations, and national laboratories) where scientists work; and of course, the scientists themselves. Whereas the logic of science is a philosophy of knowledge, the establishment of science is an actual socially situated set of institutions. Thus, the establishment of science must be assessed by examining how it really operates in society and what its consequences have been for nature and humanity, not by recourse to abstract philosophical reasoning. Since science is pursued by humans, it is intrinsically a social phenomenon and, thus, cannot be seen as a free-floating institution disembodied from other human endeavors. Although the scientific community does support the ideal of objectivity, in practice scientists are not free of the biases and prejudices; social, cultural, and economic pressures; psychological quirks; and emotional states common to all humans. Science has never been carried out on an ethereal plane, where cool, clear minds pluck unsullied truth from nature. Thus, scientific findings and theories always reflect to some degree the social milieu in which they were formed.

The scientific institutions of our time have their origins in the emergence of "modernity"—the period following the Renaissance in Europe, when feudalism was replaced by capitalism and industrialism, beginning roughly in the seventeenth century. Science through most of its history has been dominated by members of the social elite, and scientists have often sought to further the interests of those in power by engineering weapons of war, developing technologies aimed at aiding global economic imperialism, and accelerating the exploitation of natural resources and laborers for profit by capitalists (see Lesson 8). Thus, it is necessary to recognize that the modern scientific establishment from its start was not aimed simply at the goal of understanding the world in which we live but was intimately linked to existing power structures and typically focused on achieving ends dictated by the ruling class.

This link between the scientific establishment and those in power remains clear in the contemporary world. As highlighted at the beginning of this lesson, it is a matter of no small importance that so much of scientific effort has been directed at developing weapons. A very substantial share of the research that took place over the twentieth century in physics, chemistry, and to a lesser extent biology—from work on rocketry and explosives to work on poison gases and deadly microbes—was done at the behest of, and with funding from, military interests. Furthermore, another substantial share of research effort is driven by raw financial interests, where corporations seek to increase profits by developing technologies of production and new products for the market, without particular regard for human well-being, environmental sustainability, or the lives of other creatures (see Lesson 5). For example, a considerable amount of experimentation on nonhuman animals is done merely to develop new consumer goods, such as cosmetics, that cause much animal suffering and do little to enhance human quality of life, for the sole purpose of generating greater profits for corporations. Similarly, the development of genetically modified organisms (GMOs) is to a large extent driven by the desire of large corporations to increase profits since products stemming from genetic engineering (for example, GM crops, pharmaceuticals) may potentially have vast markets. In this, the corporations pushing such technologies do not have it in their interest to highlight the social and environmental costs associated with GMOs since the profits will flow to the corporations while the costs will be shared with society as a whole.

Science and scientists cannot be seen as disinterested parties seeking truth for its own sake. This is not to say that individual scientists are not typically honest and well-meaning. Furthermore, while it has often served the interests of the ruling class, the scientific community has also brought to light the impacts of societies on the natural environment, such as in its analyses of global warming, ozone depletion, and escalating rates of species extinction. However, it is necessary to recognize that the structure of the scientific establishment, particularly in its connections to the ruling class, cannot be relied upon to serve the interests of the mass of humanity or of the other creatures with which we share the Earth. Due to the nature of the scientific establishment, it is, therefore, essential that environmental sociologists and other scholars continually engage in a critique of science. However, it is also important that in this critique we not lose sight of the importance of studying the natural and social world in a rational manner so that we can understand the processes that generate environmental and social crises.

The outright rejection of the logic and methods of science because of the environmental and social problems generated in the modern world by technology is fraught with danger. In fact, generating skepticism toward science at times has been a key tactic of powerful interests seeking to subvert environmental protection. Most notably, the fossil fuel industry has waged a tireless campaign to discredit the science demonstrating the emerging crisis of human-generated climate change—where the scientific consensus is clear in its assertion that human activities are contributing to global warming—in much the same way that the tobacco industry sought to misrepresent scientific findings about the health effects of smoking. The assault on climate science and scientific research more generally was particularly severe under the presidency of George W. Bush, which took every opportunity to undermine global warming research and particularly the presentation of that research to the public (see Lesson 14). The Bush administration, for example, sought to cut funding for scientific research that highlighted environmental problems, censored government scientists, and intimidated other scientists who conducted research and presented findings that contradicted the administration's political positions.

In light of these various considerations, environmental sociology has generally engaged the science question in a nuanced way. Environmental sociologists have examined how scientific claims about the environment are produced, contested, and presented to the public. Here, the main questions have been about how the environment is perceived by society and how some perceived conditions and changes in the environment come to be identified as "problems." These debates focus on to what extent social (and scientific) perceptions of the environment are "socially constructed"—that is to say, perceptions are created in the social realm through discourse—rather than being reflections of the real external natural world.

As I have already mentioned, taking a strong social constructionist position undermines the entire field of environmental sociology because it in effect denies that there is an environment independent of human perception of it, or at least that we can have reliable knowledge of the natural world. However, milder forms of social constructionism have proved valuable in helping us to understand the social and political processes through which scientific and other claims are shaped and manipulated by social actors and how these social processes often can create public perceptions of the environment that are distinctly at variance with objective environmental conditions.

Researchers have focused on how the environmental movement and other social actors present information about the environment and make the case that human modifications of the environment are problematic. It is clear that environmental writers, such as Rachel Carson and Aldo Leopold, and the larger environmental movement, including national organizations such as the Sierra Club and grassroots environmentalists such as Earth First!, played key roles in increasing public awareness of the human effects on the environment, emphasizing some environmental conditions more than others (see Lesson 15). Thus, public environmental concern did not simply come from a diffuse and general public awareness of the environmental effects of modern societies but was generated by the concerted efforts of a variety of social actors. The environmental movement plays a key role in both disseminating and interpreting scientific knowledge about the ecological consequences of human actions and questioning the wisdom of such actions. Similarly, other social actors, such as conservative think tanks, have worked to deny the existence of environmental crises and to "deproblematize" human-generated environmental change (see Lesson 6). These actors frequently question whether environmentalists are correct in their identification of human effects on the environment and/or portray human-induced change as beneficial rather than detrimental.

In these types of debates, scientific claims are of central importance because they often serve as the starting point for the creation of socially salient ideas about what is happening in the environment, and the validity and interpretation of the science is highly contested. For example, claims about global warming have been challenged by conservatives, particularly in the United States, despite the scientific consensus, with industry-funded antienvironmental groups claiming variously that humans are not affecting the environment or that global warming will in fact be good (or at least neutral) for societies. Similarly, the science of genetic engineering has been at the center of heated controversy over the development and use of GMOs, with various activist organizations questioning the safety of GMOs for human health and the environment and biotechnology firms and their allies denying the existence of any serious risks.

Recognizing the social influences on scientific findings is clearly important since research agendas are often determined by those with the resources to fund research, rather than stemming from disinterested consideration of the intellectual merits of various topics. Although empirical evidence is a central part of answering questions about the natural world, data do not speak for themselves. Rather, what data are collected and how they are collected, analyzed, and interpreted are not independent of the social context of research. For example, timber companies are unlikely to fund research that demonstrates the detrimental environmental consequences of logging, and, unsurprisingly, scientists funded by timber interests are unlikely to design studies that highlight such consequences.

These issues are not limited to research done by corporations but also play out in universities and colleges since many researchers who are not employed by corporations still receive funding from corporate sources. The influence of corporations on university research has become more intense as governments have cut funding to public institutions, increasingly pushing universities to seek private sources of funding. Furthermore, public universities, still being partially dependent on government support and concerned about cuts to their funding, are subject to political pressures from elected officials who are often sympathetic to corporate interests. For these reasons, a variety of scientists, from foresters to geneticists, even if scrupulous and fair-minded, are often limited in the type of research they can do and present. Thus, with good reason, many sociologists do not accept scientific findings uncritically and often take into consideration in their evaluation of factual assertions whose interests are served by various research programs.

In a similar manner, environmental sociology has analyzed the growing variety of technologically generated risks in modernity. Much of the debate in this area centers on to what extent the "experts," primarily scientists, can be relied on to fairly assess the risks associated with new technologies. For example, who should decide whether or not to build nuclear power plants or allow the use of GMOs? Do scientists know better than laypeople whether or not the potential benefits of such technologies outweigh their potential costs? Although at first glance it may seem that scientists are the best candidates for making such decisions since they have specialized knowledge about the technologies to be considered, on further consideration the issue appears to be much more complex.

Since scientists depend on empirical evidence to make their assessments, when data are absent they do not necessarily have greater insight than laypeople. In the case of many technologies, such as GM crops, questions are often about the long-term consequences of large-scale use; and this cannot be assessed with high certainty for new technologies that have only been tested over limited time periods in a restricted number of settings. For example, scientists did not foresee the threat that chlorofluorocarbons represented to the ozone layer until long after they came into widespread use. And, as I noted at the start of this lesson, there was considerable uncertainty about how large of an explosion the first atomic bomb would yield, despite the fact that it was studied by many of the greatest scientific minds in the world. (Did the scientists and military bureaucrats have the right to make the decision to conduct the Trinity test, despite the potential consequences for all of humanity and nature?) Scientific methods are good at assessing risk when there is a sufficient amount of data but have only limited potential to give reliable assessments in the absence of such data.

Since the potential costs and benefits of new technologies are not evenly distributed across society, issues of justice and fairness are central to risk assessment; and these are not entirely reducible to empirical questions. After all, in making calculations about risk by estimating the potential costs and benefits of new technologies, is an economic measure (such as dollars) the most appropriate, or should the life of humans and other creatures be assessed with a different metric? Clearly, there are ethical questions to be considered that will not yield to scientific analysis.

Furthermore, it is increasingly the case that scientists have financial stakes, beyond simply the funding of their research, in the technologies they advocate and, thus, commonly have a conflict of interest when asked to assess whether the benefits of new technologies are likely to outweigh the risks. For example, many geneticists hold patents for gene-based technologies and/or own shares of companies that stand to profit from biotechnology applications. Thus, the extent to which such scientists can be relied upon for an objective evaluation of technological risks is quite dubious. Clearly, questions about how scientific knowledge should be applied and how decisions are made about which risks are worth taking are matters of no trivial importance. Environmental sociology, then, has studied how the public has sought to democratize science, as well as how the social elite has often sought to insulate decisions about technological applications and scientific ethics from public scrutiny.

I have only touched on many of the complex issues that environmental sociologists face in engaging science. There are three key points to take from this lesson. First, environmental sociologists, by necessity, generally take a realist stance toward environmental problems. That is to say, they recognize that concern for the environment is in substantial part due to real changes occurring in the natural world, not merely because of cultural changes in values, beliefs, and perceptions. Thus, environmental sociology is dependent on a scientific approach to understanding the human–environment interaction, where knowledge is sought through rational investigation of empirical evidence. Second, existing in some degree of tension with the first point, environmental sociologists also recognize that social perceptions of the environment are affected by political, economic, and social processes, where those in power often manipulate scientific knowledge to further their own interests. Therefore, it is necessary to situate scientific knowledge in its social context. Third, environmental sociologists recognize that the effects of science on the environment have been double-edged. On the one hand, the logic of science has allowed for a growing understanding of the natural world and how humans have affected the biosphere. This rational knowledge allows for the recognition of environmental problems and an emerging understanding of what needs to be done to address them. On the other hand, science has given humans unprecedented power to manipulate nature, and this has contributed to a growing suite of technologies that generate new and greater threats to ecosystems and disrupt the metabolic exchange between society and the environment. Environmental sociology grapples with these many facets of science in an effort to understand society and nature. It is to be hoped that such understanding will help us to bring about a just and sustainable world.

SOURCES

Beck, Ulrich. 1992. *Risk Society: Towards a New Modernity*. Newbury Park, CA: Sage.

Burningham, Kate. 1998. "A Noisy Road or Nosy Resident? A Demonstration of the Utility of Social Constructionism for Analysing Environmental Problems." *Sociological Review* 46(3):536–63.

Conner, Clifford D. 2005. *A People's History of Science: Miners, Midwives, and "Low Mechanicks."* New York: Nation Books.

Ehrlich, Paul E., and Anne H. Ehrlich. 1996. *The Betrayal of Science and Reason: How Anti-Environmental Rhetoric Threatens Our Future*. Washington, D.C.: Island Press.

Gould, Stephen Jay. 2003. *The Hedgehog, the Fox, and the Magister's Pox: Mending the Gap Between Science and the Humanities*. New York: Harmony Books.

Levins, Richard, and Richard C. Lewontin. 1985. *The Dialectical Biologist*. Cambridge, MA: Harvard University Press.

McCright, Aaron, and Riley E. Dunlap. 2000. "Challenging Global Warming as a Social Problem: An Analysis of the Conservative Movement's Counter-Claims." *Social Problems* 47(4):499–523.

Merchant, Carolyn. 1980. *Death of Nature: Women, Ecology, and the Scientific Revolution.* San Francisco, CA: Harper.

Mooney, Chris. 2005. *The Republican War on Science.* New York: Basic Books.

Rhodes, Richard. 1987. *The Making of the Atomic Bomb.* New York: Simon & Schuster.

Rosa, Eugene A. 1998. "Meta-Theoretical Foundations of Post-Normal Risk." *Journal of Risk Analysis* 1:15–44.

Yearly, Steven. 2002. Pp. 274–85 in "The Social Construction of Environmental Problems: A Theoretical Review and Some Not-Very-Herculean Labors." In *Sociological Theory and the Environment: Classical Foundations, Contemporary Insights,* edited by Riley E. Dunlap, Frederick H. Buttel, Peter Dickens, and August Gijswijt. New York: Rowman & Littlefield.

York, Richard and Brett Clark. 2006. "Marxism, Positivism, and Scientific Sociology: Social Gravity and Historicity." *Sociological Quarterly* 47(3):425–50.

8

Technological Change and the Environment

Kenneth A. Gould

One of the primary ways that human societies mediate their relationship with the natural world is through the development and use of technology. Societies use technology to overcome obstacles to surviving and thriving that they perceive in nature and to modify the natural world in ways that meet certain human needs and desires. The social creation of new technologies transforms both societies and the natural world upon which human societies depend. Therefore, in order for us to understand the dynamic relationship between social systems and ecosystems, we need to understand the role played by technology in shaping that relationship.

WHAT IS TECHNOLOGY?

So what is technology? In simplest terms, technology is how we make "stuff" and do "stuff." In order to make certain kinds of stuff and do certain kinds of stuff, we organize and reorganize social relations and nature. And technological change is most commonly produced by social actors and institutions. It doesn't fall from the sky, and it doesn't emerge in some predetermined path of linear progress. Specific social groups (corporations, governments, and other forms of social organization) make it their business to move technological change in specific directions and for specific purposes. For instance, take a look at the classroom when you go back to class to discuss this lesson. A classroom is, in part, a technology for making or doing stuff. In this case, the stuff to be made is educated people and the stuff to be done is education. The classroom is organized, created, and maintained by a social institution (your college). Manifest in your classroom are both social relations (the relationships between people) and relations between the social system and the ecosystem. Is your classroom organized with chairs in a circle or with all the seats facing a central point? The physical organization of the classroom (the technology of education, if you will) tells you much about the social relations within it, as well as the social expectations. With seats in a circle, you expect to have to talk to others in the room quite a bit. With the chairs facing a central point, you expect to be spoken to and for you to speak much less, and then perhaps only to the person occupying the central point of focus (the lectern). In a circle, you expect social relations to be more egalitarian, with each participant playing a more equal role. With chairs facing a central point, you expect social relations to be more hierarchical and authoritarian, with a single power holder (your professor) commanding most of the attention.

What you can see by looking at the physical structure of your classroom is an indication of the social structure of the classroom. That is, the way that the technology of education (your classroom) is organized both reflects and determines social relations. The same is true of any technology for doing and making anything. The technology itself, a computer, a factory, a hog farm, a television, a cell phone, or a nuclear weapon, manifests specific social relations. Technology consists of both physical, tangible "things" and the social relations they imply. No technology is separable from its social relations, even though those relations are intangible and take a little more work to actually "see."

You will have missed the early part of your class thinking about the ways in which the physical parts of the technology of education reflect and determine the social relation parts of the technology of education, instead of paying attention to what's being said. That's okay. You can get notes from the person next to you. Now think about the relationship to nature manifest in the classroom. What is all the stuff in the classroom made from? Your notebook, made from trees. Your seat, made from plastic, made from oil. Maybe some aluminum made from bauxite here and there. All of the physical things in your classroom have their origins in nature and have been transformed, through technologies (social relations and physical hardware), into something else to meet human goals.

You probably have electricity in your classroom too, to power lights, computers, projectors, etc. That means that your classroom is physically hard-wired to some technology for transforming some natural element or process into electricity. Look at the electrical sockets in your classroom. You could follow the wires from those sockets all the way back to the cogenerator, power dam, coal-burning power plant, nuclear reactor, photovoltaic cells, or windmill that has been constructed to convert natural resources or processes to meet human goals. Perhaps the socket leads to a coal-fired power plant that burns coal mined in some region quite distant from your own. People there are busy transforming nature in their location in order to allow you to have lighting so you and your professor can produce education in your location. And that electricity is probably transmitted through copper wires, made somewhere off-campus, from copper mined in yet another distant community by still other people. In all likelihood, there aren't coal or copper mines on your campus. So your classroom and you are connected to other parts of the country and the world, using natural resources from distant ecosystems.

Your classroom, and any other technology you use or are a part of, connects you to a variety of relationships with the natural world, both immediate and far removed. And the technologies for converting natural resources into other stuff (electricity, books, seats, etc.) also connect you to other sets of social relations, with people you may never know or see, who mine coal and copper or work in factories producing wires or wood pulp for paper.

So technology is a series of entanglements with social systems and eco-systems, close and far, obvious and hidden. Your cell phone, your pen, your computer—all represent a series of relationships between you and others and between you and the natural world. Those relationships are not random. They reflect the social origins of the technologies, the goals of those who designed the technologies, the interests of those who require or request you to use the technologies, and the ways in which society has been organized to use and change nature.

TECHNOLOGICAL CHANGE

Social scientists who analyze technology and technological change have used a variety of schema to identify various phases or periods in the development of technology. You have probably heard some of these eras of specific technological applications described with terms such as "the bronze age" or the "iron age." Note that the materials used signify these eras of technology. Lewis Mumford, in his classic work *Technics and Civilization*, identified three distinct eras of modern technological development: "paleo-technic," "eotechnic," and "neotechnic." The paleotechnic phase was typified by the use of wood as the primary material and the use of moving water and wind as the primary energy sources. The eotechnic phase was typified by the use of iron as the primary material and the use of coal to generate steam as the primary energy source. The neotechnic phase, he argued, was typified by the use of steel as the primary material and the use of electricity. Here again, the elements of nature, modified through human intervention, are central to our categories of technological phase. The ways human societies use and transform nature are key to our understanding of what various technologies are.

We can categorize different technological eras in various ways, by changes they produce in society and nature, both large and small. For our purposes here, let's look at two very large, very broad, and very transformative eras of technological change, both of which completely revolutionized the ways that human societies are organized and the ways that those societies relate to, modify, and rely upon nature. These two periods of technological transition were so transformative of society and the natural world that they have been viewed by most as revolutionary: the agricultural revolution and the industrial revolution.

The Agricultural Revolution

The realization that by planting seeds of desirable plants, people could transform ecosystems to make them produce large volumes of preferred food crops radically changed the relationship between human societies and nature. Prior to the technology of agriculture, human societies were primarily organized for a hunting and gathering survival strategy. In order to get the food they required, groups of people collected the plants and other foods they found in nature. This meant that, as local plant and animal stocks were depleted, people had to migrate to other areas in search of food. They developed patterns of migration that followed the seasonal availability of food plants and the seasonal migration of other animals (which also followed seasonal patterns of the availability of food and water). The technology of agriculture changed all that, allowing humans to modify their local ecosystems to meet their food needs, rather than modifying their societies (through migration) to meet local ecosystem conditions.

In a real sense, the power balance between environment and society was shifted toward greater human agency and greater ecosystem malleability. Humans cleared portions of local ecosystems of their natural species of plants, animals, and habitats and replaced them with increasingly vast fields of human-selected species of plants. This large-scale transformation of land from natural ecosystems to farm fields has continued ever since as prairies, savannas, and forests are cleared. Plants were selected for attributes most desired by humans (food and textiles), and that selection began to replace the process of natural selection in the evolution of certain species. A similar process occurred with the domestication of animals used for meat, dairy, and textiles. Animals were taken from the wild and raised and reproduced to serve human needs. Pastures were cleared, ecosystems transformed, and species gradually modified to serve human goals.

With settled agriculture, human populations could remain in a single location, modifying the environment to facilitate settlement. Settlement allowed for the building of permanent structures, rather than the portable or disposable shelters logically necessary for societies of nomads. Settlement also allowed for the accumulation of material possessions. Keeping material possessions to a minimum makes good sense if you'll have to move them from place to place all the time (something that anyone who has ever moved quickly realizes). If you can plan to be in a locale indefinitely, you can begin to fill your permanent structures with "stuff," thus creating an incentive for the production of more material things. So, in a real sense, the technology of agriculture is what began the process of human societies constructing permanent houses and filling them with material possessions.

The successes of agriculture also led to the creation of what sociologists call a "labor surplus." Where soils were fertile and water available, agriculture was very successful and large quantities of food could be produced by fewer and fewer people. This process of increasing yields and decreasing demand for human labor has continued so that now, in countries like the United States, vast food surpluses are produced with a very small percentage of the population engaged in actual primary food production. But even very early in the process, fertile regions allowed for growing numbers of people to eat, without themselves being engaged in food production. With large populations permanently settled in a single location without survival-oriented work to do (food collection or production), other activities and new ways of organizing people in more complex ways emerged. Along with permanent houses, permanent ritual sites, large-scale irrigation works to support agriculture, and other engineering projects requiring vast amounts of human labor were organized. Pyramids, temples, aqueducts, and astronomical observatories were constructed by harnessing surplus labor (often involuntarily). How the Egyptian pyramids were built is no mystery. The answer is agriculture. It is worth noting that much of this large-scale construction was organized to support agricultural success and expansion physically (irrigation works), to appeal to nature through religion for adequate rain and fertility (temples), or to track seasonal changes to determine appropriate planting and harvest schedules (astronomical observatories).

Supporting larger populations in one place required more complex social organization in governance and the production and distribution of a wider variety of goods and services. Labor surpluses also allowed for the creation of standing armies, and agricultural expansion increased the value of transforming and taking more land, especially in fertile areas. With hunting less essential to survival but conflict over access to arable land more vital, the primary trajectory of weapons technology turned from the killing of other animals to the killing of humans. Agricultural societies gave rise to the first central state authorities, commanding standing armies and controlling access to land and the distribution of food. While we may think of ourselves as living in industrial or even postindustrial societies, it is easy to see that many features of both human social organizations and their relationship to ecosystems actually stem from the radical social system and ecosystem shifts that came with the technology of agriculture.

The Industrial Revolution

The field of sociology was initially developed by people attempting to understand the vast transformations of social organization that emerged in the nineteenth century with the rise of industrialization. While the great agricultural civilizations emerged primarily in Asia, Africa, and Latin America, the first great industrial civilizations emerged in Europe. European social analysts like Marx, Weber, and Durkheim established the scientific study of societies and social change in efforts to understand the new patterns of social relations generated by the emergence of industrial production. The Industrial Revolution produced the second great technological transformation of the relationship between social systems and ecosystems, although, as noted in Lesson 1, the ecosystemic aspect of change was not of particular interest to early sociologists. The industrialization of production generated a vast array of social changes, far too numerous to address at length here. Among these, however, it is worth noting the creation of new classes (such as those Marx termed the "proletariat," or industrial working class, and the "bourgeoisie," the capitalist class) and the formation of industrial cities (London being the first city to reach 1 million in population since the fall of Rome).

In terms of the society-environment relationship, industrialization ushered in societal dependence on enormous inputs of nonrenewable resources, particularly fossil fuels. Industrial civilization was, and remains, predicated on nearly limitless supplies of relatively cheap and portable nonrenewable energy inputs. It was the capacity to convert coal into steam, and thus energy, on an ever-increasing scale that gave industrial society its form and its trajectory. Our current society can be thought of as one designed specifically to thrive in, and to survive off of, endless increases in energy inputs. Those conditions appeared to be sustainable at the dawn of the industrial era, when the exhaustion of necessary resources appeared unlikely. In the current era, it is the foreseeable end to increasing supplies of such energy, and it is the environmental impacts of using that energy (see Lesson 14) that is causing many to consider the need to wholly reorient the path of human society.

The technological changes that coalesced into the Industrial Revolution were intended primarily to vastly increase human ability to produce an increasing range of synthetic products, from textiles to machines themselves. Just as the agricultural revolution made the large-scale production of food possible, the Industrial Revolution made the large-scale production of other goods possible. And just as agriculture required the growing transformation of natural ecosystems into farm fields, industry required the growing conversion of elements of ecosystems (trees, coal, metals, etc.) into natural resource inputs in the production of products. Of course, as industrial production expanded and new markets for new products were expanded to meet the increased supply, the pace and scale of the extraction of natural resources and their conversion to natural resources increased, with two major results.

First, ecosystems and habitats, at first locally and later globally, were pillaged to meet the needs of industry for raw materials. We can think of these as ecosystem "withdrawals." These withdrawals would eventually lead to socially generated problems of natural resource depletion such as deforestation and oil scarcity. Second, the capacity of industry to produce on increasingly vast scales resulted in the world being increasingly full of social products and by-products. The products, although useful for a time, eventually find their way into dumps, landfills, the oceans, and incinerators. The by-products tend to be returned to ecosystems as industrial air-, water-, and land-based emissions. In addition, many of the products create by-products themselves in the course of their use, such as cars producing air emissions, discarded batteries, and used motor oil. We can think of these socially created artificial elements injected by industrial societies back into ecosystems as ecological "additions." These new additions to nature would quickly give rise to problems of environmental pollution (such as pesticide toxicity and greenhouse gases). The Industrial Revolution is therefore most notable in terms of the social system–ecosystem interaction for increasing the social capacity for, and rate of, conversion of natural resources into products and by-products. The result has been wholesale disruption of local and global ecosystems that natural scientists have only just begun to comprehend.

In giving rise to the modern city, the new industrial technologies also quickly gave rise to the familiar socioenvironmental problems that are part of urban landscapes: urban smog and resulting respiratory disease, the accumulation of trash and the difficulty of disposing of it in a safe and hygienic manner, the contamination of freshwater supplies and the threat of waterborne illness, and the social inequities in exposure to these urban environmental hazards. These environmental hazards were, and are, compounded with other key features of the urban social environment, such as issues of inadequate housing, congested infrastructure, and problems of the provision of adequate and equitable services such as health care, housing, employment, and justice. In addition, the urban environment cut off large portions of the human population from direct daily contact with natural environments, which had been a key fact of human existence since the dawn of the species. This disconnection from nature would lead many in "modern industrial society," including sociologists (see Lesson 1), to conclude that society was no longer dependent on nature and that the two could be thought of as separate concerns.

THE TECHNOLOGICAL TRAJECTORY

As you can see, both the revolutions in agricultural technology and industrial technology completely transformed the relationship between social systems and ecosystems. In the broadest sense, the greatest change that emerged from each was an enormous increase in the incentive and capacity to adjust natural systems to meet social needs, rather than adjusting social systems to meet naturally occurring ecosystem realities. In this process, the human capacity for technological innovation, our ability to develop new techniques to transform the natural world, has been key. As social systems now come to realize the dramatic negative social implications of their vast transformation of ecosystems, it is important to ask, where is our technological trajectory headed? Why? Who or what determines the path of technological innovation? And how might we choose a path of technological innovation that resolves some of the conflict between social systems and ecosystem?

Social Institutions and Technological Decision Making

Social institutions pursuing specific social goals largely control the progress and direction of technological change. These institutions exert substantial control over the research and development process in numerous ways, including influence on educational institutions, research facilities, research and development funding, and remuneration of outcomes. At each point of the research and development process, these social institutions are able to influence the agendas of scientists and engineers and, thus, the trajectory of technological innovation. There is no "runaway technology," as some environmentalists have argued. Nor is there a clear "natural evolution" of technological direction, as most might assume. The direction of scientific and technological research and development is a result of human intentionality and decision making (see Lesson 7). As a result, the history and current direction of technological research and development are reflective of the power and the political and economic interests of the social institutions that control the process.

The main social institutions determining the technological research and development agendas are universities, states, and corporations. Each of these institutions has specific interests, which are reflected in their agendas for scientific research and technological innovation and which thus shape the social system–ecosystem interactions that the rest of the world inherits. Universities have historically been viewed as the institutions with the greatest dedication to the "objective" pursuit of scientific truths and as being somewhat independent of political and economic pressures. In universities, it was often the scientists and engineers who set the research and development agendas, and they were largely immune from the influence of the political and economic goals and rewards stemming from states and corporations. However, as the costs of research and development increased and public funding for universities declined, states and corporations gained greater influence over the agendas and goals of science and technology workers within universities. As a result, the interests of states and corporations ripple through the university system and reduce the capacity of these formerly more autonomous institutions to chart a distinct technological research and development direction.

Governments are the primary source of funding for basic scientific research. The knowledge base upon which applied science will be built is thus influenced by the ways that state decision makers prioritize certain paths of inquiry and distribute funding for it. The goals of states in funding basic science are fairly clear. First, states fund basic science and some applied research and development to enhance their military power. Since governments are the market for weapons systems, they have a vested interest in making sure that the creation of ever more powerful military technology is a major thrust of technological innovation. As a result, the pursuit of more effective military systems has become one of the dominant goals—if not *the* dominant goal—of the technology research and development agenda of the species. The enormous amount of funding offered by the state for military research and development directs the human technological trajectory toward destructive ends while sapping funding from quality of life–enhancing research along other paths of human inquiry (such as health, environmental protection and remediation, renewable energy, etc.). Since military technology is particularly environmentally destructive, energy-inefficient, and natural resource–intensive, it has a significant negative impact on the nature of social system interactions with ecosystems.

The other goal of states in sponsoring research and development is the pursuit of global "economic competitiveness." By using tax revenues to subsidize the research and development agendas of corporations based within their borders, states try to boost their gross domestic products. Increasing the economic power of the country increases the relative power of a state, giving it greater influence over the global arenas in which it competes with other states. Because of this, increasing the economic power of the state becomes a technological goal in its own right, along with increasing the military power of the state. And those two goals are intertwined in a military–industrial complex because the greater tax revenues gained through successful international economic competition make more funding available to support military research and development, and greater military power facilitates greater access to the global natural resources, waste sinks, markets, and labor pools which are needed for economic growth.

The interests of corporations in technological research and development are somewhat less complex than those of states. Corporations pursue technological innovation to enhance profitability. Corporations are the leading institutional source of funding for technological innovation and the primary employers of engineers. As a result, the goals of corporations have greater influence over the human technological trajectory than those of any other social institution. Corporations use the government subsidy of basic research as the basis for their applied research (see Lesson 7) that produces profit-enhancing products to be sold to states (military hardware), other corporations (including labor-replacing technologies), and individual consumers (consumer goods). Lines of research that will lead to products that may produce social or ecological benefits but do not promise to generate profits are not funded and not pursued. Corporate profitability is then, in some sense, the ultimate criterion for determining much of the human technological trajectory. Given that technology is such a big factor in shaping the relationship between social systems and ecosystems, we can see that corporate interests have come to be a major—if not *the* major—factor in determining how social systems and ecosystems will interact.

The goal of corporate profitability influences the direction of technological innovation in other ways. Corporate profitability sets much of the research agendas of scientists both within the firm and within the university. Through sponsorship of university research, corporations create a system of incentives and disincentives for the pursuit of various lines of scientific inquiry and engineering development. By providing the laboratories in which research and development are conducted, corporations control the scientific and engineering infrastructure of society. By offering shared profit incentives with educational institutions and university researchers, corporations influence the direction of higher education. The nature and structure of scientific and engineering education tend to reflect the social agendas of the institutions that fund it. Corporations have also been known to overtly and covertly squelch lines of scientific investigation that may threaten the goal of corporate profitability, as we have seen in research on the health effects of tobacco, the environmental impacts of acid rain, and the contribution of carbon dioxide emissions to global climate change.

SCIENCE, TECHNOLOGICAL INNOVATION, AND POWER

The trajectory of technological innovation is greatly influenced by a relatively small number of decision makers in governments and corporations who establish research priorities, provide research facilities, and determine the distribution of funding. The result is a global technological infrastructure, system, and direction that reflects the interests of a privileged few and pursues those interests despite the many obvious negative consequences for social system–ecosystem dynamics. The fact that the bulk of technological decisions are made in corporate boardrooms and opaque government institutions shields technological innovation agendas from democratic processes. Although the outcomes of research and development decisions often become obvious to the public at large, the decision-making processes which ultimately lead to these outcomes are generally unavailable for public input and public influence. We all must live with the technological consequences in terms of products that are and are not available, technologies that do and do not exist, employment opportunities that are created and destroyed, and public health and ecological impacts that are generated; but we are generally denied a role in determining those consequences.

Democratic input into research agendas is quite limited. What often passes for democratic controls on technology are mechanisms for "public consultation" arranged after new technologies are created. These public consultations are often organized by the very institutions that sponsor technological research and whose interest is to gain public acceptance for the new innovations. These public forums are designed primarily to reduce public fears, which are viewed by those who have a vested interest in technology as irrational (see Lesson 6). The research on the social and ecological implications of technology is often highly politicized (see Lessons 7 and 14) and commonly intended to boost the chances for public acceptance of existing and new technologies. This makes it difficult for people to reach informed conclusions about the costs and benefits of technological change.

The Myth of "Progress"

Another factor that keeps the general public from participating in science and technology decision making is the myth of "progress," a set of ideological constructs promoted by the institutions that control the research and development process. Most people tend to think that research takes a natural course determined by free inquiry and the evolution of ideas and that technologies are routed along a linear progression where one development automatically follows from another. That is, people are led to believe that there is in fact no institutional agency in the technological trajectory and that what little human agency exists is in the hands of individual experts pursuing either public good or private gain. The ideology of capitalism argues that the pursuit of private gain naturally leads to the common good. The combination of the myth of technological neutrality and the ideology of capitalist ethics produces complacency in regard to research and development on the part of the public. This complacency serves the interests of the institutions that do have agency in determining the societal technological path and the social system–ecosystem relations that go with it.

While it is true that democratic citizenries could demand and exert greater influence over the research that states support, the ideological power of objective science (see Lesson 7), technological neutrality, and capitalist ethics keep this possibility from entering the public consciousness. Science and technology decision making has, for the most part, been organized out of politics. The result is that powerful individuals and institutions are left to use the human technological capacity in pursuit of their own interests largely unchecked by the majority. In no other arena are the long-term consequences for human society and the environment as great and the political discussion so muted. Conflicts do emerge from time to time (on nuclear technology, genetic technology, etc.), but even then the political discourse largely revolves around a ban on the implementation of a specific technology rather than a quest for democratic control over the processes that generate technology.

The Democratization of Technological Innovation

If we are to seriously pursue a more environmentally sound relationship between social systems and ecosystems, we may find it useful to make the technological innovation processes subject to democratic controls in which the potential social and ecological impacts of technologies can be assessed by informed publics and under conditions in which citizens are empowered to determine the goals of research and development, the prioritization and funding of that research, and the manner in which technologies will be implemented or prohibited. This input must occur at the earliest stages of the innovation process, determining the purpose of basic lines of inquiry in order to use our scientific and technological capacity for the maximization of democratically determined social and environmental benefits. That would be a very different model than the one in place currently, in which institutions produce and implement technologies without public input and then the public must overtly object to negative social and ecological consequences once they appear. After-the-fact protests and control efforts in which the public expresses opposition to prior technological decisions are certainly less than optimal for democratic governance and the creation of a technological trajectory that serves social and environmental goals.

SOURCES

Beder, Sharon. 1997. *Global Spin: The Corporate Assault on Environmentalism*. White River Junction, VT: Chelsea Green.

Gedicks, Al. 2001. *Resource Rebels: Native Challenges to Mining and Oil Corporations*. Cambridge, MA: South End Press.

Gould, Kenneth A. 2006. "Promoting Sustainability." Pp 213–230 in *Public Sociologies Reader*, edited by Judith Blau and Keri E. Iyall Smith. New York: Rowman & Littlefield.

Gould, Kenneth A. 2007. "The Ecological Costs of Militarization." *Peace Review* 19(3):331–4.

Lukes, Steven. 1974. *Power: A Radical View*. London, UK: Macmillan.

Mumford, Lewis. 1934. *Technics and Civilization*. New York: Harcourt Brace Jovanovich.

Noble, David F. 1977. *America by Design: Science, Technology, and the Rise of Corporate Capitalism*. New York: Alfred A. Knopf.

Nye, David E. 1996. *American Technological Sublime*. Cambridge, MA: MIT Press.

Schnaiberg, Allan. 1980. *The Environment: From Surplus to Scarcity*. New York: Oxford University Press.

White, Geoffry., ed. 2000. *Campus Inc*. Albany, NY: Promeheus Books.

9

Population, Demography, and the Environment

Diane C. Bates

The world's human population as of May 11, 2008, at 4:44 p.m. (EDT) was 6,667,028,294, with more than one person added every second. Social scientists have long considered human population a main determinant of environmental quality, particularly given the attention to population dynamics in ecology. However, population dynamics, including, but certainly not limited to, growth, go well beyond merely counting the number of people in a location. For example, population declines can create health and safety hazards in communities; the age and class structure of a population predict what sorts of environmental and health threats are likely to emerge from risks present in a given location; the stability and composition of a population affect its ability to respond to and recover from environmental threats. Social theory on the relationship between human populations and the environment has historically focused on population growth at different geographic levels, such as states, nations, or the entire world; but understanding population dynamics is important for all students of environmental change. Most people experience population change at the local level rather than on the national scales more typical of demographers and social theorists. For example, residents of the northeastern rustbelt may note how three decades of uneven population decline have left neighborhoods with vacant buildings, overgrown lots, and abandoned industrial and commercial space. Likewise, residents of the suburban sunbelt cannot help but observe how more and more people keep moving into the area and converting open space into residential subdivisions, office parks, and shopping centers. This chapter ties together these local experiences with the larger study of the interaction between human populations and our environment. It first defines several key terms in understanding population dynamics, then proceeds to a discussion of the main controversies in population theory. It closes with a discussion of an empirical case study that highlights how population growth in the South American country of Ecuador has affected the nation's forest resources.

Population refers to the number of people living in a specific geographic area at a specific point in time. *Demography* is the discipline in the social sciences that studies the characteristics of human populations, including how they change. In the United States, the Census Bureau compiles the most comprehensive demographic data, including the decennial census and the annual American Community Survey. Census Bureau data represent the highest-quality demographic data available on a national scale and can be accessed freely at its website (www.census.gov). At the international level, the United Nations Statistics Division compiles census and other statistical information from member nations and publishes them annually in the *Demographic Yearbook* as well as making some of these data available on its website (www.unstats.un.org). Some of the most important demographic variables include population density, population growth rates, birth and death rates, and migration. *Population density* indicates the average number of people who live in a specified area unit, usually a square mile or square kilometer. *Population growth* measures changes in population over time by taking a population at one time and adding all the births and immigrants who arrive before a later time, while subtracting the deaths and emigrants. Rates are calculated by dividing the number of births/deaths/immigrants/emigrants for every 1,000 people in a given population. Although it does not distinguish between natural change (births and deaths) and migration, a crude population growth estimate can be calculated by dividing the population at a later time by the population at an earlier time. In addition to counting the number of people in a population, demographers typically collect and publish data on the characteristics of populations, such as age and gender structure, consumption levels, and subpopulations, such as racial or ethnic groups. The quantitative specificity of demography, however, tells little about the relationship that human populations have with their nonhuman environments. Unfortunately, the relationship between population change and environmental quality is not as straightforward or easy to define as demographic variables. Indeed, the relationship between human population growth and the environment has been the subject of social theory and social investigation for centuries.

MALTHUS, SOCIAL DARWINISM, AND MORAL CONTROL

Victorian-era social theorist Thomas Malthus famously proposed a relationship between environmental quality and population growth (see Lesson 3). His *Essay on the Principle of Population* (first published in 1798) asserted that, without restraint, human population growth would eventually exceed the production of food, resulting in a massive crash in population. Specifically, he posited that human population growth increased exponentially; two people in generation 1 produced two children (generation 1 population = 2); each of those two people produced two children in generation 2 (population = 2 × 2 = 4); each one of those four people produced two children in generation 3 (population = 4 × 2 = 8); and so on. Based on his assessment of food production in Europe, Malthus reasoned that the production of food would increase only in an arithmetic or linear fashion, such that the increase between generations would be constant. Given these projections, Malthus warned that if humans did not control their own population growth, then a combination of war, disease, and especially famine would control population anyway. In part due to his own devout faith, Malthus believed that humans were unlike other animals in their capacity to exert moral control over their behavior. He therefore indicated that the most ethical course of action would be to limit human population growth, beginning with the working classes of European cities, whose lack of moral control (in his view) created large families that the poor could not feed on their own. This conclusion resonated with the era's Victorian elites in its emphasis on restraint of sexual impulses, moral condemnation of the poor, and opposition to charity designed to improve the situation of the poor, since feeding the poor would only prolong the inevitable misery and population crash.

Herbert Spencer, a founding theorist in sociology, echoed Malthus in his writings about the moral superiority of the elite, although his work also naturalized social hierarchy (Spencer 1972). According to Spencer, human society was evolutionary and progressed from less to more complexity. Spencer, like Malthus, believed that moral human individuals and groups demonstrate higher levels of progress and that these traits could be passed to the next generation. Over time, more evolved groups would come to dominate weaker groups; Spencer described this as the "survival of the fittest." In his view, the moral superiority of the European (and especially British) elite reflected its evolutionary position and this subsequently explained and legitimated European geographic expansion and subjugation of African, Asian, and Native American human groups.

Malthus and Spencer both influenced the early population theory of Charles Darwin, who explained that plants, animals, and even humans evolved in a process of competition for survival. Darwin's *The Origin of Species* (published in 1859) asserted that environmental stressors gave a reproductive advantage to individuals and species that adapted best to them; more of their offspring would survive into the next generation. This reproductive advantage (that is, natural selection) will become more pronounced in subsequent generations such that entire species evolve to become progressively more suited to their environment. Darwinian evolutionary theory revolutionized scientific thought and reduced human exceptionalist arguments, such as those advanced by Malthus. Ironically, Spencer's ideas were so well integrated into Darwinian theory that they are now sometimes referred to as "social Darwinism." *Social Darwinism*, like Malthusian theory, posits that the relationship between humans and their environment has a "natural" course but that this course can be overcome through social action, particularly restraint on population growth among those groups considered less evolved.

MODERNIZATION: THE DEMOGRAPHIC TRANSITION, THE GREEN REVOLUTION, AND NEO-MALTHUSIANISM

Following two world wars and the decline of the European global empires, Malthusian and social Darwinist thought reemerged in modernization theory, at least inasmuch as population policies assumed a connection between uncontrolled birth rates and food production. Modernization theory attempted to explain global inequality as a result of different levels of economic and cultural progress rather than as a set of innate, inherited, or moral characteristics. European domination could be explained because Africans, Asians, and Native Americans did not have the science, technology, or economic knowledge of Europeans. In a postcolonial context, European and North American knowledge would be shared with "less developed countries" in order to shepherd them into a more rationalized modernity. In terms of population dynamics, two particular elements of modernization theory stand out: the extension of modern agriculture known as the "green revolution" and the emphasis on birth control, particularly in order to achieve the so-called demographic transition.

The *green revolution* refers to a series of technological innovations to the production of food crops that were designed to increase productivity; more food could support more people. In general, these technologies reflected the system of agriculture that had been most productive in North America, particularly systems that produced single crops (*monocropping*). The green revolution introduced and/or expanded the use of mechanized tools (for example, irrigation, tractors, threshers), chemical fertilizers, and chemical pesticides in all regions of the globe. Another central technology for the green revolution was the development and introduction of high-yield varieties (HYVs) of rice, corn (maize), wheat, and other staple crops. HYVs typically produced more edible grain, while allowing plants to grow faster in more marginal environments and withstand the use of chemical fertilizers and pesticides. Agricultural scientists used advanced genetics and biotechnology to create HYV crops in international laboratories, such as the International Maize and Wheat Improvement Center in Mexico and the International Rice Research Institute in the Philippines. Green revolution technologies greatly increased food production worldwide; for example, world rice production nearly tripled from 215 million tons in 1961 at the onset of the green revolution to over 618 million tons in 2005.

Unfortunately, the green revolution created additional and distinctly modern problems. Monocrop systems, especially HYVs, typically required higher levels of chemical input (fertilizers and pesticides) than traditional agriculture. Consequently, world fertilizer consumption grew faster than crop production: from 31 million tons in 1961 to over 141 million tons in 1999. Chemical additions to agricultural crops have since been linked to salinization and a decrease in biodiversity among beneficial species and in neighboring nonagricultural lands. The high water demands of mechanized, industrial agriculture have also led to an extension of irrigation systems that has significantly and negatively altered freshwater resources, most dramatically in central Asia's Aral Sea, which has lost more than half of its volume and geographic area since the 1960s. Green revolution technologies raised the cost of production substantially by requiring the purchase of HYV seeds (which were often infertile, so seeds had to be purchased each season), chemical inputs, farm machinery, and irrigated water. The increased cost of production meant that over the long term the green revolution has favored larger producers over smaller ones and small producers have been progressively squeezed out of production of basic grains. Moreover, HYVs are typically grown in fields of single crops at a scale appropriate for mechanized agriculture, as opposed to traditional agriculture, which was tended by human workers and contained a greater variety of plant species, including nonfood species used for livestock or fiber. These changes led to massive displacement of the rural labor force and nutritional deficiencies for many small farmers in countries as different as Mexico and India. Unable to compete in agriculture, many of these small producers and agricultural workers have relocated to cities, which have expanded spectacularly since the 1950s in all regions of the globe.

While the green revolution unquestionably increased food production (albeit with social and environmental costs), advocates of modernization also held that a modern society would have low birth and death rates and, thus, low population growth rates. A *demographic transition* would occur when low growth rates were achieved through controlled fertility and low death rates were achieved through modern health care and sanitation. According to this model, in premodern societies, birth and death rates were both high but population growth remained small because the deaths more or less cancelled out the births. However, as sanitation, nutrition, and health care improved with modernization, life expectancies increased and death rates declined (especially infant mortality rates). Because of the cultural lag following technological change, birth rates remain high and population growth increases dramatically. Only when family planning norms adjust downward to longer life expectancies and higher survival rates among children will population growth slow and stabilize, indicating that a demographic transition to a modern society has occurred.

The demographic transition model is based on the historical experience of European and North American societies but has been expanded to include Asian nations such as Japan, South Korea, and Taiwan. Less developed nations in Asia, Africa, and the Americas did see their death rates decline significantly in the postcolonial period, while their birth rates remained at traditionally high levels. Consequently, population growth in less developed regions of the world expanded dramatically in the latter half of the twentieth century: Africa's population more than quadrupled in these 50 years, Latin America's more than tripled, while Asia's and Oceania's more than doubled (see Table 9-1). Even regions where the demographic transition had allegedly occurred increased their population, with North America nearly doubling its population and Europe adding a third of its population. Note, however, that these are raw population figures and do not distinguish between natural increase through births and immigration, which account for significant proportions of the increases in both western Europe and North America.

Population pyramids are often used to display the explosive population growth that occurs before a demographic transition. These graphs

Table 9–1 Population and Population Growth in Selected Regions, 1950–2000

	Population (millions) 1950	Population (millions) 1975	Population (millions) 2007 (est.)	2007 Population as Percentage of 1950 Population
Africa	224	416	965	431%
Asia	1,411	2,394	4,030	286%
Europe	548	676	731	133%
Latin America and the Caribbean	168	325	572	341%
North America	172	243	339	197%
Oceania	13	21	34	262%

Source: Population Division of the Department of Economic and Social Affairs of the United Nations Secretariat 2007: Table I.1.

present national populations by age and sex (that is, the age structure of the population) as a means for distinguishing between countries that have already made the demographic transition and those that have not. Figure 9-1 depicts population pyramids for Kenya, China, and Germany to highlight these different stages. Kenya's population pyramid in 2007 looks like a pyramid, in which the largest categories of the population are children (0–14 years); this portends a future baby boom as these young people enter into prime childbearing years (15–29). In contrast, China's population pyramid displays a population evidently in the early stages of a demographic transition: The top half of this graph looks like a pyramid, with the largest proportion of people past their prime childbearing years (ages 35–44). However, the graph tapers in age categories below these ages, indicating that people are having fewer children. Finally, the pyramid for Germany exhibits characteristics of a population that has undergone a demographic transition, as evidenced by the relatively equal distribution among age categories. In fact, Germany's age structure reveals an aging population, with almost equal proportions of older and younger people; Germany has a substantially greater number of older women (75 and older) than young girls (under 10).

Because rates of growth are highest in the poorest regions of the world, neo-Malthusian arguments emerged in the late 1960s calling for control of population and conservation of resources. Paul Ehrlich's *The Population Bomb* (1968) attempted to avoid the elitist trappings of Malthus by proposing an equation that measured environmental impact through a combination of population, affluence, and technology ($I = P \times A \times T$). Population (P) reflects the number of people, affluence (A) indicates the level of consumption by those people, and technology (T) reflects the type of technology used by those people. Environmental impact (I) thus varies not only by raw numbers of people but also by their consumption and waste patterns, sometimes now measured as their "ecological footprint," or the amount of land necessary to sustain consumption and absorb wastes. Based on higher consumption levels and use of more environmentally damaging technologies, the average North American individual is estimated to have over 12

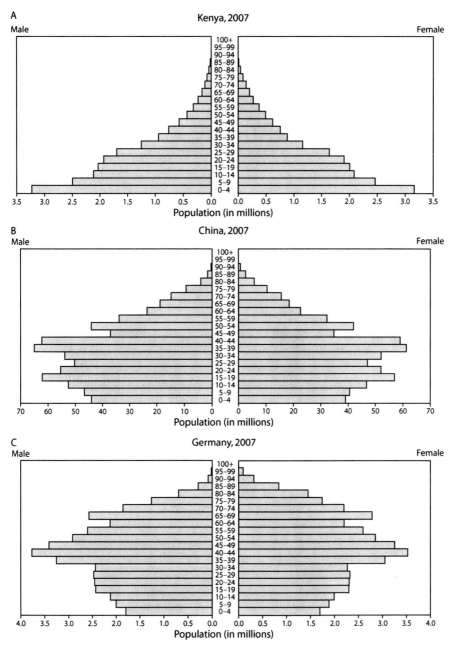

Figure 9–1 Population pyramids for Kenya (**A**), China (**B**), and Germany (**C**). *Source*: U.S. Census Bureau, International Data Base 2007.

times the ecological impact than an African (see Table 9-2). Neo-Malthusians have also expanded on Malthus' attention on food supply to include references to the carrying capacity of a geographic unit (for example, an ecosystem, a nation, or the entire planet). The *carrying capacity* represents

Table 9–2 Ecological Footprint in Hectares per Person

Africa	7.48 ha
Asia—Central	41.61 ha
Asia—Pacific	19.42 ha
Europe—Western	60.70 ha
Europe—Eastern and Central	31.36 ha
Latin America and the Caribbean	16.9 ha
North America	95.99 ha

Source: Venetoulis and Talberth 2005: Appendix I.

the total population of any given species (for example, humans) that can be supported in that geographic unit without permanently damaging the ecological systems that support that species. Damages come from extraction of resources from as well as pollution added to that geographic unit. Neo-Malthusians generally predict that, unless changes are made in terms of all components of the $I = P \times A \times T$ equation, the carrying capacity of the planet will be reached and famine, disease, war, and, at worst, complete global ecosystemic collapse will follow.

Responding to these concerns, population policy became an integral part of most nations' development plans. The West has reviled China's one-child policy for encouraging sex-selective abortions and female infanticide, but China's population growth rate has dropped significantly, from 1.9 annually in 1955 to 0.7 in 2005 (see Table 9-3; also review the age structure in Figure 9-1B). Unable to institute a policy like China's, India sent mobile sterilization teams into its rural areas to reduce its population growth rate, although these successful programs have also been criticized for sterilizing men and women based on quotas rather than the actual wishes of the people being sterilized. Funding from European and North American sources allowed for greater distribution of birth control and family planning technologies to developing countries in the 1960s and 1970s but came under increasing pressure from parties as disparate as the Roman Catholic Church, the U.S. government, and Muslim clerics, who argued against women's access to birth control and abortion. Even this debate could not stifle the excitement surrounding the United Nations Population and Development Conference in Cairo in 1994, where the links between controlling population growth and sustainable development were made more explicit (see Lesson 19). In addition to their focus on population control, the UN's Decade of the Woman, from 1985 to 1995, highlighted women's education, economic security, and health as a means for reducing birth and infant mortality rates. Women in Development programs rely on the assumption that women who have opportunities outside of motherhood and who can depend on the survival of their children will have fewer children. Whether due to this global effort or to other changes in the global social system, population growth rates have slowed somewhat since the 1980s (see Table 9-3).

Table 9–3 Annual Population Growth Rates, 1955–2005 (selected countries)

	1955	1965	1975	1985	1995	2005
China	1.9	2.1	2.2	1.4	1.1	0.7
India	2.0	2.3	2.2	2.1	1.9	1.6
Kenya	2.8	3.2	3.6	3.8	3.0	2.2
Mexico	2.7	3.1	3.2	2.2	1.9	1.3
United States	1.6	1.4	0.9	1.0	1.1	1.0
Italy	0.6	0.8	0.6	0.1	0.2	0.1

Source: United Nations Statistics Division 2007.

POPULATION AS A STRAW DOLL: MARX, FAMINE, AND XENOPHOBIA

Karl Marx called Malthus' 1798 *Essay* a "lampoon" that was popularized entirely because it legitimated the partisan interests of the English elite. Apart from this ideological component, Malthus was criticized by contemporaries and later social theorists for methodological weaknesses, notably his assumption of linear, arithmetic growth rates in food production, which apparently had no empirical foundation and was rendered inaccurate by the green revolution. Likewise, modernization theories involving food production and population dynamics have shown empirical and ideological weaknesses.

The main critiques of Malthusian, neo-Malthusian, and modernization theories about population growth point to the fundamental lack of discussion about the distribution of people and resources. A neo-Marxist critique of Malthus has been cogently and convincingly argued by John Bellamy Foster. Foster's other elaborations on Marx's work also call attention to the importance of population in terms of concentration in cities, where people have become dependent on industrial agriculture to produce food and organic waste is disposed in landfills instead of returned to agriculture. The "metabolic rift" that has developed between human food production and waste has overburdened rural natural systems by irrigation, fertilizer, and pesticide contamination and created pollution and health risks in urban areas. Given the rural population displacement and urban growth associated with the green revolution, this metabolic rift has created massive pollution problems in all regions of the world.

Critics also point to the lack of distributive concerns by neo-Malthusians. Responding directly to the assumptions of modernization theory, Amartya Sen's life work has sought to emphasize how the famines and poverty in places like sub-Saharan Africa and South Asia reflect the inhumane distribution of resources rather than any absolute shortage of food. Sen describes a world where the powerful use food as a weapon and famines reveal local and global inequalities. A well-known example of this from history involves the Irish potato famine; between 1845 and 1851, nearly 1 million Irish died of starvation or starvation-related illnesses and another million emigrated to escape the famine, while the English continued to grow and export tons of wheat from manor lands in Ireland. In contemporary times, the persistent violence in the Sudan has forced hundreds of thousands (if not millions) of small farmers to abandon their agricultural land and flee to refugee camps. Stripped of their ability to produce their own food, these refugees rely on food aid shipments. However, the delivery of these shipments is controlled by warlords who demand loyalty from the refugees and camp personnel. These examples demonstrate Sen's key concern that famines represent less of a shortage of food or (as neo-Malthusians may suggest) population exceeding its ecological carrying capacity than a manifestation of vast power differences between groups of people. When people interpret famines as examples of a population exceeding its carrying capacity, they ignore the human agents that cause famines and blame the victims for their own misery.

Apart from famines, local and global inequality directly determines how much food is available to people. A considerable portion of agricultural land worldwide is dedicated to export and luxury crops rather than basic food crops; often, these crops occupy the most productive agricultural land. I personally have seen extensive tea plantations in Kenya, coconut plantations in northeast Brazil (see Figure 9-2), banana plantations in Guatemala, citrus plantations in Mexico, strawberry plantations in Florida, and artichoke plantations in California, where the workers on these plantations suffer from basic health and malnutrition problems. Moreover, immense rangelands as well oceans of grain (such as corn in the American Midwest and soy in the Brazilian south) feed cattle instead of humans (see Lesson 5). Only more affluent consumers include meats, especially beef, in their staple diets. Since the 1980s, poorer nations have felt strong economic pressure to continue to

Figure 9–2 Coconut plantation in northeastern Brazil.
Source: Diane C. Bates.

produce luxury and export crops as these represent some of the few means to generate hard currency used to repay national debts and eventually expand local markets, social services, and infrastructure. However, world trade has generally seen a decline in the value of agricultural exports relative to manufacturing and high-tech exports; countries that rely on agricultural production for foreign exchange (like Ecuador, which sells flowers and bananas) guarantee themselves a subordinate position in the global hierarchy.

A focus on population growth in the Global South may also reflect social fears in the Global North more than real population concerns. Increased immigration from the Global South to the Global North has contributed to xenophobic, ideological beliefs about population growth in poorer countries, particularly where immigrant newcomers are socially distant from natives, as with northern Africans in the Paris suburbs, Latin Americans in the U.S. border states, South Asians in the north of England, and Asians in Australia. Workers in the Global South (agricultural and otherwise) are aware of the limits to advancement in their local economies and increasingly migrate to North America, Europe, East Asia, and the Middle East in search of better-paid work. This process of migration, in fact, has contributed greatly to the population growth rates in the Global North, where some countries (such as Germany and Italy) would register negative population growth rates were it not for immigration. Regardless of the relative size of these groups and the economic importance of immigrants in their host countries, many see the influx of newcomers as a population "problem" couched in environmental language as strain on local resources in receiving countries and an effect of "overpopulation" in sending countries. While nativism has bubbled up all over the Global North, Australia now has neo-Malthusian groups that explicitly link immigration to environmental security, such as Sustainable Population Australia. Mainstream environmental organizations, like Friends of the Earth—Australia, specifically disavow simplistic causal connections between immigration and environmental problems; but this debate "down under" portends future population–immigration–environment controversies worldwide. U.S.-based environmental groups like the Sierra Club and Zero Population Growth have already expressed neo-Malthusian concerns about population; without attention to the social complexity behind population dynamics indicated above, they risk reproducing the elitist and unscientific conclusions of nativist Australian environmental groups.

POPULATION AND TROPICAL FORESTS IN ECUADOR: A DEMOGRAPHIC CASE STUDY

This final section uses a case study to explore the complex relationship between population growth and tropical deforestation in the South American nation of Ecuador. Ecuador stretches from the Pacific coast over the Andes and into the upper reaches of the Amazon basin, containing about 12 million inhabitants. North–south mountain chains divide the small country into three distinct social and environmental regions: the Pacific coast, the Andean highlands and valleys (the Sierra), and the Amazonian lowlands (the Oriente). Prior to European contact, most of the population in what is now Ecuador lived in the temperate Andean highlands and valleys, where they were able to take advantage of how altitude created small variations in climate. These microclimates allowed pre-Columbian farmers to produce a wide variety of agricultural products, ranging from tropical fruits like the papaya to temperate staples like potatoes. The rich volcanic soils of the Sierra allowed for relatively intensive agriculture and relatively dense populations. In contrast, nearly impenetrable tropical rain forests flanked the Andes in the west (the coastal region) and the east (the Oriente). These forests prevented the expansion of agriculture from the Andes because the terrain was difficult to traverse, fast-moving rivers prevented navigation, and Andean migrants faced both tropical diseases and hostile indigenous people in the lowlands.

European colonization dramatically changed the relationship of people to Ecuador's forests, starting trends that continue into current times. The Spanish created plantation-like manor farms (*latifundia*) in the richest and most productive Sierra land, while obliging the indigenous highland people to perform labor and assimilate to Spanish customs. Because the best land was occupied by plantations, subsistence farmers planted their fields further onto steep mountainsides, contributing to alpine deforestation and erosion. Today, valley lands remain concentrated in large farms that produce commercial goods, such as dairy products and cut flowers. On the Pacific coast, the Spanish recognized the protected harbor at Guayaquil and the nearby stands of tropical timber suitable for shipbuilding. While the port city of Guayaquil grew, the Spanish also cleared forests for plantations of cacao, from which chocolate is derived, and later bananas, which remain Ecuador's most important agricultural export crop today. In order to attract labor from the Sierra, coastal plantation owners set aside productive nearby land for workers and their families. The growth of export-oriented plantations and associated urban economies has attracted many people from the Andean region, and more Ecuadorians now live in coastal provinces than in the Sierra. Only in the Oriente, with its poor access to population centers in the Sierra and worse access to the international trade networks offered through Pacific ports, have forests remained largely intact. This situation changed only since the latter half of the twentieth century after oil was discovered, providing an incentive and funds to build roads deep into the northern Oriente. The Ecuadorian government in the 1950s and 1960s also used oil revenues to develop colonization programs that made land available to poor farmers who were willing to migrate to remote coastal and Oriente forests to develop new agricultural land.

The relationship between population growth and deforestation in Ecuador appears to be a fairly simple one: As population grew, forests were removed from the country's landscape (Figure 9-3). However, Figure 9-3 obscures a more complex relationship between the use of forest resources and human activities. The coastal population has grown most, although the Oriente surpassed the Sierra in regional population early in the twenty-first century (Figure 9-4).

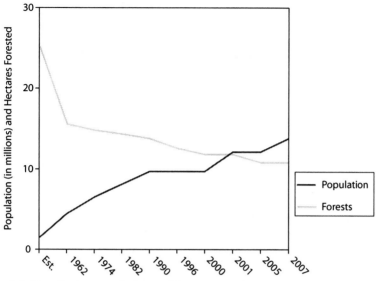

Figure 9–3 Ecuadorian population and forests over time.

Note: Original population estimate is based on 1889; original forest cover was estimated by the Food and Agriculture Organization of the United Nations (2001:120–122). Because comparable dates were not available for forest cover and population estimates, data are smoothed by adding or subtracting average annual increases or decreases between known data points. *Sources:* Minnesota Population Center 2007; Central Intelligence Agency 2007; Food and Agriculture Organization of the United Nations 2001, 2005.

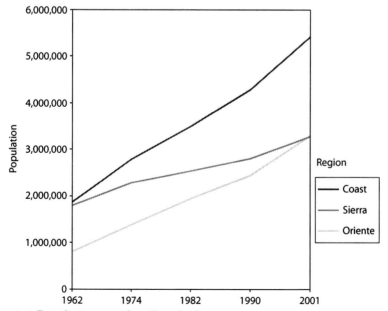

Figure 9–4 Population growth in Ecuador by region.

Source: Minnesota Population Center 2007.

Over 76% of forests on the coast have been cleared, leaving only about 2 million hectares, while just over a quarter (26%) of the Oriente has been deforested and over 7 million hectares remain; two-thirds of the forests in the Sierra have already vanished, with only 3 million hectares remaining. A simplistic, neo-Malthusian explanation of these data would predict the following: Population growth has declined in the Sierra relative to the Oriente and coast, so pressure on forests will decrease in the Andes. Population growth will eliminate remaining coastal forests and significantly reduce the size of forests in the Oriente. A more sophisticated analysis forecasts an entirely different outcome that bears out empirically. Limited just to data from the most recent years available, Figure 9-5 shows that in recent years rates of population growth were highest in the Oriente and lowest on the coast, while rates of deforestation have been highest in the Sierra and lowest in the Oriente. How can an area with the highest rates of population growth have the lowest rates of deforestation?

The simple answer is that the relationship between population growth and environmental quality is not the same from place to place, even in a country as geographically small as Ecuador. Ecuador's coast has seen high levels of absolute population growth but the lowest rates of growth in the country. Deforestation rates appear high but reflect the relatively small size of the coastal forests remaining in 1996. Sociologist Thomas K. Rudel classified

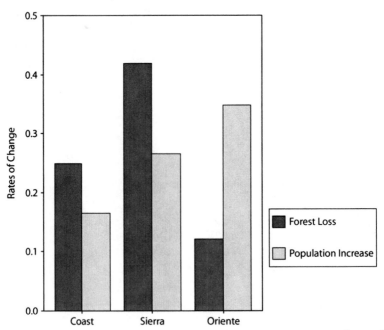

Figure 9–5 Ecuadorian rates of change of forest loss (1996–2000) and population growth (1990–2001).

Source: Minnesota Population Center 2007; Food and Agriculture Organization of the United Nations 2005.

Ecuador's Pacific coastal forests as similar to those in Central America and the Caribbean, where most primary forests were cleared early in the process of European colonization to make way for export agriculture, leaving only remnant forests in relatively inaccessible locations. The coastal economy today remains centered around export-oriented agriculture but with large urban centers and tourist zones. Deforestation still occurs when small farmers clear marginal forests to meet urban demand for food or create shrimp ponds in mangrove forests; however, plantations replaced most of the region's forests generations ago, and urban residents increasingly consume food produced elsewhere. The remnant forests that still exist are now located only in those areas most inhospitable to agricultural expansion; thus, the actual threat of population growth on remaining coastal forests is limited. Rudel even suggests that places like Ecuador's coast are excellent for promoting ecotourism (see Lesson 19) and environmentally certified agricultural products because urban and international consumers and tourists can exert great pressure on the quality of goods they purchase and relatively few locals depend directly on the forest for their livelihoods.

In contrast, Ecuador's Amazonian region shows relatively high rates of population growth but relatively low rates of deforestation, although these figures are also somewhat distorted by the region's relatively small population and large forest in 1996. Most of the Amazon basin was too remote and inaccessible to be converted to plantation crops; distance continues to limit the profitability of farms except along main transportation corridors. As is true elsewhere in the Amazon basin, these geographic obstacles have also concentrated populations in cities, while rural areas face chronic shortages of labor. Urban population growth, measured either absolutely or as a rate, affects forest conversion in two ways: The demand for agricultural products in Amazonian cities has led to forest clearing on transportation corridors and has encouraged land-extensive ranching adjacent to these corridors. Since the region's fast-growing cities absorb excess labor, farmers utilize land-extensive, rather than labor-intensive, strategies to make their farms productive. After initial clearing, small-scale cattle ranching requires little human labor, which can often be performed by women and children. In this way, a single household can clear and maintain farms of 100 hectares or more, with intensive agricultural activities concentrated nearest the transportation corridors and ranching beyond. Dramatic as this sort of deforestation may appear from roads, little deforestation occurs outside these corridors. As a consequence, inaccessibility will likely continue to protect large blocks of Amazonian forest, as demonstrated by the relatively low rates of deforestation displayed in Figure 9-5. Ecuador has also established indigenous reserves and national parks in the less populous regions of the Oriente, which may provide the institutional infrastructure necessary to protect these large forests over time.

Positive environmental outcomes seem less likely in the Sierra, which has seen the highest rates of deforestation recently and only moderate rates of population growth (see Figures 9-4 and 9-5). Pre-Columbian and planta-tion agriculture had converted most valley and gently sloped land to agri-culture long ago, leaving only remnant alpine forests. Temperate climates in Andean valleys and tenuous access to coastal ports limited the develop-ment of export-oriented agriculture, although greenhouses for cut flowers have provided some access to global markets in the past two decades. Most deforestation in the Sierra today reflects the removal of forests upslope from the region's growing cities, where poor migrants clear land to provide housing, fuel, and subsistence for their families and sell whatever surplus they may produce. In this case, population growth has a direct effect on for-est cover: More people trying to live in and from these forests leads to more degradation. Thus, although population growth in the Sierra has been slow when compared to the coast and the Oriente, this growth has had a direct negative effect on the region's forests. The loss of remnant forest buffers in the mountains that cradle Ecuador's cities creates additional environ-mental problems for these cities, including erosion, degradation of water sources, and poorer air quality. Forest conservation and management in this context are hampered by the increasing numbers of squatters, their inability to meet immediate needs except by extracting short-term gains from the forest, and the absence of control over access to these forests. In the Sierra, even slow population growth will likely have major negative effects on the region's environment.

This foray into Ecuador's forests underscores the complexity of the relationship between human populations and the nonhuman environ-ment. At the regional level, human populations can expand while creat-ing the conditions for environmental protection (as in Amazonian parks) or conservation (as with coastal ecotourism). However, growth in the number of people who are directly dependent on the environment (like squatters in the Sierra) does tend to degrade the local environment. Ecua-dor also demonstrates that the relationship between food production and population growth makes no sense on national and subnational scales; global food commodity chains and urban markets have freed human populations from their local food sources. Plantations in the Sierra and coastal regions have removed the best land from production of food for local populations, while small farmers in Amazonia clear forests mainly for urban markets. Both situations transfer the reason for food production from supporting human populations to supporting human economies. Consumer preferences for greener products may thus have a greater effect on environmental quality than population control. Finally, demographic trends are best understood within their social and histori-cal contexts. Slow population growth in the Sierra does more damage to that region's forests than faster population growth in the coastal and Amazonian regions. To understand this situation requires more than a statistical representation of population growth; a sociological and histor-ical perspective illuminates the patterns of resource use and inequality that shape this relationship.

CONCLUSION

Ecuador represents a tiny fraction of the world's growing human population, but sociologists must consider population dynamics and the demographic profiles of affected communities, whether considering environmental issues on a local, national, or global scale. How many people live in an area, their characteristics, and how that population changes in time determine how they interact with their environment. We don't yet understand the full implications of 6.6 billion people for the global ecosystem, but with more people, rising levels of consumption, and more damaging technologies, global environmental problems such as climate change and atmospheric ozone thinning point toward more serious concerns for the future. Moreover, the uneven distribution of resources, ranging from food to stop famines to political power to compel remediation of contaminated sites, underscores the importance of understanding not just population growth but contextualized demography as an element in environmental sociology.

SOURCES

Central Intelligence Agency. 2007. The World Factbook. Retrieved June 28, 2007. (http://www.cia.gov/library/publications/the-world-factbook/).

Darwin, Charles. 1909. *The Origin of Species*. New York: P. F. Collier and Son.

Ehrlich, Paul R. 1968. *The Population Bomb*. New York: Ballantine Books.

Food and Agricultural Organization of the United Nations. 2001. *Estado de la Información Forestal en Ecuador*. Santiago, Chile: United Nations.

Food and Agricultural Organization of the United Nations. 2005. Global Forest Resources Assessment. Retrieved July 8, 2007. (http://www.fao.org/forestry/site/32089/en/ecu).

Foster, John Bellamy. 1999. "Marx's Theory of the Metabolic Rift: Classical Foundations for Environmental Sociology." *American Journal of Sociology* 105(2):366–405.

Foster, John Bellamy. 2002. *Ecology Against Capitalism*. New York: Monthly Review Press.

International Rice Research Institute. 2007. *Atlas of Rice and World Rice Statistics*. Retrieved April 21, 2007. (http://www.irri.org/science/ricestat/index.asp).

Malthus, T. R. 1914. *An Essay on Population*. New York: E. P. Dutton.

Marx, Karl. 1865. "On Proudhon: Letter to J. B. Schweizer." Retrieved January 18, 2007. (http://www.marxists.org/archive/marx/works/).

Marx, Karl. 1906. *Capital: A Critique of Political Economy*. New York: Modern Library.

Minnesota Population Center. 2007. *Integrated Public Use Microdata Series—International: Version 3.0*. Minneapolis, MN: University of Minnesota.

Population Division of the Department of Economic and Social Affairs of the United Nations Secretariat. 2007. *World Population Prospects: The 2006 Revision*. New York: United Nations.

Rudel, Thomas K. 2005. *Tropical Forests: Regional Paths of Destruction and Regeneration in the Late Twentieth Century*. New York: Columbia University Press.

Sen, Amartya. 1981. *Poverty and Famines: An Essay on Entitlement and Deprivation*. New York: Oxford University Press.

Spencer, Herbert. 1972. *On Social Evolution: Selected Writings,* edited by J. D. Y. Peel. Chicago, IL: University of Chicago Press.

United Nations Statistics Division. 2007. UN Pop. Div. quinquennial estimates and projections [code 13670]. Retrieved April 20, 2007. (http://unstats.un.org/unsd/databases.htm).

United States Census Bureau. 2007a. "International Data Base: Population Pyramids." Retrieved June 30, 2007. (http://www.census.gov/ipc/www/idb/pyramids.html).

——. 2008. "World Population Clock." Retrieved May 11, 2008. (http://www.census.gov/ipc/www/popclockworld.html).

Vandermeer, John, and Ivette Perfecto. 1995. *Breakfast of Biodiversity: The Truth About Rainforest Destruction.* Oakland, CA: Food First Books.

Venetoulis, Jason, and John Talberth. 2005. *Ecological Footprint of Nations: 2005 Update.* Oakland, CA: Redefining Progress. Retrieved January 8, 2007. (http://ecological footprint.org/).

Part 3

SOME SOCIAL CONSEQUENCES OF ENVIRONMENTAL DISRUPTION

Environmental Inequality and Environmental Justice

Michael Mascarenhas

DEFINING ENVIRONMENTAL JUSTICE

Over the past several decades, public health researchers, activists, and policymakers have devoted a great deal of attention to understanding the social dimensions of environmental injustice: the notion that sources of environmental pollution are unevenly distributed among different social groups or categories. More recently, some scholars and health researchers have begun to explore the role of neoliberal policies as a major contributing factor in the production of environmental injustices. Through Canadian examples, this lesson explores the intersection between these two concepts. Those concerned with environmental injustices have focused their energies on two claims regarding the relationship between environmental pollution and race and class. The first claim posits that racial and ethnic minorities, low-income people, and indigenous peoples are more likely to live in close proximity to hazardous environmental facilities and that their communities continue to be the targets for the siting and growth of "dirty industries." The second claim argues that with an increased public awareness regarding the relationship between environmental pollution and health problems—largely born from high-profile cases such as Love Canal, New York; Three Mile Island, Pennsylvania; Woburn, Massachusetts; and Warren County, North Carolina—it has become increasingly difficult to site hazardous or dirty industries in middle-class white communities. It is the premise of the lesson that neoliberalism has contributed to both the political and economic justifications for the siting and growth of dirty industries in minority, indigenous, and low-income communities.

Consider the following data compiled by Sylvia Tesh in her 2004 book *Uncertain Hazards: Environmental Activists and Scientific Proof*:

> Nearly 70,000 chemical products have been introduced since World War II and 1,500 new ones are added each year. Total U.S. production of chemicals amounts to over 300 million tons annually. In 1994, 22,744 facilities released 2.26 billion pounds of listed toxic chemicals into the environment. In 1994 approximately 62 million people . . . lived in countries where air quality levels exceeded the national air quality standards for at least one of the six principal pollutants. In

1995 over 40 million Americans were served by drinking water systems with lead levels exceeding the regulatory action level. By September 1995, a total of 1,374 sites had been listed or proposed for listing [on the Superfund's National Priority List]. . . . In addition, EPA had identified 40,094 potentially hazardous waste sites across the nation. About 94 percent of these sites have been assessed by EPA to determine if further action is needed. By the end of 1995, EPA had removed 24,472 low-priority sites, leaving 15,622 remaining in the inventory. In 1993 over 40 percent of the Hispanic population, and over 25 percent of the Asian/Pacific population was exposed to poor air quality. Three out of every five Black and Hispanic Americans live in communities with uncontrolled toxic waste sites.

In her 1998 ethnography *The Tainted Desert: Environmental Ruin in the American West,* Valerie Kuletz writes that a nuclear landscape encompasses most of the Southwest—"much of New Mexico, Nevada, southeastern California, and parts of Arizona, Utah, Colorado, and Texas. (To the north, in the West, we can also add parts of the state of Washington and Idaho)." This area, she writes, includes "large land masses for uranium mining and milling, the testing of high-tech weaponry, and waste repositories" that include weapons' stockpiles and nuclear production facilities. This region is also "home to the majority of *land-based* American Indians today on the North American continent."

In recent years the rural center that makes up the Sarnia-Windsor-London triangle in southern Ontario expanded the capacity of the region's landfill as well as approved a 4 million gallon per day sewage treatment plant (for the city of London). These new waste industries are in addition to numerous other landfills that dot the countryside, heavy agricultural use, and the highway of electromagnetic towers (and wires) that span this area, not to mention heavy industry, particularly in the Windsor and Sarnia area. It is also home to eight First Nations' territories.

I cite these data partly to make the reader aware of the extent of environmental pollution but also to illustrate the numerous environmental conditions that this pollution affects. Environmental justice activists and scholars present a broad concept of the environment in which we live, work, learn, and play. The environment from this perspective is not a people-free biophysical system but rather the ambient and immediate surroundings of everyday life activities and relationships linking people with their immediate environs. These include, but are not limited to, residential environments, working environments, and recreation environments. Turner and Wu describe this: "It encompasses the air people breathe walking down a city or country street, the water drawn from their taps or wells, the chemicals a worker is exposed to in an industrial plant or strawberry field, and the forests people visit to hike, extract mushrooms, and engage in spiritual practice." This conception of the environment links labor and public health, recreation and housing, and culture and history. Furthermore, this understanding of the environment breaks the boundaries between nature and society, work environments and open spaces, and urban and rural places.

The U.S. Environmental Protection Agency (2007:1) defines *environmental justice* as follows:

[t]he fair treatment and meaningful involvement of all people regardless of race, color, national origin, or income with respect to the development, implementation, and enforcement of environmental laws, regulations, and policies.

Environmental inequality (or *environmental injustice*), then, refers to a situation in which a specific group is disproportionately affected by negative environmental conditions brought on by unequal laws, regulations, and policies. A specific form of environmental inequality is the phenomenon of *environmental racism*, or the deliberate targeting of communities of color for toxic waste facilities, the official sanctioning of poisons and pollutants in minority communities, and the systematic exclusion of people of color from leadership roles in decisions regarding the production of environmental conditions that affect their lives and livelihoods.

HISTORY OF THE ORIGINS OF ENVIRONMENTAL JUSTICE

Over years of painstaking research and emotionally charged activism, environmental justice scholars have been able to successfully link questions of social justice, equity, rights, and people's quality of life. Originally forged from a synthesis of the civil rights movements, antitoxic campaigns, and environmentalism, environmental justice has focused on the class and racial inequalities of pollution. The growth of tragic and high-profile cases like Love Canal, New York, and Woburn, Massachusetts, has increased the publicity and power of this largely grassroots movement. A feature length movie, *A Civil Action*, starring John Travolta was made about the Woburn Case. Furthermore, such publicity later inspired legislation in the United States that identified hazardous waste sites—commonly known as "Superfund sites"— and established a protocol for remediation. In 1994, President Clinton signed Executive Order 12898, charging all federal agencies with integrating environmental justice concerns into their operations.

Beginning in the early 1970s, a substantial body of literature began to emerge in the United States documenting the existence of environmental inequalities among particular social groups, specifically minority, aboriginal, and poor communities. In 1982 a major protest was staged in Warren County, North Carolina, over a polychlorinated biphenyl (PCB) landfill in a majority African American town. Several hundred protesters (many of them high-profile civil rights activists) were arrested, and the issue of environmental justice was thrust into the national spotlight and onto the political agenda. In 1983, 1 year after the Warren County protests, the U.S. General Accounting Office conducted a study of several southern states and found that a disproportionate amount of landfills (about three out of every four) were located near predominantly minority communities. This regional study was followed in 1987 by a national study, *Toxic Wastes and Race in the United States*, by the

United Church of Christ Commission on Racial Justice. This groundbreaking study found that race was the most significant factor in determining where waste facilities were located in the United States. Among other findings, the study revealed that three out of five African Americans and Hispanic Americans lived in communities with one or more uncontrolled toxic waste sites and 50% of Asian/Pacific Islander Americans and Native Americans lived in such communities. A follow-up study in 1994 concluded that this trend had worsened. In 1990, sociologist Robert Bullard published his now classic book *Dumping in Dixie: Race, Class, and Environmental Quality.* This was the first major study of environmental racism that linked hazardous facility siting with historical patterns of segregation in the South. This study was also one of the first to explore the social and psychological impacts of environmental racism on local populations and to analyze the response from local communities against these environmental threats.

In addition to the growing body of research, conferences, such as the Urban Environment Conference in New Orleans in 1983 and the University of Michigan Conference on Race and the Incidence of Environmental Hazards in 1990, brought together researchers from around the nation who were studying racial and socioeconomic disparities in the distribution of environmental contaminants. These conferences were attended by several leading "activist-scholars" who, while working closely with community activists, came together to present and debate their findings and implications. The scientific analyses presented at these and other conferences began to frame the toxics struggle in terms of power, class, and racial inequality. Since 1990, scholars and activists have produced an extensive and sophisticated literature on the various and complex dimensions of environmental hazards and their intersection with race and socioeconomic position; however, this research has not been without much debate and controversy.

DEBATES WITHIN ENVIRONMENTAL JUSTICE

Although the vast majority of studies on environmental justice conclude that racism is the major driving factor, there has been much debate about the degree to which this form of injustice is a function of racial inequalities or socioeconomic position or some combination of the two. This controversy has come to be known as the "race versus class debate". Robert Brulle and David Pellow argue that this controversy has done much to sharpen the methodological and conceptual approaches to analyzing environmental injustices; however, they also point out that many scholars and activists have argued that the debate misses the point and that the production of industrial toxins and their generally unequal distribution deserve to be the main focus of research efforts and political change.

Although research points to a relationship between environmental injustice and social hierarchies, the existence and extent of environmental inequalities and their relationship to race, class, or both are still the subject of much political and empirical debate. For example, in his 2005 meta-analysis of 49 environmental equity studies, Evan Ringquist found that there was overwhelming evidence of environmental inequities based upon race but little evidence to support the notion that similar inequities exist with respect to economic class. However, Gary Evans and Elyse Kantrowitz document evidence of an inverse relationship between income and other indices of socioeconomic status with environmental risk factors "including hazardous wastes and other toxins, ambient and indoor air pollutants, water quality, ambient noise, residential crowding, housing quality, educational facilities, work environments, and neighborhood conditions." The poor, especially the non-white poor, Evans and Kantrowitz argue, "are the most likely to be exposed not only to the worst air quality, the most noise, the lowest-quality housing and schools, etc. . . . but also to lower-quality environments on a wide array of multiple dimensions." This exposure to multiple suboptimal physical conditions, rather than any singular environmental exposure, is what makes the relationship between socioeconomic status and health so elusive. These studies highlight the complexity and multiple dimensions of compromised environmental conditions that impact particular groups of people.

More recently, a 2006 report from the United Nations Development Programme also echoed a similar finding between poverty and environmental inequality. The report *Beyond Scarcity: Power, Poverty and the Global Water Crisis* found that the crisis of water and sanitation is, above all, a crisis of the poor throughout the world. The World Bank has also published statistical data on global air and water pollution. For example, in low-income countries from the 1970s to the late 1980s, the average levels of suspended particulate matter in cities increased by 8% (from 300 to 325 μg/cubic meter of air), while cities in the middle-income countries over the same period of time witnessed improved air quality (from approximately 180 to 150 μg/cubic meter of air).

Brulle and Pellow point to a number of complexities that hamper the establishment of a clear link between environmental inequality and health disparities among certain segments of the population. These complexities include "the lack of appropriate statistical measures, varying individual exposure levels, lengthy incubation periods, confounding influences on health, such as access to health care and individual behaviours," that range from diet and exercise to employment and housing conditions. As a result of these complexities, Brulle and Pellow argue that researchers know very little about the ways in which health risks from environmental conditions interrelate with and contribute to health disparities between different social groups and communities.

DIMENSIONS OF THE ENVIRONMENTAL JUSTICE MOVEMENT

In spite of these empirical and political challenges, the environmental justice movement has had a significant impact on the direction of environmental policy, research, and activism in the United States (see Lesson 15). The nature and extent of the movement's impact can be divided into five dimensions, which range from local struggles to more global concerns. A detailed description of the five dimensions of the environmental justice movement is given by David Pellow's 2005 work. The following brief description borrows from Pellow's comprehensive analysis.

Local Struggles

Without a doubt, it is at the local community level where struggles for environmental justice have had the most profound impact. Some examples include the forced closing of large polluting industries. For example, waste incinerators and landfills in Los Angeles and Chicago; power plants in South-gate, Los Angeles, and San Jose, California; and oil refineries as well as metal plating and chrome plating facilities in San Diego and Los Angeles were all forced out of business due, in large part, to local community struggles. Other examples include the prevention of polluting operations being built or expanded. Pellow points out that this is clearly the case in

> the chemical plant proposed by the Shintech corporation near a low-income African American community in Louisiana; securing relocations and home buyouts for residents in polluted communities like Love Canal, New York, Times Beach, Missouri, and Norco, Louisiana; and successfully demanding environmental clean ups of locally unwanted land uses (LULUs) such as the North River Sewage Treatment plant in Harlem, New York.

These local struggles have made it extremely difficult for polluting industries to locate or expand incinerators, landfills, and related LULUs anywhere in the nation without much controversy and conflict.

Institution Building and Cultural Impacts

The environmental justice movement has successfully built up local organizations and regional networks and forged partnerships with preexisting institutions such as churches, schools, neighborhood groups, and cooperatives. While this dimension represents an important piece of the environmental justice movement, maintaining and building environmental institutions or networks that can systematically respond to growing environmental injustices have been difficult in some areas of the country, and many regional networks have often fallen victim to shifts in political ideology or fiscal shortfalls and budgetary cuts. Given this challenge, Pellow argues, the building of enduring institutions and sustainable communities may, in fact, be the environmental justice movement's greatest challenge.

On a broader cultural and discursive level, Pellow writes,

> the language and discourse of environmental justice have entered the lexicon of public health, corporate responsibility, climate change debates, urban planning, transportation development, and municipal zoning processes in cities around the U.S. where these issues might never have been considered two decades ago.

These changes constitute a significant dimension of the environmental justice movement.

Legal Gains and Losses

While few and relatively recent, the litigated cases emerging from environmental justice conflicts have not been successful in changing the systemic and institutional causes that continue to produce and reproduce compromised environs in some communities. Early on, environmental justice activists and attorneys devised a strategy to apply civil rights law to cases of environmental injustice. Again, Pellow summarizes:

> Specifically, they argued that Title VI of the 1964 Civil Rights Act would be applicable to EJ cases. Title VI prohibits all institutions that receive federal funds from discriminating against persons based on race, color or national origin. Unfortunately, the courts have uniformly refused to prohibit government actions based on Title VI of the Civil Rights Act without direct evidence of discriminatory intent.

The U.S. Environmental Protection Agency (EPA) has also been of little assistance on the legal front. Since 1994, when the EPA began accepting Title VI claims, more than 135 have been filed and none has been formally resolved. Furthermore, Pellow writes,

> only one federal agency has thus far cited environmental justice concerns to protect a community in a significant legal case. In May 2001, the Nuclear Regulatory Commission denied a permit for a uranium enrichment plant in Louisiana, based on its findings that environmental justice concerns were not taken into account in that siting proposal.

National Environmental Policy

In spite of serious challenges for the environmental justice movement at both institution building and legal recourse, the movement has succeeded in affecting environmental policy at both the national and state levels of government. The most prominent among these achievements occurred in 1994 when then President Clinton signed Executive Order 12898, charging all federal agencies with integrating environmental justice concerns into their operations. The passage of environmental justice laws or policies in more than 40 states, including California, Massachusetts, Indiana, Tennessee, Rhode Island, and Minnesota, has added to the development of a comprehensive environmental policy regime. However, Pellow argues that in spite of these legislative advances, many of these new environmental policies are either very specific (for example, related to brownfields) or too general and diffuse to bring about substantial and long-term environmental equality. In response to this shortcoming, many activists have shifted their focus away from the national and state levels of government back to local communities, "where their work has a more tangible influence and where polluters are more easily monitored."

Globalization and Environmental Justice

The impact of globalization and transnational capitalism and the growth of multilateral and international trade agreements have seriously undermined local government attempts to regulate environmental and public health conditions and, as a result, have connected the local with the global in uneven and unjust ways. Perhaps the most vivid example of globalization and environmental injustice comes from Lawrence Summers, a now retired chief economist of the World Bank. In his now infamous memo Summers argued that the World Bank should encourage the movement of pollution from the rich core countries to those of the periphery because the cost of illness associated with pollution would be less in economically marginalized communities. This was because, according to Summers, those in the periphery were likely to earn lower wages than those in the core and to have a shorter life span; both would suggest that the economic cost of their illness, in terms of either sick days off or cumulative sickness from working in polluted environs, would be substantially lessened. Summers argued that a clean environment was worth more to people in industrialized states than to those in the periphery, and since the cost of pollution would be less in poor countries, it made perfect economic sense to export "dirty" industries to the periphery.

In other words, "global" environmental problems also bear down disproportionately upon minorities, the poor, and aboriginal peoples. The unequal distribution of environmental "bads" is, of course, compounded by the fact that globally and nationally developed countries and their citizens are the major polluters (see Lesson 19). In response to this trend, environmental justice activists and scholars have engaged in collaborations, resource exchange, networking, and joint action that transgress national boundaries and connect the Global North and South.

NEOLIBERALISM AND (HOW IT EXACERBATES) ENVIRONMENTAL INJUSTICE

For environmental justice scholars and activists, environmental problems are social problems; the two are often inseparable. This is according to Andrew Szasz because "toxic victims are, typically, poor or working people of modest means. [Thus] [t]heir environmental problems are inseparable from their economic condition." As Szasz clearly argued, integrated in demands for clean and healthy communities are larger assertions for "the restructuring of the current relationship between economy and society." More recently, however, sociologists Daniel Faber and Deborah McCarthy have argued that contemporary environmental governance reform (commonly referred to as "neoliberalism") and contemporary environmental and social injustices (that neoliberalism produces) are different sides of the same coin. In fact, they assert that neoliberalism and contemporary environmental and social injustices "are now so dialectically related (if not essential) to each other as to become part of the same historical process" (p. 45). Understanding the relationship between neoliberalism and environmental justice is an important first step in analyzing the macro institutions that produce uneven development on a daily basis. It is this relationship that I now turn to.

It has been said that neoliberalism is the most powerful ideological and political project in modern global governance reform (see Lesson 3). Yet, despite its familiarity, defining what neoliberalism is and what its social and ecological consequences are has not been an easy task. Part of this difficulty comes from the fact that neoliberalism represents a complex assemblage of ideological commitments, discursive representations, and institutional practices. And because of this complexity, the social and environmental consequences of neoliberalism remain difficult to quantify and qualify. Furthermore, upon closer inspection of particular neoliberal projects, one is more likely to find a complex and hybrid political imaginary, rather than a straightforward implementation of a unified philosophy.

Scholar David Harvey defines neoliberalism as a theory of political economic practice which posits that humanity's well-being can best be advanced by liberating individual entrepreneurial freedoms and skills. The institutional framework that best facilitates these political and economic practices is characterized by strong private property rights, a self-regulating market, and free trade. The appropriate, and only, role of the neoliberal state, according to this theory, is to guarantee the proper functioning of such markets. Furthermore, if markets do not exist (in such areas as land, water, education, social security, health care, and environmental pollution), then they must be created through state action, if necessary.

Social scientists have highlighted several important components to neoliberal reform over the last 30 years. First, there were sweeping amendments to virtually every provincial statute that dealt with environmental protection or natural resource management. Second, there were major reductions in the budgets of provincial and local environmental and natural resources agencies. And finally, there was a dramatic restructuring of the roles and responsibilities of provincial and municipal governments and the private sector.

Neoliberal reform has resulted in major changes in the use of industrial, agricultural, and municipal lands. Many rural areas have experienced the growth of large industrial feedlots (see Lesson 12). For example, livestock farms in southwestern Ontario have the highest livestock concentration in the province. Similarly, pig farms are also higher than provincial averages in these areas, the same areas that are also home to seven aboriginal communities. In fact, First Nations communities are located either downstream, downwind, or downgrade of these major industrial agricultural lands, all which were able to dramatically expand their operations with the rolling back of provincial environmental laws and regulations.

In addition to agriculture, energy is another predominant land use activity in southwestern Ontario. This area, particularly the Sarnia River, is referred to by locals as "chemical alley"—arguably Canada's largest concentration of petrochemical industries and associated water and air pollution. Between

1974 and 1986, a total of 32 major spills, as well as 300 minor ones, contributed to approximately 10 tons of pollutants in the St. Clair River. Furthermore, since 1986, the Ministry of the Environment has recorded an average of 100 spills per year. This does not include the significant agricultural runoff of pesticides and fertilizers, as well as other nonpoint pollution sources from nearby livestock producers that enter the watershed and river every year. Furthermore, because the St. Clair River connects Lakes Huron and Erie, it is also a major shipping route; and the necessary dredging of contaminated sediments to permit heavy marine traffic poses yet another serious environmental problem. The St. Clair River is also a source of drinking water for Walpole Island and Aamjiwnaang First Nations.

Neoliberal reform in Ontario has reduced monitoring and reporting requirements for industry and severely impaired the ability of provincial ministries and local agencies to regulate and monitor environmental conditions. As such, the recognition of environmental harm and environmental pollution has become a much more difficult endeavour. This is particularly true for First Nations communities, which simply do not have the capacity to provide the monitoring technologies and expertise to demonstrate scientifically the relationships between health disparities and environmental inequalities. Neoliberal reform in Ontario has reduced or eliminated opportunities for public participation in land use decisions, such as environmental problems arising from "normal" farm operations and location of waste disposal sites. These impacts were again disproportionately discriminatory toward First Nations partly because of where they were located—downwind, downgrade and downstream—but also because of a lack of legitimate opportunities to participate in environmental governance that affects their health and welfare.

Indigenous peoples, like First Nations in Canada, are increasingly becoming the target of the externalized social and environmental costs associated with neoliberal policy reform. This is because indigenous peoples still maintain sovereignty over vast resource streams, many still held in common, such as water, oil, diamonds, forests, and, of course, labor, to name only a few, which are desperately needed for this phase of capitalist expansion. This is still true in spite of a brutal history of colonialism that has devastated many indigenous cultures and lands, leaving only a social and environmental skeleton of its previous wealth. Neoliberalism, then, is a concerted effort by those in power to disconnect, and in some cases remove, indigenous peoples from their resources and land.

Indigenous lands also represent a space, conveniently located on the margins of our spatial consciousness, to cheaply and inconspicuously dump the vast wastes of this phase of capitalist expansion. In an attempt to delineate new frontiers for capitalist expansion, many core nation-states have increasingly shifted their focus between external and internal forms of expansion. Individual nation-states of the Global North have differed in their institutional response to the challenges of transnational capitalism. In most cases, Harvey suggests, "some combination of internal motivation and external pressure lies behind such transformations." For example, the United States, the current global "empire", has largely chosen to expand its markets, and its fiscal crisis, to the global periphery through the direct use of its military and other coercive powers. However, as Kuletz so clearly points out, the United States has also led the way in forms of internal colonialism, particularly with regard to its Native Americans. However, other less powerful empires, like Canada and China—nation-states rich in resources yet weak in military power—have exclusively focused on internal colonialism to facilitate this phase of capitalist expansion.

The concept of "internal colonialism," Kuletz writes, "has been used by political scholars, such as Gramsci, to describe political and economic inequalities between regions in a specific society." Similar in fashion to colonialism, where the wealth and well-being of "core" countries are augmented at the expense of the "periphery," internal colonialism is based on unfair and unequal exchange relations, like resources for pollution, between the urban and rural spaces. The presence of internal colonialism, Kuletz suggests, where one's existence (in the core) is premised on the exploitation and marginalization of others (in the periphery), usually of a different cultural, racial, or class background, argues against the liberal notions of democratic pluralism and freedom. But whereas colonialism was marked the deliberative and direct use of state apparatus to remove and disperse indigenous peoples from traditional territories, this phase of primitive accumulation is translated by deregulation, privatization, and a diminution of state-supported social protections.

In addition to studying how globalization and neoliberal orthodoxy have affected the health and well-being of aboriginal peoples, environmental justice scholars and activists have studied other social groups that have been, and continue to be, the recipients of this form of institutional discrimination. For example, David Pellow's historical and ethnographic study *Garbage Wars: The Struggle for Environmental Justice in Chicago,* analyzed the historical origins of environmental inequalities in Chicago's communities of color and in workplaces where municipal and industrial solid wastes were collected, processed, and eventually dumped. Pellow's analysis reveals the bitter irony of how recycling facilities—ostensibly built to prevent waste from entering landfills and incinerators in already overburdened neighborhoods— were creating occupational hazards for both workers and communities of the South Side of Chicago (workers and communities that were predominantly immigrant, African American, Latino, and Asian American). "Despite its promises," Pellow points out, "recycling was just one more example of environmental inequality, stemming from a long line of waste management practices as old as the local city dump and as old as human civilization."

Another example of environmental justice scholarship has been the analysis of the rapidly growing phenomenon of urban poverty. The 2003 United Nations Human Settlements Programme (UN-Habitat) Report *The Challenge of the Slums: Global Report on Human Settlements 2003* represents the first truly global audit of urban poverty. The new report breaks with traditional United

Nations circumspection and self-censorship to squarely indict neoliberalism, especially the International Monetary Fund's structural adjustment programs, as the chief cause of the rapid increase in urban poverty. In his review of the UN report, *Planet of Slums: Urban Involution and the Informal Proletariat*, Mike Davis writes that there may be more than a quarter of a million slums on earth.

The world's highest percentages of slum-dwellers are in Ethiopia (an astonishing 99.4% of the urban population), Chad (also 99.4%), Afghanistan (98.5%), and Nepal (92%). The poorest urban populations, however, are probably in Maputo and Kinshasa, where (according to other sources) two-thirds of residents earn less than the cost of their minimum required daily nutrition. In Delhi, planners complain bitterly about "slums within slums" as squatters take over the small open spaces of the peripheral resettlement colonies into which the old urban poor were brutally removed in the mid-1970s. In Cairo and Phnom Penh, recent urban arrivals squat or rent space on rooftops, creating slum cities in the air.

Whereas the classic slum was a decaying inner city, the new slums are more typically located on the edge of urban spatial explosions. This land use pattern, referred to as "slum sprawl," is as much of a problem in the developing world as suburban sprawl in the rich countries. Davis writes:

> The urban poor, meanwhile, are everywhere forced to settle on hazardous and otherwise unbuildable terrains—over-steep hillslopes, river banks and floodplains. Likewise they squat in the deadly shadows of refineries, chemical factories, toxic dumps, or in the margins of railroads and highways. Poverty, as a result, has "constructed" an urban disaster problem of unprecedented frequency and scope, as typified by chronic flooding in Manila, Dhaka and Rio, pipeline conflagrations in Mexico City and Cubatão (Brazil), the Bhopal catastrophe in India, a munitions plant explosion in Lagos, and deadly mudslides in Caracas, La Paz and Tegucigalpa. The disenfranchised communities of the urban poor, in addition, are vulnerable to sudden outbursts of state violence like the infamous 1990 bulldozing of the Maroko beach slum in Lagos ("an eyesore for the neighbouring community of Victoria Island, a fortress for the rich") or the 1995 demolition in freezing weather of the huge squatter town of Zhejiangcun on the edge of Beijing.

The urban and working poor, indigenous peoples, and other social groups that have been disadvantaged politically or economically by globalization are among the growing groups of humanity that the neoliberal state is unable and, in some circumstances, unwilling to provide for. If refugees represent such a disquieting element in the order of the modern nation-state, then indigenous peoples represent the resource element of globalization (see Lesson 18). Both groups break the continuity between human and citizen, nativity and nationality. Agamben notes this becomes most evident in moments of crisis where both international humanitarian organizations and individual states prove themselves, despite their solemn invocations of "sacred and inalienable" human rights, absolutely incapable of resolving the problem of a globalized humanity.

CONCLUSION

Racism and classism—either overt or covert—have clearly played an integral role in the setting and maintenance of these uneven and exploitative land use patterns. "Whether by conscious design or institutional neglect," argues sociologist Robert Bullard, "communities of color in urban ghettos, in rural 'poverty pockets,' or on economically impoverished Native-American reservations face some of the worst environmental devastation in the nation". I suggest that neoliberalism has aided in the legitimacy and effect of this uneven and unjust social and environmental relationship.

Environmental justice scholars and activists argue that certain minority populations are forced, through lack of access to decision-making and policy-making processes, to live with a disproportionate share of environmental "bads"—and suffer the related public health problems and quality of life burdens. In addition, research has shown that not only are minority populations more likely to live in environmentally degraded and dangerous places but the amount of environmental and health protection afforded these groups by the governments and regulatory agencies is substantially less than that generated for whites and more wealthy people.

Much more information is needed to accurately assess the relationship between socioeconomic status and environmental inequality. In particular, longitudinal databases that sample across a continuum of income levels and incorporate multiple environmental conditions will provide the data needed to connect health, socioeconomic status, and environmental inequality. These databases would allow scientists and policy makers to examine the relationship between disenfranchised groups and exposure to cumulative environmental risks, and then determine if that exposure accounts for their higher mortality.

On a final note, other social scientists concerned with environmental equality and justice have argued that the victims of environmental inequalities will be afforded the same protection as others only when they have access to the decision-making and policy-making processes that govern the locations of hazardous materials and polluting industries. In other words, more accurate information regarding environmental risks and more opportunities for legitimate participation in environmental policy-making processes may provide environmental justice for all social groups.

SOURCES

Agamben, Giorgio. 1998. *Homo Sacer: Sovereign Power and Bare Life*. Stanford, CA: Stanford University Press.

——. 2004. "We Refugees: Refugees, Nation State, Citizens, Rights of Man." Saas Fee, Switzerland: European Graduate School. (http://www.egs.edu/faculty/agamben/agamben-we-refugees.html).

Agyeman, Julian, Robert D. Bullard, and Bob Evans. 2003a. "Joined-up Thinking: Bringing Together Sustainability, Environmental Justice and Equity." Pp. 1–16 in

Just Sustainabilities: Development in an Unequal World, edited by J. Agyeman, R. D. Bullard, and B. Evans. Cambridge, MA: MIT Press.

——, eds. 2003b. *Just Sustainabilities: Development in an Unequal World.* Cambridge, MA: MIT Press.

Brulle, Robert, and David Pellow. 2006. "Environmental Justice: Human Health and Environmental Inequalities." *Annual Review of Public Health* 27:3.1–3.22.

Bullard, Robert D. 1990. *Dumping in Dixie: Race, Class, and Environmental Quality.* Boulder, CO: Westview Press.

——. 1993. *Confronting Environmental Racism.* Boston, MA: South End Press.

——. 1994. "Unequal Protection: Environmental Justice and Communities of Color." San Francisco, CA: Sierra Club Books.

Davis, Mike. 2004. "Planet of Slums: Urban Involution and the Informal Proletariat." *New Left Review* 26:5–34.

Evans, Gary, and Elyse Kantrowitz. 2002. "Socioeconomic Status and Health: The Potential Role of Environmental Risk Exposure." *Annual Review of Public Health* 23:303–31.

Faber, Daniel and Deborah McCarthy. 2003. "Neoliberalism, Globalization, and the Struggle for Ecological Democracy: Linking Sustainability and Environmental Justice." Pp. 38–63 in *Just Sustainabilities: Development in an Unequal World.* Edited by J. Agyeman, R. Bullard, and R. Evans. Cambridge, MA: MIT Press.

Foster, John Bellamy. 1993. "'Let Them Eat Pollution': Capitalism and the World Economy." *Monthly Review* 44:10–11.

Gedicks, Al. 1994. *The New Resource Wars: Native and Environmental Struggles Against Multinational Corporations.* Montreal, Canada: Black Rose Books.

Getches, David, and David Pellow. 2002. "Beyond Traditional Environmental Justice." Pp. 3–30 in *Justice and Natural Resources: Concepts, Strategies, and Applications,* edited by K. Mutz and G. Bryner. Chicago, IL: Island Press.

Hardt, M., and A. Negri. 2001. *Empire: The Crisis of Political Space.* Cambridge, MA: Harvard University Press.

Harvey, David. 2003. *The New Imperialism.* Oxford, UK: Oxford University Press.

Kuletz, Valerie. 1998. *The Tainted Desert: Environmental Ruin in the American West.* New York: Routledge.

Larner, Wendy. 2000. "Neo-liberalism: Policy, Ideology, Governmentality." *Studies in Political Economy* 63:5–25.

Nue, Dean, and Richard Therrien. 2003. *Accounting for Genocide: Canada's Bureaucratic Assault on Aboriginal People.* New York: Zed Books.

Pellow, David. 2004. *Garbage Wars: The Struggle for Environmental Justice in Chicago.* Cambridge, MA: MIT Press.

——. 2005. "The Movement for Environmental Justice in the U.S.: Confronting Challenges and Charting a New Course." *Transatlantic Initiative to Promote Environmental Justice.* Budapest, Hungary: October 27–30, 2005.

Ringquist, Evan. 2005. "Assessing Evidence of Environmental Inequalities: A Meta-Analysis." *Journal of Policy Analysis and Management* 24:223–47.

Szasz, Andrew. 1994. *Ecopopulism: Toxic Waste and the Movement for Environmental Justice.* Minneapolis, MN: University of Minneapolis Press.

Szasz, Andrew, and Michael Meuser. 1997. "Environmental Inequalities: Literature Review and Proposals for New Directions in Research and Theory." *Current Sociology* 45:99–120.

Taylor, Dorceta. 2000a. "Introduction." *American Behavioral Scientist* 43:504–7.

———. 2000b. "The Rise of the Environmental Justice Paradigm: Injustice Framing and the Social Construction of Environmental Discourses." *American Behavioral Scientist* 43:508–80.

Tesh, Sylvia. 2000. *Uncertain Hazards, Environmental Activists and Scientific Proof.* Ithaca, NY: Cornell University Press.

Turner, Robin Lanette, and Diana Pei Wu. 2002. *Environmental Justice and Environmental Racism: An Annotated Bibliography and General Overview, Focusing on U.S. Literature, 1996–2002.* Berkeley, CA: Institute of International Studies, University of California, Berkeley.

UN-Habitat. 2003. *The Challenge of the Slums: Global Report on Human Settlements 2003.* London: Earthscan Publications Ltd.

United Church of Christ Commission on Racial Justice. 1987. *Toxic Wastes and Race in the United States.* New York: United Church of Christ.

United Nations Development Project. 2006. *Beyond Scarcity: Power, Poverty and the Global Water Crisis.* New York: Palgrave Macmillan.

U.S. Environmental Protection Agency. 2007. "Environmental Justice." Washington, DC: U.S. Environmental Protection Agency, http://www.epa.gov/compliance/environmentaljustice/index.html.

11

The Sociology of Environmental Health

Sabrina McCormick

When I was eight, I lost almost everything: my room, all the stuff in it—toys, dance costumes, purple barrettes, green tights, sparkly lip gloss. I had to leave them behind when we abandoned our house on Bishop Lake. That summer, a crew had sprayed our house for powder post beetles. Quickly, my mother got sick and dizzy. She had a piece of furniture tested. The crew had illegally sprayed our house with chlordane, a chemical used as a pesticide. Before that year, 3.6 million pounds of chlordane were applied to corn, fruits, lawns, and houses every year. But the initial testing of chlordane was not sufficient. Eventually, the Environmental Protection Agency discovered that the chemical can contaminate air, water, and soil and that it causes damage to the nervous and blood systems, lungs, and kidneys. That year regulations were put in place to ban chlordane. That was when I first learned how the environment impacts health.

One of the most pressing concerns in any society is the health of its people. Many of the most common yet seemingly mysterious illnesses are clearly caused, at least in part, by exposures in the environment. Although most conceptions of illness causation have focused on the individual for the past few hundred years, there is growing concern about environmental causes of illness as more and more people realize that there are direct and intimate relationships between the world around us and our own health. However, health-care researchers, practitioners, and providers face many obstacles in remedying environmental illness. In this lesson, I describe the field of environmental health and the obstacles that impede better address of it. I review several landmark cases that have shaped our understanding of environmental illness. To exemplify some of the obstacles to understanding and dealing with environmental illness, I describe illnesses caused by heat waves—a critical issue that exemplifies how environmental conditions affect human health.

SHIFTING TO ENVIRONMENTAL HEALTH

In the early twentieth century, health-care practitioners began to trace illness causation, prevention, and treatment to the individual, rather than the environment in which we live. Regarding the individual as the locus of illness resulted from the rise in *germ theory*—the idea that microorganisms that are transmitted between people are the cause of disease—and the power of polluting industries. *Miasma theories*, which acknowledged environmental contaminants and exposures, fell away as large-scale polluters were released from responsibility for the health effects of their actions. Power, politics, and science got intermixed in medical understanding and treatment (see Lesson 7). These processes reflect how underlying sociological aspects of life get embedded in bodies and health. As such factors shaped our understanding of what causes illness, a new model underlying medical thinking arose in the shape of the biomedical model.

E.G. Mishler describes the biomedical model as the unquestioned conceptual model on which medical thinking is based. The model's key assumptions are the doctrine of a specific etiology (the search for causes of disease) and the neutrality of medicine. This model does not acknowledge the social, political, or economic facets driving the development of medical knowledge. The largest government institutions, the pharmaceutical sector, and major health foundations have provided support for the biomedical approach and have focused little on environmental causes of disease. There is only one government institution that has been given the responsibility to address environmental health, the National Institute of Environmental Health Sciences (NIEHS). The NIEHS is one of 21 institutions housed within the National Institutes of Health.

Despite most health care and research being based on the biomedical model, concerns about environmental causes of illness have become more common, especially among people whose lives are touched by environmental illness. The field of environmental health is generally concerned with human exposures to human-made toxins and other harmful exposures in air, food, and water. These exposures are often shaped by social and physical structures. As a result, the field of environmental health also addresses the neighborhoods, schools, and homes in which we live. An individual's or group's racial, ethnic, age, or gender identity shapes experiences in these places and is therefore also of importance in environmental health. For example, asthma rates in inner-city areas have been skyrocketing. These areas are inhabited largely by poor people of color who live adjacent to bus terminals and polluting facilities where air pollution is rife. Recent research has connected this air pollution with asthma rates. This case of environmental illness reflects how race, class, neighborhood, and air interrelate to impact human health (see Lesson 10).

The field of environmental health addresses population-level factors, a broader conception than that encompassed by the biomedical paradigm. An environmental conception of disease demonstrates that the individual-level focus of a biomedical approach omits broader political and environmental factors that might force polluters to reduce emissions or to face losses by stopping the production of certain products. An environmental framework looks at changes in industrial production practices as the source to changes in health outcomes. In the example of asthma, an environmental framework would bring to light the lack of regulation of small air particles emitted by smokestacks and the need to cut vehicle emissions to protect public health.

In the conception of environmental health, the individual is seen in relationship with the social world. It calls attention to the difference between a focus on sick individuals and one on sick populations. A number of sociological processes play a role in environmental health assessments, such as gender inequality, racial and ethnic identity, social norms and structures, political economy, and environmental justice. This means a population-based approach to illness. An individual risk factor approach seeks to answer the following question: Why are some individuals sick? Conversely, a population-based line of inquiry asks the following: Why are some groups sick while others are not? Finding the answer to the second question can be much harder than discovering the answer to the first. Due to the difficulties with conducting research that produces scientifically legitimate answers to these types of questions, innovative methods and topics of study are generally adopted in the environmental paradigm. They include geographic information systems (GIS) study—or the mapping of geological sites and human patterns of disease—survey methods, and novel epidemiological and toxicological methods. Collaboration with laypeople can also characterize these research projects.

Concerns about environmental causes of illness arose with the environmental movement and with the environmental justice movement, which focused on how exposures were more extreme for minorities or the poor (see Lesson 15). Today, several health social movements have drawn attention to the role of environmental factors in illness. For example, the environmental breast cancer movement has changed our conception of breast cancer causation from individual-level risk factors like diet, exercise, and alcohol consumption to human-made chemicals and radiation. The movement seeks to overturn an individual-level approach to health by politicizing connections between health, the environment, and industrial production. In other words, they point to the social production of disease. Environmental breast cancer activists claim that the biomedical model of disease prevention, which focuses on genetics and lifestyle, blames women for getting cancer, therefore conveniently removing the responsibility from polluters and government regulators. There are many other movements that attempt to do the same thing. Many of them have arisen because of the most catastrophic and debilitating environmental illnesses today.

TRAGEDIES: MAKING THE CASE FOR ENVIRONMENTAL HEALTH

The biomedical focus of health care has sidelined environmental health, often creating a crisis. Sometimes that crisis is immediate and obvious. There have been catastrophes where thousands of people die overnight. In other cases, these problems grow over years, becoming obvious only to those who feel the brunt of them. Tragedies have often brought environmental health concerns to the attention of policymakers and the public, while other illnesses have slid under the rug.

In the late 1950s in Minamata Bay, Japan, a mysterious illness began to infiltrate local communities, most of which ate fish out of the bay. Neurological symptoms like numbness, slurred speech, and brain damage plagued them. Little explanation ensued until it was discovered that the Chisso Company had been dumping mercury into the bay for 40 years. The company had been producing plastics and chemicals there. When locals became upset about getting sick, the company pressured them to settle for a small amount of compensation while it continued to profit from manufacturing. Many people received nothing. Meanwhile, people in several other locations in the world have gotten what is now called Minamata disease.

In a quiet, rural area in Michigan in the early 1970s, livestock began to drop dead from no known cause. Farmers in the surrounding area got sick. Infected milk was recalled. In a period of months, public health officials discovered that polybrominated biphenols (PBBs), highly toxic chemicals used as flame-retardants, had contaminated cattle feed trucked around the state. Public health officials investigated the source of the contamination and claimed it was an individual farmer who had sold this hazardous feed. Pushed by angry communities and farmers, government agencies slowly came to realize that a lack of government responsibility had allowed it and ultimately threatened public health. Eventually, the crisis was contained but only after a statewide scare.

One warm night in 1984 in the small Indian city of Bhopal, a cloud of gas shot out of a smokestack and formed a plume that shifted and dropped onto the town below. Thousands died. A plant run by Dow Chemical, formerly known as Union Carbide, had leaked methyl isocyanate, an extremely toxic chemical, into the air after an accident in the plant. The company attempted to shirk responsibility, claiming that a worker caused the accident and that only a small number of deaths resulted. Legal battles ensued for over 20 years. Eventually, some of those who lost loved ones or their livelihoods received compensation. Others never did.

Possibly the most famous case in the United States to ignite attention around environmental illness is the exposure and displacement of communities in Love Canal, New York. In the late 1970s people in the Love Canal area began to mysteriously get ill. Lois Gibbs, a young mother and president of the local homeowners association, began to bring the community together to investigate why. They discovered that their homes and school had been built on the former waste site of Hooker Chemical. The site had been covered up, but toxins had followed the below-ground plume and leached into their basements. Scientific and legal battles began over who was responsible and what had to be done. Without exact scientific evidence about what was causing illness, the residents found it difficult to find Hooker at fault. In 1978, President Carter declared an emergency and evacuated the community. Eventually, the government paid hundreds of families for their losses. This event instigated the Superfund law, which could be used to declare a site toxic and mandate cleanup by the polluters.

These are some of the landmark cases that helped found the field of environmental health. More recently, there have been other tragedies to bring environmental health to light. Possibly the most public tragedy with the most hidden environmental health costs is the World Trade Center disaster. When the World Trade Center was destroyed, the burning buildings polluted the air, releasing human-made toxins that had been hidden in building materials for years. At first, government officials claimed that nearby areas were safe and that residents could return to their homes. Studies since then have shown that firefighters who worked intensively in the area and people who lived there have developed a "World Trade Center cough" and other illnesses. Women have given birth to babies of lower than normal weight. The site has not been safe, despite the assurance of government agencies. New research has found many exposures in the area, although their health consequences are not entirely clear.

These kinds of severe events are taking place all over the world. In 2007, the illegal practice of shipping toxic waste across borders came to light when a waste site was created to accommodate sulfurous sludge sent from a Dutch company aboard a Panamanian ship to the West African country of Ivory Coast. The open-air site was adjacent to homes in the port city of Abidjan. Soon after the $20,000 fee was paid and the sludge was dropped in the site, the community began to develop headaches, skin lesions, and difficulty breathing. Eventually, 15 people died and thousands incurred health problems. Activists arose in the area, and a lawsuit was won against the company, which promised to clean up the site. The long-term impacts on the local environment and community are unclear.

Such tragedies where environmental toxins have threatened public health have been the most obvious cases of environmental illness. They have forced public officials to be more wary of environmental contaminants and the built environment. A crisis often reflects social problems that otherwise go unnoticed. However, if a problem persists long enough, it can be seen in chronic illness as well.

CHRONIC MISHAPS

A number of environmental health concerns have taken years to realize. Often in these cases, a particular group is chronically exposed to an environmental contaminant that eventually leads to illness or disease. Lead poisoning is a perfect example. In the early to mid-twentieth century, lead became an important ingredient in paint and gasoline. Health studies showed that it was problematic, but a powerful lead industry distracted policymakers from these studies, allowing lead to go unregulated. Over the years, it became clear that air pollution with lead in it was causing severe respiratory problems. Similarly, children exposed to lead paint were acquiring neurological damage. Ironically, children were used in advertising campaigns for the paint. As a result, the government required the removal of lead from gasoline and paint. However, the legacy of lead remains in the air and in the homes where it has yet to be removed.

Cancer is of more recent and widespread concern. Cancer is possibly the most contentious and most important environmental health issue facing the United States. One in three Americans will get cancer in their lifetime. The most common cancers are lung, breast, and colon. Most attention to prevention of cancer is directed toward diet and exercise. However, a growing body of research shows that there are environmental exposures that cause cancer. For example, pesticides and other chemicals have been linked to heightened cancer rates. There is a great deal of resistance to these studies on the part of both the industries that make chemicals and the pharmaceutical companies that profit from cancer treatments. While diet, exercise, and other factors that individuals can control are important, of growing concern is the lack of protection against carcinogenic exposures from the government.

One group of chronic exposures that may lead to cancer is toxins in personal care products. Makeup, deodorant, lotions, shampoo, and other products are not regulated by the Food and Drug Administration. As a result, these products often include ingredients for which there are limited health data or that are linked with illness. Daily usage of these products could be adding up, especially for some groups like women who use makeup on a regular basis. There is little public awareness about these ingredients, but they may be contributing to a number of different kinds of illness. Some research has shown connections between certain chemicals in these products, like methylparaben, and increase in cancer. In Europe, many of these ingredients have been banned. In the United States, they are still legal.

While war causes many immediate deaths, it also causes more long-term health problems that are often ignored. The toxins used in bombs and munitions contaminate both the communities in which the war is waged and the soldiers on the battlefield. One controversial case of this has been Gulf War–related illness. After the Gulf War in the early 1990s, many soldiers came home with strange symptoms, like neurological disorders and fatigue. Over time the term "Gulf War illness" was attached to these disorders. There was little explanation for them, other than exposures to depleted uranium, an ingredient of bombs that American military handled regularly. Meanwhile, populations living in the area where the munitions remained even after the war were exposed.

Environmental illnesses can have a broad range of causes. They can be caused by something you choose to use or exposures that are out of your control. Illness can arise immediately or take years to manifest itself. One individual can face many exposures at once, making it difficult to identify the real cause of illness. Consequently, environmental factors are hard to identify and target. The most tragic cases where death and deformation result almost immediately help clarify the relationship between contaminant and illness. However, most people do not face such dire circumstances. Therefore, connecting environmental exposures to one's own illnesses is difficult to do. Similarly, "proving" that environment impacts health is also often challenging. The following case study of illness and death caused by heat waves demonstrates that, while it might appear obvious that heat makes people sick, politics and conflicting interests can obstruct medical interventions.

DYING OF THE HEAT

Like other tragedies that have forced us to realize that the environment impacts health, climate change (see Lesson 14) is making an impact on health around the world. An estimate by the World Health Organization tallies global deaths at 160,000 people every year due to illnesses induced by global warming. These trends are forecast to increase in severity as temperatures rise, creating one of the greatest public health issues of this century. There are five main health concerns regarding climate change: (1) air pollution–related illness, (2) temperature-related illness, (3) vector-borne disease, (4) water- and food-borne disease, and (5) illness or injury from extreme weather events. While to date these changes have been gradual, abrupt changes may also occur that create immediate catastrophes and public health crises. These problems will vary in extremity depending on the social and physical environment in which people live.

With an increase in global warming, extreme heat events, otherwise referred to as "heat waves," are forecast to increase. In the United States, heat- and cold-related illnesses have become a major focus because of their impacts around the country. Extreme heat often causes death, especially in urban areas. Approximately 400 people die of heat-related illness in the United States each year, and this number is projected to rise dramatically with climate change. In fact, on average more deaths occur due to heat waves than any other natural disaster in the United States. Heat waves lead to poor health in two main ways. Extreme temperature rise leads to heatstroke, while cardiopulmonary problems and respiratory illness are linked to shifts in air pollution concentrations.

Heat waves affect groups differently based on their race, gender, age, and medical and socioeconomic status. Minority communities and poor people are more impacted by heat waves than others. They often lack air conditioning at home or access to cooling facilities. They also often live in urban areas where heat islands are more common due to lack of green space, dark roofing, and other urban characteristics. The elderly in minority communities are particularly at risk. They lack the social networks and ability to gauge how hot they are that can help prevent illness. Some studies also show that women have worse outcomes. Since the elderly are predominantly women and have more difficulty dealing with heat, gender is likely to play a role.

Usually, people living in inner-city areas without access to parks and cooler areas are impacted by heat waves much more than those living in suburban or rural areas with access to air conditioning. This raises the question of health inequalities. Health inequalities occur when some populations are disproportionately impacted by a particular disease or illness, often because they are poor, have less access to health care, or in the case of environmental burdens, have greater exposure to harmful substances. Because heat waves impact minorities in cities more than other groups, environmental justice groups have raised a public outcry about the health impacts of climate change more generally.

Since the 1980s, environmental groups in the United States have addressed climate change; however, only a subset of environmental justice organizations have made health-related issues a priority. These groups have developed a "climate justice framework" composed of 10 points. These points focus on the accountability of polluters, the participation of affected people in policy making, and inclusion of inequalities in planning for climate change health outcomes and were used in the "Climate Justice Declaration." The declaration brings together principles from environmental justice and climate activism to emphasize how climate change would result in adverse health outcomes. It shows how such illnesses would be exacerbated by lack of access to health care and mitigation measures, disparities in health insurance coverage, and increased susceptibility of inner-city communities and communities of color.

Since the framework was established, groups proposing the climate justice agenda have burgeoned in California, New York, Alaska, Michigan, Illinois, and the United Kingdom. Prestigious academic institutions have also utilized the framework's language and approach in developing new studies. It has also been used internationally as a way to frame the global burden of greenhouse gas emissions generated by developed nations. While this discursive innovation and public contention has filtered into national environmental discourse, it is unclear how great an influence it has had in the political arena.

While public concern has grown about the health impacts of climate change and heat waves specifically, less attention has been dedicated to health concerns in policy making. Policy addressing climate-related health and illness originated in the late 1980s and early 1990s. Initially, only limited attention was given to such concerns. While political developments are still in their infancy, in some areas they are moving quickly to account for rapid, recent climate developments. New reports, policies, and institutions have been generated in order to prepare for and possibly mitigate impending public health crises, but little analysis has been done of these developments.

The first major federal report that dealt with human health impacts of climate change was produced by the U.S. Environmental Protection Agency in 1989, entitled "The Potential Effects of Global Climate Change." It drew attention to vector-borne disease and illnesses from extreme weather events and recommended that federal agencies like the Departments of the Interior, Energy, and Health and Human Services, among others, in conjunction with local agencies begin preparations. However, the majority of its focus was on ecosystems, and information regarding human health was limited to descriptions of sensitivities rather than recommendations or projections.

In 1992, the United Nations established the Framework Convention on Climate Change, which called for national governments to conduct risk assessments of health threats posed by global climate change. While the need for public health measures was mentioned, human health was sidelined in the framework. The following year, the Office of Technology Assessment developed a congressional report entitled "Preparing for an Uncertain Climate." This document only mentioned that there were possible human health impacts from climate change, especially extreme weather events, and gave almost no attention to the need to prepare for them. The Environmental Protection Agency demonstrated greater attention to health concerns in 1997 when it recommended that medical and public health practitioners better educate the public about heat events and that interventions for vulnerable populations be created. In 1998, Congress mandated the creation of the U.S. National Assessment of the Potential Consequences of Climate Variability and Change. It included thousands of stakeholder and scientific participants, eight federal agencies, 20 regional workshops, and assessments of 16 regions. Health concerns were a greater focus than in previous government documents.

Climate-related health policy developments have been shaped by political tensions and normative overtones, resulting in less effective preparatory measures. One of the most important policy advances reflects this process. In 1990, Public Law 101–606, the U.S. Global Change Research Act, was passed to stimulate a 10-year plan for national agencies such as the Environmental Protection Agency, the Department of Energy, and the National Institute of Environmental Health Science, among others, to develop an understanding of and necessary responses to climate change. Health-related impacts were one aspect of that bill. The Clinton administration, with Vice President Al Gore at its environmental helm, supported this initiative. However, when President George W. Bush entered office, his constituents encouraged him to stop reports in development, and a debate ensued over the components of the bill.

In order to resolve this conflict, new bounds were imposed on the assessment that removed discussion of greenhouse gas emissions and adaptation measures. The executive summary of the assessment developed in response to the 1990 bill was released in 2000 and included a major focus on health. However, it framed health impacts as uncertain and included few policy recommendations. The opacity of the political process makes it unclear what scientific findings or political interests shaped this development. Such instances as these, which are currently little understood, provide an opportunity to examine the policy-making process.

There are measures that can and need to be taken to protect the public's health from temperature rises caused by climate change. However, there are many scientific and political obstacles to making that happen. They are similar to the impediments to protecting the public from other environmental illness. Many public officials resist acknowledging that heat is increasing because it might result in better regulation of the air pollution which causes global warming. In addition, there are medical and scientific factors that make it difficult for policymakers to deal with illnesses caused by heat waves. For example, it is difficult to determine who has died due to the heat as opposed to other ill-nesses. If an individual had a preexisting heart condition which was worsened by a heat wave, is it the heat or other heart-related risk factors that caused the death? Scientists have yet to pin down exactly when cities will begin to have more heat waves. Therefore, it is challenging to plan for them. Lack of scien-tific and medical certainty is an issue that plagues many endeavors to connect the environment with human health. Biomedical research conducted in a lab or in large populations that isolates particular factors or genes is much easier. Therefore, more credibility is often given to that kind of work.

The public health impacts of climate change are just one of the emerging concerns of environmental health specialists. Others include the accumula-tion of chemicals in the human body, decreasing availability of clean water and resulting water-borne illnesses, and environmental crimes that lack inter-national regulations but that cause many illnesses around the world. These concerns need to be addressed in political and scientific spheres. The field of environmental health has room to grow in substantiating the concerns of social movements, citizens, and policymakers.

BODIES IN THE ENVIRONMENT

Problems with the environment are reflected in our bodies. But acknowledg-ing the environmental causes of illness is a controversial venture. It requires that polluters become more responsible and policymakers less attuned to powerful economic interests. The cases discussed in this lesson demonstrate that making connections between health and the environment is often first achieved by those who suffer environmental illness. In order for them to gain compensation for their losses and to stop these exposures, public officials must also accept their claims. A key component to this latter process is sci-entific proof. If an affected community has research that proves an illness is connected to certain exposures, it is much easier to gain the proper treatment and prevention.

A key political principle that may improve environmental health is the precautionary principle (PP). Born in Europe and spreading quickly across the United States, the PP is regarded as a defensive public health approach to reducing or banning chemicals even in the absence of understanding whether or not they harm human health. Usually, the government uses risk assessment to test how many people will become ill if a chemical is released onto the market. Risk assessment is a type of cost–benefit analysis that uses human lives as a measurement of cost. When a manufacturer generates a new chemical and tests it for harm to human health, the analysis includes a number of human lives that will be lost. The PP takes the opposite approach of arguing for the prevention of lives lost by disallowing products onto the market that cause environmental illness.

Issues of environmental health are local and global. They affect people in the most intimate ways and yet are increasingly caused by global issues. As transnational companies move around the world, often shirking environmental restrictions, communities immediately adjacent to manufacturing facilities, oil refineries, and other plants face harmful exposures. However, toxins and contamination also defy borders. They move through the air and water around the world. As we learn more about them, it becomes all the more plain that communities, states, and nations must collaborate to stop them and prevent the tragic illnesses that have occurred in the past and continue to make us ill.

In my own case, my mother used the legal system to gain compensation for the house that we lost. She also sued for the emotional damages we maintained by losing everything. The company that had illegally sprayed the chemical reimbursed us for a fraction of what had vanished from our lives. A large company had more power to decide the outcome of my life than we did, as a small family. I experienced the political economy of environmental illness in an obvious way. But all of our lives reflect the social and environmental landscape in which we live. A crisis may bring it to light more clearly, but chronic mishaps also occur over time, sometimes remaining hidden.

SOURCES

Bernard, S. M., J. M. Sarnet, A. Grambsch, K. L. Ebi, and I. Romieu. 2001. "The Potential Impacts of Climate Variability and Change on Air Pollution-Related Health Effects in the United States." *Environmental Health Perspectives* 109(Supplement 12):199–209.

Brown, Phil, and Edwin J. Mikkelsen. 1997. *No Safe Place: Toxic Waste, Leukemia, and Community Action.* Berkeley, CA: University of California Press.

Campbell-Lendrum D., A. Pruss-Ustun, and C. Corvalan. 2003. "How Much Disease Could Climate Change Cause?" Pp. 133–58 in *Climate Change and Human Health: Risks and Responses,* edited by D. Campbell-Lendrum, C. Corvalan, K. L. Ebi, A. K. Githeko, and J. S. Scheraga. Geneva, Switzerland: World Health Organization.

Cordova, Robert, Michel Gelobter, Andrew Hoerner, Jennifer R. Love, Ansje Miller, Calanit Saenger, and Disha Zaida. 2006. "Climate Change in California: Health, Economic, and Equity Impacts of Climate Change: A New Report by Redefining Progress." Redefining Progress, accessed on April 4, 2008 (http://www.rprogress.org/publication/2006/CARB_ES_0306.pdf).

Kovats, R. Sari, Diarmid Campbell-Lendrum, and Franziska Matthies. 2005. "Climate Change and Human Health: Estimating Avoidable Deaths and Disease." *Risk Analysis* 25(6):1409–18.

Mishler, E. G. 1981. *Social Contexts of Health, Illness, and Patient Care.* New York: Cambridge University Press.

Morgan, M. Granger, Robin Cantor, William C. Clark, Ann Fisher, Henry D. Jacoby, Anthony C. Janetos, Ann P. Kinzig, Jerry Melillo, Roger B. Street, and Thomas J. Wilbanks. 2005. "Learning from the U.S. National Assessment of Climate Change Impacts." *Environmental Science and Technology* 39(23):9023–32.

Pettit, Jethro. 2004. "Climate Justice: A New Social Movement for Atmospheric Rights." *IDS Bulletin* 35(3):102–106.

Tesh, Sylvia. 1988. *Hidden Arguments: Political Ideology and Disease Prevention Policy.* New Brunswick, NJ: Rutgers University Press.

12

From Farms to Factories

The Environmental Consequences of Swine Industrialization in North Carolina

Bob Edwards
Adam Driscoll

F rom the Appalachian Mountains in the west to the beaches of the Outer Banks, North Carolina's natural beauty attracts millions of vacationers, retirees, and outdoor enthusiasts each year to enjoy its varied landscapes. The ecological diversity of rural eastern North Carolina's bountiful wetlands, rivers, estuaries, and sounds is no exception. Yet, over the last 25 years these natural resources have come under increasing stress from pollution. When one thinks of industrial polluters, the images that readily come to mind are those of factories belching black smoke into the air or pipes dumping unknown factory chemicals into a river. Rarely is a farm one of the first associations. Yet, a 1998 Senate Agriculture Committee report estimated that the annual volume of livestock wastes—including pork, poultry, and beef—in the United States is 130 times greater than our annual production of human wastes and constituted the largest contributor to the pollution of America's waterways. The industrialization of agricultural production techniques has changed the very nature of farming, and something that may have been harmless to the environment has become a pollution giant. Moreover, in recent decades the agriculture industry has undergone a thorough restructuring of ownership that has pushed small and family farmers out of business and put ownership or control of most food production in the hands of a small number of large corporations.

A case in point can be found in the North Carolina pork industry. The traditional pattern of numerous independent farmers raising hogs in small numbers, often to supplement income from field crops like cotton, tobacco, corn, or soybeans, is all but extinct. Anecdotally this is borne out by the absence of pigs at county fairs in eastern North Carolina over the last decade. Large, vertically integrated corporations own the pigs from birth to bacon; thus, showings and competitions among individual farmers and students have gone by the wayside. Gone as well are the benign environmental impacts of traditional pork production, which have been replaced by ones that may best be described as corrosive. This lesson examines the North Carolina case to better understand these profound changes and their environmental impacts.

Furthermore, we argue that the North Carolina hog industry illustrates ongoing trends in all protein production, including beef, poultry, and most recently fish.

FROM FARMS TO FACTORIES

Between 1985 and 2000 the North Carolina pork industry changed dramatically in several ways. First, and most obviously, the industry expanded dramatically, but the fivefold increase in hog population and waste rests on more subtle, but consequential, changes in the structure and technology of pork production. This section discusses the growth of the hog industry from 2 million to 10 million head and its concentration on the coastal plain of eastern North Carolina. Second, we describe the confined animal feeding operation (CAFO) technology typical of pork and other livestock production nationwide. Third, we conclude by describing how the above changes in the industry combined to transform it into one of the state's worst polluters and introduces our concept of "externalities of scale."

Industry Expansion

Between 1982 and 1992 the North Carolina swine population reached about 4 million. Production had become horizontally integrated and increasingly utilized capital-intensive CAFO technologies. These industry changes, along with active promotion by the state government, a massive new processing facility, and the growing popularity of pork, set the stage for meteoric expansion to over 10 million hogs by 1997. Suddenly, North Carolina had more pigs than people, with hogs outnumbering humans by 5 to 1 on the coastal plain and by as much as 50 to 1 in individual counties. Pork surpassed poultry and tobacco as North Carolina's top agricultural commodity. Yet, the number of hog farms declined dramatically over this same period, leaving the state with far fewer, but much larger, hog operations concentrated in one region, as shown in Figure 12–1. Overall, these changes catapulted North Carolina to the vanguard nationally as the United States' leading innovator in the expanding and rapidly globalizing pork products market.

This explosion in the hog population was accompanied by a simultaneous geographic implosion. In 1982 only one North Carolina county lacked commercial hog farms; by 1997, following the period of intensive growth, approximately 95% of all swine production had concentrated in the eastern counties of the coastal plain, particularly in the southern portion of this region. The top 10 hog-producing counties in the southeastern region of the state accounted for a full 77% of the state's hog population in 2006. Figure 12–2 provides an excellent visual representation of the industry's geographic concentration.

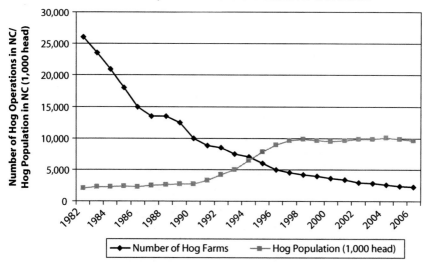

Figure 12–1 The North Carolina hog industry's consolidation and growth from 1982 to 2006. Growth is represented by the state hog population, while consolidation is exhibited in the number of hog farms in the state. *Source*: North Carolina Department of Agriculture.

Confined Animal Feeding Operations

Prior to the surge in industry growth, production techniques varied somewhat among traditional, small farmers, with hogs kept in different sorts of shelters and variable pastureland available to them. Similarly, feed consisted of a wide range of food sources, from on-farm scraps and crop by-products to 100% off-farm purchased feed. Traditionally, hog farming was conducted by numerous independent farmers raising hogs in small numbers on pasture or dirt lots. In North Carolina most hog production merely supplemented a farmer's income from field crops like corn, soybeans, or tobacco. Farms specializing in hog production were rare, while supplemental hog farming was widespread. In 1982 there were over 11,000 farms that produced swine for commercial sale and 58% of those producers had herds smaller than 25 hogs. Perhaps the most important feature of traditional production, hog waste was frequently used as fertilizer for commercially viable crops on the same farm. The combination of small herd sizes and less geographically concentrated hog populations meant that this form of waste disposal produced no adverse environmental consequences.

Traditional hog farms of this type are all but extinct in North Carolina. Today, the typical hog operation utilizes CAFO technology. CAFOs are frequently dubbed "assembly-line swine" by their critics who want to emphasize that swine CAFOs more closely resemble industrial facilities than the traditional farms just described. Swine CAFOs often house in excess of

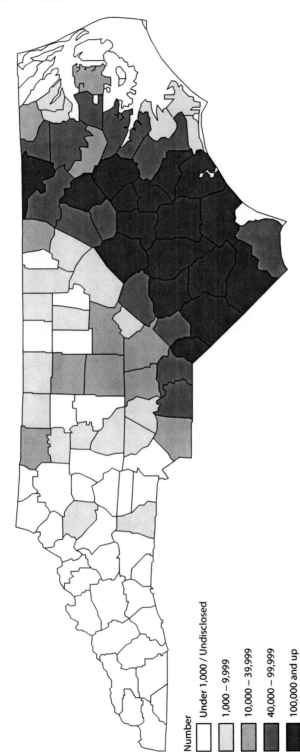

Figure 12.2 Distribution of swine production in North Carolina by County.

Number

Under 1,000 / Undisclosed

1,000 – 9,999

10,000 – 39,999

40,000 – 99,999

100,000 and up

50,000 head, with operations such as Circle Four Farms of southwestern Utah producing over a million head each year in a single facility. Yet, herd sizes of 2,000–5,000 are more the norm. Herd sizes vary depending upon which developmental stage of hog growth the CAFO is designed to accommodate. Contemporary production uses a three-stage process and CAFOs. At the first stage of the process are sow farms, where breeding sows give birth to litters of pigs, which are raised until weaned at about 15 pounds. "Wean to feeder" facilities are the second stage of the process. Pigs are sent to a "feeder to finish" facility when they reach about 40–50 pounds. They remain at a feeder to finish operation until reaching slaughter weight of about 250 pounds. All three stages, from birth to slaughter, take about 5.5 months.

A swine CAFO consists of three essential parts, the hog house, the waste "lagoon," and the "sprayfield." Hog houses are long, rectangular buildings with a center aisle and confinement pens along each side. Confinement pens vary in size depending on the stage of development of the pigs. In sow farms a single breeding sow occupies each pen. Pens do not provide much room for the sow to move around. In later stages, the confinement pens are sized to accommodate between 10 and 30 animals at the size they would be when they leave that CAFO for the next stage in the process. In other words, when 30 freshly weaned pigs of about 15 pounds each are first put in a confinement pen, they have room to maneuver and fill about one-third of the pen. However, by the time they are ready to be moved to a feeder to finish facility they have grown to about 40–50 pounds and their increased body mass has filled all the free space in the pen. Thus, on their last day at a given stage of the process, pigs cannot move or lay down as they have grown to fill all the available space and are so packed in that they physically touch each other. This design is obviously efficient with floor space. It also enables operators to observe all pigs easily and to tend to them in small numbers one pen at a time.

Since the animals occupy the confinement pens around the clock, waste disposal is a critical issue. Hog house (confinement barn) flooring is made of slats suspended over concrete subflooring. The spaces between each slat are small enough that hooves do not go through them but large enough that urine runs between them and feces either falls between them or is pushed through as it is stepped on by the animals. Thus, all feces and urine that does not evaporate ends up on the subfloor. Periodically, water is flushed along the subfloor to transport the swine excreta out of the hog house. This forms a liquid "slurry" of swine feces, urine, water, and anything else that falls through the slats of a hog house. The slurry is then pumped into an adjacent waste "lagoon."

CAFOs utilize a refined and greatly expanded and concentrated version of the waste disposal techniques characteristic of small-scale traditional hog farms, where waste was used as fertilizer for commercially viable crops. In current practice, the slurry of liquid and solid excreta from the confinement buildings is transferred to waste lagoons and subsequently sprayed on "sprayfields." Sprayfields typically contain a type of grass that is not a marketable crop as in the traditional model of swine waste disposal. Rather, it is chosen for its capacity to metabolize some of the nitrogen and phosphorus in swine waste.

Each swine CAFO must have a waste lagoon of appropriate size; the bigger the CAFO, the bigger the lagoon. Waste lagoons are open earthen pits 25–30 feet deep and several acres in surface area. Newer lagoons have a clay liner, but older lagoons are unlined pits dug directly into the coarse, sandy soil typical of the coastal plain. Swine waste remains in the waste lagoon to process anaerobically and evaporate. Anaerobic processing is a way to describe naturally occurring bacteria breaking down the waste material that does not evaporate. In fact, evaporation of waste and its dispersion downwind, or more technically *evapotranspiration*, is a key component of the lagoon–sprayfield waste disposal design. The intention is that a large proportion of the swine waste will be dispersed downwind until it falls as rain into waterways or onto the land.

The other key feature of waste disposal practices is the sprayfield. Eventually, lagoons fill up from the mix of slurry and rainwater. As the lagoon level rises, its free board decreases. "Free board" refers to how far the level of waste in the lagoon can rise before overflowing. When elevated slurry levels reduce free board sufficiently, the slurry is pumped out of the lagoon and sprayed on an adjacent field, called a "sprayfield." Though reminiscent of the crop fields traditional farmers fertilized with their livestock waste, sprayfields typically do not grow crops with any market value. The grasses planted on sprayfield crops are selected for their ability to metabolize organic pollutants. To think of them as giant well-fertilized lawns mowed often but having no or limited commercial value would not be too far off the mark. Sprayfields dispose of swine slurry in three ways. First, the waste evaporates during the spraying process. Second, it is metabolized into the grass. Third, it soaks into the ground and contaminants are filtered out as the slurry seeps through the soil.

The last point to emphasize about CAFOs concerns their design and labor requirements. CAFOs are a "capital-intensive" technology. In short, capital-intensive technologies cost a lot of money to construct and get started but require relatively little labor to operate (see Lesson 5). Animals enter a confinement barn pen when they arrive and typically remain in that pen until they move on to the next stage of the process. Dispensing of feed and medicines to prevent diseases from spreading through the confined herd is automated. Operators tend to the dispensers but typically do not interact with the hogs unless a problem is observed. In fact, a recruiter for one of North Carolina's larger corporate integrators routinely sought to persuade farmers to construct a 3,000-head, second-stage hog operation by describing it as a "housewife operation." He then went on to explain that the farmer's wife could operate the entire CAFO during the middle of the day while the kids were at school.

Externalities of Scale

The industrialization and restructuring of the North Carolina hog industry has had tremendous consequences on how hog waste is managed and disposed. It is being produced in an unprecedented volume at a very high geographic concentration and is even altered in its makeup relative to the waste produced on traditional hog farms 30 years ago. These changes in the volume, concentration, and makeup of hog waste illustrate a concept we describe as "externalities of scale." This concept refers to a constellation of adverse, but not yet fully understood, economic, social, and environmental impacts associated primarily with current large-scale pork production and waste disposal practices but not present in the more dispersed, small-scale production practices typical at the beginning of the period described here. In smaller traditional operations, for example, hog herds that number in the low hundreds can be rotated over different pasturelands. The fields are large enough to fully absorb the nutrients from the hog waste (or to fully bioreme-diate the pollution), and those nutrients go on to fertilize future crops. With a low enough hog to land ratio, there is no pollution and you have a zero-discharge system.

In concept, large-scale CAFOs use such a system with their lagoons and sprayfields. However, full bioremediation is impossible for a CAFO with herd sizes in the thousands as sufficient land is not available. When more waste is applied to a field than the soil can absorb (oversaturation), hog waste washes off of fields and into the local watershed. Even if the soil can absorb the phys-ical waste, when more nutrients are placed in the soil than the crops can utilize, the surplus nutrients leach out into the ground water. At one point, three hog-producing counties were generating more nitrogen than could be absorbed by all of the crops in the entire state! Since waste is being passed onto the public and the CAFO owners are generating a profit from this waste, an externality is being created. Because the formation of this externality is primarily due to the scale on which this process is being performed (excess waste is being generated only by large-scale operations), we describe it as an "externality of scale." These externalities also include economic impacts like disruption of livelihood and loss of property values, health impacts on those who work in or live in close proximity to CAFOs, and broader environmental impacts which can indirectly affect human health and economic vitality in downstream communities.

When dealing with externalities of scale, the volume of hog waste being produced by the industry in eastern North Carolina must be addressed. Hogs excrete more waste than humans. Though this fact is undisputed, claims of how much more fluctuate widely from two to three times more to as much as 10–15 times more depending upon who is making the claims and their stake in the issue. Clearly, the truth lies somewhere between these extremes and in all likelihood closer to the low end of the range, around four times. The reasons for this lie in a hog's growth rate. Consider that a market hog reaches slaughter weight of 250 pounds at less than 6 months of age. Thus, each space in a CAFO produces two hogs per year. More to the point, each CAFO-raised pig gains 250 pounds in 6 months, for a rate of 500 pounds per year. This tremendous growth rate requires a correspondingly tremendous rate of consumption and subsequent excretion. Even a human who reaches

250 pounds at age 18 gains only 14 pounds a year. Moreover, maintaining that weight requires less consumption and excretion than gaining it in the first place. When a hog's rate of weight gain levels off, it is slaughtered and replaced by another rapidly growing hog.

Opponents of current CAFO and waste disposal practices often illustrate their concerns by suggesting that the 9–10 million hogs in eastern North Carolina represent the same excretory impact as 35–40 million people. Don Webb, founder of the Alliance for a Responsible Swine Industry, seldom misses the opportunity to portray the region as a giant cesspool, where the waste of 10 million hogs is simply laid on the land for nature to take its course. Others suggest that it is like four New York Cities moving to eastern North Carolina without the benefit of sewage treatment. Some critics emphasize that if 9–10 million humans lived in eastern North Carolina utilizing open-pit cesspools, it would be a public health crisis of epic proportions and a national embarrassment. Irreverent opponents joke about miracles of "immaculate excretion" when it comes to CAFO-raised swine. Far more objective sources like the North Carolina Swine Odor Task Force (1995) estimated that hogs produce nearly 1,700 pounds of *solid* waste per head per year. With 11.3 million hogs being raised and slaughtered in the year 2006, the pork industry created approximately 9.2 million tons of solid waste in eastern North Carolina alone. This is waste being produced on a scale far outside the level at which on-farm disposal is a feasible option.

Additionally, it is worth noting that this tremendous volume of waste is not being spread evenly over the eastern region. As hog farms have intensified and industrialized their production, they have concentrated more pigs on less area. An analysis of farm-registration data shows that hundreds of these farms lack sufficient acreage to absorb the volume of waste being produced. An even greater number do not cultivate a sufficient portion of their land to ensure that waste gets properly absorbed. So in addition to more waste being produced, it is being concentrated onto smaller areas, creating more of a runoff problem. Basically, the CAFO lagoon system stacks the waste into fewer and bigger piles.

In addition to the volume and concentration differences, the very makeup of the hog waste generated by CAFOs is substantially different from that of traditional hog farms. In CAFOs many things beside excrement can fall through the slats in the floor and get flushed along with the waste into the lagoons, including afterbirths, trampled and stillborn piglets, old batteries, broken bottles of insecticide, and antibiotic syringes. A more important component of CAFO hog waste, however, is excess antibiotics, vaccines, and insecticides. The extremely high concentration of hogs at high temperatures (often higher than 90°F) in close proximity to their own wastes creates the most unsanitary conditions imaginable. Most CAFO operations depend on the subtherapeutic use of antibiotics as a substitute for disease control practices. Animals are routinely infused with antibiotics and vaccines and doused with insecticides (oxytetracycline, tulathromycin, ceftiofur, and tiamulin) in a preemptive attempt to combat the numerous pathogens that are festering in the relative filth of the hog barn. Whatever chemicals are not absorbed by the animals exit the barns as a component of the waste. Antibiotics can promote the growth of antibiotic-resistant bacterial strains in an already bacteria-rich medium. The toxic quality of hog waste is most clearly exhibited in the color of the waste lagoons, where the interaction between the bacteria, blood, waste, and chemicals turns the liquid, not a decent healthy brown, but various unnatural shades of pink.

"Externalities of scale" refers to the way that the social and environmental costs of new forms of production may exceed those of more traditional or less concentrated methods. New production methods can be both technological, as with the shift to CAFOs, and structural, relating to how production is organized and how its costs and benefits are distributed. This aspect of externalities of scale is discussed more later when we discuss the horizontal and vertical integration of this industry as well as its globalization. This aspect of externalities of scale refers to how adverse social and environmental costs of production are often concentrated in socially and politically marginalized regions around the world, while most of the economic benefits of that production are channeled out of production zones to large corporations and their stockholders. In other words, the places and communities that suffer the costs of production most directly receive a much smaller share of its benefits (see Lesson 10). In the next two sections we discuss the social and environmental costs of concentrated pork production on North Carolina's coastal plain.

SOCIAL IMPACTS OF SWINE INDUSTRIALIZATION

The radical expansion and industrialization of the North Carolina swine industry has had a wide range of far-reaching consequences. The externalities of scale created by this industry transformation are costs that extend into the realms of health, economics, and quality of life. This section describes the health risks created by this new style of hog production. Additionally, we discuss the impacts of hog CAFOs upon members of surrounding communities' quality of life. The third portion of this section deals with the economic impacts of this new model of agriculture. Finally, this section concludes with a discussion of the unequal distribution of these externalities among communities with high percentages of minorities and high levels of poverty.

The Health Risks of Hog Waste Exposure

A substantial body of research has accumulated on the adverse health impacts of occupational exposure to concentrated hog wastes for swine confinement house workers. In poorly ventilated swine buildings, workers can be exposed to a number of hazards, including harmful levels of gases (methane, ammonia, hydrogen sulfide, and carbon monoxide), dust, infectious agents, and airborne bacteria. These hazards contribute to a wide range of respiratory disorders, from headaches and shortness of breath to hydrogen sulfide poisoning, bronchitis, atopic asthma, and acute organic dust toxic syndrome. There have been cases reported of workers being killed by exposure to high concentrations of hydrogen sulfide gas or by falling into a waste lagoon. In one such report, a worker performing repairs on a hog lagoon in Michigan was overcome by fumes from the lagoon and fell in. In an effort to rescue him, the worker's nephew, cousin, older brother, and father all jumped in separately and in sequence. All four rescuers were overcome by the noxious liquid and met the same fate.

More recent studies have examined health and quality-of-life impacts among those living near swine CAFOs and have consistently found indications of adverse effects. Many studies have shown that the smell from swine CAFOs can be experienced by nearby residents as a sickening and irritating odor, as well as a mood-altering source of tension, depression, fatigue, and anger. Additionally, multiple studies have shown that residents living near hog CAFOs are experiencing higher rates of respiratory, sinus, and nausea problems caused by the dust and gases being released. Symptoms associated with proximity to a large-scale hog operation include, but are not limited to, burning eyes, runny nose, headache, cough, diarrhea, nausea and vomiting, dizziness, shortness of breath, and chest tightness. Moreover, the contamination of local drinking water, through lagoon leakage or sprayfield runoff, can allow pathogen transfer between pigs and people and lead to such human diseases as salmonellosis, giardiasis, chlamydia, meningitis, cryptosporidiosis, worms, and influenza. Additionally, waste lagoons have been linked to increased levels of nitrates in drinking water, which can cause methemoglobinemia, or "blue baby syndrome," a rare but potentially life-threatening condition for infants. These numerous health risks associated with hog wastes clearly demonstrate the need to treat it as a dangerous pollutant.

Quality of Life

In addition to the direct health risks associated with proximity to a large-scale hog operation, there have been numerous findings of negative impacts of hog CAFOs on nearby residents' quality of life. Individuals living near lagoons or hog barns can find themselves virtually trapped in their own houses, unable to open windows or go outside and sit on the porch in nice weather. Clothes hung out to dry are said to come back in smelling of hog waste. While difficult to quantify, the impact of hog waste on individuals' quality of life certainly constitutes an environmental impact. Some hog CAFO neighbors have found themselves trapped in their homes in a different way. Research clearly indicates that the value of homes in close proximity to hog CAFOs is less than comparable homes farther away. Similarly, the value of existing homes declines significantly if a nearby farmer decides to construct a CAFO. Thus, some neighbors who decide to just move away from the CAFO cannot do so because they are unable to sell their homes and cannot afford to continue to make payments on them while renting or buying another house elsewhere.

Economic Impacts

The North Carolina Pork Council has vigorously touted the industry as the economic backbone of eastern North Carolina. According to current estimates, the North Carolina hog industry generates $6.7 billion in annual sales and supports 46,000 jobs. An economic input as large as this in an impoverished region is substantial and important. Yet, the "economic miracle" of the North Carolina pork industry comes with economic costs as well. First, no one disputes that the industry restructuring and conversion to CAFOs drove thousands of small farmers out of business and contributed to a wave of farm loss in North Carolina. Hog farmers who did not contract with corporate integrators were pushed out of the business entirely. The main mechanism for this came from slaughterhouse policies that would only contract to slaughter hogs in lots of 1,000 or more. Independent producers, even those in co-ops of 40–50 farmers, could not amass 1,000 slaughter-ready hogs on the same day. Only large corporate integrators could meet this requirement.

The pork industry may be the economic "backbone" of North Carolina, as was claimed during the 1990s, but the state's single largest industry currently is tourism, which depends on the perception of an uncontaminated environment. North Carolina has about 300 miles of coast along the Atlantic Ocean and another 3,000 or so miles of inland coast along its sounds and tidal river systems. All of these areas are popular vacation and recreation destinations. They are also attracting a substantial inflow of retirees. Neither vacationers nor retirees want to smell a swine CAFO. Nor do they want to wonder what's in the water. Prominent national media coverage of hog operations in North Carolina between 1995 and 1997 and then again following the massive flooding from Hurricane Floyd that inundated the region in 1999 threatened to diminish the area's appeal as a vacation or retirement destination. Such fears motivated substantial segments of the state's business community to join with environmentalists in pushing for stricter regulations of the industry.

Environmental Injustice

Thus far we have discussed social, health, and economic impacts in general terms. However, the evidence is indisputable that these impacts have not been distributed evenly among the population of North Carolina, or even among residents of the eastern region. First, hog production, and thus any adverse impacts flowing from it, is concentrated in one region of the state. The region lies between Interstate 95 and the Atlantic coast and has been on the periphery, both economically and politically, throughout its history. Much of eastern North Carolina is socially isolated and has higher rates of poverty, a higher proportion of African American residents, and lower rates of homeownership and college graduation than other parts of the state. Much of the region is a rural analogue for what the sociologist William Julius Wilson referred to as truly disadvantaged areas of concentrated poverty and social isolation (see Lesson 10).

Low-income, African American, and politically marginalized communities up and down the coastal plain complain that a disproportionate number of hog operations are locating in their communities, leaving them to suffer the consequences without sharing the benefits. At least five separate scientific studies have confirmed the accuracy of their claim of disproportionate exposure, finding that African Americans regardless of income and low-income residents regardless of race are significantly more likely to live in close proximity to hog waste or to CAFOs. Whatever the adverse impacts of current waste disposal techniques are, African American and low-income residents of eastern North Carolina are more likely to suffer them.

ENVIRONMENTAL IMPACTS

The Earth is a multifaceted ecosystem of systems within systems. Adverse impacts produced in one place diffuse globally, eventually affecting all places even if to a negligible degree. Nevertheless, the environmental damage caused by an industry's production will be most apparent in the specific places where that production is concentrated. Both the human and biotic communities living in zones of concentrated production will be more likely to pay the costs of environmental damage. This brings us again to our notion of "externalities of scale" and raises two interrelated questions about the environmental impacts of swine production: What kind of place is this zone of concentrated production ecologically? How well suited is it to tolerate the environmental stressors of hog CAFOs? This section explores and describes those costs, starting with a discussion on the unsuitability of eastern North Carolina for this particular mode of waste disposal. Following that is a description of the ways the lagoon system allows hog wastes to end up in the environment. Finally, this section concludes by discussing the direct impacts untreated hog waste can have on the ecosystems of eastern North Carolina.

Regional Vulnerability

Newcomers to the region are often overwhelmed by just how flat it is. The upper deck of the East Carolina University football stadium in Greenville may well be the highest point in the entire region. The Tar River in Greenville, 90 miles from the Atlantic Ocean, is no more than 10 feet above sea level when not in flood stage. This flat region, like other low-lying coastal zones, was once primarily swamps, or more accurately wetlands. Prior to European settlement, the vast majority of the coastal plain was wetlands, and much of it still is. Settlers in eastern North Carolina used slave labor to dig a vast network of ditches throughout the region to drain wetlands so that they could be planted for agriculture. Without the network of drainage ditches, much of the region would still be under water, or at least wetlands. Yet, this is the same region where the hog industry is concentrated. In this area the water table is close to the surface regionwide. So by the time one digs 25–30 feet down to construct a waste lagoon, it is quite likely that the bottom of the lagoon will be very close to the water table, if not already in it.

Additionally, with the land so flat the waterways move very slowly. When swine waste is applied to land already saturated from rain, it runs off into the system of drainage ditches which serve as a direct transport into creeks and rivers. Nutrients like nitrogen and phosphorus run off and enter the slow-moving estuarine waterways. Similar effects come as nutrients in evaporated livestock waste condense and fall as rain onto wetlands or rivers. In other types of river systems in less flat land, rivers would carry these pollutants downstream and eventually out to sea quickly, transferring the environmental problem into an ocean "sink." Yet, in eastern North Carolina the nutrients remain in the slow-moving rivers and contribute to problems of eutrophication and hypoxia. Finally, the soils of eastern North Carolina are coarse and sandy, making them highly permeable to both liquid waste and small particulate matter. Combined, these geological and ecological features make the region extremely ill-suited for the application of waste from 9 million hogs.

Non-Point Source Pollution Still Pollutes

According to industry public relations statements, the lagoon/sprayfield system does not discharge hog wastes into waterways. Yet, as we describe in this section, substantial amounts of pollutants get into waterways from swine CAFOs. How can both statements be true? The answer lies in the important distinction between "point source" and "non-point source" polluters and pollution. Point source polluters are industrial facilities that are regulated under the federal Clean Water Act and must obtain a discharge permit from the U.S. Environmental Protection Agency, which regulates the type and amount of pollutants each facility is allowed to discharge. Municipal sewage treatment plants fall into this category. By contrast, non-point source pollution comes mainly from urban storm water runoff and agricultural runoff. Swine CAFOs are non-point source polluters, and because they are legally categorized as farms rather than industrial facilities, they are not governed by the Clean Water Act. Therefore, by legal definition, they do not "discharge" pollutants. So when the industry claims that it does not discharge hog waste into waterways, all it is really saying is that hog CAFOs are non-point source polluters rather than point source dischargers. In truth, the waste lagoon and sprayfield system is consciously designed to transport pollutants off the farm through the primary mechanism of evaporation rather than pumping them through a pipe.

Pollutants from swine waste most often leave the farm by runoff from sprayfield and waste lagoon leaks and occasionally by lagoon ruptures and discharges associated with flooding or very heavy rains. Any overapplication of hog waste to sprayfields results in waste running off into local waterways, as described. Don Webb, a former hog farmer and founder of the Alliance for a Responsible Swine Industry, claims that millions of gallons of hog waste are reaching the state's eastern waterways every week in this fashion.

Additionally, lagoon discharges or ruptures pose another threat to surface water. When the contents of a lagoon are not pumped onto sprayfields in a timely fashion, the lagoon can fill to the point of overflowing. This leaves lagoons especially vulnerable to heavy rainfall, a high risk in a region where eight hurricanes and 21 additional named tropical storms have made landfall during the last 12 years. There have also been some cases of spectacular lagoon ruptures directly spilling millions of gallons of waste into the surrounding area. In 1995 heavy rains contributed to a series of lagoon failures, which was highlighted by a 22 million–gallon spill at Oceanview Farms, a 10,000-head operation in Onslow County. In 1998 alone the state of North Carolina documented 107 lagoon discharges, of which 31 reached surface waterways. These spills happen with alarming regularity and transfer high volumes of pure hog waste directly into the eastern waterways.

Hog waste lagoons are also vulnerable to flooding. As described, eastern North Carolina is quite flat, with very low elevation, a very high water table, and high amounts of rainfall annually, and is prone to hurricanes. These factors combine to make the region very vulnerable to intense flooding. In 1996, floodwaters from Hurricane Fran submerged over 10 lagoons, spilling an unknown volume of waste into the Neuse River. In 1999, Hurricane Floyd, on the heels of Hurricane Dennis, caused widespread flooding over a period of several weeks, with nearly every river basin in the eastern part of the state exceeding 500-year flood levels. The floodwaters inundated approximately 50 waste lagoons and filled many others beyond safe capacity. Many hog barns themselves were flooded, and over 30,000 hogs were killed.

Finally, swine waste can enter underground aquifers and contaminate the groundwater supplying private and public drinking water wells by leaking waste lagoons or the leaching of sprayfield waste. Eastern North Carolina soils are coarse and sandy and drain quite quickly. A study by North Carolina State University showed that 38% of older, unlined swine waste lagoons leached nitrogen compounds into the groundwater at "strong" or "very strong" levels. Perhaps more troubling are the results of a North Carolina Division of Environment and Natural Resources study, finding that 25% of *newer lined* lagoons may contaminate groundwater. A state program offered free testing of private wells located near hog operations. After 15 months of testing, the program found that more than one-third of the 948 wells tested showed some contamination, with nitrates being the primary contaminant. Ultimately, the state health officials warned more than 89 families to not drink the water from their own wells. These are well-documented cases where individual households' drinking water was directly contaminated by nearby hog lagoons and sprayfields.

Pollutants found in swine wastes can leave the farms and lagoons in more forms than direct liquid waste. Airborne emissions from hog confinement houses, waste holding lagoons, and fields onto which wastes are sprayed have been found to contain such substances as methane, hydrogen sulfide, endotoxins, and ammonia. The North Carolina governor's 1999 report on lagoon and sprayfield conversion states that atmospheric deposition occurs as "approximately two-thirds of nitrogen in swine excretions is emitted to the air in accordance with the design of a lagoon and sprayfield system." Consequently, 20% of North Carolina's total atmospheric nitrogen emissions come from swine facilities, which account for 53% of the total in the eastern region. Atmospheric nitrogen and phosphorus enter surface water indirectly as they are carried downwind and redeposited on nearby lands and waterways. So waste from hog CAFOs can find its way into the environment even when a perfectly functioning lagoon and sprayfield system is employed.

The Environmental Impacts of Hog Waste

As sociologists, our primary concern with the hog industry is how it negatively impacts human beings. It is worth briefly describing, however, the various ways in which hog waste can negatively impact the natural environment. The primary effect of hog waste on waterways is the nutrient loading that occurs in the local watershed. This eutrophication of the streams and rivers promotes excessive plant growth and decay and can lead to both algal blooms and oxygen depletion in the water. Both can be fatal to fish and plants that normally live in the waterways. In the wake of the 1995 spills, there were widespread fish kills that totaled an estimated 10–15 million dead fish. In another instance, where a hog farmer had been discharging waste directly into a swamp that bordered a creek, the pollution killed trees up to 18 inches in diameter. The swamp was studded with dead trees, and stands of them continued downstream along the creek. In sufficient quantities, these nutrient loads severely stress aquatic ecosystems.

The pathogen content of hog waste can have negative effects on ecosystems as well. Fecal bacteria and protozoans can disrupt a food system and, in sufficient quantities, can kill larger animals directly. Bacteria can thrive on river bottoms for weeks after initial exposure. In one instance in 1994, a recreational lake in Duplin County with seven nearby hog farms was found to have a fecal coliform count (an indicator of fecal contamination) 60 times the allowable level for swimming. At high enough levels, the bacteria and nutrients contained in hog waste are a threat to the balance of any aquatic ecosystem.

INDUSTRY RESTRUCTURING

Over the last 25 years, the North Carolina pork industry expanded dramatically, shifted to CAFO-style production technologies, and spatially concentrated its externalities of scale in a peripheral and ecologically vulnerable region, as we have seen. Beyond the substantial social and environmental impacts already discussed, equally profound changes in the structure of pork industry ownership have occurred as well. In short, 25 years ago thousands of small farmers produced North Carolina's pork. They bought feed from local feedlots and sold pigs to a network of small slaughterhouses, which in turn sold butchered pork to meat wholesalers. Each step along the process consisted of numerous independent businesses. Today, the situation could hardly be more different. Currently, one large multinational corporation, Smithfield Foods, owns outright or exerts contract control over more than 90% of the North Carolina pork industry, from breeding to feed sales to finishing farms to slaughtering and processing and eventually to branded pork products for retail consumption worldwide. This shift has important implications for public policy to protect the environment, for the strategies and activities of environmental movements, and for understanding how peripheral zones of concentrated production like eastern North Carolina connect to globalized processes of production and consumption. In this section, we briefly describe the two phases of this change: (1) the horizontal integration of all aspects of pork production and (2) the vertical integration of the entire industry from birth to branded bacon products marketed worldwide.

From Independent Farmers to Corporate Producers: Horizontal Integration

The traditional system of numerous independent farmers has been replaced by one of corporate contract farming, where large firms, known as "integrators," own the pigs and pay farmers to raise them. Recall that many hog farmers were driven out of the business by these changes as the number of hog farms fell from over 10,000 to about 2,300. By about 1995 the process of horizontal integration was complete. Under this new structure of industry ownership, hog farmers whose businesses had survived became outsourced contractors providing hog-raising services to a corporate integrator. Farmers no longer owned the pigs. Rather, they agreed to raise pigs owned by a corporate integrator and to be paid a set price per pound for the weight the pigs gained while in their care. The integrator provided the piglets, feed, and transport, while the farmer provided the land, CAFO, and labor.

One man, Wendell Murphy, influenced the horizontal integration of pork production in North Carolina more than any other. Murphy entered the hog industry as a feed mill owner but in 1973 introduced the practice of contract hog farming. By 1987 Murphy Family Farms, Inc., was clearly North Carolina's largest and most influential corporate pork integrator. The success of Murphy Family Farms rested on the implementation of contract farming and the shift to CAFO-style production technologies.

Smithfield Foods Vertically Integrates the Industry

In 1997 a moratorium on new and expanded hog operations halted industry growth and has held North Carolina's hog population and its environmental impacts constant over the last 11 years. However, the events of 1998–2001 dramatically altered the structure of the pork industry. During this period, pork production and processing in North Carolina were vertically integrated (see Lesson 6) under the ownership or indirect control of one multinational firm, Smithfield Foods of Virginia.

To appreciate this rapid shift, we have to return to the role of Wendell Murphy and his principal pork industry rival, Joseph W. Luter III, whose grandfather founded Smithfield Foods in 1936. By 1997 Murphy graced the cover of *Forbes* magazine as America's "low-tech" billionaire and main mover behind the horizontal integration of pork production. Smithfield Foods in 1997 was already the nation's largest pork processor and already slaughtered and processed over 95% of the hogs raised in North Carolina. During the growth years of the industry, a spirited and mutually benefi-cial rivalry existed between Luter, the pork processor, and Murphy, the hog producer. Each joked about the inherent superiority of his rival business model and about someday buying the other out and vertically integrat-ing all phases of the industry. Vertical integration would mean uniting the business from breeding to feed sales to finishing farms to slaughtering and processing and eventually to branded pork products for retail consumption into one big company.

As it turns out, Smithfield Foods did just that by skillfully exploiting a sustained downturn in pork prices in 1998 (Figure 12–3). This price decline caused substantial losses to corporate producers like Murphy Family Farms, while creating a windfall for Smithfield Foods. Smithfield Foods used this windfall to purchase North Carolina's largest corporate pork producers: Brown's of Carolina (1998), Carroll's Foods (1999), and finally Murphy Fam-ily Farms (2000). Vertical integration of domestic pork production and pro-cessing was good for Smithfield Foods; in the first *quarter* of 2000, just after its acquisition of Murphy Family Farms, sales totaled $1.4 billion, with quar-terly *after-tax* profits of $44.6 million, a 546% increase.

Today, Smithfield Foods owns or contracts for over 90% of all pork production and processing in North Carolina. Profits made in eastern North Carolina have been used to fund Smithfield's acquisition of 11 domestic and foreign competitors. With current operations in Canada,

Figure 12–3 National hog prices for the month of December from 1990 to 2001. *Source*: USDA National Agricultural Service.

Mexico, France, the United Kingdom, Poland, Romania, and China, Smithfield has positioned itself as a "domestic" producer in significant trade zones worldwide. Its brilliant business strategy illustrates another facet of our concept "externalities of scale." One multinational corporation financed its global expansion using profits extracted from a peripheral zone of concentrated production (see Lesson 3). The profitability of its production is increased substantially because the costs of waste disposal are paid by the human and biotic communities of eastern North Carolina.

POLITICS AND PROTEST

Thus far we have focused on changes to the pork industry, the social and environmental impacts, and the economic factors that propelled them. The transformation of North Carolina's hog industry from a sustainable small-scale system into the corporate-owned "swine factory" system we now have did not occur in a historical or political vacuum. A combination of events and individuals guided this shift and provided the driving force behind this 20-year overhaul. This section describes and details those events and individuals, starting with the role of the North Carolina state government in facilitating, regulating, and eventually collaborating with the hog industry. Next, we examine a vigorous and important coalition of community and environmental groups that mobilized to protest industry impacts and pressure the state government to act.

The Shifting Role of the State Government

Industry Facilitator To understand why the hog industry could grow so quickly in North Carolina, we need to return to the influence of Wendell Murphy. In addition to being the leading hog producer in the state, Murphy had been the college roommate of four-term Democratic governor James Hunt and served in the North Carolina General Assembly from 1982 to 1992. While in office he passed legislative acts to promote pork production as an alternative to tobacco in economically distressed eastern North Carolina. These actions included a bill that exempted large, CAFO-style hog operations from county-level zoning restrictions, an amendment that granted animal and poultry feeding operations immunity from North Carolina air and water standards, and a bill providing industry exemptions from selected state taxes and fees. This body of regulations, widely referred to as "Murphy's Laws" by industry critics, effectively promoted pork production. The North Carolina government actively promoted and encouraged the growth of CAFO-based pork production from the 1980s to the mid-1990s.

Industry Regulator By 1995, North Carolina found itself at the center of a growing national and regional debate and intensifying opposition. Then Governor Hunt responded with a blue ribbon commission to study agricultural waste. The commission's eventual report recommended much stronger state regulation of hog farms as well as stiffer penalties for violators. In August 1997, after months of intense lobbying, the North Carolina General Assembly passed the Clean Water Responsibility Act (CWRA), which imposed increased regulatory controls over the industry to protect air and water quality as well as a 2-year moratorium on new and expanded hog operations. Passage of the CWRA institutionalized a major shift in the role of state government from industry booster to regulator.

Industry Collaborator While the CWRA halted industry growth, it did not eliminate public pressure for a long-term solution to the hog waste issue. With Smithfield Foods consolidating ownership of the North Carolina hog industry, it became the focal point of anti-industry sentiments and activities. It also created an opportunity for then Attorney General Mike Easley to negotiate an agreement with only one party that would apparently cover the entire industry, lead to a long-term solution, and defuse a potent issue. In the Smithfield–Easley agreement of July 2000, Smithfield Foods agreed to provide $15 million over 10 years to fund research into alternative waste disposal technologies and to pay $50 million toward cleaning up abandoned waste lagoons and compliance monitoring. Additionally, Smithfield pledged to adopt the new technology on all company-owned farms within 3 years, if the technology were to prove economically feasible. In exchange for this, the state of North Carolina implicitly agreed to maintain the status quo until the research team made its recommendations.

The agreement was widely hailed as a breakthrough success and exemplary of the potential of public–private partnerships to solve environmental problems. Most people in the state considered the issue on the road to resolution. Efforts by environmentalists to point out flaws in the agreement gained little attention from the General Assembly, the press, or the public. Nevertheless, critics pointed out several flaws. First, Smithfield's profits were so great at the time that the agreement essentially required them to exchange 4 months worth of profits for 10 years of being left alone to continue polluting as usual. Second, the agreement applied only to the 276 hog operations directly owned by Smithfield Foods. It did not apply at all to the remaining 2,000 plus operations in the state even if those operations contracted with Smithfield Foods or its subsidiaries. In March 2006 a report detailing five alternative technologies was released. Yet, none of them was deemed to be cost-effective by Smithfield Foods, and to date none has been implemented. Before discussing how the North Carolina environmental community has responded to the current situation, we review the role of organized pork industry opposition.

Protest Against Pork Industry Impacts

The transformation of pork production in North Carolina and its social, environmental, and economic impacts did not go unchallenged. A vigorous opposition began to emerge at the end of the 1980s and continues to this day. In this section we describe that opposition and its accomplishments in protecting both residents and the environment.

Early Opposition   Organized opposition to swine CAFOs in eastern North Carolina first surfaced in 1990–1991 with the formation of a number of organizations that "were tired of hogs stinking up their environment and decided to fight back." Grassroots groups like the Alliance for a Responsible Swine Industry and Concerned Citizens of Tillery (CCT) worked with environmental organizations from the state capital in an unsuccessful effort to block a proposed 32,000 head per day slaughterhouse in Bladen County. CCT persuaded 42 North Carolina environmental and citizens' groups to form the Hog Roundtable in 1993. This unique coalition brought together grassroots, legal and mainstream environmental organizations with the dual goals of protecting communities from the environmental health hazards associated with intensive hog operations, as well as forging ties between environmental justice groups and mainstream environmental organizations (see Lessons 10 and 15). The Hog Roundtable further organized opposition to pork industry expansion and sought to put the social and environmental impacts on the public agenda.

Their efforts eventually attracted serious press attention in 1995. The *Raleigh News & Observer* published an investigative series entitled "Boss Hog: North Carolina's Pork Revolution". The series amplified the claims of industry critics who charged the pork industry with polluting the state's air and water, displacing traditional small farmers with vertically integrated corporations, and using its political ties to state lawmakers to avoid economic and environmental regulations. The "Boss Hog" series touched off a firestorm of reaction from virtually every interest group in the state with a stake in the industry and went on to win a Pulitzer Prize for public service reporting. Within months of its publication, heavy rains in eastern counties caused waste lagoons at seven hog facilities to burst and sprayfields to flood, and over the next few weeks over 40 million gallons of untreated swine feces and urine spilled into the streams and rivers of the coastal region. An estimated 10–15 million fish died as a result, and 364,000 acres of waterways were closed to commercial and recreational fishing.

Partial Resolution to This Most Contentious Issue   Public opposition, scientific study, and political debate over swine operations intensified; and by 1997 the politics of swine waste was the single largest and most contentious issue in North Carolina. The state capital became the scene of a series of protests organized by proponents on both sides of the issue. Hog Roundtable groups mobilized public concerns over odor, water pollution, equity, and recreation into an effective lobby, while the North Carolina Pork Council responded with a statewide public relations media campaign, asserting that hog farms were the economic lifeblood of the state and claiming an unmatched record of environmental stewardship. After months of intense lobbying, the North Carolina General Assembly in August 1997 passed the CWRA, which imposed increased regulatory controls over the industry to protect air and water quality, as well as a 2-year moratorium on new and expanded hog operations. Since 1997, hog industry opponents have exerted enough political pressure to maintain the moratorium on swine industry expansion past its initial 2 years through a series of extensions due to expire in September 2007.

Passage of the moratorium, however, proved to be a double-edged sword. Freezing the 1997 hog population in place did prevent the magnitude of environmental impacts from escalating further, but waste from a stable population of 9 million hogs still produces substantial adverse impacts year in and year out. Passage of the moratorium also undercut the political clout of future opposition by creating the perception among the general public that the problem had been solved.

Recent Progress   In 2007, after 10 years supporting the moratorium they worked so hard to get in place, North Carolina's environmental community changed course. Rather than support another extension, they now oppose moratorium extensions and are mobilizing support for a permanent ban on lagoon and sprayfield disposal technologies. Current efforts proceed along two paths. First, concerted efforts are under way to recruit and train a network of citizen water-quality monitors to document the environmental impacts of swine CAFOs. Some citizen monitors work with volunteer pilots to photo, video, and document by global positioning systems (GPS) CAFOs from the air, while others collect surface water samples regularly at appropriate locations. Samples will be tested by an independent lab and compiled into a comprehensive, longitudinal water-quality data set. Second, analyses of the data will better document adverse environmental impacts and results will be communicated through scientific reports, press releases, and other educational materials intended to persuade the public and policymakers that a long-term solution to swine waste disposal must be implemented. Recent persuasion activities have consisted of two lobby days mobilizing citizens from around the state to visit elected representatives at the state capitol and a 51-hour occupation of the central plaza at the North Carolina State General Assembly.

As we write this, the North Carolina General Assembly debates a new hog waste bill that enjoys the support of environmental, farm, and industry groups in the state. The bill would allow existing waste lagoons to continue operations but prevent new ones from being built. Hog operations needing to replace aging lagoons would have to convert to a waste disposal system that meets new, stricter environmental standards. The state will provide $2 million a year to subsidize conversion costs as well as a pilot program to generate electricity from the methane gas emitted by hog waste lagoons.

CONCLUSIONS

This lesson has described how the industrialization of hog production in North Carolina has created a host of "externalities of scale" that were absent in traditional hog farming. These externalities include health risks, farm loss, reduced quality of life, and environmental degradation. Currently, this situation remains unresolved, with the waste from the production and slaughter of 10 million hogs still concentrated in an ecologically fragile region, with a disproportionate number of poor and minority residents.

While the environmental dangers of this industry are described only for eastern North Carolina in this lesson, they are increasingly global in scope. The industry, led by Smithfield Foods, has expanded into both nationwide and international production. In Utah, Circle Four Farms, a subsidiary of Smithfield, produces pork for the U.S. West Coast markets. Additionally, starting in 1998, Smithfield has expanded into the international market through the acquisitions of foreign hog producers and processors, such as Animex in Poland (1999), Mitchell's in Canada (2000), NORSON in Mexico (2000), AFG in China (2002), and SFGP in France (1999). In Poland, Smithfield Foods made clear its intentions to export the "North Carolina miracle" of vertically integrated industrial-style pork production. Continued diffusion of this industrial model of hog production will also extend related environmental issues to a global scale.

Furthermore, the lessons that can be drawn from CAFO-style pork production can easily be extended to apply to nearly all manner of industrial protein production. The poultry industry pioneered the mechanized model that Wendell Murphy adapted to swine. Catfish, salmon, tilapia, shrimp, scallops, oysters, and beef are all currently being raised in similar fashion. With this form of factory agriculture becoming the norm across all manner of meat production, the issues and concerns raised about pork production in North Carolina have general implications up and down the global supply chain.

SOURCES

Edwards, Bob, and Anthony E. Ladd. 2000. "Environmental Justice, Swine Production and Farm Loss in North Carolina." *Sociological Spectrum* 20:263–90.

Furuseth, Owen. 1997. "Restructuring of Hog Farming in NC: Explosion and Implosion." *Professional Geographer* 49:391–403.

Juska, Arunas, and Bob Edwards. 2004. "Refusing the Trojan Pig: The Trans-Atlantic Coalition Corporate Pork Production in Poland." Pp. 187–207 in *Coalitions Across Borders: Transnational Protest and the Neoliberal Order*, edited by Joe Bandy and Jackie Smith. Lanham, MD: Rowman & Littlefield.

Ladd, Anthony and Bob Edwards. 2002. "Corporate Swine, Capitalist Pigs: A Decade of Environmental Injustice in North Carolina." *Social Justice* 29(3):26–46.

North Carolina Department of Environment and Natural Resources. 1999. Framework for the Conversion of Anaerobic Swine Waste Lagoons and Sprayfields. Office of the Governor: Raleigh, NC.

Smithfield. 2007. "About Smithfield." Retrieved March 5, 2007 (http://www.smithfield.com/about/index.php).

Stith, Pat, Joby Warrick, and Melanie Sill. 1995. "Boss Hog: North Carolina's Pork Revolution." *News and Observer*, February 19–26, 1A–16A.

Tietz, Jeff. 2006. "Boss Hog." *Rolling Stone*, December 14. Retrieved March 5, 2007 (http://www.rollingstone.com/politics/story/12840743/).

Wilson, William Julius. 1990. *The Truly Disadvantaged: The Inner City, the Underclass, and Public Policy*. Chicago, IL: University of Chicago Press.

Wing, Steve, Dana Cole, and Gary Grant. 2000. "Environmental Injustice in North Carolina's Hog Industry." *Environmental Health Perspectives* 108:225–31.

13

Understanding Disaster Vulnerability
Floods and Hurricanes

Nicole Youngman

W e tend to think of "natural disasters" as sudden, extreme events that have their origins in the workings of the Earth's physical systems. Other kinds of disasters, like oil spills or failed dams, seem to have clearly anthropogenic (human) causes. But even though different kinds of disasters may have different *triggers*, which may or may not be the direct result of human activities, they are all caused by *interactions* among three overlapping systems: human social and cultural systems, the built environment, and the preexisting natural environments in which they are embedded. The impacts of all disasters, from tornado touchdowns to nuclear meltdowns, are directly related to how and where human societies organize themselves. And while disasters always create *community* (rather than simply individual) trauma, some residents of disaster-prone areas are much more vulnerable to extreme losses than others.

Hurricane Katrina's impact in August of 2005 demonstrated how a myriad of human and nonhuman factors can come together to produce a profoundly traumatic event. Over 1,700 people were killed in the storm, most of whom were in Louisiana, with a few hundred in Mississippi and a handful in surrounding states. The flood that accompanied the storm engulfed 80% of New Orleans, inundated nearly all of St. Bernard and Plaquemines Parishes (counties) to the city's south and east, and largely obliterated the Mississippi Gulf Coast. In this case, the disaster's trigger—the hurricane itself—was a natural and normal (though exceptionally large) event for the Gulf Coast. But while the unprecedented 30-foot storm surge that hit the Mississippi coast was directly generated by the storm, extensive development along the state's beaches, particularly the large number of casinos built in recent decades, had placed many more people and structures in harm's way than had existed there during previous hurricanes. In the New Orleans area, the effects of development were even more pronounced. The city's approximately 1,100 deaths and widespread destruction were caused by its failed flood-control system, which in turn was caused by a combination of poor engineering practices, unwise land-use decisions, and the metro area's long history of prioritizing economic growth over public safety. Not surprisingly, the city's most vulnerable residents—those who were poor, African American, and/or elderly—were hit especially hard (see Lesson 10). Rather than declaring the hurricane an "act of God" for which no one was responsible, the residents of New Orleans and its eastern suburbs responded to the disaster with an extraordinary amount of anger and a profound sense of betrayal, insisting that the Katrina flood was a human-made, not a "natural," disaster.

DISASTERS AND DENIAL

In decades past, it was all too common for "city boosters" or "growth machines"–the local government, business elites, and their allies in the media–to simply deny that natural disasters posed any real threat to the well-being of their city. Investors or residents might be scared away, after all, if they became too concerned that all their assets might come tumbling down in the face of high winds, storm surges, or suddenly shifting earth. This rhetoric of denial would sometimes go so far as to claim that a recent disaster hadn't even occurred or that its effects were minimal; even worse, news of an approaching disaster might be deliberately kept from the public in the name of "avoiding panic." In California, Los Angeles newspapers have insisted on calling local tornadoes "high winds" despite clear funnel cloud sightings, and the San Francisco earthquake of 1906 was repeatedly referred to as merely a "great fire" in its immediate aftermath. Before the Galveston hurricane of 1900, which killed several thousand people, city boosters and prominent meteorologists alike claimed that it was scientifically impossible for their city to be hit by a hurricane, insisting that Texas was a paradise of constantly perfect weather. During the Florida land rush that took place before the Lake Okeechobee hurricane in 1928, real estate con artists insisted that *mosquitoes* were unknown in south Florida; hurricanes were simply not to be mentioned at all. And in New Orleans, news of the enormous flood occurring upriver along the Mississippi in 1927 was not allowed in the newspapers until the river crest was dangerously close to the city–a strategy that likely caused considerably more panic than regular updates might have.

More recently, however, this "everything is just fine" mantra has shifted from "there is no problem" to "the problem can be kept under control." Rather than denying that natural disasters can and do occur, officials have tended to emphasize the saving grace of modern technology, particularly regarding flood control. With proper knowledge and funding, they insist, modern engineering can keep water out of where it is not wanted indefinitely; the only problem lies in finding the best ways to accomplish the task. In disaster-prone locations, this faith in technology can be as dangerous as the earlier denials of vulnerability; but without it, municipalities in risky areas simply cannot continue to exist (see Lesson 8). Even in the aftermath of a catastrophic storm, when undeniable failures have occurred, the emphasis is almost always on finding and fixing the problems, with the assumption that such efforts will prevent a recurrence of the disaster and business as usual will be able to resume.

Both of these approaches allow powerful government and business interests to avoid acknowledging any fault or liability for how natural disasters impact their communities and to ignore the more difficult questions of how to create communities that are sustainable in the face of inevitable extreme natural events. Although violent weather and seismic events are innate characteristics of the places in which they occur–and thus should be considered a part of "normal," everyday life–municipal growth machines and their allies have largely continued to treat them as though they were rare and surprising rather than likely and expected occurrences, either by ignoring the risks altogether or by claiming to have those risks under control. What should be predictable damage in disaster-vulnerable communities can then be shrugged off as unforeseeable "acts of God" that are unlikely to recur. In reality, however, they are very much the result of previous development decisions and cultural patterns that tend to ignore or downplay any potential for eventual catastrophe and shrug off the reality of risk inequalities in the name of encouraging "economic growth."

THINKING ABOUT VULNERABILITY

Despite these official efforts at denial, natural disaster vulnerability is increasing worldwide, particularly as coastal developments and populations grow rapidly and as industrialization and urbanization continue to expand. Sociologists distinguish among different types of vulnerability however, particularly between physical vulnerability and social vulnerability. *Physical vulnerability* generally refers to one's geographic location; different parts of the world, of course, are more prone to various kinds of natural disasters than others. More specific locations matter, too: living downstream or next to a dam or levee that might break, on a hillside prone to slide in heavy rains, or in a poorly constructed dwelling increases one's risk of experiencing a catastrophe. This type of physical vulnerability is sometimes referred to as "unsafe conditions." *Social vulnerability* refers to preexisting conditions, rooted in social inequalities, that affect potential disaster victims' ability to escape, survive, and/or "bounce back" from a disaster: race, class, gender, age, disability, health status, etc. Physical and social vulnerability are frequently intertwined in complex ways and can exist at the individual, household, or community level.

The New Orleans flood provides several clear examples of how physical and social vulnerability can intersect. In some ways, physical vulnerability in the city cuts across racial and class lines. Many relatively wealthy, mostly white neighborhoods in and near the city, such as Lakeview, are extremely vulnerable to flooding. Lakeview is immediately adjacent to the 17th Street Canal, which is one of the city's primary drainage canals, and to Lake Pontchartrain. Likewise, the low-income, predominantly African American Ninth Ward is low-lying and adjacent to the Industrial Canal, which connects the lake and the Mississippi River, making it also at high risk for flooding (and in fact it did flood badly during Hurricane Betsy in 1965). When floodwalls around the city broke from Katrina's storm surge, Lakeview and the Ninth Ward both had homes near the canals torn apart from the force of the water, while homes farther from the canals quickly filled to their second stories. Meanwhile, other wealthier (and, again, predominantly white) neighborhoods such as the Garden District, as well as poorer (and predominantly African American) neighborhoods such as the Irish Channel, escaped flooding because they were built on higher ground in older sections of the city.

This does not, however, mean that these two flooded communities are equally vulnerable to disasters overall. Because Lakeview residents generally have considerably more financial resources and human capital at their disposal, they are much more likely to be able to eventually return and rebuild if they so desire or to "start over" elsewhere if they prefer. This is not to say that the recovery process is not difficult at best for all of Katrina's victims; lengthy, exhausting struggles with insurance companies and government relief programs, for instance, abound throughout the Gulf Coast. But even so, wealthier victims are more likely to have had sufficient insurance in the first place, to have well-paying jobs to return to and high-quality schools and daycare available, and to have the skills and social networks necessary to negotiate the piles of paperwork and extensive new regulations that flourish in a postdisaster environment. In the first 2 years after Katrina, wealthier New Orleans neighborhoods made slow but steady progress toward rebuilding, while the Ninth Ward and other lower-income areas remained largely vacant.

Gender issues, too, play an important role in determining disaster vulnerability. While our society is considerably less patriarchal (male-dominated) than it has been in the past, women of all races and social classes still tend to find themselves dealing with considerably heavier child care, elder care, and housework responsibilities than men. For single mothers, this is obviously a huge burden, but even married women with jobs and incomes comparable to their spouses' often find themselves in this position due to cultural norms that still consider such activities "women's work." In the aftermath of a disaster, these "traditional gender roles" tend to be exacerbated, even for couples that have tried to create more egalitarian relationships. With buildings and infrastructures heavily damaged and many residents unable to return, schools and daycare centers may be unable to reopen for months after the disaster or may close permanently. Traumatized children, who may have lost their homes and belongings and/or had family members die, often "act out" in ways that can be difficult for their caregivers to predict or cope with. Widespread damage to businesses and office buildings can create long commutes for those relatively lucky residents who are able to go back to work when their jobs are forced to relocate to more distant locations.

With no outside help caring for children or elderly family members, many women end up staying home to tackle these responsibilities full-time while their male partners (who usually earn more than they do, even if both had worked outside the home previously) put in extraordinarily long hours commuting to work. Both single- and two-parent families may find themselves unable to return home at all without child care available since the situation makes it impossible for mothers to go back to work and many families rely on women's incomes to survive economically. Women also tend to find themselves with the primary responsibilities of applying for disaster aid—which often involves standing in long lines for many hours, with young children in tow—and dealing with the contractors who arrive to repair their homes, some of whom turn out to be con artists who take victims' money and promptly disappear. The stresses of dealing with these kinds of situations on an everyday basis can lead to significant marital and other family problems, particularly when men and women are facing different kinds of stresses and may have different coping strategies (for example, talking about them vs. "being strong" and "bottling up" emotions), making communication difficult.

Hurricane evacuations also provide examples of different kinds of physical and social vulnerability. For low-income residents, the physical vulnerability of living in a disaster-prone location is frequently compounded by the physical inability to leave when disaster threatens. Pre-Katrina research in the New Orleans area had clearly demonstrated that at least 100,000 residents did not have cars and thus would be unable to leave in advance of a major hurricane. This problem became all too obvious when tens of thousands of New Orleanians, almost all of them African American, fled to the Superdome and the Convention Center downtown before, during, and immediately after Katrina made landfall, remaining stranded in the blistering heat for days with little or no food, water, or sanitation. The preexisting social vulnerabilities these victims faced led directly to extreme physical vulnerability, making them exponentially more likely to become trapped (and perhaps die) in the storm or its chaotic aftermath.

Not everyone who fails to evacuate in advance of a hurricane stays behind for simple lack of transportation, however. Figuring out when and whether to go, even when told by authorities that leaving would be the best option, can be very tricky. Gas, meals, and hotels while on the road can be very expensive, especially for those whose incomes are marginal. Employers and schools may be reluctant to close down until the very last minute, prolonging the decision-making process for those who are dependent on them. Traveling with children (and pets) is difficult and stressful under normal circumstances; spending hour after hour in traffic that barely moves is much worse. Not all cars are reliable, and even vehicles in good condition can break down in the stop-and-go circumstances of evacuating in ninety-degree weather, leaving their occupants potentially stranded and in an even more dangerous situation while the storm approaches. And to make things worse, since it is impossible to predict exactly where the eye wall of a hurricane will hit more than several hours in advance, some evacuations turn out to have been unnecessary, resulting in wasted time, money, and stress for many thousands of people. It is hardly surprising, then, that many coastal residents are extremely reluctant to put themselves through such an ordeal and may choose to risk the storm instead.

Failure to truly understand one's physical vulnerability—or a stubborn refusal to accept it—can also lead to a failure to evacuate. Paradoxically, both a lack of experience with hurricanes and considerable experience "riding them out" can give coastal residents a false sense of security, leading them to underestimate the true danger of a major storm. In rapidly growing coastal areas, newer residents who have no experience with hurricanes and therefore no idea what to expect when a warning is issued may assume that the risk is manageable if they stay home. But even longtime residents, who often have been through many smaller storms (or only the edges of bigger ones) with little more than power outages and downed trees to deal with, can easily arrive at the faulty conclusion that they can get through any hurricane with only a few inconveniences. Those who have made it safely through truly horrendous storms are also likely to assume (not entirely irrationally) that since they and/or their homes survived the worst that nature could dish out, they can successfully weather any subsequent storms. Some Mississippi residents who got through Hurricane Camille in 1969, for instance—a category 5 storm with 200 mph winds and a 28-foot surge—failed to evacuate for Katrina, mistakenly assuming that no storm could possibly be any worse than what they had already experienced. A long period of time between hurricane "hits" can play a role in development and evacuation decisions, too. Coastal communities tend to develop "hurricane amnesia" when memories of the last terrible storm fade, which encourages a push for more "economic growth" in their region, increasing the area's long-term physical vulnerability as more businesses, residents, and tourists move in.

Finally, it is important to note that more than 60% of the people who drowned in Hurricane Katrina were over 61 years of age, demonstrating another mixture of physical and social vulnerability. For older people, the evacuation process can be frightening and difficult enough that "riding it out" seems like a comparatively smaller risk. While the prospect of a long road trip—perhaps to an unknown destination for an undetermined amount of time—may seem manageable or even a bit exciting for those who are younger, healthy, and have some financial resources to fall back on, the elderly frequently live on fixed incomes and often must deal with a variety of health and mobility problems: poor hearing or eyesight, difficulty walking, arthritis pain, etc. They are also likely to require medication for severe conditions such as heart problems, high blood pressure, or diabetes and thus depend heavily upon remaining close to their own familiar doctors and pharmacists. These difficulties can make traveling any distance unpleasant at best and dangerous at worst. Residents of New Orleans-area nursing homes, entirely dependent on others' evacuation decisions, were particularly at risk in Katrina. Some nursing home directors, faced with the extreme difficulty and expense of safely moving their residents (many of whom were on oxygen, severely disabled, etc.), decided that staying put was less risky—sometimes with tragic results as water rapidly filled their facilities and there was no way to get the residents out in time.

STRUCTURAL AND INFRASTRUCTURAL MITIGATION: DECREASING OR INCREASING VULNERABILITY?

Communities at risk for disasters have three basic options for trying to mitigate (lessen or prevent) their impacts: structural mitigation, infrastructural mitigation, and nonstructural mitigation. *Structural mitigation* generally refers to strategies in coastal areas and river floodplains that emphasize large engineering "megaprojects" to stop flooding and erosion, such as levees, floodwalls, groins, bank stabilization, and beach renourishment. *Infrastructures* are those things that physically tie a community together, including the drinking water, sewerage and drainage systems, roads and bridges, phone and Internet lines and towers, and power and gas lines. *Infrastructural mitigation* strategies, then, are efforts to make these systems more resilient to high winds, floodwaters, or seismic activity. Stronger building codes, too, are sometimes considered infrastructural mitigation. *Nonstructural mitigation* generally focuses more on keeping people (and property) out of harm's way in the first place: stricter zoning laws that prohibit or severely restrict building in some parts of a floodplain or coastal area, for instance, or restoring wetlands that absorb floodwaters and storm surges. In extreme cases this can mean moving entire communities to higher ground, which some small Midwestern towns chose to do after the enormous Mississippi River flood of 1993. Flood and other disaster insurance, too, can be considered nonstructural mitigation.

Infrastructural mitigation tends to be one of the first things emergency management officials and government agencies try to improve after a disaster strikes (or nearly strikes), in an effort to quickly and effectively reduce their community's vulnerability. Communications systems, in particular, are obviously crucial during search and rescue operations and all too frequently fail completely or prove to be incompatible among different agencies under extreme conditions. Postdisaster mitigation planning, then, frequently focuses on finding new ways to ensure that police, firefighters, and other "first responders" can continue to communicate with one another despite widespread devastation. During Katrina, some local police resorted to using lower-tech personal walkie-talkies as they searched for survivors; future strategies include relying more heavily on redundant, higher-tech devices such as satellite phones that are less dependent on local infrastructures for power or signal transfer capabilities.

New Orleans' experience with improving evacuation routes is an interesting case of infrastructural mitigation that was, eventually, highly effective. In a strange way, the city was actually very lucky to have gone through a couple of "near misses" before being inundated by Katrina. Hurricane Georges in 1998 and Hurricane Ivan in 2004 were both extremely powerful storms that came very close to hitting the city before veering away at the final hour. When Georges threatened, the city had not had a serious storm scare since Hurricane Betsy in 1965 and "hurricane amnesia" had long set in. Between these storms, neither residents nor the city government had considered hurricane risk a particularly salient issue, especially in a city with so many other pressing urban problems. Georges scared residents badly enough, however, that tens of thousands tried to flee all at once via I-10, the primary route into and out of the city. Not surprisingly, this led quickly to extraordinary gridlock. The trip to Baton Rouge, for instance, which normally takes about an hour, became a 9- or 10-hour ordeal. Having a huge number of motorists trapped on highways in an approaching hurricane—especially highways that, like in New Orleans, frequently pass over bodies of water—is an absolute nightmare for emergency planners, one that might have come true had Georges not turned and hit Mississippi.

After Georges, emergency planners and traffic engineers created a "contraflow" plan, which would close the interstates to inbound traffic around New Orleans and allow motorists to travel the "wrong way" on those lanes during evacuations, effectively doubling the highways' outbound capacities. When Hurricane Ivan threatened several years later and Mayor Ray Nagin advised residents to evacuate, the contraflow plan was implemented for the first time; but it ran into several snags. It took several hours to set up, was implemented only on the western side of the metro area, and created enormous bottlenecks in spots where interstates merged or where motorists were supposed to cross back over to the proper lanes to allow two-way traffic to resume. As a result, motorists were again trapped on the road for huge stretches of time as they tried to leave. For instance, drivers who tried to avoid the worst traffic by going northeast across Lake Pontchartrain before heading north found themselves trapped on I-10 over the lake for as long as 6 hours—on a stretch of highway that normally takes less than 10 minutes to traverse.

After Ivan demonstrated the severe flaws in the contraflow plan, however, a much better implementation strategy was worked out. The system was set up more quickly as Katrina approached, and motorists on different sides of I-10 were forcibly "funneled" in different directions as they reached intersections with other highways, considerably cutting back on the "bottleneck" problem, though it did require drivers to know well in advance what lanes they needed to be in to go the direction they desired. While the new plan was not perfect and traffic was still very slow, it was an enormous improvement over previous efforts and several hundred thousand New Orleans area residents (as well as many others in even higher-risk areas to the south) were able to leave before Katrina made landfall. It is, of course, important to note that this approach was only "successful" for those who had the means to leave on their own and did nothing to help those without reliable transportation.

New Orleans' experience with the contraflow plans highlights three concerns that disaster researchers have been expressing for decades. First, at-risk communities tend to rely almost entirely on structural and infrastructural mitigation techniques, at the expense of nonstructural strategies (such as restoring adjacent wetlands or moving people out of an area's most flood-prone locations) that have the potential to be far more effective over the long term. Second, these mitigation efforts tend to be "event-driven" rather than "threat-driven," designed and implemented *after* a disaster strikes rather than as a result of a careful risk analysis beforehand. Finally, structural and infrastructural techniques do not protect all members of a community equally. All these tendencies actually serve to increase rather than decrease communities' long-term disaster risks, but persuading governments, businesses, industries, and residents to place more emphasis on nonstructural mitigation methods is difficult for several reasons.

Residents and business interests that have been traumatized by a major flood or hurricane understandably want their community back the way it was as soon as possible. City growth machines must work to encourage (re)investment in their area by somehow overcoming the negative images and impressions of their community as destroyed and chaotic, in order to restore confidence in its ability to rebound from the disaster and "get back to normal." Disaster victims tend to pressure their elected officials at all levels of government to find a way to "fix" their disaster vulnerability problem, to "do something, now!!" to ensure that such an event never happens again—but without forcing the community to make any drastic land-use changes. If ideas for long-term mitigation conflict with the community's immediate goals of getting the surrounding natural systems back under control, allowing residents to rebuild their homes, and returning to the normal routine of encouraging growth and development, they will almost always be rejected out of hand.

Not surprisingly, then, the postdisaster mitigation solutions that communities decide upon usually involve more (or improved) flood control structures, along with better evacuation routes and stronger building codes. Rezoning hazardous areas and moving human development away from them altogether, which would allow floodwaters to come and go in mostly unoccupied areas and thus provide better long-term risk reduction, are rarely considered seriously. Instead, at-risk communities repeatedly try to remove the dynamic, shifting aspects of the natural hydrological systems in which they are embedded and somehow make the land and water hold still indefinitely so that the area can continue to be developed and therefore "used." This approach ensures that as much land as possible will remain open to profitable (re)development, rather than being turned into less immediately beneficial spillways, "natural" beaches, or "green space." Ironically, communities hit by floods or hurricanes often find themselves in the midst of a building boom as the real estate industry works not only to rebuild what was destroyed but also to purchase and redevelop land that had once been vacant or built with small single-family homes, turning it into high-rise hotels and condominiums. The Alabama coast, for instance, has been through this process twice in recent decades, once after Hurricane Frederic in 1979 and again following Hurricane Ivan in 2004, after which signs appeared reading "Pardon our progress as we rebuild" along the main beachfront highway, as though the coast were merely a large shopping mall.

In decades past, these efforts to "conquer nature" were considered a noble cause that served to benefit the entire community. Experience has shown, however, that constructing elaborate structural flood mitigation systems frequently backfires. Such systems tend to create a vicious cycle that encourages more and more development in disaster-prone areas, which then needs increasingly higher levels of "protection," which then encourages still more development. Levees give communities a false sense of security, something tangible that can make residents feel safe (and does, in fact, provide safety in smaller flood events) until they create an even bigger disaster when a flood too large for them to contain eventually occurs. Exceptionally large floods are actually more dangerous with levees than they would have been without, creating huge surges of rising water that wipe out everything in their path when the levees finally break, giving victims little or no warning or time to escape.

This kind of overreliance on structural mitigation is especially acute in New Orleans, which is extremely low-lying (although contrary to many media reports, only about half of the city is actually below sea level) and has no natural means of drainage. The city has always relied on an elaborate system of levees and pumps for safety from floodwaters, and as it grew over a period of 300 years, development reached farther and farther into lower and lower areas. This process was greatly accelerated in the early and mid-twentieth century, when new technologies and a growing population made it possible to drain and fill swamplands, bayous, and the lakefront area to create new middle- and upper-class housing developments. The same time period saw the construction of the aforementioned Industrial Canal, along with the Intracoastal Waterway and the Mississippi River-Gulf Outlet (referred to as the MR-GO, pronounced "Mr. Go"). Over time, these three shipping shortcuts—particularly the MR-GO—destroyed massive areas of wetlands by introducing saltwater from the Gulf of Mexico and provided new routes for storm surges to be "funneled" into the city, which happened in both Hurricanes Betsy and Katrina. In Katrina, this "funnel effect" was coupled with the "complete catastrophic failure" of several other elements of the city's flood control system, most of which had been constructed by the U.S. Army Corps of Engineers with the assurance that it would withstand up to a "fast-moving category 3" hurricane.

However, post-Katrina forensics investigations conducted by three different teams of civil engineers—one from Louisiana State University, one from the University of California at Berkeley, and one from the Corps itself—all concluded that the Corps' designs for these levees and floodwalls were badly flawed and, thus, the failure of the system was inevitable with a large storm surge. These reports clearly demonstrated that, although one could fairly argue that residents of a city with a long history of catastrophic flooding had made a conscious decision to risk such a disaster by continuing to live there, not all of the flood risk in New Orleans was actually known and, therefore, some of residents' risk was decidedly involuntary rather than freely chosen. This is, of course, even more true of many lower-income residents, who lived in some of the most risky areas because that was what they could afford rather than because they enjoyed being near the water. In short, over a period of several decades, public safety in the New Orleans area was repeatedly compromised by a faulty flood control system created for the sake of encouraging "economic growth" via the shipping and real estate industries, with catastrophic long-term effects.

The situation is further complicated by the severe loss of wetlands that South Louisiana has experienced over the last several decades. This loss is partly due to the levees along the Mississippi River, which do not allow the river to overflow and deposit any new sediment along its floodplain, making it impossible for the land-building process that created that part of Louisiana to continue. Meanwhile, the soft, highly organic alluvial soils the river had previously deposited over a period of about 6,000–7,000 years continue to subside (contract and sink), allowing the Gulf of Mexico to reach farther and farther into the state's interior, slowly destroying coastal communities and increasingly threatening New Orleans. This process is further exacerbated by the sea level rise created by global warming (see Lesson 14).

The oil and natural gas industry, too, bears a significant portion of the blame for Louisiana's wetlands loss. Over the last century, the industry has carved literally many thousands of miles of exploration canals throughout the coastal areas, interfering with the region's natural hydrology and, like the MR-GO, allowing massive saltwater intrusion that has killed vast areas of freshwater wetlands. Despite widespread knowledge and recognition of this issue, however, the oil and gas companies have never been held responsible for the damage they have created, or for the communities they have destroyed or endangered. Recent efforts to earmark some oil revenues for coastal restoration projects have focused on giving Louisiana a greater share of the royalties formerly paid entirely to the federal government. These new royalty payments to Louisiana, however, will only come from offshore drilling for new wells, encouraging further oil exploration (and further contributing to global warming) while providing nowhere near the amount of funding truly needed to "save the coast." The continued overreliance on new and improved levees, then, not only allows landowners to expect protection without changing their land-use patterns; it also lets the oil industry "off the hook" by allowing it to continue business as usual while making token but highly publicized payments to "coastal restoration" efforts.

The timber industry in Louisiana has played a role in the state's wetlands loss as well. Massive cypress forests in and around New Orleans, which had once provided significant protection from storm surges, were logged and destroyed many decades ago. Efforts to allow the forests to regrow are complicated by the fact that many of those that still exist are on private property and continue to be periodically "harvested." Today, the wood is often chipped for use in garden and landscaping mulch, which is tremendously ironic since the huge trees cut in ages past were highly valued for their incredible strength and ability to withstand a hot and humid climate. Early homes in New Orleans were often built of cypress, and today antique dealers charge a premium for old doors and furniture made with this sturdy wood. Area environmental activists have encouraged gardeners to boycott cypress mulch and have lobbied large companies like Wal-Mart and Home Depot to stop selling it, raising the ire of the owners of large tracts of cypress who insist that their rights as property owners are being infringed upon and that in any case their actions are not truly harming the environment.

FLOOD INSURANCE: ENCOURAGING RISKY BEHAVIOR

Disaster researchers have also heavily criticized the National Flood Insurance Program (NFIP) for increasing flood risks nationwide. Created in 1968, the program was intended to help people living in flood- and hurricane-prone areas recover from catastrophic floods, but unfortunately it has had a number of unintended consequences. When Hurricane Betsy hit New Orleans in 1965, one of the most salient political issues during the relief and recovery effort was the fact that the vast majority of victims' losses had been uninsured because homeowners insurance did not (and still does not) cover flood losses. The NFIP was supposed to help ameliorate this problem by providing low-cost flood insurance to those who were already living in coastal areas and flood plains, while discouraging further development in such risky areas. Municipalities had to choose whether or not to join the program, which would then make insurance available to residents with the requirement that local governments adopt land-use policies that would not increase the number of residents and businesses in high-risk areas.

This provision of the NFIP, however, has been poorly enforced since its inception. While the program has in fact provided much needed relief to homeowners who lost everything in floods—particularly for lower-income families living in floodplains because they simply cannot afford to move to higher ground—it has also inadvertently encouraged growth and development in low-lying and coastal areas by making insurance available in places that had previously been uninsurable and allowing repeat claims for properties that flood frequently. Economists refer to this phenomenon as a "moral hazard"—a change in peoples' risk-taking behavior brought about by the availability of insurance. While insurance is technically a kind of nonstructural mitigation, the problems created by the NFIP are very similar to those created by levees: helping to diminish risk in the short term, while actually making things worse in the long term.

The existence of a federal flood insurance program has also exacerbated disaster victims' already difficult task of applying for settlements from their homeowners' insurance companies. After a major hurricane, when insurance companies face many thousands of claims for the same event, it is to their benefit to award each homeowner as little as possible in order to keep their total payout lower. Because homeowners insurance will only pay for wind damage, while the NFIP only covers flood damage, property owners with both kinds of policies frequently find themselves facing the rather surreal process of dealing with appraisers whose job it is to determine what percentage of their home was damaged and what percentage of that damage was due strictly to wind or to the storm surge. Given that hurricanes bring both, this distinction can be somewhat nonsensical in ordinary terms, but homeowners insurance companies have a vested interest in declaring that most of the damage they survey is from water rather than wind, while appraisers from the NFIP may be making the opposite assertion.

Other forms of government disaster relief, too, can be rendered considerably less effective thanks to this dilemma. The "Road Home" program created in Louisiana after Hurricane Katrina, which was designed to provide flooded-out homeowners with rebuilding grants of up to $150,000, is a good example. The program was funded with federal appropriations but administered by a private company hired by the state; it was plagued with massive administration problems from its inception. This was complicated by the fact that the program was designed to augment, rather than replace, whatever settlements homeowners received from their preexisting policies. Road Home grants were decreased according to the payments applicants were supposed to receive from their insurance companies, even while insurance companies were reducing their awards so that the government program would make up the difference. Homeowners remained stuck in the middle for months or even years, with heavily damaged homes, two or three programs that were supposed to provide funding for rebuilding, and no actual checks in the mail, all while each program tried to pass off its costs onto the others. And buying new insurance or renewing existing policies post-Katrina turned out to be an even worse nightmare. With many insurance companies in the area dropping wind and hail coverage altogether, homeowners seeking to rebuild their homes or move into new ones found themselves forced to buy three separate insurance policies from three separate companies: homeowners insurance for theft, fire, and liability; a second policy elsewhere for wind and hail; and an NFIP policy for floods. Needless to say, this reality sent insurance costs skyrocketing and, in some cases, kept storm victims from being able to repair or sell their homes or to buy new ones.

DECREASING VULNERABILITY?

Finding viable solutions to the complicated, intertwined realities of flood and hurricane vulnerability is extremely difficult, to say the least. Improved evacuation planning and more sensible and equitable insurance policies are certainly important but do very little to tackle the underlying issues of disaster *resiliency and sustainability*—enabling communities to "bounce back" quickly from an extreme natural event with a minimum of damage and losses over the long term. Instead, these approaches continue to rely on a philosophy that could perhaps be characterized as "run like hell, then come back and fix it if you can." The inequalities built into our social system, however, simply do not give all potential disaster victims an equal ability to run away, or to come back and fix the damage to their lives and property after the initial danger has passed. Stricter building codes, including elevation requirements, are certainly a step in the right direction; but they tend to be fought by real estate interests and become watered down or unenforced by state and local governments, to the point of being almost meaningless—and are frequently prohibitively expensive for residents to implement without considerable financial assistance.

Even so, switching to a heavier reliance on nonstructural mitigation is problematic as well, both from a political and a social justice standpoint. Disaster relief in the United States has been increasingly federalized over the last several decades and focuses largely on upholding the institution of private property. While homeowners may be eligible for a variety of loans and grants after disasters, there are few programs aimed at helping renters or public housing residents move back home, find new permanent housing, and get back on their feet. Structural mitigation, too, is largely aimed at protecting (and sometimes even creating) private property; and communities are likely to choose those structures that take up the least amount of space (that is, levees over "green space" and floodwalls over levees) in order to allow as much development as possible. Property rights organizations are prone to fight any government attempts to restrict what owners can do with their property but still insist that owners' investments should be protected with massive projects built at taxpayers' expense, even if they are along a beach or in a floodplain.

Not all resistance to nonstructural mitigation planning comes from wealthy property owners, however. Low- or modest-income residents often fear—not illogically—that attempts to rebuild their towns or cities with radically different "footprints" after a severe flood are merely thinly disguised "land grabs" aimed at taking over and destroying their public housing projects or other neighborhoods, turning them into city-owned parks or privately developed, highly profitable condominium complexes. Increasing emphasis on nonstructural mitigation after a catastrophe involves determining who will and will not be allowed to have their neighborhoods back, which raises difficult questions of equity, justice, and fair compensation. And while some federal government policies exist to help residents move to higher ground rather than rebuild in place, they have never been implemented on a wide enough scale to help communities like New Orleans shift massive sections of their population to other parts of town, even assuming that enough people were willing to move in the first place.

While large natural disasters do provide opportunities for communities and disaster relief agencies to learn from their mistakes and improve their planning, response, and long-term mitigation techniques, they also serve to exacerbate rather than "even out" the preexisting social inequalities in devastated regions. While severe floods and hurricanes do in fact heavily impact all kinds of people across the socioeconomic spectrum, they are far from being "great equalizers" that place everyone (perhaps literally) in the same boat. Finding ways to tackle centuries of discrimination and risky land-use decisions is considerably more difficult than improving communications technologies or contraflow plans, but it is absolutely essential for truly diminishing overall disaster vulnerability.

SOURCES

Colten, Craig E. 2005. *An Unnatural Metropolis: Wrestling New Orleans from Nature*. Baton Rouge, LA: Louisiana State University Press.

Cutter, Susan L., and Christopher T. Emrich. 2006. "Moral Hazard, Social Catastrophe: The Changing Face of Vulnerability Along the Hurricane Coasts." *Annals of the American Academy of Political and Social Science* 604:102–12.

Davis, Mike. 1998. *Ecology of Fear: Los Angeles and the Imagination of Disaster*. New York: Metropolitan Books.

Godschalk, David R., David J. Brower, and Timothy Beatley. 1989. *Catastrophic Coastal Storms: Hazard Mitigation and Development Management*. Durham, NC: Duke University Press.

Haas, Edward F. 1990. "Victor H. Schiro, Hurricane Betsy, and the 'Forgiveness Bill.'" *Gulf Coast Historical Review* 6(1):66–90.

Kirby, Andrew, ed. 1990. *Nothing to Fear: Risks and Hazards in American Society*. Tucson, AZ: University of Arizona Press.

Logan, John R., and Harvey L. Molotch. 1987. *Urban Fortunes: The Political Economy of Place*. Berkeley, CA: University of California Press.

Logan, John R., Rachel Bridges Whaley, and Kyle Crower. 1999. "The Character and Consequences of Growth Regimes: An Assessment of Twenty Years of Research." Pp. 73–94 in *The Urban Growth Machine: Critical Perspectives Two Decades Later*, edited by Andrew E. G. Jonas and David Wilson. Albany, NY: State University of New York Press.

McQuaid, John, and Mark Schleifstein. 2006. *Path of Destruction: The Devastation of New Orleans and the Coming Age of Superstorms*. New York: Little, Brown, and Company.

Mileti, Dennis S., et al. 1999. *Disasters by Design: A Reassessment of Natural Hazards in the United States*. Washington, DC: Joseph Henry Press.

Murphy, Raymond. 2004. "Disaster or Sustainability: The Dance of Human Agents with Nature's Actants." *Canadian Review of Sociology and Anthropology* 41(3):249–66.

Peacock, Walter Gillis, Betty Hearn Morrow, and Hugh Gladwin. 1997. *Hurricane Andrew: Ethnicity, Gender, and the Sociology of Disasters*. London: Routledge.

Perrow, Charles. 1999 [1984]. *Normal Accidents: Living with High-Risk Technologies*. Princeton, NJ: Princeton University Press.

Platt, Rutherford H. 1999. *Disasters and Democracy: The Politics of Extreme Natural Events*. Washington, DC: Island Press.

Rose, Chris. 2006. *1 Dead in Attic*. New Orleans: CR Books.

Steinberg, Ted. 2000. *Acts of God: The Unnatural History of Natural Disaster in America*. Oxford, UK: Oxford University Press.

Van Heerden, Ivor. 2006. *The Storm: What Went Wrong and Why During Hurricane Katrina—The Inside Story from One Louisiana Scientist*. New York: Viking.

Wisner, Ben, et al. 2005. *At Risk: Natural Hazards, People's Vulnerability, and Disasters*. London: Routledge.

14

Climate Change:
Why the Old Approaches Aren't Working

J. Timmons Roberts

HOW BAD?

It seems like people are living in two worlds these days. Some are freaking out about climate change, saying that we need to radically change our behavior or the world is soon going to become uninhabitable. For them, climate change may bring nightmarish tides and hurricanes to the places where millions of people live—first to small islands, along coastlines, and in low-lying river deltas. Thousands are already dying from hurricanes and flooding, especially in poor countries, and it could get a lot worse if the oceans keep getting warmer and higher, they argue. Human-induced climate change could bring horrible heat waves, killing thousands in cities—as happened to over 5,000 people in downtown Chicago in 1995 and over 13,000 in Paris in 2003. But worst of all, they say it could kill tens of millions of poor people who rely on rain to water their crops. It will probably start with sub-Saharan Africa and the northeast of Brazil but could include parts of China, India, Central America, and even places closer to the homes of those of us living in the wealthier countries. There could be millions of what are already being called "environmental refugees" pouring across borders to escape these wastelands, creating "environmental conflicts" or even "resource wars." The groups warning of this potential apocalyptic future include worldwide networks of climate and ecosystem scientists, specialists on disasters, the environmental movement, and even some governments. Best known is the Intergovernmental Panel on Climate Change, which includes thousands of scientists from around the world and whose reports are approved by nearly all the world's governments.

Then there are the rest of the people, who either don't know about these predictions, don't believe those who are proclaiming the coming disaster, or who know about climate change, what they should do, and yet choose to continue living as if the problem didn't exist. Sometimes it seems this last group includes our parents, college administrators, politicians, the "captains" of industry, and anyone else who has any power in our smaller and wider worlds. They make explicit or unspoken arguments based on the huge economic costs which will result from changing our whole social system to address environmental concerns like climate change (see Lesson 6). They go on purchasing wasteful cars and appliances; leaving on the lights, air conditioning, and heat; and traveling like there was no tomorrow in the face of the mounting evidence of the relationship between overconsumption and climate change. Some have faith in science or technology to solve the problem; others believe that God will take care of humanity or that climate change is just God's will. But many more people than that are finding it difficult to make serious changes in their lives because all our decisions are so strongly constrained by our society. Our ecological or carbon "footprints" are so difficult to change without ample public transportation options, thermostats in our rooms, or whatever. Contemplating the changes that need to happen is just too overwhelming, and the critique of our whole existence too deep, to even begin the change. Of course, this group of "climate deniers" includes nearly all of us, to varying degrees; and recent surveys have shown a surprising number of people skeptical of climate change.

A lot of the helpless feeling, I believe, is due to our perception that our own government and others around the world are not leading the way on climate change. As people become aware of and worried about environmental crises like climate change, they quite understandably "freak out" and demand that everyone pay attention and change what they are doing. In particular, governments are expected to mobilize to address the crisis: We conducted a survey recently in 46 nations and found that in country after country people believed that government action was the most likely to make a difference. Yet the United States and many other wealthy countries have resisted committing to serious attempts to restructure the whole system of production.

This is the case right now with climate change, but it is not a new problem. Perhaps we can learn a from a similar episode in the late 1960s, when environmentalists in northern Europe and the United States led the global environmental freak-out by saying that everyone had to protect our "Spaceship Earth" before it was too late. At that time, the concerns were industrial and pesticide pollution, overpopulation, depleted natural resources, urban smog, contaminated oceans, and so on. Environmentalists argued that everyone was responsible for cleaning up the mess that our modern industrial life was making. In response to the clamor by this new social movement of environmentalism, in 1968 Sweden submitted a proposal to the United Nations (UN) expressing the alarm felt by many people at the time, declaring an "urgent need for intensified action at the national and international level, to limit and, where possible, to eliminate the impairment of the human environment." Four years of intense discussion later, the first UN conference about the environment was held in Stockholm, Sweden, in 1972: the Stockholm Declaration was signed by 113 nations.

The difficulty came when representatives from poor countries said basically "Wait a minute, we didn't cause the problem, and we can't afford to clean it up. You clean it up." These are almost the exact words used by ambassadors from developing countries. Sri Lanka's ambassador said: "we must not, generally speaking, allow our concern for the environment to develop into a hysteria." India's pointed out that there are different pollutions of the poor and rich, "the wealthy worry about car fumes; we worry about starvation." China's argued that wealthy nations wanted to keep their cars while preventing their people from even riding on buses.

So there's the rub: We're freaking out about climate change and want everything to change to address it, quickly. But others stand to lose if there is a headlong rush which says that everyone must act in the same way and that they should forget their hopes of a better life with economic growth. When pressed to share the wealth so unequally distributed across the world, the wealthy nations in the global North (North America, Europe, Japan, and Australia) have resisted major changes in the fear that they might lose some of their commanding position. To attempt to untie this difficult knot, I try in this lesson to combine the basics on climate change and efforts to address it with some key insights from environmental justice and environmental sociology that I think could help move us forward together in addressing the problem. Three and a half decades after Stockholm, negotiators are still trying to build a workable global treaty to take care of the horrifying problem of climate change, and the issues are the same: I argue that the lessons of Stockholm (that inequality and development must be addressed with environmental issues) were never really learned, that the old approaches aren't working, and that it's time for a new way forward.

ON TO KYOTO

In 1992 at Rio de Janeiro, the largest gathering of heads of state in history signed a treaty called the United Nations Framework Convention on Climate Change (UNFCCC). It was eventually ratified by 192 countries. Those countries agreed to "stabilizing greenhouse gas concentrations in the atmosphere at a level that would prevent dangerous anthropogenic interference with the climate system." There has been a huge debate about the numbers this implies, but a planet on average 2°C warmer (about 4°F) is the level at which the computer models suggest the really bad things I mentioned at the start of this lesson will take off. The spring 2007 reports of the Intergovernmental Panel on Climate Change support these numbers and suggest that we need to slow and stop the increase in our emissions of greenhouse gases to keep the atmospheric level of carbon dioxide (and other pollutants that cause climate change) below 450–550 parts per million. A crucial line in the convention was that nations should act "in accordance with their *common but differentiated responsibilities* and respective capabilities. Accordingly, the developed country Parties should take the lead in combating climate change and the adverse effects thereof." These are crucial words that allowed both the Global North and the Global South to sign the treaty, but there is still disagreement about what they mean in practice.

The third Conference of the Parties of the "Framework Convention" was held in Kyoto, Japan, in November 1997, where that historic agreement was hammered out. To date, 180 countries have ratified the protocol, with 35 countries and the European community required to reduce greenhouse gas emissions below levels specified for each of them in the treaty. The United States initially signed the treaty at Kyoto, but then President Clinton never submitted it to the Senate to ratify and become a binding agreement because it was clear it didn't have enough votes to pass (more on that later). Then, after taking office in 2001, President G. W. Bush "unsigned" the treaty, removing the nation entirely from the protocol; but he remained in the UNFCCC. All of this keeps the United States from having any binding commitment to control its impact on the global climate by cutting its emissions of greenhouse gases. The key ratification for Kyoto was by Russia in late 2004, which pushed the treaty over a key threshold and finally put the protocol into effect on February 19, 2005.

People can argue about whether the Kyoto Protocol on climate change is worthwhile or worthless, but one thing is very clear: It is not yet global. It really applies to only about 30 rich countries that have pledged to reduce their emissions about 5% overall from their 1990 levels by 2012. It does not yet include over 5 of the 6 billion people on Earth: No poor or developing nations have agreed to *any* reductions in their emissions of greenhouse gasses, nor has the United States. That is, 80% of humanity has agreed to no limits on either their emissions from their cars or industries using oil, gas, and coal (fossil fuel or "industrial" emissions) or their rights to cut or burn down every last shard of rain forest inside their national boundaries. In fact, in the 15 years of negotiations, just mentioning any "binding limits" at any future date for the developing countries was like touching the high-voltage "third rail" of the subway. Having their right to develop out of poverty taken away was simply not on the table.

Is climate change a global problem or not? We know that any time we breathe or burn any fossil fuels to create electricity or to power our stoves or cars, that carbon dioxide goes into the atmosphere and stays there an average of 100 years. There, it combines with other carbon dioxide, methane, chlorofluorocarbons, nitrous oxides, and some other greenhouse gases to trap more heat each day and night, slowly warming the planet. It doesn't matter where on the planet the carbon was emitted: The impact is the same. So it *is* a global problem. But who can afford to worry about it or, more importantly, *do something* about it? Who caused the problem in the first place?

THE CORE MESSAGE AND THE IMPORTANCE OF SOCIOLOGY

I've been studying global warming for 15 years, including studies of international negotiations, national programs, complicated statistical analyses, and some heavy-duty attempts to bring sociological theory to the issue. But for me it all boils down to one basic point, which I draw from the sociological literature on environmental justice: *We cannot deal with environmental issues without addressing inequality* (see Lesson 10). By this I mean that poverty, racism, ethnicity, gender, and other types of inequality strongly influence people's power to control the "goods" (wealth and power) and "bads" (pollution, risks, illnesses, etc.) they get in life.

I suppose this needs explanation. I would argue that environmentalists thought they could solve environmental problems like toxic industrial pollution by creating "technocratic" (technically led bureaucratic) solutions. But they only drove the problem across borders. That is, if rich states or cities in one country imposed strict controls over polluting industries or dumps, those industries or dumps often simply moved to somewhere with weaker regulations. Or, more often, they just threatened to move and got a break from enforcement which was threatening their profits or sometimes merely cumbersome for their operation. Faced with organized communities after the famous Love Canal toxic community protests in the late 1970s and early 1980s (see Lesson 11), for example, companies looked for places where people wouldn't get organized. Sometimes they moved to black people's communities, and they often moved to the U.S. South, where environmental regulations and enforcement were weaker. As Robert Bullard said, NIMBY (Not in My Backyard) became PIBBY (Put it in Blacks' Back Yard). But then the environmental justice movement got going in the late 1980s and 1990s, so it became more difficult to put waste in black communities. Some companies moved the most polluting parts of their production chains overseas, where the labor is much cheaper and environmental regulations are barely enforced. Now it's become PICBY (Put it in China's Back Yard). The problem of industrial pollution wasn't so much solved, I'd say, as simply shifted around.

So this brings us back to the core message of this lesson and I think a central message of environmental sociology: *We cannot deal with environmental issues without addressing inequality*. This may seem obvious once stated, but many environmentalists (and especially environmental scientists) have been going about their business for three decades without addressing poverty and racism. Many still believe that to solve environmental problems in today's political climate, one should *not* address other issues, for fear of alienating potential allies. And in fact, the way one sets to work is very different if one operates with this message in mind.

This is why I think sociology and the other social sciences are so important to understanding the incredibly complex problem of climate change and actually developing a solution that might work. Much of modern sociology is the study of inequality—its causes and impacts. There are even some efforts to build policy based on the insights of sociology (much more is needed), and there is plenty of sociological analysis of past policy efforts to address inequality. Of course, sociology and the other social sciences have other branches, including those that address how and why people, companies, governments, and other institutions make decisions in the real world. These are filled with crucial insights into how we might move people and all our different institutions (like family, church, school, workplaces, etc.) to take on the climate issue quickly and effectively. Or at least they might tell us what miracles we shouldn't expect!

In what's left of this lesson, I explore the extent and types of inequality in the climate issue and how our failure to address the inequality in global income and development prospects is making it impossible for the negotiations on the issue to move ahead. People like Al Gore are great at raising the issue by talking about our common problem, but without a frank discussion about who caused it and what addressing it fairly would entail, many people will resist movement. Informed citizens need more than "political junk food" and feel-good solutions—they need to understand the complexity of the problem and possible solutions, and they need to be included in efforts at addressing it meaningfully and fairly.

INEQUALITY AND WHY IT MATTERS FOR ADDRESSING CLIMATE CHANGE

Let's start with the level of inequality in impacts from climate change. Those who emphasize that climate change is everybody's problem, or a "global public bad," also obscure the ways in which its impacts are socially distributed across human populations. Some suffer worst and first from climate disasters, and they are often not those who caused the problem (see Lesson 13). People in Africa, Asia, and Latin America are facing more frequent and more dangerous droughts, floods, and storms and have suffered immeasurably more loss of life and livelihood due to hydrometeorological disasters than rich nations. An analysis I did with my former undergraduate student Brad Parks of 4,040 climate-related disasters between 1980 and 2002 found that some poor nations had rates of death and homelessness from climate disasters *200–300 times worse* than the United States. They have far less capacity to deal with and recover from those disasters.

While the effects of and the ability to handle climate change are unequally distributed, *responsibility* for the problem is even more unequally distributed. Poor nations remain far behind us in terms of emissions per person. With only 4% of the world's population, the United States is responsible for nearly 25% of all global emissions. That can be compared to 136 developing countries that together are responsible for only 24% of global emissions. Clearly, poor nations remain far behind wealthy nations in terms of emissions per person. The average American citizen dumps many times more greenhouse gas into the atmosphere than the majority of humans who live on Earth—four or five times the global average. The average U.S. citizen causes *100 times as much damage* to the climate than an average resident in the poorest countries in the world (this is true for 30 countries, see Table 14–1). I come back to these figures in a minute.

Table 14–1 Number of Citizens Emitting as Much Carbon Dioxide as One U.S. Citizen.

29 Nations with Over 100 Citizens to 1 U.S. Citizen	37 Nations with Over 20 Citizens to 1 U.S. Citizen	22 Nations with Over 10 Citizens to 1 U.S. Citizen	36 Nations with Over 5 Citizens to 1 U.S. Citizen	26 Nations with Over 3 Citizens to 1 U.S. Citizen	30 Nations with Over 2 Citizens to 1 U.S. Citizen
Ethiopia (540)	Bangladesh (90)	Philippines (19.3)	Ecuador (9.8)	Jamaica (4.8)	Ukraine (2.9)
Chad (540)	Guinea Bissau (90)	India (18.6)	Guyana (9.5)	American Samoa (4.7)	Spain (2.8)
Zaire (540)	Benin (77.14285714)	El Salvador (18.6)	Grenada (9.5)	Lebanon (4.6)	Malta (2.8)
Afghanistan (540)	Kenya (67.5)	Peru (17.4)	China (9)	Mexico (4.5)	Turkmenistan (2.7)
Mali (540)	Kiribati (67.5)	Mauritania (17.4)	Egypt (8.8)	Barbados (4.5)	Slovenia (2.7)
Cambodia (540)	Nigeria (60)	Zimbabwe (16.9)	Puerto Rico (8.9)	Croatia (4.4)	Bermuda (2.7)
Burundi (540)	Ghana (60)	Georgia (16.875)	Panama (8.9)	Uzbekistan (4.1)	Italy (2.7)
Uganda (270)	Cape Verde (60)	Tonga (16.4)	St. Lucia (8.7)	Bosnia-Herz. (4.1)	South Africa (2.6)
Mozambique (270)	Solomon Islands (54)	Indonesia (15.4)	Botswana (8.4)	Iran (4.1)	Austria (2.6)
Burkina Faso (270)	Togo (49.1)	Morocco (15.4)	French Polynesia (8.4)	Hong Kong (4.1)	Cayman Islands (2.6)
Malawi (270)	Swaziland (49.1)	Bolivia (15)	Brit. Virgin Islands (8.2)	Suriname (4.1)	Iceland (2.6)
Rwanda (270)	Cameroon (45)	Dominica (14.2)	Latvia (8.1)	Bulgaria (3.7)	Poland (2.5)
Laos (270)	Senegal (45)	Costa Rica (13.8)	Mauritius (8.1)	Switzerland (3.7)	Saint-Pierre and
Nepal (135)	São Tomé & Príncipe (30)		Gabon (6.8)	French Guiana (3.6)	Gibraltar (2.5)
Madagascar (135)	Viet Nam (27)		Algeria (6.8)	Belarus (3.4)	Kazakhstan (2.4)
Guinea (135)	Honduras (27)		Dominican Rep. (6.7)	Bahamas (3.3)	Oman (2.4)
Sierra Leone (135)	Nicaragua (27)		Belize (6.4)	Portugal (3.3)	Denmark (2.4)
Myanmar (108)	Pakistan (25.7)		Mongolia (6.3)	Malaysia (3.2)	North Korea (2.4)
Sudan (108)	Samoa (24.5)		Thailand (6.2)	Venezuela (3.0)	Cyprus (2.3)
Zambia (108)	Guatemala (22.5)		Lithuania (6.2)	Slovakia (3.0)	Netherlands (2.3)
Haiti (108)	Fiji (22.5)		Iraq (5.9)		Greece (2.2)
Eritrea (108)	Armenia (21.6)		Syria (5.9)		South Korea (2.2)

(continued)

Table 14–1 (continued)

29 Nations with Over 100 Citizens to 1 U.S. Citizen	36 Nations with Over 5 Citizens to 1 U.S. Citizen	37 Nations with Over 20 Citizens to 1 U.S. Citizen	26 Nations with Over 3 Citizens to 1 U.S. Citizen	22 Nations with Over 10 Citizens to 1 U.S. Citizen	30 Nations with Over 2 Citizens to 1 U.S. Citizen
Bhutan (108)	Albania (21.6)		Reunion (5.9)		Japan (2.1)
Gambia (108)	Kyrgyzstan (20.8)		Turkey (5.8)		United Kingdom (2.1)
	Western Sahara (20.8)		Azerbaijan (5.5)		Germany (2.1)
	Namibia (20)		Argentina (5.3)		Taiwan (2.0)
			Macau (5.3)		Montserrat (2.0)
			Romania (5.1)		Russia (2.0)
			Guadeloupe (5.1)		
			Chile (5.0)		
			Yugoslavia (5.0)		

Source: Calculated from Boden et al. 2003.

This to me is simple, true injustice: where the innocent are suffering the effects of something from which they draw little or no benefit. As members of the small island states whose cultures are likely to be decimated by rising sea levels have pointed out, to understand the links and yet willfully allow the destruction of cultures and people is plainly immoral.

Vast differences in absolute and relative income also have a tremendous impact on the ability of developed and developing countries to show up at international conferences, participate in international organizations, and hire skilled negotiators. Michael Richards of the Overseas Development Institute described the situation at COP-6, where the United States brought 99 formal delegates and the European Union brought 76, while many small island and African states had one-, two-, or three-person delegations. But it's worse than that: Wealthy nations typically show up at international conferences with lawyers, legal experts, scientists, economists, skilled diplomats, and "observers," allowing them to read every document, attend every committee meeting, and painstakingly weigh the pros and cons of many proposals. It is difficult to overstate the importance of this impact of global inequality on how the climate crisis is being negotiated.

Most of all, we need to understand that the debate about climate change occurs in a negotiating climate already poisoned by bad acts and unfilled promises from decades of other negotiations on trade and development. Poor nations feel they have repeatedly "gotten the shaft" in initiatives like the World Trade Organization (WTO), the TRIPS treaty on property rights, the International Monetary Fund (IMF), the World Bank's "conditions" on who gets loans and what they have to do to get them, and so on.

The climate in which the debate occurs is one where most poor nations are not getting richer as they were told they would. Of the world's 6.5 billion people, almost 5 billion live in countries where the average income is less than $3 a day. At the same time, on average, the people in the high-income countries get to live on 23 times that much, and the gap between the two groups is widening. About one out of four people in the world live in absolute poverty, defined as too poor to afford an adequate diet and other necessities. Malnutrition is said to stunt the growth and development of 40% of all 2-year-olds in poorer countries. In short, developing countries have very good reasons to not believe the stories they are told about how they should just trust the wealthy nations since we know what's best for them and that they should try to follow in our footsteps.

As Adil Najam put it in describing why poor countries are being "difficult" in the Kyoto negotiations:

> It is tempting to dismiss the South's persistent distrust of the North as the paranoia of historical baggage. However the South's anger is directed...by what it sees as subjugation today, and its inability to influence what might happen in the future.

Why does inequality matter so much for resolving climate change? Inequality within and between nations, of many sorts, drives desperation in the Global South (vulnerability), anger at the injustice of the distribution of goods (wealth) and bads (emissions), as well as inability and unwillingness to participate effectively in international efforts to address climate change (participation in Kyoto and other environmental treaties). Wealthy nations are able to build sea walls, intricate "disaster management plans" to prepare for and recover from climate disasters, and border fences to keep out refugees. Feeling secure that they can endure a warmer climate, wealthy nations' citizens and politicians are more susceptible to arguments by the oil, mining, and auto industries that reducing emissions would hamper our lifestyles. Poor people suffering across the world seem far away and unthreatening. As a result, Brad Parks and I argue that inequality makes it difficult to get people thinking in constructive and harmonious ways: It reinforces particularistic world views. That is, among the subordinate groups (the poor especially), inequality supports "structuralist" perspectives (that they are without power to change the system, that the system is unfair). Extreme inequality can lead to "get-even" or "zero-sum" approaches by those who are on the bottom, even when they are self-defeating. More dangerously, extreme inequality leads the wealthy to not address crucial issues facing the poor and to resist efforts to create fair solutions that may require serious sacrifices. Looking globally at the opulence of wealth beside the starvation and desperation of the poor, one must conclude that inequality is savage.

POLLUTION OF WEALTH AND POVERTY

As Indira Ghandi of India said long ago, there are two pollutions, the pollution of wealth and the pollution of poverty. In carbon terms, the worst is unquestionably the pollution of wealth: large homes, many cars, appliances of all sorts, luxury foods and products transported over tremendous distances, and so on. In the poorer nations, the greater environmental problems are simply survival: having enough to eat, a safe place to sleep, a way to take care of one's children. So there is great inequality of wealth and greenhouse gas emissions between nations and within them. We lack much data on intra-country variation in carbon emissions (especially in the poor nations), but it can be said with confidence that the world's richest people cause emissions *thousands of times* those of the world's poorest. Traveling by foot, bicycle, and bus and cooking local foods in unheated, un-air conditioned, tiny homes built of simple, local materials, fossil fuel use by the world's poor on a per capita basis is almost negligible. Still, the "pollution of poverty" must be considered. Many of the world's poor continue to gather firewood or animal waste for fuel or move into rain forests to create a farm of their own (see Lesson 9). These create important environmental damage and can contribute to land-use change (Kyoto jargon for cutting rain forests), biodiversity loss (UN jargon for cutting rainforests and polluting or overfishing coral reefs), and climate change. But fuel wood is an essentially "renewable" energy source, and rain forest cutting is about one-fifth of global emissions; so *the main threats to our atmosphere come from adding new carbon to the biosphere by burning fossil fuels.* Twenty percent of the world's population is responsible for 63% of the emissions, while the bottom 20% of the world's people are releasing only 3%. Per capita, the analysis is striking: The high-income countries (using World Bank categories) are leveling off around 2.5 metric tons (mT) of annual carbon emissions per person, while the middle-income nations are around 0.6 mT and the poorest are around 0.02 mT. One recent calculation by Robert Socolow put it very plainly: Providing the fossil fuel energy for a decent life for the billions without energy supplies will cause only a minor increase in total global energy use.

In early 2007, China became the world's largest emitter of greenhouse gases, surpassing the United States. But the Chinese argued that on a per capita basis they were still emitting only one-fifth of what Americans were. They also argued that they were not responsible for much of the gases already in the atmosphere. And they have a point: It is a basic rule of civil justice, Superfund, and kindergarten ethics that those who created a mess should be responsible for cleaning up their share of the mess. Since carbon dioxide burned now stays in the atmosphere for over 100 years, shouldn't accounting for all the damage the rich nations have done in the recent past be considered? This is a highly contentious issue indeed but one which we have to consider if we are to address inequality and climate change. When emissions since 1950 are summed, not surprisingly, the gap between rich and poor nations is much higher, and it is not narrowing or going away anytime soon. This is a legitimate thing to do since virtually all the carbon emitted since 1945 is still in the atmosphere. Carbon dioxide has an atmospheric lifetime of 120 years and methane, 12 years. The summed emissions from the high-income nations amount to 900 trillion tons of carbon, those from the 28% of the humans who live in middle-income nations only 500 trillion tons, and the poorest majority of the world has dumped only 200 trillion tons.

MEASURING RESPONSIBILITY, NEGOTIATING JUSTICE?

A major sticking point in the Kyoto Protocol debate has been precisely this: how to calculate who is polluting how much and how much they should be required to reduce their emissions and by when. One alternative that has been proposed is to look at total carbon emissions that the atmosphere can handle and divide up the rights on an equal/per capita basis. One scheme, called "contraction and convergence," proposes that we all eventually converge on a globally acceptable average. The Global Commons Institute proposal for "C and C" would allow poor nations to sell their "rights" to wealthy nations in the short term, and eventually the funding would allow them to improve their conditions and presumably increase their emissions, gradually reaching the global allowance per person. Wealthy nations would have to "contract" their emissions but could do so gradually by buying permits from the poor. Obviously, this approach has been favored by the populous poor countries, like China and India.

Some will point out that there is another, very different side to this story. China and India, with massive populations and rapid industrialization, will quickly surpass the wealthy countries in total emissions of greenhouse gases to the atmosphere. It is true that, environmentally speaking, one cannot handle the problem of global warming without addressing the boom of emissions in the developing countries. This point has been seized upon by the U.S.-headquartered oil and coal industries, which have mobilized think tanks, journalists, scientists, and senators to block any progress on the Kyoto treaty until the poor nations also agree to limits on their carbon emissions. However, to ask these nations to stop development at a level we would never consider returning to seems hypocritical. What's more, by their importance in the problem and their sheer numbers in negotiating efforts, the poor nations hold veto power over efforts to enact a global climate treaty.

The per capita approach was described as "dead on arrival" at the Kyoto negotiations in 1997, when the wealthy nations negotiated the treaty largely behind closed doors. Rather, the Kyoto approach to carbon accounting is "grandfathering" emissions; that is, in the name of political expediency, national reductions are decided on a baseline of 1990 levels. Leading the way on addressing the climate change problem aggressively have been the European Union nations, some of which wanted 20% reductions and binding limits on carbon emissions at Kyoto. Densely populated and well aware of the environmental limits to economic growth, Europe's environmental movement is the strongest in the world, with viable political parties in several nations and even a few which have gained real political power. The February 20, 2007, agreement by European Union environment ministers committed the 27 nations to 20% reductions in emissions by 2020 and even higher levels if the United States and other key nations became involved. This appears to be a major step forward in concrete commitments to address the climate issue. Europe does it, of course, in the hopes that other foot-dragging nations will follow.

Foot-dragging wealthy nations at various times have included Japan, the United States, Switzerland, Canada, Australia, Norway, New Zealand, and Russia, among others. These have been called the JUSCANNZ nations, or "the umbrella group," but the group has diverged substantially in behavior. After succeeding in getting less ambitious targets for emissions reductions at Kyoto, the group moved on to its next negotiating goals. At the top of the list was their desire to "buy" an unlimited amount of "permits," that is, purchase whatever reductions they fail to meet by the deadlines in the treaty (2012). Such purchases are called "flexibility mechanisms," and they can be in the form of buying reductions which were made in other rich nations (called "joint implementation") or in poorer nations (called the "clean development mechanism"). Some projections on how much money could be flowing between nations if trading takes off (and it already has begun) suggest that trading could soon overshadow foreign aid and military aid, in the tens or hundreds of billions of dollars a year.

A critical moment in the struggle over inequality and climate change came in the summer of 1997 before the Kyoto meeting in December. In the U.S. Senate, the Byrd-Hagel resolution passed 95–0 on July 25, 1997, making it impossible for the administration to sign any treaty that did not include the poor countries. Senator Robert C. Byrd declared on the Senate floor that "I do not think the Senate should support a treaty that requires only...developed countries to endure the economic costs of reducing emissions, while developing countries are free to pollute the atmosphere, and, in so doing, siphon off American industries." Representative Henry Bonilla stated that Kyoto "is anti-American because it imposes strict, costly penalties on Americans while allowing many Third World countries to pollute our environment at will." At the other end of the limited political spectrum on Capitol Hill, Representative John Dingell said in 1998 that "India, a mass emitter of CO_2, is not going to be bound. Our friends in China have told me that they will never be bound. So that leaves Uncle Sam, the United States, which proposes to be bound by a treaty which is going to cause enormous economic hardship."

To understand the position of the representatives, one need look no further than the hard-lobbied positions of the industries that support them: Byrd is a Democrat from the coal-dependent state of West Virginia; Bonilla is a Republican from oil-dominated Texas; Dingell represents the auto industry–dependent state of Michigan. World-system theory in sociology suggests that these are bald efforts by privileged economic groups at the top of the world inequality system to defend their position there, while making outlandishly ironic claims about and impossible demands on those at the bottom of the pyramid (see Lesson 3). The "polluting elites" are flexing their political muscle. However, there are even more factions outside the wealthy nations, tied largely to the nature of their own economic and political elites.

WORLDS APART

Many people have argued that climate change still is not a top priority issue for much of the world's population because there are more pressing problems or because their values have not reached a "postmaterialist" level when people start to care about quality of life, not only survival. These are hugely contested ideas: Most surveys show that in fact as many people in poor nations are concerned about global warming and willing to do something about it as in the rich nations. The main point I want to make here is that there is no single "developing world" and that the positions on climate change vary tremendously among the nonwealthy nations. Though the poorer nations have often negotiated together as the "G-77 and China" (the "Group of 77" actually represents about 134 nations), there are at least five distinct positions of these nations on the issue of climate change treaties.

First, when it comes to obstructing binding limits on emissions of greenhouse gases, not surprisingly the hardest line has been taken by the Organization of the Petroleum Exporting Countries (OPEC). They have adopted a very similar position to that of the U.S. oil and coal lobbying arm, saying "go slow," "do more research," "don't hurt the economy," and so on. At the COP-4 round of negotiations on the FCCC in Buenos Aires in late 1998, OPEC Secretary General Rilwanu Lukman gave a defining speech and released a press statement. It said that "as the group of developing countries that is most dependent upon fossil fuel sales, [OPEC] is concerned that the legitimate right to economic development, shared by all developing countries, is under threat from the mitigation measures [reducing emissions] that may come under discussion." More concretely, "OPEC's research, for example, suggests that OPEC Member Countries could collectively suffer losses in revenue flows of the order of US$20 billion each year as a result of the proposed mitigation measures being implemented." He continued: "Compensation is a necessary concomitant of a balanced agreement." Finally and bluntly, "how can fossil fuel producers be expected to give their wholehearted blessing to measures that could wreak havoc with their economies?" Saudi Arabia has often been the most visible negotiator for OPEC, and together, the oil producers have made the G-77 and China a very difficult group in which to gain consensus.

At the other extreme are the Alliance of Small Island States (AOSIS) nations, like Nauru, Marshall Islands, Fiji, and Tuvalu. These nations have been loudly arguing that they are "among the most vulnerable to impacts of climate and sea-level changes...the inhabitable land tends to be on the coastal fringe...climate change could mean changes in storm frequencies and intensity and lead to increased risk of flooding." These nations could all suffer "a terrifying, rising flood of biblical proportions...the willful destruction of entire countries and cultures," as described by Kinza Clodumar, president of Nauru at Kyoto in 1997. They call for immediate, drastic action to curb global warming. Their argument is that "(a) Pacific Island Countries make a small or negligible contribution to GHG [greenhouse gases]; (b) They are among the countries which are most impacted; and (c) Knowledge of relevant parameters is very low." Among the first nations ratifying Kyoto were the small island states.

There is also a silent majority of nations in the developing world. For the 134 nations in the G-77 and China, many are still barely heard from on climate. Guyana's delegate, speaking at the June 1, 1999, meeting in Bonn as representative of the group, made clear that the G-77 would "play ball" on climate change only if the redistribution of resources was immediately forthcoming. "Transfer and access to technology, including information technology and enhancement of endogenous technologies, and the provision of financial resources, in particular for the full participation of developing countries in the implementation of these decisions, are necessary...." Some countries have taken a "middle ground" approach, such as the Philippines and especially Argentina, attempting to do some brokering between the Global North and South. Finally and quite importantly, there are the "emissions entrepreneurs," states where projects are already under way to gain some of the potential investments from trading of carbon permits or technology transfer. These nations saw clearly what many others did not: how they could capture a large share of this new flow of funding if they acted quickly. The vast majority of the revenues from the clean development mechanism are going to a very small group of developing nations: China, India, Brazil, and Mexico. All of Africa, for example, has received a tiny proportion of the investments, less than 3%. The inequality is not going to automatically go away with the adoption of market mechanisms like carbon permit trading; it will need to be tempered with other programs.

BREAKING THE DEADLOCK: EXPANDING THE TERRAIN

This brings the discussion back to the original point about how issues of equity will have to be dealt with at the same time as the environment. Richard Benedick, chief U.S. negotiator on the Montreal Protocol on ozone protection, said that "The North's interests in maintaining a healthy planet can only be achieved through aggressive efforts to support national economic advancement in the South." Surveys in the Global South show huge majorities there concerned about protecting the planet, but Benedick's point is nearly identical to the lesson I am arguing that environmentalists are learning from environmental justice advocates: *We cannot deal with environmental issues without addressing inequality.* It would be nice if we could stay more focused on addressing one issue at a time or technical solutions that don't upset the political or social order, but it seems we cannot. Technical solutions can get us a major part of the way toward addressing climate change, but some serious reorganization of society will be necessary to reach the major emissions reductions suggested by many scientists (60–80% in a few decades for the wealthy nations). This also suggests the importance of sociology and its insights into the roots of inequality and identity as well as the need to develop our understanding of how environmental issues relate to inequality.

As we've seen, inequality drives the deadlock over Kyoto in four very direct and powerful ways. First, inequality within and between nations, of many sorts, drives desperation in the Global South (vulnerability). Second, it drives anger at the injustice of the distribution of goods (wealth) and bads (emissions) since "waste flows downhill." Third, it drives the inability and unwillingness of poor countries to participate effectively in international efforts to address climate change (participation in Kyoto and other environmental treaties). Fourth, in some key nations like the United States and Australia, extreme wealth has allowed the continuing delay in seriously addressing the issue. Each of these impacts of inequality is complex and must be addressed to move climate policy forward.

Things are not hopeless. Trust can be restored if the wealthy nations take meaningful steps to address these types of inequality and create binding treaties that address climate change and at least begin to rebalance global inequality in wealth by helping poorer nations get a fairer deal in their efforts to develop. Political scientist Robert Keohane stated an obvious but important point that I think most people intuitively know but which the rules of "rational actor" economics fail to grasp: People trust those who don't try to always get the best deal at other people's expense.

There is a ready stock of "fairness principles" that have been developed in past global negotiations, which could be incorporated into the Kyoto treaty. First is democracy and the feeling of inclusion in decision making for all nations. For example, there is a double majority system of voting in the Global Environment Facility, which provides one vote for each nation in one voting round and in the other round proportional voting based on how much a nation has contributed to the fund. "Procedural justice" means that decisions of this magnitude are made in a transparent and fair way.

Second, to compensate for economic losses due to cleaning up the environment and recovering from climate disasters, there will have to be a lot of funding, like that provided to poorer nations under the Montreal Protocol to protect the ozone. This will admittedly be much more complex in the case of climate change since the big losers in the effort to stop ozone depletion were a small group of manufacturers of freon and a few other chemicals used in refrigeration and foam. The greenhouse effect, by comparison, is worsened by the burning of all fossil fuels, deforestation, and much agricultural production. Much will have to change, and somehow the losers will need to be compensated; but little discussion has taken place about how and who will pay and how the funding will actually get to those who stand to lose from protecting the atmosphere. "Compensatory justice" needs attention.

To decide who pays, we need a "fairness principle" that is well accepted. I believe we have one. The "polluter pays principle" simply says that the person or company or nation who created a mess must clean it up. The principle was acknowledged in 1974 by the wealthy nations of the world at the time, the Organization for Economic Cooperation and Development (OECD). This principle suggests we should include past emissions of greenhouse gases in our calculations of responsibility for the problem, but how far back should we go? A new proposal, under development by the two men who created the group EcoEquity, is called "greenhouse development rights" and would raise money based on who has emitted the most and pay for the adaptation and mitigation needs of developing nations. I believe that any effective proposal on climate change needs to address all the major barriers to an agreement and to do so at the scope needed for this massive problem.

Regardless of what agreement is hammered out on emissions and adaptation funding for climate change, other things need to happen to build trust between the Global North and South. Wealthy nations will need to send "costly signals" that they care about the social and economic development of poor nations. They need to make rapid reductions in their own emissions, and they need to do drastic rewriting of trade treaties and development aid rules, debt relief, international court systems, and foreign policy and interventions. There will need to be a huge infusion of international aid from the Global North to help poorer nations get off self-destructive pathways of development (ones that bring few benefits but many risks and high emissions). Poor nations will need the most cutting-edge technology provided nearly free and great help developing the technical capacity to operate and innovate. Ideally, these technologies will help them "decarbonize" their development, but in some cases they will need to burn more fossil fuels, at least in the short term. To get the cooperation of owners and workers in old inefficient and high-polluting sectors (like coal mining, steel works, or much smaller enterprises), the assistance will have to include compensation and retraining, and around them there will need to be a serious redirection of local economies. This will need to happen in wealthy nations as well. Some experts are now arguing that "simply doing good development work will solve many adaptation issues." Perhaps it will, but many projects will have to be specifically undertaken just to help with the adaptation needs directly (like building key seawalls or irrigating fields in many places). This could require funding of billions of dollars in aid from Global North to South each year, so we need some consistent and high levels of funding, not the voluntary funds we currently have.

Many people are feeling climate change already, and we all have to worry about this problem to come up with innovative, inclusive solutions. As residents in wealthy nations, we need to drive less and fly less and turn the lights, heat, and air conditioning down. But we need to also push for structural changes locally, nationally, and globally. Politicians, college administrators, parents, and business leaders need to take the issue seriously and actually do something about it. They need to get their own houses in order and to be part of forging a new global agreement of what would be a fair way to solve this problem. Global institutions like the WTO, the IMF, the UN, and so on will have to be rebuilt. As sociologists, we need to offer a broader approach that brings our understanding of the importance of inequality together with our environmental concern. The failures of past environmental negotiations to address global inequality cannot block the creation of a truly just one on climate change: A new approach is needed.

SOURCES

Boyd, Emily, Nathan E. Hultman, Timmons Roberts, Esteve Corbera, and Johannes Ebeling. 2007. "The Clean Development Mechanism: Current Status, Perspectives and Future Policy." Environmental Change Institute Oxford, Tyndall Centre for Climate Change Research UK, and EcoSecurities LLP. Working paper.

Brechin, Steven R. 1999. "Objective Problems, Subjective Values, and Global Environmentalism: Evaluating the Postmaterialist Argument and Challenging a New Explanation." Social Science Quarterly 80(4):793–809.

Bullard, Robert. 1990. Dumping in Dixie: Race, Class, and Environmental Quality. Boulder, CO: Westview.

Ellis, J., H. Winkler, J. Corfee-Morlot, and F. Gagnon-Lebrun. 2007. "CDM: Taking Stock and Looking Forward." *Energy Policy* 35:15–28.

Gelbspan, Ross. 1997. *The Heat Is On*. Reading, MA: Addison-Wesley.

Inglehart, Ronald. 1995. "Public Support for Environmental Protection: Objective Problems and Subjective Values in 43 Societies." *PS: Political Science and Politics* 28(1):57–72.

Intergovernmental Panel on Climate Change Working Group II. 1995, 2001, 2007. Climate Change. Bonn: IPCC.

Najam, A. 1995. "An Environmental Negotiating Strategy for the South." Internationl Environmental Affairs 7(3): 249–287.

Oxford University Environmental Change Institute/AC Nielsen Survey Group. 2007. "Global Nielsen Survey: Consumers Look to Governments to Act on Climate Change." Press release (http://www.eci.ox.ac.uk/news/070605pr-nielsensurvey.pdf).

Redclift, Michael, and Colin Sage. 1998. "Global Environmental Change and Global Inequality: North/South Perspectives." *International Sociology* 13(4):499–516.

Roberts, J. Timmons, and Bradley C. Parks. 2007. *A Climate of Inequality: Global Inequality, North–South Politics, and Climate Policy*. Cambridge, MA: MIT Press.

Shue, Henry. 1992. "The Unavoidability of Justice." Pp. 373–97 in *The International Politics of the Environment: Actors, Interests and Institutions*, edited by Andrew Hurrell and Benedict Kingsbury. Oxford, UK: Clarendon Press.

Simms, Andrew. 2002. *An Environmental War Economy*. London, UK: New Economics Foundation.

World Bank. n.d. *World Development Report*. New York: Oxford University Press.

World Resources Institute. 1998. *World Resources 1998–99*. New York: Oxford University Press.

Part 4

SOME SOCIAL RESPONSES TO ENVIRONMENTAL DISRUPTION

15

U.S. Environmental Movements

Robert J. Brulle

T he U.S. environmental movement is perhaps the single largest social movement in the United States. With over 6,500 national and 20,000 local environmental organizations, along with an estimated 20–30 million members, this movement dwarfs other modern social movements such as the civil rights or peace movements. It is also the longest-running social movement. The first local environmental organizations were founded before the Civil War, and several still existing national environmental organizations, such as the Sierra Club, the National Audubon Society, and American Forests, were founded in the late nineteenth century.

The question facing social scientists is how can we understand and examine this enormously complex social movement? There are three commonly used approaches. First, sociologists examine the belief systems that define the various components of this social movement, which is termed *discourse analysis*. Second, the development of the social movement over time is examined using *historical analysis*. Third, the techniques used to garner financial resources for the organization are examined through the perspective of *resource mobilization analysis*. By combining all three of these perspectives, one can gain a more complete picture of the environmental movement.

DISCOURSE ANALYSIS OF THE U.S. ENVIRONMENTAL MOVEMENT

The first approach is to view this movement as a group of distinct communities, each based on a particular worldview. For example, if you were asked to describe organized religion in the United States, you could list all of the various denominations, such as Catholics, Jews, Episcopalians, and Baptists. When you describe religion using these terms, what you are saying is that there are a number of different religious communities, each based on a particular set of beliefs.

This approach can be applied to describing the U.S. environmental movement. Just like organized religion, the environmental movement is made up of a number of different communities, each based on a particular worldview (see Lesson 2). Sociologists label these different worldviews as "discursive frames." A *discursive frame* is the set of cultural viewpoints that inform the practices of a community of social movement organizations. Each discursive frame provides a cultural viewpoint from which the environmental organization acts. This discursive frame defines the goals and purposes of the organization and provides guidance for the actions of the organization.

For example, the Wilderness Society belongs to the discursive community defined by the discourse of preservation. This discursive frame focuses on the preservation of intact ecological systems and protection of biodiversity. Oriented by this viewpoint, the Wilderness Society seeks to create and maintain wilderness areas and to ensure long-term ecological diversity in these areas. Conversely, the Center for Health, Environment and Justice is informed by the discursive frame of environmental health (see Lesson 11). It seeks to protect the health of urban area residents by eliminating toxic chemicals from their environment. So while both of these organizations have an environmental focus, their discursive frames are distinct.

When you look at the U.S. environmental movement from this perspective, it is clear that it is comprised of several distinct communities, each based on a unique discursive frame. Thus, to understand this movement, it is important to recognize its multiple foci based on unique discursive frames. There are 11 major discursive frames that define the environmental movement in the United States. Thus, to understand the environmental movement, you must be familiar with each one.

Wildlife Management

The oldest and first manifestation of concern over the natural environment appeared in the United States over the issue of hunting. Around the middle of the nineteenth century, wealthy Americans became concerned about the depletion of wildlife for hunting. These sportsmen organized the first environmental organizations. These organizations lobbied for the creation of bag limits on both game animals and fish. This expanded into a national movement toward the end of the nineteenth century with the appearance of organizations such as the Boone and Crockett Club and the National Audubon Society.

In the early 1930s, this movement underwent a profound shift. Up until this time, the only strategy was to control the demand on fish and game animals through limiting the number of animals that could be taken or limiting the hunting season to a specific time period. However, due to the loss of habitat, this strategy was unable to ensure that a sufficient number of game animals was available. Thus, a new strategy of wildlife management was created. This strategy focused on both reducing demand and increasing the supply. To increase the supply of game animals, wildlife refuges were established. This strategy of managing both the supply and demand of game animals has worked successfully since its development. This approach defines a major environmental discourse in the United States, with the following key components:

- The scientific management of ecosystems can ensure stable populations of wildlife.

- The wildlife population can be seen as a crop from which excess populations can be sustainably harvested in accordance with the ecological limitations of a given area. This excess wildlife population thus can be utilized for human recreation in sport hunting.

The discourse of wildlife management defines both a unique viewpoint and the practices of a distinct community of organizations. This community is centered on wildlife conservation issues, and it defines its objective as conserving or rationally developing wildlife resources to provide for human recreational needs. It uses phrases such as "maximizing the supply of game" and "conserve our wildlife resources." Some major organizations in this discursive community are Trout Unlimited, Ducks Unlimited, and the National Wildlife Federation.

Conservation

Perhaps the most influential early discursive frames in the U.S. environmental movement were developed by the conservation movement. Around the turn of the twentieth century, there was a great deal of concern regarding the overexploitation of natural resources by market forces. This concern led to the creation of the conservation movement. These organizations, such as the American Forestry Association (founded in 1875), advocated government control to ensure that these resources would continue to provide an adequate supply for the economy. This philosophy was put into practice during the administration of Theodore Roosevelt in the creation of the national forests. From 1900 to around 1960, this perspective dominated American environmental policy.

From the viewpoint of the discourse of conservation, nature is a resource to be used by society to meet human needs. This forms the basis for collective action to ensure that natural resources are used by applying the criteria of rationality and efficiency to achieve the maximum utility to society. Key components of this perspective are as follows:

- Physical and biological nature is nothing more than a collection of parts that function like a machine.
- Humans need to use the natural resources provided by nature to maintain society.
- Nature can be managed by humans through the application of technical knowledge used by competent professionals.
- The proper management philosophy for natural resources is to realize the greatest good for the greatest number of people over the longest period of time.

Organizations based on this discourse define their objective as conserving or rationally developing our natural resources to meet long-term human needs. They use phrases such as "ensure wise use of natural resources" and "bring about efficient conservation and development." Some organizations in this discursive community are the Society of American Foresters, American Forests, and Scenic America.

Preservation

The third environmental discourse to emerge in the United States during the nineteenth century was preservation. As economic development expanded across the United States, there was growing concern regarding the disappearance of "wild" lands. In 1890, a dramatic proclamation was issued by the U.S. Census Bureau. The census reported that it could no longer define a frontier line. For a country that had previously thought of the West as an inexhaustible source of natural resources and land, this was a profound psychological shock. This meant that the United States was running out of natural resources and wild areas.

This led to concern over the loss of wilderness and the animals that occupied those areas. Based on this concern, a number of organizations arose, such as the Sierra Club (founded in 1892). These organizations advocated for the preservation of wilderness as both a natural and a spiritual resource. This discourse took the form of preservation. It defines a spiritual and psychological relationship between humans and the natural environment. In this discourse, nature in the form of wilderness, untouched by human activity, has intrinsic value. Nature also serves as a site for self-renewal through the experience of its aesthetic beauty. This translates into a concern over the preservation of scenic areas, wilderness, and wildlife. Key components of this perspective are as follows:

- Natural systems are self-creating evolutionary wholes that cannot be reduced to the sum of their parts. Hence, nature is not a machine but an intact organism.
- Human actions can impair the ability of natural systems to maintain themselves or to evolve further.
- Wilderness and wildlife are important components in supporting both the physical and spiritual life of humans.
- Human values go beyond those measured by the national income accounts to include the preservation of wild lands and life.
- Continued existence of wilderness and wildlife is critical to the spiritual well-being of humanity.
- Protection of wilderness areas and wildlife for the current and future generations is an essential environmental task.

Several key features identify organizations based on this discourse. First, the organizations define their objective as preserving wilderness in a pristine state, untouched by humans. This includes leaving all of the plants and wildlife that inhabit that area to develop in a "natural" manner, that is, unaffected by human influences. They use phrases such as "preserve and protect" and "ensure the continued existence of wilderness areas." Some preservation organizations focus only on a specific species or geographic region. This is reflected in the name of the organization. Some examples of these types of organizations are the Sierra Club, the Wilderness Society, and the Nature Conservancy.

Reform Environmentalism

The most dominant discourse of the present day is reform environmentalism. This discourse is, in fact, so dominant that it is generally used to refer to the multiple discourses that make up the current environmental movement. However, this was not always the case. Up until around 1966, environmentalists were commonly referred to as "conservationists." This changed in the mid-1960s. In an enormous expansion of the environmental movement, reform environmentalism rose to its current position of dominance in under a decade.

Concern about pollution has been around since the mid-1800s. The development of industrialization brought the burning of coal, the concentration of factories, and human crowding in urban areas. This created environmental problems in the industrial cities in the United States, including crowded tenement districts, air and water pollution, garbage disposal problems, and occupational hazards in the rapidly expanding factories. The brunt of these environmental problems was borne by the working class and the poor. As shown in Lesson 16, this environmental pollution had adverse impacts on workers' health and economic opportunities.

Concerns over urban environmental pollution first manifested themselves in the sanitary movement. The sanitary movement arose after the Civil War to address community health problems. Its aim was to improve urban living conditions, and it dealt with problems such as sanitary water supplies, sewage systems, garbage, and air pollution. This was followed by concern over the excess of refuse and garbage in urban areas. Several protests occurred and a number of civic organizations were founded in the 1890s to demand urban cleanliness. This movement became known as the "municipal housekeeping movement." It primarily took the form of antilittering campaigns, education about sanitary procedures, city cleanup days, and advocating effective sanitation ordinances. Finally, around 1900, labor unions began pressing demands to address the exceptional levels of exposure to environmental pollution in urban factories.

However, these issues were not a major focus of the leading discursive frames of the early environmental movement in the form of wildlife management, preservation, or conservation. Following a number of highly publicized environmental pollution incidents and spurred on by the publication of Rachel Carson's book *Silent Spring,* pollution concerns rose dramatically among the American public. This gave rise to a new discursive community oriented around a concern that links human health and survival to environmental conditions. In this discourse, nature has a delicate balance and humans are part of it. This perspective emphasizes that nature is an ecological system, that is, a web of interdependent relationships. Humanity is part of this ecological system. Hence, human health is vulnerable to disturbances in the ecosystem. This animates action to identify and eliminate the physical causes of environmental degradation. Key components of this perspective are as follows:

- Natural systems are the basis of all organic existence, including that of humans.
- Humankind is an element within natural ecosystems, and hence, human survival is linked to ecosystem survival.
- Ethical human actions (actions which promote the good life for humankind) necessarily promote action toward all life on Earth in an ecologically responsible manner.
- Proper use of natural sciences can guide the relationship between humanity and its natural environment.

Organizations based in this discourse identify their purpose as protecting the Earth's ecosystem and human health. These organizations tend to use phrases such as "to protect and enhance human welfare and combat environmental deterioration" and "this organization is dedicated to improving environmental quality and public health." Some of the well-known organizations in this discursive community include Greenpeace, Environmental Defense, and the Natural Resources Defense Council.

Deep Ecology

Following the rise of reform environmentalism in the 1960s and 1970s, there was increasing disillusion with the results that the existing environmental movement was able to realize. One area of concern was the increasing exploitation of the few remaining natural areas in the United States. These concerns gave rise to the formation of the deep ecology movement in the early 1980s. Although part of the environmental movement, it is much more radical in its belief that the requirements to maintain intact natural systems should take precedence over human needs. At the core of this discursive frame is a belief in the intrinsic value of all nature that will ground a respectful way of living in and with the natural, nonhuman world. In this discursive frame, nature is seen as a value in its own right, independent of human existence. Humanity is only one species among many and has no right to dominate the Earth and all of the other living organisms. This creates an ethic of radical wilderness advocacy. Unlike preservation, which seeks to keep what remains, deep ecology seeks the restoration of fully functioning ecosystems, in which the evolution of life, unaffected by human actions, can continue. It also advocates the inherent rights of all nonhuman beings to exist in their natural state. In this sense, deep ecology makes a moral argument for the preservation of the natural environment. Key components of this discourse are as follows:

- All life on Earth, in its richness and diversity, has intrinsic value.
- Humankind's relations to the natural world presently endanger the richness and diversity of life.
- Human life is privileged only to the extent of satisfying vital needs.

- Maintenance of the diversity of life on Earth mandates a decrease in the human impacts on the natural environment and substantial increases in the wilderness areas of the globe.
- Changes (consistent with cultural diversity) affecting basic economic, technological, and cultural aspects of society are therefore necessary.

The organizations based in deep ecology generally define their objectives as acting to preserve the rights of all nonhuman beings to a natural existence, unaffected by human intervention. These organizations define their aims using phrases such as "defending the intrinsic rights of species to life" and "placing ecological considerations first in any decision-making process." Some of the well-known organizations in this discursive community include Earth First! and the Sea Shepherd Conservation Society.

Environmental Justice

A second component of the U.S. environmental movement that arose in the early 1980s was the environmental justice movement (see Lesson 10). Like deep ecologists, environmental justice advocates had a profound sense of disappointment over the results of the 1960s and 1970s environmental movement. However, the concern of this community was not wilderness. Rather, it was the unequal burden of pollution that was placed on poor and minority communities. Thus, they were concerned with exposures to persistent toxic pollution, in the form of local toxic waste dumps, high levels of air pollution, or unhealthy and polluted living conditions. From these concerns, a unique community arose that focused on urban environmental issues in systematically disadvantaged areas.

The discursive frame of environmental justice accepted the link between human survival and ecosystem survival as defined by reform environmentalism. However, instead of focusing on the physical causes of environmental degradation, this frame sees environmental problems as creations of human social order. Hence, the solution of environmental problems lies in social change. Key components of this viewpoint are as follows:

- Domination of humans by other humans leads to domination of nature.
- The economic system and nation-state are the core structures of society that create ecological problems.
- Commodifization and market imperatives force consumption to continually increase in the developed economy.
- Environmental destruction in low-income/racially distinct communities or third-world countries originates in the exploitation of the people who live in these areas by the dominant social institutions.
- Resolution of environmental problems requires fundamental social change based on empowerment of local communities.

Thus, environmental justice organizations focus on the social creation and resolution of environmental problems. While these groups focus on a large number of issues, they all seek to protect local communities from the adverse effects of environmental degradation. Additionally, regardless of their specific focus, groups based in the discourse of environmental justice define their objective as changing the social order in some manner to solve environmental problems. The means to carry out this goal include holding government and corporations accountable through democratic processes or by bringing legal suits to end toxic waste dumping. Some organizations with this orientation describe their purpose in phrases such as "create economic democracy through localized decision-making," "develop grassroots capabilities to involve local citizens in the resolution of their communities' environmental problems," and "abolish environmental racism." Some of the leading environmental justice organizations include the West Harlem Environmental Action Coalition, the Southwest Network for Environmental and Economic Justice, and the Indigenous Environmental Network.

Environmental Health

A discursive community closely associated with the environmental justice community is the environmental health movement (see Lesson 11). While the environment has always played a key role in community health, the relationship between environmental pollution and specific illnesses is still not widely acknowledged. However, in a number of diverse locations, individuals noticed a strong relationship between environmental pollution and their health. Some of the key examples are the extremely high rate of breast cancer among women on Long Island and the increasing rates of asthma among children exposed to automobile exhausts.

From this concern, a movement took shape in the late 1980s that focused on the relationship between environmental pollution and human health. This movement defined a unique discourse that encompassed the perspective of environmental health. Key components of this viewpoint are as follows:

- Human health is the outcome of interactions with physical, chemical, biological, and social factors in the natural environment, especially toxic substances and pollution.

- To ensure community health requires a livable and healthy community, with adequate social services and elimination of exposures to toxic or polluting substances.

- The precautionary principle (no technology or material can be used unless it is proven environmentally harmless) should guide industrial development.

The organizations in this discursive community seek to reduce the use of toxic materials and to ensure a safe and clean environment for all peoples. Organizations in this movement describe their purpose in phrases such as "preventing exposure to toxic materials that cause breast cancer," "creating safe schools to protect our children's health," and "ensuring that medical waste from hospitals is disposed of in an environmentally responsible way."

Some examples of actions taken by these types of organizations include demanding that all toxic materials are removed from schools to ensure that children are not exposed to them and calling for the safe disposal of industrial wastes. Some of the leading environmental organizations in this discursive community include the Center for Health, Justice and the Environment and 1 in 9: The Long Island Breast Cancer Action Coalition.

Ecofeminism

The fourth environmental discourse to develop in the 1980s was ecofeminism. This discursive community grew out of the feminist movement. Thus, it links the development of a patriarchal society and the domination of women by men to the domination of nature by humanity. Specifically, ecofeminism defines the problem of ecological degradation as originating in the treatment of nature as an object to be possessed and dominated, instead of a partner to be cooperated with. This cultural treatment of nature is tied to the development of a patriarchal society and the domination of women by men. Just as men dominate women, humanity dominates nature. Thus, the resolution of our ecological problems entails a shift from a manipulative and controlling culture toward both women and nature to a culture of cooperation. Key components of this discourse are as follows:

- Earth is home for all life and should be revered and nurtured.
- Ecosystem abuse is rooted in androcentric concepts, values, and institutions.
- Relations of complementarity rather than superiority between culture/ nature, human/nonhuman, and male/female are desirable.
- The many problems of human relations and relations between the human and nonhuman worlds will not be resolved until androcentric institutions, values, and ideology are eradicated.

There are very few ecofeminist organizations in existence. Those that do exist focus on empowering women to function as decision makers. Some examples of phrases used by ecofeminist organizations include "representing the viewpoints of all women in international affairs" and "facilitating the development of women in leadership roles in the environmental movement." In addition, they seek to correct the perspective in economic development programs that fail to recognize the role of women and the household economy in the overall system of economic production. The largest and best-known ecofeminist organization in the United States is the Women's Environment and Development Organization.

Ecospiritualism

In 1967, a landmark essay by Lynn White, titled "The Historical Roots of Our Ecologic Crisis," appeared in *Science* magazine. In this essay, White argued that the Western biblical tradition, on which both the Jewish and Christian faiths are based, was the root of the environmental crisis. Since the Bible created a separation of humans from nature, humans were seen as masters of and apart from the rest of creation. This image, White argued, created a wholly anthropocentric view of nature, in which humanity was commanded to subdue the Earth. So the exploitation of nature for human needs was natural and appropriate. The remedy for our ecological crisis was clear. He argued that if the biblical belief system created a disregard for the natural environment and led to our ecological crisis, we needed to develop a new religious viewpoint that would accommodate humans living in harmony with nature.

This viewpoint posed a major problem for Western theologians. The ecological crisis created doubt of the Christian idea that a providential god was providing for humanity. Following this essay, a number of different religious thinkers developed unique perspectives that integrated concern over the natural environment into religious belief systems. Out of these writings, a unique discourse of ecospiritualism emerged. Key components of this discourse are as follows:

- Nature is endowed with spiritual value.
- Humanity, as part of nature, has a moral obligation to preserve it intact.
- Religious beliefs need to be developed that embody this ethic.
- These beliefs can then inform actions to create an ecologically sustainable society.

This new viewpoint spread through the U.S. religious community, and by 1995, virtually all of the major churches in the United States issued proclamations on environmental degradation. Additionally, in 1993, the National Religious Partnership was formed. This organization is composed of the United National Council of Churches, the U.S. Catholic Conference, Consultation on the Environment and Jewish Life, and the Evangelical Environmental Network. This action united the major Protestant, Catholic, Jewish, and Evangelical communities into one organization focused on developing and implementing religious approaches to combat environmental degradation. Recently, this viewpoint has gained increasing support in large Evangelical churches. So while this discursive community is rapidly expanding, it has a unique structure. Its organizations are not single-focus social movement organizations. Rather, they involve religious organizations that are expanding their role into environmental affairs.

It is important to realize that there is no absolute line that defines the environmental movement. Rather, it is a gradient, moving from organizations that have an exclusive focus on environmental issues to those that deal with environmental issues as part of a group of associated issues. The final two discursive frames examined in this lesson fall into this category.

Animal Rights

The first related discursive frame is animal rights. Concern about the treatment of animals dates from 1866 in the United States, when the American

Society for the Prevention of Cruelty to Animals (ASPCA) was founded. Although the primary focus of this movement has always been on domestic animals and pets, it has also been a significant actor regarding the treatment and preservation of wildlife. For example, Henry Bergh, who founded the ASPCA, was a key force in trying to stop the indiscriminant slaughter of bison in the 1870s.

This concern over animals has developed into a well-defined discursive community. In this discursive frame, all species are seen to have intrinsic rights to realize their own evolved characteristics and to live an independent life free from human direction or intervention. Key components of this discourse are as follows:

- All of creation is endowed with an ability to define itself and evolve.
- Life thus has a right to be left to develop according to its own character.
- Humanity has no right to infringe on these rights of other animals.

The organizations in this discursive community usually focus on the protection of both domestic and wild animals. There are a large number of organizations that focus on the rehabilitation and release of injured or sick wildlife. Some of the better-known animal rights organizations in addition to the ASPCA include the Free Willy Keiko Foundation and People for the Ethical Treatment of Animals (PETA).

Antiglobalization/Greens

The second discursive frame related to the U.S. environmental movement is the antiglobalization/greens frame. This frame, which arose in the 1990s, focuses on the rise of a global economy and the impacts of this process on both the quality of life and the environment. Specifically, it sees the process of economic globalization and the weakening of national labor and environmental standards as encouraging a "race to the bottom" as nations lower these standards to attract business investments. Key components of this discursive frame are as follows:

- All humans and their communities deserve to live in an equitable, just, and environmentally sustainable world.
- Global abuses—such as ecological destruction, poverty, war, and oppression—are linked to global capitalism and the political and economic forces that have allowed the development of social inequality and injustices.
- The coercive powers of international financial institutions need to be eliminated so that national governments are accountable to the democratic will of their population.

This community of organizations is still developing. The first large-scale collective action of this community in the United States was the series of demonstrations in conjunction with the meeting of the World Trade Organization in Seattle in 1999. This community is loosely organized in the U.S. Network for Global Economic Justice, a coalition of over 200 social movement organizations. Some of the better-known organizations in this community include the Ruckus Society and the Pesticide Action Network of North America.

Distribution of Organizations by Discursive Frame

The number of organizations in each discursive frame is shown in Figure 15–1. As this graph shows, the largest number of organizations are found in the long-established discursive frames of reform environmentalism, preservation, and conservation. Together, these three discursive frames represent 78% of the environmental movement. All of the other discursive frames represent 5% or less of the total organizations. Thus, although a great deal of attention is given to the newer discursive frames in the academic literature, the environmental movement continues to be concentrated in these more conventional and long-lived discursive frames.

HISTORICAL DEVELOPMENT OF THE U.S. ENVIRONMENTAL MOVEMENT

The second approach to understanding the U.S. environmental movement is to examine its historical development over time. The current environmental movement is the result of the cumulative historical development of the different discursive communities over the past 150 years. This growth in organizations is shown in Figure 15–2. To simplify this presentation, the number of

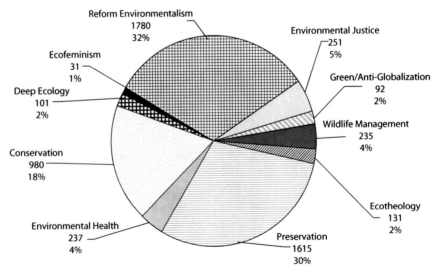

Figure 15–1 U.S. national and regional environmental organization distribution by discursive frame.

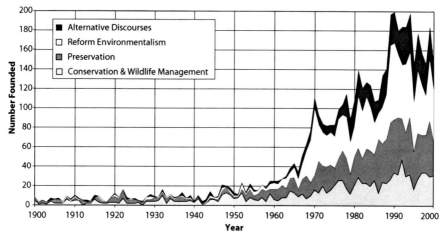

Figure 15-2 U.S. national and regional environmental organizations, 1900–2000.

discourses illustrated has been reduced. First, due to the relatively small number of organizations with the discourse of wildlife management and its close ideological similarity with conservation, these two discursive frames have been combined. Second, due to their small numbers, organizations with the discursive frames of animal rights, deep ecology, ecofeminism, ecospiritualism, environmental health, environmental justice, and antiglobalization/green have been combined into one category, labeled "Alternative Discourses." As this graph illustrates, there was a substantial increase in the numbers of organizational foundings starting in the mid-1950s up until around 1967. This was followed by explosive growth in 1968–1970 and again in 1988–1990.

To further examine this growth by different discursive frames, the relative growth rates of the different communities are shown in Figure 15–3. This graph clearly shows that the discursive frames of preservation and conservation/wildlife management were dominant until the end of the 1930s. In the 1940s, there was a significant rise in the number of alternative discursive organizations. This was due primarily to the increase of environmental health organizations founded during World War II. Additionally, the founding of preservation organizations dramatically declined in the 1940s. However, in the 1950s, preservation foundings increased rapidly, and conservation/wildlife management foundings started a long, slow decline. Additionally, reform environmental organizational foundings started a long and steady increase, which culminated in an explosive rate of growth around 1970. Additionally, as more alternative discursive frames were developed in the 1970s and 1980s, there was a slow but steady growth in these organizations in the time period from 1960 on.

What Figure 15–3 shows is that there are unique developmental dynamics to each discursive community. It is the cumulative impact of these different developmental dynamics that has led to the highly differentiated environmental movement we encounter today.

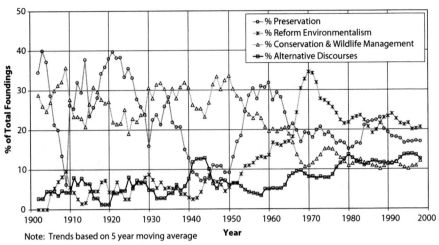

Figure 15–3 Foundings by discursive frame.

Note: Trends based on 5-year moving average.

ECONOMIC RESOURCE MOBILIZATION

The third approach to understanding the U.S. environmental movement focuses on the economic resources that each discursive community has available to promote its particular environmental agenda. The mobilization of economic resources is an extremely important determinant regarding the effectiveness of a discursive community to realize its goals. Every year, all nonprofit organizations are required to inform the U.S. Internal Revenue Service (IRS) of their income and expenses. Based on this information filed with the IRS in 2003, Table 15–1 shows the total income of these different discursive communities.

As Table 15–1 shows, fully 50% of the funding of the environmental movement is under the control of the organizations with a preservationist frame. This is followed by the other three mainstream discursive frames of reform environmentalism, wildlife management, and conservation, which range between 20.4% to 12.2% of the total income. The alternative discourses have very low levels of economic resources. Even if they are all combined, they total less than 5% of the total income distribution.

This economic distribution is mirrored in the income ranking of individual organizations. Table 15–2 shows the total and percent income distribution for the wealthiest 50 U.S. environmental organizations. Income among environmental organizations is highly skewed to a few extremely wealthy organizations. The Nature Conservancy, a large land trust organization, receives nearly 19% of the total environmental movement's income.

It is important to note that this list shows only the top 50 organizations. There are another 1,339 organizations that are not shown in this table. Between them, they divide the remaining 25.2% of total income. Thus, the

Table 15–1 Income Distribution by Discursive Frame - 2003

Frame	N	% of N	Total Income	% of Total	Mean	Median
Animal Rights	35	2.5%	95,542,298	1.9%	2,729,780	420,819
Conservation	223	16.0%	627,813,084	12.2%	2,815,305	345,421
Deep Ecology	34	2.4%	17,763,087	.3%	522,444	270,092
Ecofeminism	4	0.3%	2,027,480	>.1%	506,870	115,100
Ecospiritualism	12	0.9%	8,776,361	.2%	731,363	149,452
Environmental Health	33	2.4%	36,683,659	.7%	1,111,626	503,346
Environmental Justice	38	2.7%	57,301,562	1.1%	1,507,936	385,728
Green/Anti-Globalization	9	0.6%	8,844,870	.2%	982,763	571,318
Preservation	536	38.6%	2,590,627,143	50.3%	4,833,260	296,873
Reform Environmentalism	404	29.1%	1,048,293,688	20.4%	2,594,786	395,409
Wildlife Management	62	4.5%	656,084,214	12.7%	10,582,003	310,477
Total	1,390	100.0%	5,149,757,446	100.0%	3,704,861	348,058

Table 15–2 Income Distribution - Top 50 U.S. Environmental Organizations, 2003

Organization	Income	% of Income
Nature Conservancy	9,72,368,622	18.85
Wildlife Conservation Society	3,47,533,674	6.74
Sierra Club Foundation, The	2,41,236,005	4.68
Conservation International Foundation	2,29,267,098	4.44
Population Council	1,97,888,299	3.84
World Wildlife Fund	1,75,582,103	3.40
National Audubon Society	1,72,642,826	3.35
Trust For Public Land	1,53,915,522	2.98
National Wildlife Federation	1,32,004,722	2.56
Sierra Club	88,203,029	1.71
Tides Center	69,567,396	1.35
American Land Conservancy	68,110,320	1.32
Fresh Air Fund	65,459,125	1.27
Chesapeake Bay Foundation	61,007,116	1.18
Conservation Fund	60,133,583	1.17
Rocky Mountain Elk Foundation	55,418,970	1.07
Environmental Defense	51,657,887	1.00
Natural Resources Defense Council	50,063,972	0.97
World Resources Institute	48,241,872	0.93
Brandywine Conservancy	39,007,586	0.76
Earthjustice	34,266,715	0.66
Ocean Conservancy	31,981,555	0.62
Ducks Unlimited	31,475,354	0.61
Institute Of Ecosystem Studies	30,206,097	0.59
Association Of Village Council Presidents	29,865,852	0.58
Pheasants Forever	27,824,126	0.54
Yosemite Foundation	25,967,512	0.50

(continued)

Table 15–2 (continued)

Organization	Income	% of Income
Wilderness Society, The (Tws)	23,180,201	0.45
National Parks Conservation Association	22,147,238	0.43
Defenders Of Wildlife	21,779,921	0.42
National Arbor Day Foundation	21,337,542	0.41
African Wildlife Foundation	18,861,831	0.37
Student Conservation Association	18,714,956	0.36
Water Environment Federation	18,687,081	0.36
People For The Ethical Treatment Of Animals	18,652,096	0.36
Wetlands America Trust	17,171,656	0.33
Anti-cruelty Society	16,932,539	0.33
International Fund For Animal Welfare	16,634,365	0.32
Energy Federation Inc Incorporated	15,537,392	0.30
Environmental Careers Organization	15,468,856	0.30
Save The Redwoods League	14,546,107	0.28
American Forest Foundation	14,351,443	0.28
Coastal Conservation Association	14,265,263	0.28
Center For International Forestry Research	12,466,225	0.24
Aspen Center For Environmental Studies	12,402,810	0.24
Water Environment Research Foundation	12,042,492	0.23
National Save The Sea Turtle Foundation	11,349,324	0.22
Manomet Center For Conservation Sciences	11,212,735	0.22
Greenpeace Foundation	10,986,369	0.21
National Environmental Trust	10,715,102	0.21

vast majority of environmental organizations have very limited economic resources available to them. It is no surprise then that the organizations that mostly appear in the press and before Congress are those with sufficient funding to build and maintain a strong staff and organizational structure. Accordingly, one of the key areas of focus in current research into the environmental movement is why these funding differentials exist.

CONCLUSION

The U.S. environmental movement is not a monolithic structure. Rather, it is composed of a number of different discursive communities. Each of these communities has its own specific issue focus. Additionally, they developed under different historical and political circumstances and have widely varying levels of economic resources. To understand this highly complex social movement requires that we use the full range of social movement perspectives.

One certainty is that this is not a static movement. Over the past century, it has developed several new discursive frames and will most likely continue to do so in the future. There are several areas of potential development. For example, there has always been an uneasy alliance between trade unions and the environmental movement. Will they be able to develop a united political program? (See Lesson 16.) Additionally, the rise of environmental justice and the greens as significant actors in the movement has shaken the more established environmental organizations. How will these newer approaches work within the overall environmental movement? Finally, the discursive frames that were once dominant have been replaced by other approaches. What discursive frames will become dominant in the future? How this movement will evolve in the future is an open question. However, as it has in the past, it will continue to be a major player in the politics of the United States.

SOURCES

Bernstein, S. 2001. *The Compromise of Liberal Environmentalism*. New York: Columbia University Press.

Brulle, Robert J. 2000. *Agency, Democracy, and Nature: The U.S. Environmental Movement from a Critical Theory Perspective*. Cambridge, MA: MIT Press.

Buell, F. 2004. *From Apocalypse to Way of Life*. London, UK: Routledge.

Bullard, Robert D. 1990. *Dumping in Dixie: Race, Class and Environmental Quality*. Boulder, CO: Westview Press.

Dowie, M. 1996. *Losing Ground: American Environmentalism at the Close of the Twentieth Century* Cambridge, MA: MIT Press.

Fox, Stephen. 1981. *The American Conservation Movement: John Muir and His Legacy*. Madison, WI: University of Wisconsin Press.

Hays, Samuel P. 1972. *Conservation and the Gospel of Efficiency: The Progressive Conservation Movement, 1890–1920*. New York: Athenaeum.

Hays, Samuel P. 1987. *Beauty, Health, and Permanence: Environmental Politics in the United States, 1955–1988*. New York: Cambridge University Press.

Nash, R. 1967. *Wilderness and the American Mind*. New Haven, CT: Yale University Press.

Oelschlaeger, Max. 1991. *The Idea of Wilderness: From Prehistory to the Age of Ecology*. New Haven, CT: Yale University Press.

White, Lynn Townsend, Jr. 1967. "The Historical Roots of Our Ecologic Crisis." *Science* 155(3767):1203–1207.

16

Labor and the Environment

Brian K. Obach

I magine that you have worked in a lumber mill in a rural area in the Pacific Northwest for the last 15 years. Your father worked in the timber industry, as did his father before him. The timber industry is the primary economic engine in your area. Tourism has been growing, and the wilderness enthusiasts who come to town have also helped to bolster the economy through spending on lodging, supplies, and services. But the jobs associated with serving these visitors do not pay very well, and the mill remains the main employer. However, timber sector jobs have been disappearing in recent years. Several mills elsewhere in the region have shut down, and the mill at which you are employed has laid off several workers. So far, you've been able to keep your job; but unemployment is high, and there is much fear and concern among the mill workers about their employment situation.

The company says that the industry is being harmed by environmental groups that charge that logging is destroying the habitat of an endangered owl. The mill owners say that measures being promoted by "big city environmentalists" would "lock up" a good deal of forest land that the industry depends upon. Lawsuits filed by some environmental groups have already delayed logging on some parcels, and the company claims that this is what led to the recent layoffs. Along with your last paycheck the company included a request that everyone write to their congressional representatives to oppose any new logging restrictions. Many of your fellow workers have already done so, and talk about these "damn environmentalists who want to destroy our jobs" is common throughout the community. What do you think you would do in this situation? How do you think you would feel about environmentalists and the need for forest protection?

People form opinions and take political action on the basis of many different factors. As sociologists we recognize that people have different interests and are exposed to different ideas and influences depending on their social position, that is, their economic class, the region they live in, their age, their race, their gender, their education, and other important facets of their lives. Unless you are returning to school, as a college student you are probably fairly young, you are already relatively well educated, you might have a part-time job or work over the summer in the service sector, and, while you may not necessarily be well off now, your education level will likely place you in a job that does not involve manual labor and which will provide you with a relatively decent income in the future. On the basis of your social position and the influences to which you are exposed within that location, your views on many issues are likely to be different from those of a middle-aged career mill worker.

Research demonstrates that, as with most issues, views of environmental protection vary depending on one's social position. Thus, in order to understand (and to shape) our environmental future, it is important that we examine what influences people's attitudes regarding the need for environmental protection. Age has been found to be among the most important factors that shape opinions about the environment, with younger people expressing greater environmental concern than their older counterparts. But one's employment situation has also been found to shape perspectives on the environment.

If you were the mill worker described above, you might view the need for forest protection with some skepticism. Logging restrictions would pose a potential threat not only to the basic economic interests of you and your family but to your whole way of life and the community in which you live. If the mill were to shut down, you would find yourself out of work, your community would likely deteriorate without its primary economic engine, and you would be cut off from some of the cultural traditions that extend back in your family for generations. In addition, your employer, who not only signs your paychecks but whom you probably consider to be knowledgeable about the industry, is telling you that environmentalists are responsible for this threat. Many of your friends and coworkers share the view that environmentalists are a problem. And what's more, these environmentalists are outsiders who you do not know and do not necessarily trust. You know that logging has been done in your area for decades, even by members of your own family; and there have not been environmental problems before. What would these environmental activists, lawyers, and lobbyists based in Washington, D.C., or other big cities know about the forest that they probably never even visited in the first place? It is likely that if you were in that mill worker's social location, you would be suspicious about these environmental claims and possibly even hostile to environmental advocates and the cause that appears to threaten your livelihood.

This is not to suggest that every person in such a position is going to react to this situation in exactly the same way. Human beings are extremely complex, and while we know that social position *influences* the beliefs and behaviors that people develop, that position does not *determine* the opinions and attitudes of every individual. You probably hold some views different from your classmates, even though some of them share a generally similar social location. We could possibly better understand these differences with some fine-tuning regarding your particular experiences or variations in some specific features of your social location. Or perhaps we may have to attribute some variation to an autonomous individual "free will" or some unknowable complexities of human behavior. Similarly, some mill workers may still support environmental protection, even in the face of many strong social influences to act otherwise. Based on family upbringing or some bad experiences with bosses, some mill workers may doubt any statements made by their employers, including claims about the threat posed by environmental protection. Others may have had experiences that made them aware of the ecological damage caused by some modern logging practices, perhaps witnessing the degradation of a favorite childhood fishing stream.

Despite these complexities, it is clear that one's employment situation and the associated influences can affect the way one views issues, including that of environmental protection. Examining the relationship between labor and the environment will help us to answer important questions: Will environmental measures harm the economic condition of workers? Or might a failure to act to protect the environment harm some industries and destroy jobs? Who will be most affected by environmental measures and in what way? How will employment concerns shape workers' perspectives on environmental protection? How will such concerns shape their political behavior? Are there ways to effectively address both environmental concerns and the economic interests of working people? What is the role of government, of labor unions, of employers, and of environmental organizations in this process? Our future as a society will depend on what policies we develop to address environmental issues. Those policies will be shaped, in part, by mobilized segments of the public, people whose views about the need for environmental protection are in turn shaped by their employment situation. Thus, it is of crucial importance that we seek to understand the relationship between work and the environment.

ENVIRONMENTAL PROTECTION AND JOBS

Workers have obvious reasons to be concerned about environmental measures if they pose a direct threat to their jobs. But in reality, environmental regulations threaten very few jobs and, in many cases, actually *add* to employment. A 1997 study conducted by the Organisation for Economic Co-Operation and Development found that in economically developed nations "direct and indirect environment-related employment ranges between 1 and 3 percent of the labour force." Although certain industries may experience job loss due to some environmental measures, the study found that the net effect of environmental policies on employment is "on the whole...slightly positive."

Environmental policies can generate employment in many ways. In some cases the additional measures required by environmental regulations create a demand for workers to carry out those tasks. For example, the manufacture and maintenance of pollution control equipment represents work created as a result of environmental policy. Similarly, environmental cleanup work and habitat restoration employ many people. As suggested above, environmental protection also creates and sustains jobs in other sectors. Ecotourism has grown dramatically in recent decades, and in many regions, where attractive environmental features have been preserved, communities have prospered by selling services to tourists (see Lesson 19). Thousands more are employed as researchers, lawyers, lobbyists, and policymakers—all associated with protecting the environment. In the United States roughly 2 million people work in jobs that are directly or indirectly related to environmental protection. In recent years, recognition of the need for more environmentally sound products, such as vehicles, energy sources, and building materials, has spurred many new industries, creating tens of thousands of jobs globally. Given environmental imperatives and international measures being taken to address them, nations that have taken the lead in promoting environmentally sound, energy-efficient practices are likely to thrive economically relative to those that fail to act. Thus, pursuing these goals will have a dramatic, positive impact on employment.

It is also important to keep in mind that in some cases a failure to act to protect the environment may harm certain employment sectors. For example, manufacturing industries grew dramatically along the Hudson River in New York State during the early to mid-twentieth century. However, the pollution that these factories released into the river, including many toxic substances, ultimately decimated the fishing industry, which was an important part of the regional economy. Thousands of workers in the region lost their jobs as a result, and the fishing industry never fully recovered.

But despite the fact that environmental protection measures result in net job gains and protect workers in industries dependent on a healthy environment, in some rare instances particular jobs may be threatened by environmental policies. These factors are never as significant as other major influences on employment, such as trade policy, corporate restructuring, technological change, and the general ups and downs of the business cycle characteristic of capitalist economies. The relatively small impact of environmental regulation is not surprising given that environmental protection costs typically make up less than 2% of a firm's expenditures. Yet environmental compliance can still cost jobs in some instances. One economic analysis indicates that roughly 3,000 jobs are lost annually in the United States due to environmental regulation. This represents a tiny fraction of jobs lost nationally. In fact, more workers lose their jobs as a result of natural disasters than they do from measures taken to protect the environment. But any job loss represents serious hardship for the affected workers; therefore, concern about the economic impact of environmental policies can shape people's support or opposition to such measures.

Who actually stands to lose their job as a result of environmental protection? Some early studies found that environmental measures have contributed to job loss in the metal, chemical, and paper industries. But environmental economist Eban Goodstein found that workers in the extractive industries have borne the brunt of the job loss. For example, his research indicates that the Clean Air Act resulted in the loss of about 10,000 coal mining jobs in the 10 years following its passage. He found that a similar number of timber industry workers lost their jobs following the implementation of measures designed to protect the endangered northern spotted owl in the Pacific Northwest, the basis for the scenario introduced above.

While there is some evidence to suggest that environmental measures can cost jobs, tying job losses directly to environmental policies is very difficult. In the case of manufacturing industries, automation and outsourcing have had a dramatic effect on employment in recent decades, with environmental costs representing a small tangential element of the major trend of job loss in the manufacturing sector. Some even dispute the role of environmental measures in job losses in the timber industry. One study showed that timber employment had been decreasing for decades *before* owl habitat protection measures went into effect. There is even evidence to suggest that conservation measures *slowed* job loss since the unchecked pace of forest clearing would have resulted in more rapid industry decline. And again, other corporate actions, such as automation and the export of raw logs for processing overseas, have a greater effect on employment within the industry than environmental protection. But job losses in any way associated with environmental measures set the stage for political conflicts that can have serious implications for the kinds of environmental policies that will be enacted.

LABOR–ENVIRONMENTAL CONFLICTS

Even though the number of workers negatively affected is very small and the role of environmental measures in their plight is disputed, there have been a number of high-profile conflicts that allegedly pitted "jobs versus the environment." Most notorious among these are the "timber wars" of the 1980s and 1990s previously cited.

It is important to recognize that job loss fears and the associated political conflicts are likely to be more intense in the extractive industries because of their geographic location. Mining and timber extraction are often carried out in isolated rural communities in which the industry serves as the primary base of the local economy. Thus, entire communities can be mobilized if they believe that the whole of the local economy may be undermined. Even though environmental measures generate jobs in other areas of the economy, the extractive industry workers who lose out may not have the skills necessary to take advantage of those opportunities, nor are those jobs likely to be available in the communities in which they reside. Job loss fears are likely to be further heightened if workers already face economic insecurity, and employment in manufacturing and in extractive industries has declined precipitously in recent decades, leaving many workers in these industries anxious about their employment situation. Given this combination of factors, tight-knit rural communities that depend heavily upon a single industry are likely to unite and mobilize politically against perceived threats, especially those they see as coming from distant outsiders insensitive to their needs and way of life. It is these cases that have received the most attention and that have created the erroneous perception that there is an inevitable trade-off to be made between jobs and the environment.

Although authentic employment impacts from environmental measures are very rare, employers who do not want to assume the cost of environmental protection often exaggerate the job impact that such measures will have. As in the lumber mill scenario, business owners will use what some refer to as "job blackmail" as a means to mobilize workers and communities to build political pressure against environmental measures. Politicians themselves may seek to exploit such fears for political gain. While running for president in 1992, George Bush, Sr., claimed that if his more environmentally sympathetic opponents were elected "we'll be up to our neck in owls and outta work for every American." Exaggerated claims such as this coming from politicians or industry leaders heighten tensions and foment conflict between workers and environmentalists.

In addition to economic threats, employers seeking to mobilize opposition to environmental measures may take advantage of the cultural differences that exist between blue-collar workers and the middle-class professionals who often fund or make up the active membership base of many large environmental organizations. In *Coalitions Across the Class Divide*, Fred Rose argues that educational differences and work experiences provide middle-class professionals with different understandings about the natural environment, about work, and about the value of scientific expertise relative to direct experience. These cultural differences can be used to heighten fears about unfamiliar outsiders who threaten the workers' way of life. The situation is made worse when environmental advocates are insensitive to worker concerns or when they harbor stereotypes about ignorant blue-collar workers who don't understand what is really good for them. These cultural differences by themselves can result in suspicion that inhibits compromise and the pursuit of mutually beneficial approaches to environmental problems. But this cultural gap is particularly difficult to overcome when employers or politicians exploit these differences to foster divisions around environmental issues and their job implications.

THE ROLE OF LABOR UNIONS IN ENVIRONMENTAL CONFLICT

As sociologists we know that we can learn a great deal about people by examining the conditions under which they live, and clearly one's employment situation is a very significant aspect of one's life. After all, for most people, it is through their labor that they earn their livelihood. It is also what many of us spend much of our lives doing. As a college student you may already be working at a part-time or full-time job. But even if you are not currently employed, enrollment in college is probably tied to your aspirations for future employment. Because it is so central to our lives, sociologists, from the founding of the discipline, have placed a great deal of attention on economic institutions. The classical theorists each focused on aspects of the economy, from Emile Durkheim's analysis of the division of labor to Max Weber's research on the origins of capitalism to Karl Marx's detailed examination of class within capitalist economies. Marx in particular was attuned to the conflicts that emerge around economic issues and the power that some groups have relative to others; thus, the general branch of theory emerging from his work is sometimes referred to as "conflict theory."

We could apply conflict theory to our example to understand how mill owners exercise power in order to advance their interests within the economy. This power can be seen on the macro level, in terms of influence over the political and economic systems, down to the micro level control that an individual supervisor can exercise over an employee. Timber industry owners and other capitalists have power in that they can choose to disinvest and close down their business or move it elsewhere, thus dramatically affecting the lives of hundreds or even thousands of workers. They can also influence government policy through lobbying and campaign support, thus shaping the laws that govern every member of society. At the micro level, they can use their power and influence at the workplace to pressure individual workers into opposing environmental measures that may threaten profitability. Although those who own the means of production, in this case the lumber mill, have a great advantage when seeking to influence government action, such as environmental policy, in some cases there are other workplace actors who can play an important role in influencing individual workers and even, at times, in influencing larger policies and the general distribution of power within society. The organizations that play this role are labor unions.

Capitalist economies tend to foster organization among workers in order to counter the imbalance of power within a system based on the private ownership of the means of production. Most individual workers, because they lack assets of their own off of which they can live, are forced to sell their labor to those who own the means of production. These capitalists employ workers to produce goods so that they can obtain profit by selling those goods on the market at a rate higher than that which it cost them to have the goods produced. One way in which capitalists can increase profits is by minimizing labor costs, that is, by paying workers as little as is necessary. Workers usually understand their lack of power as individuals within this situation. After all, a single worker is rarely of great value to any large enterprise; and in any case, within market economies there is always a pool of additional unemployed workers to draw from if any single worker needs to be replaced. But at times workers recognize that if they were to join together and act collectively they would be better positioned to challenge their employer and to demand better treatment. Workers, and disadvantaged people generally, have done this in one way or another throughout history; and in the context of the workplace environment in capitalist economies, this takes the form of labor unions.

Through the formation of unions, workers pledge to act together as a unit in order to counterbalance the advantage of the employer. While the employer can carry on unharmed without any single employee, if all of the workers were to walk off the job simultaneously, that is, if they were to strike, they can impose significant costs on the business owner. Of course, employers still have a great advantage because, unlike the workers, they have the wealth necessary to secure their own survival (not to mention their very significant influence over other institutions such as the political system, the police, and the military); but at least under some circumstances, employers may find it to be in their interest to make concessions to workers in the face of a strike or other workplace disruption.

Because conflicts between workers and owners are so common, most nations have developed labor relations systems to manage these relationships. The system of labor relations varies a great deal from nation to nation. In some countries, such as China, independent unions are illegal and workers are allowed to organize only through unions closely tied to the Communist Party, which controls the government. In others, such as Colombia, unions are not prohibited but they have few enforceable rights, which leaves them vulnerable to violent repression by employers or their agents. Other nations, such as Sweden and Germany, have labor relations systems in which unions are afforded a number of legal protections that enable them to operate almost as equals with employers in making important decisions about issues such as workplace organization and compensation levels.

In the United States, unions have few protections relative to other industrialized democracies. Laws are designed and enforced in ways that make it fairly easy for employers to impose their terms on unions or to prevent workers from forming unions altogether. During the late nineteenth and early twentieth centuries, prior to the creation of a formal industrial relations system, only skilled craft workers were successful at establishing lasting unions. But by the mid-twentieth century, through the use of militant tactics and newly developed legal protections, unskilled manufacturing workers were able to form unions of their own. Although the labor relations system that developed placed workers at a grave disadvantage, the period of great economic growth and prosperity that followed World War II allowed employers to accommodate U.S. unions while still profiting immensely. Although many workers were left without unions during this period, those who were union members, even unskilled blue-collar workers, advanced economically and built the middle class in the United States.

However, when the economy went into recession in the 1970s, employers sought to protect profits by taking advantage of weak labor protections to challenge unions and drive down wages. Since then, a number of political and economic developments have furthered organized labor's decline in the United States. Technological developments have made it easy for employers to disburse production to places where unions are weak or nonexistent, while at the same time reducing the need for workers through automation (see Lesson 5). Free-trade agreements and economic globalization have allowed employers to move or threaten to move production to take advantage of low wages or weak regulations abroad. This further diminished labor's bargaining power within a labor relations system that accorded them few real protections to begin with.

As a result of these factors and an aggressive anti-union assault by employers, the United States has seen its rate of unionization decline precipitously from roughly 35% of the workforce in 1955 to about 12% today. The decline has been most severe in the manufacturing sector, labor's traditional stronghold. A wave of public sector unionization that occurred in the 1960s and 1970s enabled labor to prevent their numbers from declining further, the public sector being an area where employers are not desperate to protect profit and where jobs are not easily relocated. But private sector service employment, the largest employment sector of the U.S. economy, is still largely nonunionized; and together with the decline of unionized manufacturing employment, the U.S. labor movement is among the weakest compared to movements in other economically developed democracies.

Despite their current weakness, unions have a potentially very significant role to play in relation to environmental policy. Unions help to synthesize worker concerns and enable individuals to act collectively to advance their interests, and clearly workers, like all people, have an interest in a safe and healthy environment. In fact, survey research indicates that union members report stronger support for environmental measures than the average worker. Unions could serve as vehicles for advancing these sentiments, and sometimes they have. Yet their position on environmental issues is complicated and inconsistent. In some instances unions have mobilized workers to promote environmental protection, yet in other cases they have sided with employers to oppose environmental measures.

Some of this has to do with the particular industry in which the union members are based. For those workers who face real potential threats to jobs, it is easy to see why their union might oppose certain environmental measures. For example, the United Mine Workers have opposed a number of air pollution measures that they perceived would harm their industry and contribute to job loss. Similarly, the United Auto Workers have, in the past, opposed measures that would require improved auto fuel economy out of fear that it would weaken U.S. competitiveness in this industry. But there are other factors that shape union behavior more broadly.

In order to understand the positions that U.S. unions take on matters of the environment, it is important to first examine some key features of the U.S. industrial relations system and some crucial developments in U.S. labor history. The legal framework of the industrial relations system in the United States and the way that unions have structured themselves tend to channel unions into focusing on specific job-related issues, most significantly compensation. The primary way in which unions and employers establish terms regarding employment is through collective bargaining. Through this process the two parties create a contract that specifies the rights and responsibilities of each side in the employment relationship. The National Labor Relations Act, the most significant piece of legislation defining the industrial relations system in the United States, specifies the mandatory subjects of bargaining as "wages, hours and working conditions." Working conditions can include issues related to the environment, especially when workers must handle hazardous materials. But because collective bargaining is usually focused on the specific workplace, larger issues related to environmental degradation are not considered in the context of collective bargaining and most emphasis is placed upon wages and other forms of compensation.

Of course, unions do not act on behalf of worker interests at the workplace exclusively; unions also serve as the primary political voice for working people, and in this capacity, unions could play a significant role in efforts to advance environmental legislation. But because the labor relations system encourages unions to focus on specific job-related matters, their political work also tends to stay within this framework. Even labor federations, which are designed to advance broader political goals of interest to the array of unions that make up the federation, tend not to address many issues that are not directly tied to workplace or economic concerns. So despite the fact that environmental sentiments may be strong among union members, their unions rarely involve themselves with such issues, especially when environmental measures may threaten their own economic interests or those of other union workers. Thus, for the most part, labor's political priorities have focused on job protection and economic expansion, policies that tend to threaten the environment through unchecked material consumption (see Lesson 5).

In addition to the way in which the labor relations system channels unions away from environmental action, certain historical developments have served to limit the scope of issues with which unions concern themselves. As mentioned, following World War II unions gained acceptance from major employers in manufacturing industries, and through the efforts of their unions, workers were given a share of the wealth that was generated during those prosperous years. But this was also the peak of the cold war, and unions were caught up in the anticommunist hysteria that gripped the nation as a whole during that era. This anticommunist sentiment led to the purging of many radical labor leaders and activists from the union movement. The more radical elements within organized labor tended to seek broad social change goals that went beyond wages, hours, and working conditions. They sought to improve society and to empower the working class as a whole. When they were forced out of the labor movement, the remaining more conservative leaders focused narrowly on advancing the material interests of their particular members, and goals outside of that framework tended to be deprioritized or removed entirely from the labor agenda. In this context, environmental issues were usually addressed only when they had immediate job implications.

Despite the channeling effect of the American labor relations system and the conservative tendencies of the labor leadership, some unions still weighed in, on occasion, in support of environmental protection. While at times there were clear job gains to be had through environmental measures, as with labor's strong support for the creation of public sanitation systems, in other instances unions backed environmental policies even when they did not have direct implications for the economic concerns that they took as their primary focus. For example, unions were early supporters of clean water and clean air legislation. The American Federation of Labor-Congress of Industrial Organizations (AFL-CIO), the main labor federation representing almost all unions at the time, endorsed the creation of a wilderness preservation system as early as 1960, years before the rise of the modern environmental movement.

These examples of labor support for environmental protection in and of itself are relatively rare. But one area where labor has been active historically is that of environmental health and safety. Health and safety issues have always been on labor's agenda, although this has never been given the same attention as wages and benefits. But because unions seek to protect worker health, this creates fertile ground for cooperation with some in the environmental community (see Lesson 15). Historically, unions were supportive of environmental groups that took industrial pollution as their focus. This environmental health movement emerged from a different social context from that of the wilderness advocates who also began to mobilize in the late nineteenth and early twentieth centuries. While early conservationists and preservationists tended to be elites seeking to protect resources for industrial or recreational uses, environmental health advocates were rooted in working-class urban areas where working people and their families were being subjected to the toxic effluence from industrial production.

This link between environmentalism and worker health has, to this day, provided an opportunity for unions and environmental advocates to come together. After all, the toxic materials that can threaten worker health inside the plant are the very ones that threaten the outside community and the natural environment when they leave the plant. The 1980s saw heightened cooperation between unions and environmentalists around these issues. Spurred on by their common political adversary, President Ronald Reagan, who sought to roll back all manner of government regulation and services, unions and environmental organizations worked closely together to advance the regulation of hazardous materials.

An important leader in labor's workplace health efforts and a key figure in advancing greater cooperation between unions and environmental advocates was Tony Mazzocchi. Mazzocchi was a leader of the former Oil, Chemical and Atomic Workers union (OCAW), where he was an outspoken advocate for workplace health and safety. He helped to usher through the Occupational Safety and Health Act, the central national legislation that addresses workplace health issues. But Mazzocchi was also a committed environmentalist, and he sought to bridge the gap between unions and environmental advocates. He saw the shared concerns of workers and environmentalists, but he also recognized the tensions spawned by job loss fears associated with some environmental measures. In order to overcome these concerns, he called for the creation of a federal program that would provide workers displaced by environmental measures with a "just transition" to new employment through continued compensation and educational opportunities. He viewed this as a way to neutralize the job blackmail that employers commonly used to mobilize workers against environmentalists, while protecting workers from having to bear a disproportionate share of the cost of environmental protection.

Although no program as extensive as Mazzocchi's proposal has ever been implemented, there have been some efforts to provide displaced workers with support. For example, the Clinton administration created a program that provided economic assistance and retraining for workers who lost jobs resulting from forest protection measures. Critics charge that such policies rarely provide the support that workers need to compensate for the losses they experience; but the principles that Mazzocchi advanced still represent perhaps the best means by which to overcome the tension that can emerge between labor and the environment, and many still advocate for such a program.

LABOR AND THE ENVIRONMENT TODAY

Given the basic structure of our economic and political institutions, there are always likely to be some tensions, real or perceived, between labor and the environment. When workers are unorganized, they are particularly vulnerable to job loss claims from employers who seek to mobilize them against environmental measures. And even when workers are organized, when unions cling to a narrow agenda of economic self-interest and job protection, they can compound the problem by siding with employers against environmental advocates. But there are some signs that more unions are willing to expand their agendas to include issues of broader concern to workers and that they are open to cooperation with other movements, including the environmental movement.

This new approach was introduced in 1995 when the old-guard leadership of the AFL-CIO was defeated by a reform slate of candidates. The new AFL-CIO president, John Sweeney, promised a different direction for labor, with a focus on organizing new members and reaching out to other progressive movements. This newfound willingness to join in alliance with other movements can be interpreted as an act of necessity on the part of organized labor. Unions have lost so much of their power that they recognize the need for support from others in order to advance their goals, and, by necessity, that entails offering reciprocal support for other causes.

From labor's perspective, these alliances must still be strategically assessed in terms of whether they stand to advance core economic goals. After all, the basic structure of the labor relations system remains in place, and workers still expect that their union will primarily act to advance their work-related interests. Thus, unions, and for that matter environmental organizations, are still constrained in the extent that they can fully support one another's goals when there is not a direct link to the primary mission of their own organizations. But there does appear to be a growing willingness on the part of both labor and environmental advocates to seek out those opportunities for cooperation. This shift can be tied to the larger economic trends that affect both movements.

One major economic trend that threatens the interests of both workers and environmentalists is what is known as "trade liberalization" (a trade policy that is part of a broader "neoliberal" political perspective). *Trade liberalization* refers to the removal of government restrictions on trade and the flow of capital between nations (see Lesson 10). Historically, governments have regulated trade and taxed the importation of goods in order to protect domestic industries, to raise funds, or to prevent the sale of goods considered unsafe or otherwise harmful to consumers. Proponents of trade liberalization, including many large corporations with operations spread across several countries, argue that restrictions on trade or overseas investment inhibit the efficiency of the free market, thus driving down profits and increasing the costs of goods. Critics charge that trade liberalization simply provides employers with the opportunity to relocate operations in order to take advantage of low wages and weak workplace and environmental regulation abroad.

Opposition to trade liberalization is an important force in bringing workers and environmentalists together. Unrestricted trade greatly diminishes the ability of workers and environmentalists to improve conditions domestically as all nations are caught up in a "race to the bottom" as they seek to entice private investment through lower wages and weaker regulation. In recent years some of the most significant examples of labor–environmental alliance building have occurred as a result of mutual opposition to trade liberalization. In the early 1990s some environmental organizations joined with organized labor in opposing the North American Free Trade Agreement. But the most dramatic instance of mutual effort in this area came during the 1999 protests against the World Trade Organization (WTO) in Seattle, Washington. There, tens of thousands of unionists and environmental advocates, among others, came together to speak out against the neoliberal policies being advanced through the WTO. Although headlines focused on the violence that erupted when police engaged protesters, the most notable aspect of the event was the coming together of such a diverse coalition. While each group had its own reasons to oppose the WTO agenda, the event nonetheless demonstrated the possibility of a united labor-environmental movement. But this kind of cooperation has come in starts and stops. Soon after the WTO protest, goodwill was undermined by divisions between some unions and environmentalists over energy policy.

Still, unions and environmentalists are becoming more creative about finding ways to cooperate and to identify common ground. Issues of health and safety have continued to serve as an area of intermovement cooperation. New organizations have sprung up in recent decades, following in the footsteps of the early public health organizations that addressed environmental concerns during the early industrial period. Antitoxics organizations have formed to fight the environmental and health effects resulting from the use of poisonous chemicals in manufacturing and agriculture. Environmental justice organizations, composed primarily of working-class people of color, have formed to fight against environmental health threats which disproportionately plague their communities (see Lesson 10). These organizations typically develop out of local struggles against immediate environmental health threats. While still generally considered to be part of the broader environmental movement, their members tend to have more in common culturally and economically with unions than do traditional middle- and upper-class conservation and preservation organizations. But even the larger professional environmental groups have in many cases integrated health and social justice issues into their agendas, thus creating more opportunity for overlap with their union counterparts.

This is in addition to many new efforts to identify and build coalitions around common interests. For example, the Apollo Alliance is a coalition of unions, environmental advocates, and others formed in 2003 in order to press forward an agenda of rebuilding America's industrial base through a focus on clean energy technology. Unions and environmentalists have identified this as an area of mutual interest, advancing environmental protection while creating good union jobs. The Just Transition Alliance is another coalition of unions and environmental advocates seeking to foster intermovement cooperation based on the principles originally advocated by Tony Mazzocchi.

All of these alliance-building efforts, even when initially based upon calculated self-interest, open the door to still further cooperation. Many cases provide evidence to show that instrumental cooperation of this sort can grow into a true merging of interests. As unionists get to know and work with environmental advocates, stereotypes about insensitive elitists or deluded "tree huggers" begin to fall away, and they come to recognize that environmentalists are sincere people concerned about real threats to the environment and to human well-being. Similarly, environmentalists who work with labor advocates come to understand that unionists are not selfish or ignorant "hard hats" but people who are trying desperately to protect the basic economic security that many workers feel slipping away. As this mutual understanding grows, both unions and environmental organizations are more likely to integrate all of these concerns into their advocacy agendas.

LABOR AND THE ENVIRONMENT TOMORROW?

At this historical juncture advocates for both workers and the environment face tremendous challenges. Although the environmental movement has been successful at raising awareness about threats to the environment, efforts to actually stave off environmental crisis have not made substantial progress. National environmental policies and global treaties designed to address important issues such as global warming, species loss, and forest preservation have failed to fundamentally alter the historical trajectory of ongoing ecological degradation. Workers are also losing ground. Economic inequality is growing globally and within most nations. Little progress has been made to alleviate the extreme poverty that plagues a significant percentage of the world's population. Economic globalization has undermined the ability of both unions and environmentalists to hold accountable increasingly mobile corporate actors. Thus, on both fronts, many conclude that the prospects for rapid, significant changes are poor. But these meager hopes are greatly diminished when workers and environmental advocates are placed at odds with one another. Both have an interest in challenging the private interests that seek to exploit workers and the environment. Although their positions within existing political and economic institutions can, on some occasions, place them at odds on the basis of certain narrowly defined interests, an alliance between these movements or a new movement that embodies their respective goals represents perhaps the greatest hope of achieving a world that is both sustainable and just.

Let's return now to the hypothetical scenario with which we began, only now you are the son or daughter of the mill worker. Your mother, who by now has lost her job at the mill, is currently enrolled in an accounting program at a nearby college, where her tuition is being paid by a federal program that has also extended her old mill salary for 2 years while she is retrained. She hopes to get a job with a computer software firm that recently moved to the area, attracted by the high quality of life in the region, which can be attributed, at least in part, to strong environmental protection measures. Other former mill workers have taken jobs at a new artificial wood manufacturing facility that uses recycled plastics and paper milk cartons to make a highly durable wood substitute. This facility was developed through a federal program that brought together environmental technology investors with the Paper, Allied-Industrial, Chemical and Energy International Union. These unionized workers now earn more than they had at the former mill. You are working at a camping supply store during the summer serving the growing tourist population, but you are going away to college in the fall to study history and business. You plan to return to your community after graduation to open a bed-and-breakfast with an adjoining historical education center that focuses on the history of the timber industry. Consider how you might feel about environmental protection policies from this vantage point. As in the original scenario, your views are going to be shaped by your social position, and a significant aspect of that is your labor force status and associated economic prospects. But institutional and policy changes have greatly altered the constraints and opportunities presented to you, and this is likely to affect your attitudes about environmental protection, perhaps in ways that would lead to still more environmental policy improvements.

The need to drastically change the way that society interrelates with the rest of the natural environment is imperative. But existing institutional arrangements in many cases perpetuate ecologically destructive practices. The distribution of power in our society and the conditions under which people live and work create a confluence of forces that inhibit desperately needed changes. Our role as sociologists is to seek to understand how these institutional arrangements operate and, more importantly, to identify ways to reshape those institutions such that we are able to create a socially just and ecologically sustainable society. Examining how work life can be made compatible with such goals is a central part of that mission.

SOURCES

Dewey, Scott. 1998. "Working for the Environment: Organized Labor and the Origins of Environmentalism in the United States: 1948–1970." *Environmental History* 1:45–63.

Dreiling, Michael. 1998. "From Margin to Center: Environmental Justice and Social Unionism as Sites for Intermovement Solidarity." *Race, Class and Gender* 6(1):51–69.

Foster, John Bellamy. 1993. "The Limits of Environmentalism Without Class: Lessons from the Ancient Forest Struggle of the Pacific Northwest." *Capitalism, Nature and Socialism* 4(1):1–18.

Goodstein, Eban. 1999. *The Trade-Off Myth: Fact and Fiction About Jobs and the Environment*. Washington, DC: Island Press.

Gottlieb, Robert. 1993. *Forcing the Spring*. Washington, DC: Island Press.

Gottlieb, Robert. 2001. *Environmentalism Unbound*. Cambridge, MA: MIT Press.

Gould, Kenneth, Tammy Lewis, and J. Timmons Roberts. 2004. "Blue–Green Coalitions: Constraints and Possibilities in the Post 9–11 Political Environment." *Journal of World-System Research* 10(1):90–116.

Kazis, Richard, and Richard Grossman. 1991. *Fear at Work*. Philadelphia, PA: New Society Publishers.

Obach, Brian K. 2004a. "New Labor: Slowing the Treadmill of Production?" *Organization and Environment* 17(3):337–54.

Obach, Brian. K. 2004b. *Labor and the Environmental Movement: The Quest for Common Ground*. Cambridge, MA: MIT Press.

Organisation for Economic Co-Operation and Development. 1997. *Environmental Policies and Employment*. Paris: OECD Publications.

Rose, Fred. 2000. *Coalitions Across the Class Divide*. Ithaca, NY: Cornell University Press.

17

Environmental Movements in the Global South

Tammy L. Lewis

The term "environmentalist" means different things to different people. In North America, someone who recycles and buys "green" products might call himself or herself an environmentalist, as might someone who is concerned with the environmental effects of overpopulation, while another environmentalist argues that capitalism destroys nature. In the North American tradition, environmentalism has been strongly associated with membership in environmental organizations, such as the Sierra Club and the Nature Conservancy. Environmentalists in the Global South (lower-income countries of Latin America, Africa, and parts of Asia) also cover a broad range of beliefs and practices and do not fit neatly into one single box. In the Global South, there is less emphasis on membership in environmental organizations as defining an "environmentalist." While there are overlapping concerns between environmentalists North and South, I begin by outlining some fundamental differences between environmentalists and environmental movements in the Global North and the Global South.

DIFFERENCES BETWEEN ENVIRONMENTALISM IN THE GLOBAL NORTH AND IN THE GLOBAL SOUTH

In *Environmentalism: A Global History*, Ramachandra Guha asks readers to consider the differences between the "ecology of affluence" and "environmentalism of the poor." Guha, and others writing from the perspective of the Global South, argues that there is a strong environmentalism in the "third world" (the term that used to be used for what is now called the "Global South") that looks different from the environmental movement in the United States and other nations in the Global North (for example, Canada and countries in Western Europe).

The first and most visible difference is simply in organizational structure and tactics. The U.S. movement is considered "professionalized" in that it is made up of formal organizations, with paid leaders and staffs, large budgets, lobbying arms, and extensive fundraising mechanisms. This differs from collective action groups based on volunteer labor, with small to no budgets, that organize people to engage in direct action to preserve their local means of subsistence (the "environment").

The organizational differences are actually a result of different origins. Many southern struggles are struggles in defense of economic livelihood. They arise from threats to people's economic survival. For instance, local "environmental" opposition forms when local economic resources are threatened. One of the most popular examples of this is the rubber tappers' movement in Brazil from the 1980s. Briefly, the rubber tappers extracted rubber from trees in a sustainable manner to earn a living. When the trees were threatened by cattle ranchers who wanted to clear the forests for ranching, the rubber tappers' union resisted the ranchers and fought for control of the land they had long used to make a living. Rubber tappers resisted environmental change because it threatened their economic well-being. Whether we classify this as an "economic" movement or an "environmental" movement is an interesting question. Later, I will discuss this question in greater detail. For now, the point is that southern environmentalism is often tied to economic rights.

This leads to the third big difference in environmentalism North and South: the understanding of how humans fit into nature. Guha argues that a major difference between environmentalism in the Global South and that in the Global North has been the South's view that the environmental struggle is inseparable from the struggle for social justice. The nature–society dichotomy that is prevalent in Western thought is not as widespread in other cultures (see also Lessons 1 and 18). Therefore, movements in other societies see humans as part of the environment, and thus, the struggle for human rights is integrated into a movement to preserve the environment. When working to save the environment, these groups see that they are working to save themselves.

Environmentalism in North America was founded with the idea of preserving nature for nature's sake (what we might now call "biodiversity preservation") and for the good of humanity (see Lesson 15). John Muir, first president of the Sierra Club (1892), argued for protecting undeveloped and undisturbed habitats (like national parks) so that the public could visit these areas for spiritual uplift and recreational activities. Later, U.S. conservationists such as Gifford Pinchot (chief of the U.S. Division of Forestry, 1898) would argue that we needed to conserve lands for future development and the "wise use" of resources (though still not viewing humans as "in" nature).

Today, that we have environmentalism within both wealthy and poor nations challenges conventional wisdom that environmentalism is simply an elite movement. Before the growth of the environmental justice movement in the United States, and even since, there was a stereotype of environmentalists as "elitists." In the United States, this stereotype has some validity if we look only to the history of land preservation and conservation. Muir, Pinchot, and others advocating for land protection were elite, well-educated white men. However, if we expand our historical lens and take a broader view of environmentalism in the early part of the 1900s, we see that there were movements in U.S. cities, often led by women, who were fighting for adequate sanitation and appropriate trash disposal. While they are not commonly thought of as part of the United States' "environmental" history, today we might call them "urban environmentalists".

Just as the charges of "elite" environmentalism are largely false in the United States, they are also false across the globe. Though affluence creates opportunities to participate in the movement, nonetheless concern about the environment is not limited to elites. In fact, concern about the environment is high North and South, and in some cases, there is more concern in the Global South. Not only "elite" (rich) nations are environmentalist. Steven R. Brechin and Willett Kempton have analyzed responses to public opinion data from around the world that show that richer nations do not have a higher level of environmental concern than poorer nations. In fact, in many cases, the opposite is true. For example, 77% of Mexicans surveyed perceive air pollution to be a serious problem and 81% perceive species loss as "very serious." By contrast, in the United States, 60% perceive air pollution as a problem and 50% perceive species loss to be "very serious." In their analysis, they showed that wealthier nations were more willing to pay more for environmental protection. However, poorer nations were more willing to pay in time (a resource more available than money for many in these nations) than were the respondents in richer nations. In sum, Brechin and Kempton conclude that environmental concern is not just a concern for the rich; the concern is global.

In the Global South, as with environmental justice activists in the Global North (often working class and racial and ethnic minorities), concerns are directed at the immediate environment and the immediate threats to well-being.

GRASSROOTS CASES FROM INDIA, NIGERIA, AND BOLIVIA

Three brief examples from three different continents will illustrate how environmental actions (variously called "movements," "campaigns," and "environmentalisms") in the Global South are intertwined with livelihood struggles and how they are closely tied to attempts to promote social justice. There are numerous examples to draw from; I have selected one case each from Asia (the Chipko movement in India), Africa (the Movement for the Survival of the Ogoni People in Nigeria), and Latin America (the "water war" in Bolivia). While reading about these cases, keep in mind the environmental justice struggles going on in the United States (see Lesson 10). Some of these struggles take place in indigenous communities and others take place in industrial workplaces (see Lesson 16). They also occur in places where people live, especially in working-class and minority communities (see Lesson 12). So, while we make a distinction between environmentalism of the rich and environmentalism of the poor, these are not just differences between rich and poor nations, for there is also diversity of movement types within nations. The three cases that I present are well-known, often-referenced, historically important cases.

Asia: The Chipko Movement in India

The Chipko Movement began in 1973 and is perhaps the first internationally recognized "ecology" movement from a developing country. It became well known because of its use of direct action and due to the participation of women in the struggle.

After years of coping with flooding and the need to travel long distances for fuel wood, problems caused by deforestation and soil erosion, peasants in the Himalayan village of Mandal decided to put a stop to logging in the state-owned forests around their village. The village activists, many of whom were women, literally placed their bodies between the loggers and the trees. The loggers stopped; they did not cut the trees. This practice spread to other areas—the Reni forests and other parts of the region. This was not a centralized movement. Rather, disparate communities replicated the protest. Numerous slogans were repeated throughout the countryside, including the famous "What do the forests bear? Soil, water and pure air."

Though "chipko" literally means "to cling," the movement was popularized as the movement of "treehuggers." The action was within the Gandhian tradition of nonviolent direct action, and it was directed at the state. Because of women's participation, this movement has also been considered a feminist movement. However, in a thorough historical examination of the movement, Guha argues that in many ways the Chipko Movement is neither an environmental movement nor a feminist movement. Instead, he contends, it is simply a peasant movement against state attempts to control village life; in this case, their means of survival (the environment). Regardless of how we label Chipko, its interpretation as an "environmental," "feminist," and "peasant" movement serves to further demonstrate how southern environmental movements represent a more integrated understanding of social justice and the relationship between social systems and ecosystems.

Chipko is just one of many cases from the vast continent of Asia. Many others could have been highlighted. For instance, J. Peter Brosius has written extensively about the struggles of the Penan (an indigenous group), who reside on the island of Borneo in Malaysia. Their efforts to preserve the Sarawak rain forest were transformed into an international campaign for indigenous rights. In Asia, damming rivers for hydroelectric power has been a controversial issue, especially where it has caused the displacement of people. In India, the Sardar Sarovar Dam on the Narmada River has drawn international attention, as has the damming of the Yangtze River by the Three Gorges Dam in China. As China continues its rapid development, we can expect to see growing problems related to industrial development, such as air and water pollution in cities and their associated environmental health problems.

Africa: The Ogoni Resistance in Nigeria

The Chipko Movement was essentially a battle between the people and the state. The Movement for the Survival of the Ogoni People (MOSOP) focused its attention on a transnational corporation (TNC): the Royal Dutch Shell

Corporation. However, this was not a simple people versus TNC battle; in this showdown, the state played a complicating role. The military government sided with Shell. Why was that? Simple. In Nigeria, 80% of the state's revenues come from oil revenues.

Shell had been drilling in the oil-rich regions of Nigeria since 1958. When they started, the people were promised "development." However, years and years passed and the promises were not delivered. In Ogoniland, half a million indigenous Ogoni lived in poverty and ecological devastation. Their villages were crossed by pipelines and surrounded by open gas flares. Oil spills polluted land and water, hurting fishing and farming. According to the *Ecologist* magazine, "From 1982 to 1992, 1.6 million gallons of oil were spilled from Shell's Nigerian fields in 27 separate incidents." The Ogoni were promised clean water, schools, and health care; but after over 30 years of drilling, they were much worse off. Both Shell and the Nigerian government benefited from the extraction within the Ogoni territories; the local Ogoni paid the costs.

MOSOP was founded in 1990 by author and outspoken Ogoni, Ken Saro-Wiwa and others, to oppose the environmental destruction created by Shell's oil production and because Shell did not compensate the Ogoni, as it said it would. MOSOP attempted to bring international attention to the mess that Shell had made on their lands. They demanded compensation and wanted Ogoni control of their own environment. MOSOP was not simply an environmental organization. It worked, and still works, for democracy, to protect the practices of the Ogoni, and for social and economic development. MOSOP called for an international boycott of Shell. Greenpeace and Amnesty International became involved in the case.

The military government did not like the problems that MOSOP was causing for Shell and for its revenues. The state used its power to quell resistance. There were violent conflicts in the region, with the police repressing demonstrations and torturing activists. In January 1993, the Year of Indigenous Peoples project brought 300,000 people to the region in protest. That same month Shell withdrew its staff from the area. The Nigerian government sent security forces to dispel dissent and make the area safe for Shell. They continued to torture, detain, and kill Ogoni activists.

In 1995, Ken Saro-Wiwa and eight other activists were arrested. The government claimed that they had murdered Ogoni leaders. International observers did not believe they committed these crimes and called the military tribunal that found them guilty "unjust." In the end, the Nigerian government hung Ken Saro-Wiwa and the eight activists. This brought more international attention to Nigeria and turned Ken Saro-Wiwa into a martyr (these events are chronicled in the documentary *Ken Saro-Wiwa: An African Martyr*).

Sadly, this case from Africa highlights the deadly course that fighting for environmental and human rights can take. The MOSOP case was exacerbated by the Nigerian government's entrenchment with Shell. The people wanted schools and hospitals. The TNC and state wanted profit. The state ruled by force to silence protest and ensure its revenues. Most believe that the Nigerian military and Shell worked hand-in-hand to ensure this. Though the state in Africa has a reputation for corruption, this rather blatant case of the state's reliance on growth for its own capital accumulation is simply the grossest manifestation of what happens when capital accumulation outweighs a state's need for political legitimacy. Also, lest we think that violent repression of environmental activists happens only somewhere else, I recommend a book by Andrew Rowell, *Green Backlash*, which highlights attacks against environmentalists fighting the growth coalition in many nations, including the United States. One example is Judy Bari, the Earth First! and labor activist whose car was bombed in 1990.

Latin America: The "Water War" in Cochabamba, Bolivia

The final case study is a more recent one. It came to a conclusion in 2000 and is heralded as a success for the people against the transnational giants of neoliberalism. I also discuss it because it illustrates an urban movement that intertwines environmentalism with radical democracy and I expect that as more and more of the Global South moves to urban areas, these areas will be the sites of future environmentalisms.

Cochabamba, population over 600,000, is the third largest city in Bolivia. Due to pressure from international financial institutions like the World Bank, the government of Bolivia began privatizing what had formerly been public resources. While the laws that started the trend dated back to the mid-1980s, the issue came to the fore in 1999/2000 when the state attempted to privatize water in Cochabamba. This was required by the International Development Bank as part of the conditions of a loan. At the time, half of Cochabambans were connected to a central water system and the rest used community water systems organized by neighborhood groups and nongovernmental organizations (NGOs). The government changed the laws so that the latter forms of water acquisition would be illegal. Instead, a company, Aguas del Tunari, a subsidiary of Bechtel, a TNC based in San Francisco, would run the water system.

The people protested. They saw access to water as a fundamental human right. The common good was being sold so that a corporation would benefit. People refused to pay. Neighborhoods were organized. Demonstrations were held. Oscar Olivera, a union organizer in the shoe factory, and others formed the Coordinadora (the Coalition in Defense of Water and Life). The Cochabambans were not willing to give up the right to decide how their natural resources would be used, bought, and sold. In the end, through multiple mass demonstrations, the people won. They retained the right to access their water. This also reinvigorated Bolivian conceptions of democracy. Olivera explains:

> What is happening more and more today is that *democracy is becoming confused with elections*. At one time democracy—at least to us—meant participation in the distribution of wealth; collective decision-making on issues that affect us all; and pressure and mobilization in order to influence state policies. Now the only acceptable meaning of "democracy" seems to be *competition in the electoral market*. (italics in original)

Today, Bolivia has its first ever indigenous president, Evo Morales, who was part of the "water war." Bolivians are considering how to deal with their gas—how they will choose to use this resource and distribute its benefits. This movement, like the others discussed, is not just an environmental movement; it is about social justice, the environment, and the nature of globalization.

Latin America is rich with such cases of resistance. For example, Lesson 4 discusses the U'wa resistance to Occidental drilling in their indigenous lands in Colombia. In another case of resistance, the indigenous people of Ecuador's Amazon region took Texaco to court in New York for environmental damage. The globalization of the economy makes it more and more likely that actors in the Global South will fight agents in the Global North. In this David and Goliath fight, Cochabamba shows us that David can sometimes win.

CONSEQUENCES OF GLOBALIZATION OF OTHER INSTITUTIONS ON THE ENVIRONMENT

From these examples, it might make sense to conclude simply that globalization (particularly economic) is bad for the environment. In the Bolivian and Nigerian cases, local populations responded to threats from TNCs that were aided in their quest for natural resources through national governments (growth coalitions). However, other aspects of globalization have been positive for the environment. For example, most organizations have been "greened" to some degree: states, international NGOs, intergovernmental organizations, and international financial institutions. In general, we are living in a historical era in which "the environment," as a concern, is taken seriously. This environmental moment does not show signs of ending anytime soon.

Take the following examples as evidence that the environment is an enduring concern. Over the last century, states around the globe have increasingly become more "green." A few ways this has been measured has been in the number of national environmental ministries, national laws requiring environmental impact statements, and the number of national parks worldwide. At the international level, the number of NGOs and international governmental organizations dedicated to the environment continues to grow, year after year. International financial institutions, such as the World Bank, have enacted environmental standards for their lending programs. United Nations (UN) conferences on the theme of the environment have created an international forum for environmentalism to be discussed globally. In 1972, the UN Conference on the Human Environment was held in Stockholm, Sweden. This was followed 20 years later by the United Nations Conference on Environment and Development (popularly termed the "Earth Summit") held in Rio de Janeiro, Brazil. In 2002, this was followed by the World Summit on Sustainable Development in Johannesburg, South Africa.

There is a complicated relationship, then, between southern environmentalism and globalization. For the environment, globalization is a double-edged sword. On the one hand, there is resistance to economic agents of globalization, represented by TNCs. On the other hand, people in the Global South are often aided by institutions that have been greened by globalization, such as international governmental organizations. In this sense, the idea of a "local" movement really does not make much sense. There are groups that are focused on specific geographical areas, but they are connected to the "global" world. Earlier, I mentioned the rubber tappers of Brazil and their struggle against local ranchers. This was a fight among Brazilians, for the most part. However, it drew on the "globalization of environmentalism." Let me illustrate.

The case of the rubber tappers is chronicled in at least two films, one a documentary and the second a dramatization (*The Killing of Chico Mendes* and *The Burning Season*). To make a long and very interesting story short and to the point, essentially what happened was that there was a conflict between rubber tappers and cattle ranchers in the Acre province of Brazil. Chico Mendes was a union organizer for the rubber tappers (*seringueros*). In the 1970s, he began organizing rubber tappers in Brazil against the cattle ranchers who were clearing lands for pasture. There were violent confrontations between the two groups. This local battle became international when the World Bank and the Inter-American Development Bank (IADB) approved loans to build a road which would essentially open up the land for more clearing. Locals were not consulted in the process. Mendes worked with NGOs in the United States, notably, the Environmental Defense Fund, and eventually came to Washington, D.C., to convince the U.S. Senate that it should not support the IADB loan. The Senate withdrew its support, the IADB suspended its loan payments, and the road was stopped. Mendes and the rubber tappers short-circuited the Brazilian government to halt its road development plans. Eventually, the government, the *seringueros,* and the ranchers came to an agreement to create an "extractive reserve," that is, an area like a national park that the rubber tappers can use to tap rubber yet maintain as a forest (this fits into a "sustainable development" scheme, as discussed in Lesson 19). This innovative idea joined the interests of local people's livelihoods with the larger "environmental" interests of the "global" environmental community. As with other southern campaigns, we should ask, were the rubber tappers really environmentalists or were they framing their interests creatively to best appeal to the shifts in international thinking regarding the environment? If they had framed this battle as one of human rights or workers' rights, it may not have succeeded in this time in history. Unfortunately, this story does not have a happy ending. Mendes went on to help other communities facing similar battles. In 1988, he was gunned down and killed by cattle ranchers. In some areas of Brazil, he is considered a hero. In 1989, the Brazilian government agreed to protect 50 million more acres in extractive reserves. This case shows how "local" environmental groups were able to gain support from global environmental actors to win (or at least make some gains) locally.

In my own work, I have looked at the consequences of transnational cooperation around conservation movements with a focus on Latin America.

In Ecuador, international NGOs have had a positive effect on conservation. Ecuadorian conservationists tell me that the Ecuadorian government has protected additional areas because of actions taken by transnational environmentalists and that, without these actors' interventions, the state of the Ecuadorian environment would be worse off. In the 1980s, international NGOs created a funding mechanism for conservation called a "debt-for-nature swap." In short, what happens is that conservation groups negotiate with banks on behalf of southern nations so that instead of states making their full loan payments, a fraction of their payment is channeled within their country to pay for conservation and to fund conservation organizations. A number of swaps took place in Ecuador, which kept funds in the country for environmental activities and were tremendously important for conservation. In Ecuador, international conservationists succeeded in helping to protect a large percentage of land. This was the up side. The down side was that it created competition among Ecuadorian environmental groups for resources that were distributed by agents from the Global North. The competition that started in the late 1980s persists in Ecuador today and hinders the cooperation of Ecuadorian conservationists. Again, the "globalization of environmentalism" has had some complicated outcomes.

RESISTANCE TO ECOLOGICAL IMPERIALISM

When international NGOs work in Ecuador to protect lands for the "good of humankind," what does this mean for locals? For sovereignty in Ecuador? Whose needs are being met? What if Japan wanted to buy a chunk of the Pacific Northwest to protect it? How would people in Oregon respond? Who controls the environment and decisions regarding its use?

Transnational environmentalism has been criticized by some from the South as a form of "ecoimperialism." This critique parallels criticisms of development: "Development" was intended to change "backward/traditional" societies into "modern" societies; however, much official development has led to greater inequality between the Global North and the Global South, and many nations that started out poor are now poorer and further in debt and have less control over their choices. The critique of transnational environmentalism is that organizations "helping" with environmental issues are creating the same problem. By becoming involved in the Global South, actors from the Global North are attempting to exert control over foreign environments. For example, Arturo Escobar looks at what he calls the "dominant biodiversity discourse" that comes from the West and suggests that there are multiple ways that other actors understand biodiversity. He believes that international conservation projects based on the Western, "global" conception of biodiversity (which he calls the "resource management dominant view") are just one way of understanding and that locals have alternative conceptions of the nature–culture relationship. In the current formulation, the "globalization of the environment" has opened doors to funding flows between North and South. This makes more and more possibilities for the North to "manage" the South.

Along this same line, Akhil Gupta argues "In contrast to the humanistic pronouncement of 'sharing one world,' made mostly by leaders and activists from the North, is the view of representatives of poor countries that the environment is a crucial arena where conflict between the haves and have-nots manifests itself." There have been specific instances of local groups in the Global South resisting the North's environmentalism. Back again to Ecuador, in 1995 angry fishermen from the Galapagos Islands took their machetes and rounded up researchers from the Charles Darwin Research Station. They held the researchers hostage for 4 days. Why? The government limited fishing in the area on the basis of the northern environmental scientists' assessment. The fishermen's access to fish, and thus their economic survival, was limited by northern recommendations to limit withdrawals. This conflict in the Galapagos, between the local economy and international environmental protection, has been ongoing. This conflict, like ones around sustainable development, highlights conflicts between the Global North and the Global South at this moment in history in which the North focuses on the environment at the expense of development and vice versa (see also Lesson 19).

CONCLUSION

Environmental movements in the Global South must attend to the concerns of those who are poor and want economic development and those who are poor and suffering from the negative effects of economic development. In many cases in the South, there have been outright attacks against environmentalism, as in the case of attacks and killings of activists working for the U'wa and Ogoni as well as Chico Mendes, since environmentalism often comes into conflict with states' interests. Economic globalization is one of the biggest foes of the environment in the Global South and an issue that is bigger than what most single-campaign organizations can focus on. When I ask environmentalists in Latin America if they've been successful, they respond "Yes, we've slowed environmental degradation, but as long as we continue on this economic development path, the environment is bound for destruction."

Grassroots environmentalism in the Global South is more akin to environmental justice struggles in North America than to the "professionalized" movement industry represented by mainstream groups like the Sierra Club and the Environmental Defense Fund. I end with a quote from Ramachandra Guha which again asks us to consider the relationship between "environmental" issues and "social issues":

> Commercial forestry, oil drilling, and large dams all damage the environment, but they also, and to their victims more painfully, constitute a threat to the rural livelihoods: by depriving tribals of fuelwood and small game, by destroying the crops of farmers, or by submerging wholesale the lands and homes of villagers who have the misfortune to be placed in their path. The opposition to these interventions is thus as much a defense of livelihood as an "environmental" movement in the narrow sense of the term.

SOURCES

Brechin, Steven R. and Willett Kempton. 1994. "Global Environmentalism: A Challenge to the Postmaterialism Thesis?" *Social Science Quarterly* 75:245–69.

Brosius, J. Peter. 2001. "Local Knowledge, Global Claims: On the Significance of Indigenous Ecologies in Sarawak, East Malaysia." Pp 125–57 in *Indigenous Traditions and Ecology*, edited by J. Grim and L. Sullivan. Cambridge, MA: Harvard University Press and Center for the Study of World Religions.

Collinson, Helen, ed. 1996. *Green Guerrillas: Environmental Conflicts and Initiatives in Latin America and the Caribbean*. London, UK: Latin American Bureau.

Escobar, Arturo. 1995. *Encountering Development: The Making and Unmaking of the Third World*. Princeton, NJ: Princeton University Press.

Escobar, Arturo. 1998. "Does Biodiversity Exist?" *Journal of Political Ecology* 5:54–6.

Frank, David John, Ann Hironaka, and Evan Schofer. 2000. "The Nation-State and the Natural Environment over the Twentieth Century." *American Sociological Review* 65:96–116.

Gedicks, Al. 1993. *The New Resource Wars: Native and Environmental Struggles Against Multinational Corporations*. Boston, MA: South End Press.

Gedicks, Al. 2001. *Resource Rebels: Native Challenges to Mining and Oil Corporations*. Boston, MA: South End Press.

Guha, Ramachandra. 1989. *The Unquiet Woods: Ecological Change and Peasant Resistance in the Himalaya*. Berkeley, CA: University of California Press.

Guha, Ramachandra. 2000. *Environmentalism: A Global History*. New York: Longman.

Gupta, Akhil. 1998. *Postcolonial Development: Agriculture in the Making of Modern India*. Durham, NC: Duke University Press.

Humphrey, Craig R., Tammy L. Lewis, and Frederick H. Buttel. 2002. *Environment, Energy, and Society: A New Synthesis*. Belmont, CA: Wadsworth/Thompson.

Lewis, Tammy L. 2000. "Transnational Conservation Movement Organizations: Shaping the Protected Area Systems of Less Developed Countries." *Mobilization* 5(1):105–23.

Olivera, Oscar, in collaboration with Tom Lewis. 2004. *¡Cochabamba! Water War in Bolivia*. Cambridge, MA: South End Press.

Rowell, Andrew. 1995. "Oil, Shell and Nigeria." *Ecologist* 25(6):210–13.

Rowell, Andrew. 1996. *Green Backlash: A Global Subversion of the Environmental Movement*. New York: Routledges.

Smith, Jackie. 1997. "Characteristics of the Modern Transnation Social Movement Sector." Pp. 42–58 in *Transnational Social Movements and Global Politics*, edited by Jackie Smith, Charles Chatfield, and Ron Pagnucco. Syracuse, NY: Syracuse University Press.

Taylor, Bron Raymond, ed. 1995. *Ecological Resistance Movements: The Global Emergence of Radical and Popular Environmentalism*. Albany, NY: State University of New York Press.

18

Indigenous Cultures:

Environmental Knowledge, Practice, and Rights

Bahram Tavakolian

AN ANTHROPOLOGICAL PERSPECTIVE

What can a cultural anthropologist contribute to a volume on environmental sociology? As an anthropologist I take it as a given that the greater the variety of cultures we know about, the greater our understanding of the human condition and the potentialities of human relationships with the natural environment. A comparative or cross-cultural approach is the essential element of most anthropological research and analysis. In addition, it appears that cross-cultural similarities and differences are not merely random in their distribution, nor can they be reduced to explanations dependent upon only one or two factors. While the "variables" that are most responsible for similarities and differences in the ways of life of different populations are a major part of anthropological concern, these variables also must be understood in their immediate cultural contexts. In the anthropological view, cultural institutions, such as power, economics, gender, family, and systems of beliefs and values, need to be examined *holistically,* or as part of a set of interconnections within a "whole" or total pattern. Indeed, such a contextual understanding is essential before institutions and their practical purposes and symbolic meanings can be accurately compared with seemingly similar institutions in other societies. Lacking a holistic understanding, we risk taking cultural practices and beliefs out of context and misinterpreting or mistranslating them across cultural lines, or as the late Clifford Geertz once observed, comparing apples and oranges.

To gain an awareness of the meanings that different populations attribute to the worlds around them, anthropologists attempt to learn about the subjective cultural knowledge that human beings develop within specific cultural settings. The diverse voices of multiple respondents both within and across cultural systems remind us of the considerable variation in what people think, know, believe, and practice. In addition, however, the anthropological researcher must somehow comprehend and communicate information about this diversity across cultural lines, in particular to students, readers, and other researchers in typically literate, urban, industrial, stratified, highly specialized, and "scientific" societies. An *intersubjective* approach, which seeks to integrate culturally specific knowledge with a more universal conceptual vocabulary and analytic framework, is therefore also a necessary component in the anthropological perspective.

In addition, neither are cultural similarities found only among peoples who inhabit similar environmental zones (e.g., desert, savanna, steppe, tropical forest, coastal maritime, tundra, and polar regions), nor are such zones conducive to the development of only a single form of cultural adaptation. Thus, the expansion of anthropological research throughout the past 150 years has demonstrated considerable reason to dispute a one-to-one relationship between environmental conditions and social or cultural characteristics. Instead, we must understand the processes through which unique cultures and the interconnected aspects of their ecologies, technologies, social institutions, and cultural beliefs and values have developed over time but not assume that only one or a few "causal factors" or "determinants" are the sole bases for explanation and interpretation. A *processual* approach has as its dual objectives the explanation of *diachronic* (over time) processes and changes as well as *synchronic* (same time) interpretations of how cultural institutions and behavioral practices are interconnected within the contemporary period.

It seems to me that a comparative, holistic, intersubjective, and processual, perspective raises a number of issues and concerns that are of interest to both anthropologists and sociologists and across a broad range of societies in the contemporary world. The most provocative question of all may be the one raised by Philippe Descola and Gisli Palsson when they ask "Does nature really exist?" To students in the West, answers to this question may seem obvious and irrelevant, if not silly; but an anthropological approach brings to mind a long list of ethnographic examples from every continent except Antarctica of peoples who reject a dualistic separation between nature and society. Emilio Moran echoes this view by pointing out that many indigenous peoples consider the dividing line between the person and the environment to be a very permeable one, such that the environment is part of the makeup of the person and, of course, people are part of the environment.

Through use of multiple cross-cultural examples, a comparative perspective encourages us to learn that among many peoples of the world "the environment" is not merely a setting or a complex of material circumstances and natural resources. It is also a set of ideas and practices that people have developed in relation to their natural, sociopolitical, and symbolic surroundings, including their connectedness—or "environmentality" to use Arun Agrawal's term—to other life forms as well as to topographic features and climatic conditions.

Environmental Ideas and Knowledge

Such a cross-cultural examination reveals considerable diversity both in how "nature" is conceptualized by different societies and in how the flora, fauna, terrain, and energy of the physical environment are utilized in practice. Thus, the commonsense view that we typically assume in the West, of nature as an entity with primarily objective, physical, and often marketable characteristics, is both historically and culturally unusual, rather than either universal or inevitable. Descola, Palsson, and their coauthors in *Nature and Society* use a comparative ecological approach to reveal substantial historical and cultural variation in how people in different societies imagine and adapt to the constraints and possibilities of their environments. A major aspect of this variation is the significance of symbols, beliefs, values, and meanings in shaping how nature is subjectively and morally known and treated. As mentioned, there is no one-to-one correlation between environmental characteristics and cultural patterns. Rather, culture is an autonomous factor in its relations with the natural environment and may be both constraining and enabling in its influences on patterns of environmental knowledge and adaptation. One attribute of most indigenous cultures is that they know and live within their environments in situations of considerable intimacy, as part of everyday life and routine activity rather than as a separable domain or condition of existence.

Does this mean that indigenous peoples and their cultures are uniformly "closer to nature" than other populations? Do they invariably demonstrate greater wisdom in their understanding of and response to the rest of nature? For that matter, is ideological oneness with nature the same as "kindly use" of the environment? Quite the contrary, according to Shepard Krech III: The stereotype of the "ecological Indian" is more likely to be an example of subtle racism than it is an ethnographic reality. Furthermore, what does "closer to nature" actually mean? We must be careful not only to avoid the racist notion that any population has "instinctual" feelings or senses that tie them to their surroundings but also to disassociate a monistic understanding of the unity and interconnectedness of people and nature from such contemporary Western philosophies and practices as veganism, not to mention the newly coined concept of "freeganism" by which, ideally, all consumption is freed from its impact on the need for further production, through use of food rescued from dumpsters, among other practices.

Instead, if we carefully conduct holistic examinations and look for the many linkages between material, structural, and ideational elements within diverse cultures, we will be better able to understand technological strategies, sociopolitical adaptations, and symbolic representations in relation to their own natural and social environments. In the anthropological view, indigenous forms of environmental knowledge and practice are not "poor substitutes" for Western culture and environmental relations. Rather, they must be understood and appreciated within their own geographical, historical, and cultural contexts. In addition, by identifying multiple roots of environmental practices, a holistic investigation of interconnections among cultural institutions can help ask further questions about "how" and "why"; that is, what are the processes by which cultural–environmental relationships have emerged and changed over time? As I will turn to in the next section of this discussion, some anthropologists, such as Marvin Harris and other "cultural materialists," prefer an analysis of ecological patterns that emphasizes material aspects of culture and their "shaping" influence upon other cultural characteristics. Other researchers have given their primary attention to ideational and symbolic characteristics of culture, and I will refer to them as "cultural idealists." Both theoretical approaches are feasible and informative, and in my view a more complete and accurate understanding of the relationships between culture and environmental knowledge and practice requires a synthesis of aspects of both frameworks.

ECOLOGICAL PROCESSES: MATERIAL ADAPTATIONS

By "material aspects of culture" I am referring to such factors as population size, growth rates, and distribution (demography); the forms of technology and production patterns that characterize different societies and communities; and the variety of floral and faunal species that people utilize within their territories. Some analysts, following the line of thought presented by the late Marvin Harris's "cultural materialism," consider these cultural elements to be the primary factors that shape or constrain ways that people are socially and politically organized, as well as the degrees and kinds of differences that exist among a society's members in access to resources, power, wealth, status, and control. Harris is well known for his analysis of such practices as food prohibitions, cannibalism, female infanticide, warfare, and male supremacy with respect to their ecological implications and the material advantages that accrue from them.

According to Eric Ross, one of Harris's students and followers, material conditions and adaptations also influence the kinds of ideas, symbols, and values that people use to explain their relations to nature and to one another. Thus, a food taboo may be based, for example, on the belief that certain animal species represent reincarnated ancestral spirits and should not be hunted or consumed. Among the Achuara Jivaro of eastern Peru, such ideational restrictions are placed on the hunting of relatively large and more difficult to locate deer, tapir, and capybara. The alternative emphasis on the acquisition of more abundant, more easily found, and more efficiently hunted species of small game also contributes to better use of the time, territory, and organization devoted to hunting activities.

ECOLOGICAL PROCESSES: CULTURAL MEANINGS

A different kind of interpretation of ecological processes that is favored by cultural idealists emphasizes ideational aspects of culture and proposes that people organize their relations to their environments through their subjective thoughts, symbols, images, ideas, beliefs, moral requirements, and rituals. Through his many years of research with the Achuar of the Upper Amazon in Ecuador, Philippe Descola has demonstrated that interspecies material, social, and ideational relations are not limited only to a few materially valuable or costly species, as is suggested by Ross. Rather, almost all plants and animals are considered to be comparable to persons and social groups in their qualities and affiliations. There is even a gendered breakdown in nature comparable to human social and economic patterns, such that game animals are the affines, or "in-laws," of men, who are the primary hunters in the population, while women are associated with cultivated plants as well as the labor of horticultural production.

The Achuar extend their own kinship system to the male woolly monkey, who—like the Achuar themselves—is supposed to breed only with his bilateral cross-cousin. In contrast, the hummingbird is not faithful to his mate(s) but constantly pursues new conquests. As Descola writes, "just as there are a few shameless individuals among the Achuar, so too certain species of animals evidence their asocial character by behaving like beasts." People as geographically disparate as Yonggom gardeners in Papua New Guinea and Koyukon hunters, trappers, and fishers in Alaska share a commonality with one another with respect to their symbolic unification of human and other species. They treat other animals as equivalent to human beings in their possession of agency, spiritual power, and the right to respectful and reciprocal treatment. Both populations seek to attract other species to lend themselves to being captured, killed, and consumed. They do not assume human domination or unrestricted rights of consumption. Rather, they maintain ties to other species that are dependent on both the continued survival of these species and on symbolic restrictions on the ways that these species become part of human utilization patterns.

A particularly interesting example of "indigenous analysis of social and environmental relations" is found in Stuart Kirsch's *Reverse Anthropology*, based upon his research with the Yonggom people of New Guinea. The Yonggom believe that both people and other animals are *agentic*—or have the ability to initiate action—and belong to a single speech community. Hence, animals are not merely hunted but must be verbally and ritually cajoled into allowing themselves to be hunted and captured. In return, human beings must practice reciprocal relations with other elements of their environments, including mines and rivers as well as plant and animal species, for unrequited reciprocity is the source of resentment, anger, danger, and misfortune. As far away as the Alaskan boreal forest, Koyukon hunters practice a similarly humble, respectful, and interagentic relationship with the species of fish, birds, and mammals they depend upon for their subsistence. Without an intersubjective understanding of these beliefs and ideas, it would be very difficult to interpret a variety of ecological practices among the Achuar or Yonggom or Koyukon, who clearly "know" and "see" their settings and surroundings differently than inhabitants of urban, industrial, and "constructed" environments.

But rather than suggesting that only one of these interpretive frameworks— cultural materialism or cultural idealism—is more correct or analytically valuable than the other, it is more fruitful for a holistic ecological analysis to think of both perspectives as telling us a significant and essential portion of the story and of each requiring the other to complete its own viewpoint. In this manner, the two perspectives and the cultural elements they focus upon may be seen to be involved in a dialectical, complementary, and synthetic relational process with one another, rather than a deterministic one in which ideas and practices, or meanings and adaptations, are artificially separated from one another.

INDIGENOUS ECOLOGICAL PRACTICE

Given the variety of ways in which nature is made "real" across different cultures, rather than having a universal conceptual identity and material value, a major aspect of anthropological concern is what relationship there is between cultural conceptualizations of the environment and the ways that potential resources of the environment are defined and utilized (see Lesson 2). As I have already mentioned, many peoples may attribute qualities of agency and responsibility and reciprocity to other species and are also more respectful of the "rights" of nonhuman species. Does this necessarily mean, however, that indigenous cultures—especially foragers, gardeners, and pastoralists—leave smaller "ecological footprints" by consuming and wasting less of the environment's bounty? Conversely, are societies whose members seek to control and dominate nature more likely to experience greater social inequalities and cyclical shortages in access to material resources, as well as greater frequency of competition and conflict over material access both within their own societies and with other societies? A related question is what happens to environmental relations and cultural patterns as a consequence of economic development, the penetration of market economies, and both economic globalization and so-called cultural modernization?

These are among the questions that I examine in the following section of this lesson as I lay out some ways in which such issues matter not only among indigenous peoples but for us all—other species included. To reiterate a point made in the beginning of this discussion, in no way do I mean to suggest that indigenous peoples represent a "type" of human being but only that, by and large, their smaller populations, more limited technologies, as well as self-imposed ideational restrictions on levels of consumption and waste contribute to more sustainable and resilient relations between human populations and other elements of nature.

In addition, it becomes obvious that the difficulties that indigenous peoples may have in adjusting to contemporary environments are not primarily ecological but often political. That is to say, indigenous peoples have typically been successful in adapting sustainably to their local environments for many generations, if not centuries and perhaps even millennia. That their lifestyles are under attack and increasingly jeopardized by contemporary conditions is typically not a consequence of their irrational or inefficient practices. Quite the contrary. They have been able to survive on relatively limited resources despite the political and economic pressures placed upon them by the expansions of other populations into their traditional territories. They are the "long-term success stories," according to John Bodley (1999), while Western institutions and practices are both relatively recent and environmentally suspect. The survival of indigenous peoples in marginal lands into the twenty-first century is a measure of their resiliency but also an indication of the much greater burden placed upon their former territories and resources by the presence of other populations and ways of life.

Finally, another aspect of anthropological concern I will address later in this lesson is a reminder that the cultural and technological successes of human populations have not immunized them from having to live within the constraints on energy and other resources found in the Earth's environment. As phrased by William Catton and Riley Dunlap, one of the obstacles to understanding ecological conditions and their impacts upon human populations is *human exemptionalism,* or the idea that modern human societies have somehow overcome the limits experienced by other species in needing to balance population with resource and energy restrictions and consumption with production. There are obvious limits to growth on our planet as a result of population growth, resource scarcity, and both pollution and environmental degradation. Indigenous peoples demonstrate an awareness of this aspect of the human condition in a way that we may hope will eventually become understood within all human populations.

THE CULTURAL ECOLOGY OF NOMADIC PASTORALISM

I first became attracted to ecological anthropology after reading an essay by Fredrik Barth, the well-known Norwegian anthropologist, entitled "Ecologic Relations of Ethnic Groups in Swat, North Pakistan." Barth conducted field research with Pashtuns (then still known by the British Indian designation of "Pathans"), Kohistanis, and Gujars in the Northwest Frontier Province of Pakistan; and in this essay he demonstrated the intricate ecological, economic, and political interrelationships between three ethnically, linguistically, and technologically distinct populations. Each group inhabited a different ecological microniche and carried out a different form of technoeconomic adaptation. In combination with one another, they optimized the relationships between human populations and the natural environment through unique and interdependent strategies of territorial location and land use.

In the district of Swat, Pashtuns represent the largest and most powerful group, owning most of the land and cultivating wheat, maize, and rice in irrigated fields. Through their greater numbers and complex, stratified, and specialized political structure, Pashtuns were able to take over most of the area from earlier populations of Kohistanis (or "mountain people"), who were forced into higher and agriculturally more marginal areas. To supplement their cultivation of maize and millet on narrow, terraced fields at higher altitudes, Kohistanis practice a mixed economy that depends equally upon the raising of sheep and goats through *transhumant* (across ecological zones) migrations between fields and pastures. Unlike the highly stratified Pashtuns who depend upon a double-cropping agricultural schedule and surplus production to support their more specialized population, Kohistanis are more subsistence-oriented in their production system and relatively more egalitarian in status and wealth relationships. They also refrain from many of the symbolic meanings that Pashtuns associate with patriarchy, power, honor, and bravery, all of which depend upon Pashtun patterns of stratification and a specialized division of labor, not only between women and men but also between families and men of higher and lower status.

Meanwhile, Gujars, the third and smallest ethnic group in the region, migrated into the area from more southerly regions. Gujars depend upon herding sheep, goats, cattle, and water buffalo; and they serve as clients of powerful, landowning Pashtuns. Gujars provide agricultural labor in exchange for pasture use and for surplus grain produced by Pashtuns. In addition, their herds provide meat, milk, and wool for Pashtuns; and livestock also help to fertilize the agricultural fields and prepare them for planting by eating stubble and breaking up the soil.

From Barth's description, the cultural–environmental relations in Swat seem to represent an almost ideal, intricate, symbiotic ecological pattern, in which three groups with diverse technologies, social structures, values, and meanings are able to coexist in a limited territorial space and to make efficient and productive use of its potential environmental resources. In Barth's interpretation, each ethnic group is characterized by unique adaptations to its own ecological microzone while also benefiting from the complementary activities and surplus production of other groups. While Barth did examine the political contexts of access to environmental resources, which was itself an important development in cultural–ecological analysis, he might have gone much further in investigating the ways that human–environmental relationships are outcomes not merely of local political processes but also of relations between localized populations and the nation-state.

More than a decade later, through field research in the late 1960s with nomads and farmers in southeastern Turkey, Daniel Bates developed a more powerful explanation of ecological mutualism—or the interdependence between different cultural groups within a single environmental location. Bates examined the combination of natural and political constraints that affect the technoeconomic and structural characteristics of social groups. He presented particularly valuable insights about the role of the state in controlling the power and territorial distribution of specific ethnic groups and their modes of technoeconomic activity. Historically, the role of the Turkish state has been to allow ethnically and linguistically "Turkish" Yörük sheep and goat herders to practice transhumant nomadism, while restricting the ability of Kurdish and Turkmen populations from doing the same. However, the Yörük themselves are constrained in their use of pasture and migration routes and schedules by state-based regulation of pasture ownership and legal intervention in instances of crop damage done by their herds on the cultivated fields of villagers. Through use of a holistic and processual per-spective, Bates was able to show that what would constitute optimal graz-ing and migration patterns in connection with Yörük social institutions and cultural values is mitigated by nonbioecological, state-based, and political aspects of environmental relationships. Despite many similarities with pas-toralist ecology in northwest Pakistan, the unique characteristics of Turkish history, politics, ethnicity, and availability of pasture and migratory routes all play a crucial part in the ecology of Yörük pastoralism.

Between 1976 and 1977, I had the opportunity to conduct field research with Pashtu-speaking Sheikhanzi pastoral nomads in western Afghanistan. My focus was on the material adaptations to their natural environment made by the Sheikhanzai, that is, their population size and herd composi-tion, migration routes and schedules, patterns of land and water owner-ship and use, and economic relations with sedentary populations and with markets and merchants. I also conducted a holistic investigation of how the latter technoeconomic factors were interconnected with patterns of mar-riage, family, coresidence relationships within camp groups, gender roles, social status, political leadership, religiosity, and cultural values. During the field research I became interested in the effects of national and international development projects on local populations, especially with respect to their neglect of the cultural factors involved with directed programs of economic and social change.

Like Barth, I was interested in how diverse and unrelated ethnic groups interacted within an economic nexus; but like Bates, I observed considerably more friction, competition, and animosity—fortunately, mostly verbal rather than physical—among rival, often ethnically distinct populations. Similar to Bates's analysis, a major contrast I found with Barth's interpretation of ecological symbiosis was the interventionist role of the state and the appar-ent favoritism that government officials showed for sedentary populations (though, oddly, in this instance, across ethnic lines, with Pashtu-speaking government officials often favoring non-Pashtun sedentary villagers who were more amenable than nomads to government schools, taxes, and military conscription). But a more significant factor than state-based politics alone that helped to explain the conflictual relations between ethnic groups in western Afghanistan was the basic ecological context of the resident populations and their discrepant, contradictory, and competitive—rather than mutualistic or symbiotic—patterns of resource utilization and coexistence.

For those of you unfamiliar with pastoralism, imagine a group of inter-related families—as many as 10,000 Sheikhanzai and upward of 2 million Pashtun nomads in Afghanistan—who have no permanent abode and are on migration almost half the year to take their sheep, goats, and camels to grassy pastures, water sources, and markets. The people live in black goat-hair tents throughout the year, and they establish social clusters of four or five camp groups, with 2–10 tents per camp, in their summer pasture areas in the highlands of central Afghanistan, while they live in much larger camps of 30–35 tent households throughout the winter months in the western desert plains near the Iranian border. You don't need to know all the details, but it is important to understand that people such as the Sheikhanzai must rely upon an intimate knowledge of climate, the availability of water, types of forage, adequacy of feeding and rest cycles for animals, risks from wolves, competition for pasture access with other populations, and market prospects for surplus animals and animal/dairy products.

The difficulty of maintaining such a form of social organization and ecological adaptation in the modern era is that lands that are utilized without legal title are increasingly vulnerable to pressures by state institutions and their concessionaires as well as by other social groups in the region. The Sheikhanzai found the migration routes and pastures they had used for multiple generations reduced in size each year as a result of the expansion in cultivation by villagers, almost always belonging to other ethnic and linguistic groups and therefore not subject to the forms of economic reciprocity and conflict resolution that tied the Sheikhanzai to one another and to other Pashtun nomads.

Another obstacle to their traditional ecological patterns that Sheikhanzai nomads began to experience (well before the communist revolution in Afghanistan in 1978 and the subsequent Soviet invasion and occupation from 1979 to 1989) was the increasing inroads made by capitalist market pressures on pasture land and herding activities. Beginning in 1974 the World Bank established a program for the "rationalization" of pastoralism that attempted to encourage the adoption of range management schemes comparable to those established in Kenya and Tanzania among Maasai and other pastoralist populations. Such programs involved coercive *sedentarization* (the requirement of permanent settlement) of nomadic pastoralists and an overall reduction of the pastoralist population, along with market-based controls on herd sizes and livestock prices. In addition, the World Bank venture focused upon the raising of sheep for slaughterhouses and export, not only excluding goat and camel raising from the program but also deemphasizing the dairy products and wool provided by both sheep herds and goat flocks. Most significantly, the program assumed private ownership of animals, and specifically ownership by males, whereas the traditional Sheikhanzai pattern emphasized household-based ownership and considerable de facto control in the hands of women over dairy and wool production and distribution of surplus goods.

What the World Bank failed to recognize was the considerable power and decision-making ability held by Sheikhanzai women, who owned household tents, belongings, and even livestock and pasture rights. The World Bank's assumption of universal patriarchy among pastoralists demonstrates the lack of the cross-cultural, contextual, and holistic perspective I emphasize throughout this lesson. In addition, the World Bank project did not attempt to understand how women's power is associated with their control of dairy production activities as well as their status and rights within kinship units that include their brothers, fathers, and frequently husbands (often patrilateral first cousins).

Ecologically the program would have been disastrous for pastoralism if it had been successful in defining the purposes of sheep and goat herding primarily in terms of market prices for sheep carcasses. For one thing, the basic character of seasonal migrations by Sheikhanzai and other nomads was misunderstood by the World Bank–funded development agents as a quaint holdover from earlier times and perhaps even a reflection of human "wanderlust." This simultaneously romantic and racist image of exotic nomads, supposedly free from the constraints of government, settlement, and civilization, ignores the climatic and floral patterns that affect water and pasture resources, not to mention the severe contrasts between the seasonal temperatures of deserts and mountain valleys. The spring and fall migrations of the Sheikhanzai and their herds allow them to escape the extremes of heat in the summer and cold in the winter and to utilize pastures throughout the year that can be replenished in subsequent seasons and years as grazing sites. A sedentary existence would have been harmful to the quality of pastureland and the health of livestock, not to mention disintegrating the social ties that exist between multiple camp groups and villages in sparsely populated and agriculturally marginal areas. And, of course, it would have eliminated the economic production roles of women and their corresponding power in aspects of decision making about migration, herd size, livestock distribution, and both marital and political relationships and replaced them with monopolies of power held by the highest-status and most profit-oriented male livestock owners.

Essentially, the World Bank program paid little heed to the natural constraints of the environment and the livestock raised there, and it gave even less consideration to the social and cultural meanings and purposes of pastoralism. For the Sheikhanzai, nomadic pastoralism is not merely a way of making a living but a way of life. As such, it contains values and meanings of autonomy and self-sufficiency that are not available to sedentary village populations regulated by state institutions and market conditions. The Sheikhanzai utilized livestock markets without being dependent upon them. They sold surplus animals and wool to urban merchants when they wanted to obtain cash but not as a necessity within their own economic system.

In contrast, the World Bank adopted a culturally specific view of range management from Australia, declared itself successful in previous implementation efforts in eastern and southern Africa, transported it to Afghanistan, and blamed Sheikhanzai cultural resistance and backwardness for the failure of the program. Furthermore, their goals were in line with central state efforts to bring recalcitrant populations such as the Sheikhanzai into line with state policies and controls (see Lesson 4). The World Bank failed in its own right by giving little or no attention to the cross-cultural, holistic, processual, and intersubjective goals I have emphasized in this lesson. Their project did not succeed in attracting Sheikhanzai participants, and had it done so it would have succeeded in destroying both pastoralism and the pastoral environment for generations to come.

ENVIRONMENTAL IMPERIALISM: WHY DOES IT MATTER, AND TO WHOM?

In a book whose title at first seemed only ironic and now appears tragically prescient, John Bodley's *Victims of Progress* offers "a critique of the ethnocidal national and international policies toward indigenous peoples." Today, we refer to *ethnocide*—or the forcible eradication of unique cultures—in terms of euphemisms such as "globalization," "market expansion," and "cultural homogenization." But the latter tendencies are part of the same long-term process as the empire building by colonial powers in the nineteenth century and the first half of the twentieth century. Today, the agents of change are generally transnational corporations and the impersonal "market" rather than nation-states and world empires, but the negative outcomes for indigenous peoples and cultures not only resemble earlier colonial experiences but occur at a much more rapid pace (see Lesson 19).

Despite warnings from Bodley, Arturo Escobar, Anna Tsing, and many others, state and commercial attempts to take over indigenously owned land and to eliminate indigenous environmental knowledge, social organization, and subsistence practices have continued to expand almost unabated but not without indigenous objection and resistance. While some programs have failed because of their own mistaken assumptions and expectations and have disappeared over time, such as the World Bank project in Afghanistan, others have so modified and destroyed land and traditional technologies that entire villages and regional populations have had no other recourse but massive emigration and recruitment as agricultural and sweat-shop labor. As Deborah Barndt carefully documents in her discussion of the North American trade in tomatoes, the "tangled routes" of globalized agriculture have provided considerable economic progress for agribusiness and often only destitution for emigrants as well as those left behind to serve as the labor for commercial agricultural enterprises.

In addition to the harm to indigenous peoples and their cultural practices, the cultural and political hegemony of Western capitalism has frequently succeeded in producing a sense of the environment, both in the West and abroad, as merely a source of marketable and consumable resources. The intrinsic value of the environment as a landscape full of historical memories, a region of scenic beauty, a zone of spiritual consequence, or a site of personal and social identity is of little consequence in the effort by commercial, political, and military interests to define the world's environments simply in terms of Western interests and objectives. *Environmental imperialism*, in my usage, is the appropriation of the homes, forests, agricultural lands and pastures, and riverine or coastal lands of indigenous peoples for foreign economic and political goals. Whether with respect to the pastures and livestock of the Sheikhanzai, the forests and rivers of the Yonggom, or the agricultural lands and activities of Mexican peasant farmers in Chiapas, environmental imperialism, often as a by-product of globalization within the contemporary world capitalist system, is as devastating to cultural autonomy, identity, and continuity as more direct forms of colonial annexation and political domination. In addition, the coercive cultural changes that accompany the cultural transformations experienced by indigenous peoples jeopardize the sustainable patterns of environmental knowledge and practice that have sustained these populations over extensive periods of time.

But does it have to end in this way for indigenous peoples? Is globalization not only politically and culturally "good" but also economically "necessary" and "inevitable"? Unfortunately, most people in the West, including ordinary citizens and not just politicians and corporate leaders, would agree with the latter sentiments. To most of us in the advanced, industrial capitalist societies, it seems only logical that the path that we have traveled for the past two centuries is desirable because of the "standard of living" that it has provided for us—at least some of us—and it would seem almost immoral not to share the benefits of our wisdom and success with other peoples. But, aside from the question of who should be empowered to make such decisions, are we even sure of their long-term impacts on ourselves, let alone on people who have never been offered the opportunity to engage in the process of debating the alternatives?

Not only does continued environmental imperialism demonstrate the arrogance of power—of human domination over other species of life, of the West over the rest, and of the haves over the have-nots even in Western industrial societies—but it also risks destroying the very "goose that laid the golden egg." In the posture that many in the West have adopted for themselves and that Catton and Dunlap have labeled the "human exemptionalism paradigm," there is the assumption of unlimited innovation, growth, progress, and technological fixes. Unfortunately, for both the paradigm and life on planet Earth, global environmental problems have proven resistant to easy technological solutions, including the "green revolution," and have been exacerbated by the destruction of physical and biotic environments and cultures that had previously demonstrated long-term stability and resilience in deserts, steppes, and rain forests throughout the world.

Many indigenous peoples have already been the "victims of progress," and it seems now that some of the perpetrators of so-called progressive efforts to bring about growth at any price, with concomitant expectations of consumption and heavier demands upon energy and natural resources, have begun to realize that existing processes of energy consumption, pollution, and land degradation cannot continue. While our standard of living has supposedly improved, at least on average, the quality of life with respect to social relations and both personal and spiritual satisfaction has declined. Also, for very practical and economically oriented reasons, even major energy corporations and manufacturers have begun to see the necessity for "green business." Increasing numbers of politicians, labor organizers, and citizens argue for supporting local businesses and becoming more concerned about local environments. With enough communities decrying "Not in my backyard," both in the West and in the world as a whole, there is hope—contrary to Larry Sanders's suggestion that less developed societies are "underpolluted"—that there will be no place for the exploiters and polluters to go. "Things fall apart. The center cannot hold," wrote W. B. Yeats. But perhaps that is a good thing, after all, if it contributes to a reinvigoration and spread of localized, agentic, and responsible environmental knowledge and practice as has been documented among the many remaining and remarkably resilient indigenous peoples of the contemporary world. Furthermore, the adoption of parallel forms of knowledge, practice, and a sense of reciprocal environmental rights and responsibility would be a valuable antidote to the patterns of consumption, environmental destruction, and waste that so often characterize environmental relations in the Western industrial world.

SOURCES

Agrawal, Arun. 2005. *Environmentality: Technologies of Government and the Making of Environmental Subjects*. Durham, NC: Duke University Press.

Barndt, Deborah. 2002. *Tangled Routes: Women, Work and Globalization on the Tomato Trail*. Lanham, MD: Rowman & Littlefield.

Barth, Fredrik. 1956. "Ecologic Relations of Ethnic Groups in Swat, North Pakistan." *American Anthropologist* 58 (6):1079–89.

Bates, Daniel G. 2005. *Human Adaptive Strategies: Ecology, Culture, and Politics*, 3rd ed. Boston, MA: Pearson.

Bodley, John H. 1999. *Victims of Progress*, 4th ed. Mountain View, CA: Mayfield.

Catton, William R., and Riley E. Dunlap. 1978. "Environmental Sociology: A New Paradigm." *American Sociologist* 13:41–49.

Descola, Philippe. 1994. *In the Society of Nature: A Native Ecology in Amazonia*. Cambridge, UK: Cambridge University Press.

Descola, Philippe, and Gisli Palsson, eds. 1996. *Nature and Society: Anthropological Perspectives*. London, UK: Routledge.

Dove, Michael. 2006. "Indigenous People and Environmental Politics." *Annual Review of Anthropology* 35:191–208.

Ellen, Roy, Peter Parkes, and Alan Bicker, eds. 2000. *Indigenous Environmental Knowledge and Its Transformations*. London, UK: Routledge.

Grim, John A., ed. 2001. *Indigenous Traditions and Ecology*. Cambridge, MA: Harvard University Press.

Harris, Marvin. 1979. *Cultural Materialism: The Struggle for a Science of Culture*. New York: Random House.

Kirsch, Stuart. 2006. *Reverse Anthropology: Indigenous Analysis of Social and Environmental Relations in New Guinea*. Stanford, CA: Stanford University Press.

Krech, Shepard III. 1999. *The Ecological Indian: Myth and History*. New York: W.W. Norton.

Moran, Emilio. 2006. *People and Nature: An Introduction to Human Ecological Relations*. Malden, MA: Blackwell Publishing.

Ross, Eric B. 1978. "Food Taboos, Diet and Hunting Strategy: The Adaptation to Animals in Amazon Cultural Ecology." *Current Anthropology* 19(1):1–36.

19

The Paradoxes of Sustainable Development
Focus on Ecotourism

Kenneth A. Gould
Tammy L. Lewis

WHAT IS SUSTAINABLE DEVELOPMENT?

When we ask our classes "What is sustainable development?" they usually respond, confidently, along the following lines: "It's development that doesn't deplete natural resources." Ok. We push this a bit. We follow with, "What is development?" They respond this time, pausing: "Making things better?" Ok. We press on. What should be sustained? The environment? The economy? Human welfare? What should be developed? Who should be developed? Is development growth? And so on. The answers become murkier, and what sounded so nice and neat at first begins to unravel upon deeper scrutiny.

The most commonly used definition of *sustainable development* is from a 1987 report by the World Commission on Environment and Development titled *Our Common Future*. In the report, the term is defined as "development that meets the needs of the present without compromising the ability of future generations to meet their own needs." The term gained popularity at the 1992 Earth Summit (officially titled the United Nations Conference on Environment and Development). At the Earth Summit, heads of state of 178 nations met to address both the "environment problem" and the "development problem." Tensions between the relative priorities of countries in the Global North and those in the Global South were a key feature of the discussions. Many southern nations viewed alleviation of the crushing poverty in the Global South and the growing economic inequalities between the Global North and Global South as central issues. In contrast, many northern nations viewed habitat protection (particularly rain forests) as central, with southern poverty secondary and North–South inequality largely peripheral. In that context, the concept of sustainable development was appealing since it presumed that economic growth and environmental protection could be reconciled. Northern and southern economies could grow, and biodiverse habitat could be saved. The priorities of both the Global North and the Global South could be addressed in a "win–win" scenario of improving material standards of living and greater environmental protection. Up until that point, many viewed "environment" and "development" as adversaries. Sustainable development opened up new avenues to discuss alternative ways to protect the environment and "develop" societies.

While the definition from *Our Common Future* has the greatest recognition, a range of definitions have emerged since that time. The common thread among these definitions is what *Our Common Future* identifies as the three main, but not equal, goals of sustainable development: (1) economic growth, (2) environmental protection, and (3) social equity. Different interest groups highlight different goals. For example, industrialists focus on economic concerns, environmentalists on environmental protection, and some governments and nongovernmental organizations, especially those concerned with poverty alleviation, on social equity.

The ideas embodied in the term "sustainable development" were not entirely new in 1987. The concept of sustainable development draws upon environmental discourses from the 1970s and 1980s, such as limits to growth, appropriate and intermediate technology, soft energy paths, and ecodevelopment. For instance, the limits to growth debate was centered on a study produced by the Club of Rome in 1972 titled *The Limits to Growth*. In short, the study presented evidence that severe biophysical constraints would impinge upon the economic growth and development of societies. It predicted ecological collapse if current growth trends continued in population, industry, and resource use. The study generated tremendous debate and critique about the quantity of remaining, exploitable resources and what could be accomplished with technology. In addition, the limits to growth idea became politically unpopular in the Global South. Governments from poorer nations did not believe it was fair that they limit their economic growth in order to protect the global environment for the benefit of wealthier countries in the Global North, which had already depleted substantial resources for the benefit of their own economic growth. This was a precursor to debates around issues such as the Kyoto Protocol and global warming (see Lesson 14). Sustainable development tried to bypass the idea of limits by postulating the possibility of growth within existing environmental constraints.

The change in a common understanding of the relationship between "environment" and "economic development" that has occurred from the 1970s to the present is remarkable. While the limits to growth debate asked whether environmental protection and continued economic growth are compatible, the mainstream sustainable development language of today assumes that the two are complementary and instead focuses on how sustainable development can be achieved. The sustainable development discourse does not assume that there are fixed limits; it is progrowth and protechnology. *Our Common Future* clearly states

> The concept of sustainable development does imply limits—not absolute limits but limitations imposed by the present state of technology and social organizations on environmental resources and by the ability of the biosphere to absorb the effects of human activities. But technology and social organization can both be managed and improved to make way for a new era of economic growth.

International aid agencies, such as the United States Agency for International Development (USAID), and international financial institutions, such as the World Bank, adopted the sustainable development framework for the design of their programs. The emergence of the concept also coincided with the reframing of problems as "global problems." No longer was it enough to "think globally, act locally." In an era of sustainable development and globalization, the new interpretation of environmental problems suggested that we must "think globally, act globally."

A range of critics have attacked sustainable development. A leading criticism points to the lack of clarity in the meaning of the term. What should be "sustained"? The economy? The environment? Human welfare? What should be "developed"? Does development mean productive growth, which is typically measured by growth of gross national product (GNP)? Does it refer to environmental growth, such as an increase in environmental resources? Does it refer to growth in human welfare, including better health and working conditions? Similarly, when the "sustainable development" definition refers to "needs," whose needs are these? The definition of "needs" in the Global South contrasts sharply with the concept of "needs" in the Global North, which tends to expand into consumer "wants." How much socioeconomic inequality is sustainable? What type of objective criteria could be constructed to determine if we are moving toward or away from sustainable development?

In part due to the lack of consensus of meaning, critics argue that being in favor of sustainable development comes commitment-free. Bruce Rich (former World Bank employee and Environmental Defense Fund senior attorney) notes "Sustainable development is a mother-and-apple-pie formulation that everyone can agree on; there are no reports of any politician or international bureaucrat proclaiming his or her support for unsustainable development." The "sustainability" tag is used to describe so many desirable institutions that it has lost meaning. Who could argue against sustainable cities? Sustainable agriculture? Sustainable tourism?

THREE PERSPECTIVES ON SUSTAINABLE DEVELOPMENT

Free-Market Environmentalism

Sustainable development ideology works in a culture in which there is an almost unquestioned belief that the operation of the free market is the best way to address social problems. It does not question the existing economic or political arrangements. Instead, it calls for individuals and corporations to take voluntary actions to improve the environment. William Sunderlin (1995) calls this approach to environmental problems "free-market environmentalism." From this perspective, one can be hopeful that individuals, through green consumerism and boycotting harmful products (voting with their dollars), can pressure producers to change environmentally harmful processes, thus changing corporate behavior. Proponents of this perspective believe that everyday citizens transform culture by putting their beliefs into actions through commitments to ideals such as "sustainable consumerism."

Many corporations also embrace the voluntary aspect of sustainable development. Business leaders making up the Business Council for Sustainable Development, including Germany's Volkswagen, Japan's Mitsubishi, Brazil's Aracruz Cellulose, and the United States' 3M, see themselves as part of the solution to the global environmental crisis. Corporations have created a number of voluntary agreements, such as the CERES principles. CERES stands for Coalition for Environmentally Responsible Economies. Corporate signers pledge to participate in voluntary environmental reporting and ongoing environmental improvements. Businesses such as American Airlines, Bethlehem Steel, General Motors, and Sunoco have signed the CERES principles. Associating with such voluntary principles provides positive public relations benefits, without requiring dramatic shifts in actual corporate behavior, and signals that there is little need for government intervention. Another example is the International Organization for Standardization's ISO 14000 framework. It is a way for industries to measure and evaluate their corporate environmental programs' movement toward sustainable business development.

An example of a corporation ostensibly attempting to follow sustainable development principles is 3M. Minnesota Mining and Manufacturing (3M) produces a number of consumer products, including tape. 3M was an early initiator of voluntary environmental actions through its Pollution Prevention Policy (3P). According to 3M's literature, "3P was established because it is more environmentally effective, technically sound and economical than conventional pollution standards." The company tries to prevent pollution at the source rather than by managing its wastes. They view this as a way to save treatment and disposal costs and reduce environmental impacts. 3M has four strategies to do this: product reformulation, process modification, equipment redesign, and recycling/reuse of waste. An example of 3P was the redesign of a resin spray booth that cost $45,000 to implement and saves $125,000 a year in resin incineration disposal. 3M has saved money, reduced pollutants, and won awards since implementing its strategies. Its stated goal is to move toward zero emissions. This is also the goal of "industrial ecology" and "ecological modernization."

Ecological modernization approaches (see Lesson 3) also fit into this line of reasoning. Theorists in this tradition argue that there is a material environmental problem that can be improved through industrial production that is cleaner, more efficient, and more profitable. Leading proponents of this theory Arthur Mol and Gert Spaargaren state "More production and consumption in economic terms (GNP, purchase power, employment) does not have to imply more environmental devastation (pollution, energy use, loss of biodiversity)." Simply put, they believe green capitalism-based sustainable development is possible.

Policy/Reformist Sustainable Development

A policy-oriented approach to sustainable development similarly does not question existing political or economic structures; instead, it looks to how policies can be reformed to integrate sustainable development. Like "free-market environmentalists," the policy-oriented environmentalists/developmentalists embrace the ideology of economic growth. For instance, even Al Gore, the most "environmental" president-elect, still advocated for "greening" within the bounds of economic growth. Political actors at all levels (local, state, national, and international) take a reformist approach to sustainable development. In other words, don't change the system; adapt it to meet the goals of environment, economy, and social equity. Often, an assumption of this approach is that poverty is linked to environmental degradation; thus, ending poverty through economic growth will also curb environmental damage. Policy actors are concerned with how sustainable development can be put into action, especially through existing "development" programs. Rather than reconstruct their entire way of doing things, these actors try to adapt sustainable development into themes of current programs.

For countries in the Global North, such as the United States, incorporating sustainable development into policies has led to refocusing the activities of their aid agencies (such as the USAID). USAID supports many environment and development projects in the Global South, such as pollution prevention programs in India and Chile, biodiversity protection in Madagascar and Peru, and the training of energy professionals in Ecuador and Nigeria. USAID believes that poverty can be eliminated by economic growth (rather than redistribution) and that environmental quality will then improve. Other nations in the Global North, such as Canada, have also incorporated sustainable development into their aid agencies. International financial institutions, such as the World Bank, have also "greened" their image, and their activities now have emphases on the environment. For example, the World Bank is partnered with the United Nations' Environment Program and the United Nations' Development Program to administer the global Environment Facility, which transfers funds to the Global South for environmental programs.

If sustainable development is a goal, there is also the question of how we know if we're getting closer. While GNP per capita tells us about economic growth, it doesn't really explain anything about the environment or equity or quality of life. A number of measures have been proposed to examine sustainable development. These include measures of a community's, institution's, or nation's "ecological footprint"; the sustainable national income (SNI); and the genuine progress indicator. As an example, let's look at the SNI. This measure is used to compare actual levels of economic activity with sustainable levels of activity. It takes into account additional costs, such as costs of environmental restoration, to traditional income statistics. While higher consumption levels lead to traditionally "better" economic statistics, the SNI accounts for the environment-degrading effects of consumption, such as the negative effects of vehicle use and eating vegetables out of season. Using this measure, many development schemes are accounted for as net losses rather than gains because the environmental costs are calculated as outweighing the economic benefits.

Critical Structural Approach to Sustainable Development

A structural approach to sustainable development offers a radical critique, examining the degree to which the mechanisms of sustainable development serve to reproduce global inequality. In particular, the critique focuses on three linkages between the Global North and the Global South: trade, aid, and debt. Critics of sustainable development argue that the unequal relationship between the Global North and the Global South during the post-World War II "developmentalist" period is reproduced in the sustainable development paradigm; thus, it is simply old wine in new bottles. In this view, the sustainable development concept emerged to avoid addressing difficult conflicts between the environment and economic growth, the Global North and Global South, the rich and poor; and unless those conflicts are addressed, neither long-term environmental protection nor poverty alleviation will be achieved. Such critics do not believe that sustainable development offers a real alternative to old practices that serve those in power at the expense of the "have-nots" and the environment. Instead, they see sustainable development as currently practiced as a ploy to co-opt demands for more effective efforts to protect the environment and address poverty and inequality.

Theorists writing in the critical structural tradition, such as Allan Schnaiberg and Kenneth Gould on the "treadmill of production," James O'Connor on the "second contradiction of capitalism," and John Bellamy Foster on "ecological Marxism," would disagree with the basic premise of sustainable development by arguing that it is within capitalist logic to maximize profit at the expense of the environment (see Lesson 3). Thus, any action, voluntary or not, that would limit profit making would be ultimately impossible for corporations to pursue as the need to remain competitive outstrips any desire to be better environmental citizens. Economic logic will always win over ecological and social logics as long as free markets dominate. They argue that limiting proenvironmental and proequity actions to those efforts that can also be profitable will be insufficient to reverse the trends toward environmental degradation and greater social inequality. From that perspective, the very logic of the global economy demands ever-increasing levels of ecological withdrawals and additions in order to sustain itself. The conclusion is that only dramatic changes to the structure of the global economy, the goals that drive it, and the distribution of what it produces (both goods and bads) could bring us to a socially and ecologically sustainable relationship between social systems and ecosystems.

Frederick Buttel argues a middle ground, taking us back to a policy perspective. He suggests that efficiency in the use of resources and in the minimization of waste could be a means for capitalists to reduce costs and increase profits and that this could be especially true if policies penalize resource destruction and pollution and reward more environmentally benign behaviors. However, he also questions whether capitalism can be sustainable, in the line of argumentation taken by theorists in the "treadmill of production" tradition.

While these competing theoretical frameworks provide us with lenses through which to view, analyze, and evaluate sustainable development as a concept, ultimately sustainable development can only protect environments (or fail to) as an actual enterprise. It is the real-world application of the concept that we must turn to in order to understand the difficulties, contradictions, and trade-offs that sustainable development paths present. To provide a look at real-world efforts to achieve sustainable development, we turn to the example of ecotourism. Ecotourism has been promoted as a means of simultaneously achieving economic growth and environmental protection, while alleviating rural poverty in the Global South. Ecotourism therefore offers us a good opportunity to explore the application of the sustainable development concept in action.

ECOTOURISM: A POTENTIAL MODEL FOR SUSTAINABLE DEVELOPMENT?

Ecotourism has been heralded as a model for sustainable development. International aid agencies, national governments, nongovernmental organizations, and indigenous groups have pushed ecotourism as a means to protect land and important biological diversity while at the same time providing long-term social and economic benefits through sustained resources use. Ecotourism and "wildlife tourism" have the potential to be big moneymakers. Tourism is one of the fastest-growing industries in the world according to the World Tourism Organization.

Like sustainable development, the concept of "ecotourism" is full of hidden conflicts and contradictions. Where ecotourism is promoted as a vehicle of sustainable development we find paradox. Just as sustainability has been employed in many different ways and to many different ends, so has ecotourism been used to label a wide variety of seemingly contradictory rural development forms. In some cases, ecotourism has been used to indicate a type of ecologically low-impact tourism development. But ecologically low-impact tourism could include touring New York City on $20 per day, which is an activity not commonly understood as ecotourism. In other cases, ecotourism has been used to refer to the touring of relatively intact natural ecosystems. However, this could include touring Amazonia on $1,000 per day, which could easily be a high-impact form of traditional luxury tourism. A more precise application of the ecotourism concept might apply to ecologically low-impact touring of relatively intact natural ecosystems, but that would include a remarkably small set of the phenomena to which the term has commonly been applied. Ecotourism is then a socially contested term used to define, legitimate, promote, and constrain a wide variety of nature-based tourism development schemes.

Perhaps we could gain greater clarity through reference to sustainable development, defining ecotourism as a form of nature-based tourism that contributes to sustainable rural development. The analysis of transnational ecotourism as a form of sustainable development is therefore a way for us to tease out the implications of the wide variety of applications of both the ecotourism and sustainability concepts and one which requires us to explore the connections between transnational processes, national development trajectories, regional political economies, and local efforts to provide a reliable economic base for rural communities as well as local control over decision making.

The remainder of this lesson explores ecotourism in Belize to illustrate the complexities of sustainable development. We examine Belize's ecotourism industry because it has taken a conscious effort to enact ecotourism. Between the 1970s and the 1990s, tourism was second only to sugar production as Belize's primary source of foreign exchange and its fastest-growing industry. As a result of ecotourism's importance, the government of Belize placed increased emphasis on environmental protection, making commitments to use tourism to protect rather than destroy the environment. Ecotourists visit rain forests, wetlands, coasts, and coral reefs to view both nature and archeological sites. Accommodations range from small rustic lodges built with local materials traditionally used by the Maya to luxury jungle resorts with pools, bars, private cabanas and landscaped gardens. What's the reality of ecotourism development in one small country? We briefly examine some of the paradoxes of ecotourism, which highlight that to achieve sustainable development—that is maximizing economic growth, social equity, and environmental protection—there are inevitably trade-offs between the three systems.

ECOTOURISM AND NATIONAL DEVELOPMENT IN BELIZE

One of the key impacts of globalization on the nation of Belize has been its rapid entrance into the transnational ecotourism market. The Belizean government has made a policy commitment to environmental stewardship to prevent the degradation of coral reefs, wetlands and rainforest, and in Patty Pattullo's terms, to utilize "tourism to protect the environment rather than destroy it and so contribute to sustainable development." However, such a government commitment may prove to be unsustainable in the face of growing transnational pressures to open its rich natural resource base to transnational corporations (TNCs) and to repay a mounting international debt. Belize's resources are attractive to tourists but also to TNCs as exportable raw materials. If ecotourism can't provide the income the country needs to support its citizens and pay its debts, resource exports will.

The social sustainability of Belize's nature tourism development trajectory will depend upon its ability to provide a reliable economic base that rural communities can depend on. The ecological sustainability of Belize's nature tourism path will depend upon its ability to offer sufficient economic incentive for the government and landowners to forego more ecologically destructive economic alternatives, as well as the willingness of those social actors to keep the scale and nature of tourism facilities within ecological limits.

RAIN FOREST TOURISM IN THE ORANGE WALK DISTRICT: CHAN CHICH LODGE

Belize's western rain forests are sparsely penetrated, inhabited, and developed. The Orange Walk District in northwest Belize is the center of the nation's sugar industry. In the far west of Orange Walk, cane fields give way to tropical forest, allowing for the development of nature tourism. Within a few kilometers of the Guatemalan border, the Chan Chich Lodge offers a unique luxury rain forest experience. Chan Chich is a private reserve owned by the nation's largest private landowner. He is a seventh-generation "white" Belizean and the wealthiest person in the nation. His initial plan for his Orange Walk estate was to clear the rain forest and develop the land as an enormous citrus grove. Part of his land was already in orange production when his expansion plans inspired a "save the rain forest" campaign. Widespread national outrage at the sale of the major part of his 700,000 acres (over 12% of the nation) to two Houston-based investors and Coca-Cola Foods for under US$9 per acre created major political obstacles to this agroexport scheme. Seizing ecological resistance as an opportunity, he embarked on an "ecotourism" initiative, developing part of his private rain forest for nature consumers, while selling off only a portion for agricultural development. His Chan Chich Lodge was featured on a Discovery Channel special soon after opening in 1989 and immediately became one of the premiere jungle lodges in the nation.

Chan Chich Lodge is the one of the most expensive rain forest tourism destinations in the country. It is located in dense jungle amid numerous unexcavated archeological sites. It is also located within what amounts to the private "nation within a nation" of the owner. Access to Chan Chich is through the owner's private airport, the second largest airport in Belize. The airport is located in the privately owned town of Gallon Jug, where tourists are met by luxury tour buses that take them to the lodge on a private paved road, which is one of the best roads in Belize. After crossing the private suspension bridge, tourists enter the ancient Mayan plaza, which now hosts the lodge building, pool, bar, hot tub, and 12 luxurious private cabanas amid carefully landscaped gardens. Chan Chich attracts wealthy northerners searching for a rain forest experience within a bubble of Western amenities. In addition to an extensive network of trails, the lodge offers horseback riding out of private stables, canoeing on the private Laguna Verde, air-conditioned bus tours of the owner's agroexport enterprise, and international cuisine provided by its American chef. The lodge is managed by an American expatriate couple, whose American expatriate relative serves as bartender. The rest of the staff is Belizean, drawn primarily from the sugarcane fields of the Orange Walk District. The lodge grounds are elaborately landscaped and require constant maintenance to keep the jungle from reclaiming the site. Belizean workers are endlessly on hand and knee, pulling weeds and trimming flowering plants.

The quality of the rain forest experience offered at Chan Chich is truly remarkable, with numerous species of rare fauna wandering through the plaza. A 10-minute walk into the jungle over Mayan ruins offers glimpses of the local wildlife for which most tourists come to the rain forest. The constant raking of the elaborately marked trail system by the Belizean staff provides relatively risk-free access to an ecosystem hosting numerous deadly snakes. Most of the amenities provided in the lodge and cabanas are purchased in Miami, and in-room water coolers offer the owner's own brand of bottled water. Electricity lines follow the private road from Gallon Jug, and most food supplies are brought in from outside of the estate. Roof thatching is from local materials, and the tropical hardwood for construction comes from the jungle clearing of the agroexport operation, cut at the owner's commercial sawmill.

In contrast to the multistory homes of the American expatriate senior staff, the Belizean tourism workers live with their families in two well-hidden compounds, one of which is immediately adjacent to the lodge's open-burn dump. The housing, electricity, and water are provided to the staff for free. As most regional employment outside of the estate is in the sugarcane fields that dominate the Orange Walk District economy, jobs at Chan Chich are quite attractive. Cane field work is long, hard, and dangerous; and agricultural workers earn roughly US$6 per day. In contrast, a Chan Chich waitress will earn US$10 for a 9-hour workday. While the bulk of employment is in kitchen staff and grounds maintenance, the three skilled guide jobs offer better wages and slightly more autonomy. But even for the guides the work is often unfulfilling. Ten-hour days, 6 days a week filled with raking miles of trails is boring work, with actual tour guiding offering brief moments of respite. There is substantial resentment of the American expatriate management and the impossibility of advancement beyond guide work. This is despite the fact that the local environmental knowledge of the guides is truly astounding. The Belizean workers are aggressively supervised by the vigilant Americans. The master–servant relationship between the "white" managers and mestizo and Mayan workers sets the tone for the deference that northern elites expect from local workers.

The long-abandoned town of Gallon Jug to which tourists arrive was rebuilt by the estate owner to serve his plantation operations and includes one of his three homes, which sits atop a landscaped hill overlooking the town. The remoteness of this frontier agroexport operation has produced a classic company town, where agricultural workers live in company housing, shop in the company store, and have no local alternative employment options. The nearest non-estate-owned town is over 30 miles away, so agricultural and tourism wages are immediately recirculated into the owner's private economy.

In terms of ecological protection, the lodge has served to provide fairly high returns to the private landowner from an intact rain forest. It has managed to keep the scale modest by keeping the cost to nature consumers high, thus limiting the clientele to the top of the global stratification system. However, the origins of the lodge and its primary role are not income generation but rather legitimation of the owner's status as a dominant economic actor in the nation. Providing a private nature preserve offers political cover for forest clearing development schemes. However, private preserves exist at the whim of the landowners and therefore offer no guarantee of long-term protection. Unless national protest can pressure the Belizean state to intervene, the land base of this preserve may be put to whatever use the landowner desires. The fact that the lodge is an adjunct to forest clearing agribusiness and represents the primary route of capital penetration into otherwise "pristine" rain forest indicates that, rather than providing sustainable development for rural populations, Chan Chich provides the primary source of local ecological disruption where little or no rural population previously existed in recent history. However, it does provide the only economic counterweight to more ecologically destructive agroexport and resource extraction schemes.

In terms of social sustainability, the relationship between American managers and Belizean staff is problematic. The enormous control leveraged on workers in this isolated jungle outpost, the impossibility of locally owned tourism development, and the limited opportunities for occupational advancement provide similar relations of production as seen in a traditional plantation economy. As the workers are brought in from the non-rain forest areas of the Orange Walk District to populate company towns, it is impossible to speak of sustaining indigenous rural communities. Local populations have no decision-making authority over local ecosystem uses. In addition, although Chan Chich does provide jobs for a number of families, the limited employment capacity of this single facility is inadequate to provide for a fully sustainable local economic base.

FOREST TOURISM IN "THE CAYO": MOUNTAIN PINE RIDGE AND FIVE SISTERS LODGE

The Cayo District is Belize's western mountain frontier, known for its dense jungle, rugged mountains, sparse population, and lack of economic development. Within "the Cayo," the Mountain Pine Ridge is an ecologically unique region. The state-designated Mountain Pine Ridge Preserve protects the largest expanse of pine savanna ecosystem in Belize (although not from the invasive pine beetle that has ravaged the forests in recent years). Entrance to the preserve is through a single dirt logging road with access controlled at a gated government checkpoint operated by the Forestry Department. Access into and within the Mountain Pine Ridge Preserve is by logging roads, and no additional transportation infrastructure has been constructed to facilitate tourism. Ecotourist access is facilitated by the infrastructure created for logging.

The forests of Mountain Pine Ridge have been selectively logged since the 1930s, and the state still sells logging concessions within the preserve (much like a national forest in the United States). The logging is an export-oriented operation, with unprocessed logs and lumber cut at small local saw-mills shipped to the United Kingdom, Japan, and the United States. Most of the logging operations are Belizean-owned. Although select logging allows for fairly rapid regrowth of the forest, the necessity of firebreaks, logging roads, and wet weather skidding produces significant erosion problems. The preserve includes spectacular wild rivers with numerous undeveloped falls, caverns, and mountain peaks. The elevation provides a mild climate, while the surrounding geography allows for quick access to tropical rain forest at lower elevations with some of the densest jungle in all of Belize.

Nature tourism facilities in the Pine Ridge rely on access to small and large parcels of state-owned land within the Cayo including Caracol (the largest Mayan archeological site in the world) and Chiquibul National Park (a premier expanse of ecologically rich jungle habitat). Daily tours to these and other state-owned natural wonders provide the primary attraction for tourists, and the fees for these guided day trips serve as a primary source of revenue for small local tourism operators and nature guides. The land within the preserve is a mix of private and public land as much of the private land was not nationalized at the time of "preserve" designation. Most of the private inholdings are foreign-owned, the majority of those landowners being Americans.

There are four major nature tourism lodges within the preserve. Three of these are foreign-owned and were built quickly with large initial capital investments. The Five Sisters Lodge is the only Belizean-owned major lodge within the preserve and has been built slowly over the years with comparatively meager capital investments. The lodge began with a mestizo and creole family's purchase of 10 acres of land in 1991 that included the Five Sisters Falls and the land immediately above it on the banks of Provisional Creek. The owner and his family began construction of a small lodge building and four cabanas from local materials traditionally used by the Mayan inhabitants of the region, including palm frond thatching for which the government collected royalties for extraction from the preserve. Five Sisters opened in 1995 and has been slowly expanded with reinvestment of profits generated from the initial four cabanas. Five Sisters has 12 cabanas and a lodge building that together can host as many as 40 guests in peak season.

In the early years of operation the lodge had no electricity and relied on propane tanks and kerosene lamps. Eventually, a small hydroelectric dam was constructed above the falls to provide a local renewable and independent power source. Food for the lodge is purchased in nearby San Ignacio. Fresh water is provided through rainwater collection tanks. "Gray water" is treated on site, and sewage is fed into an in-ground septic tank, which is pumped out and transferred to the district landfill. This family-owned lodge is the least expensive option for ecotourists within the 300 square mile preserve. Its 10-acre land base remains the smallest of the four private lodge inholdings.

In addition to family labor, the Five Sisters Lodge now employs as many as 25 people on-season and 19 people off-season. As the lodge is rarely full off-season, much of the May through October work is in maintenance and construction. The numerous lodges in the Cayo compete for trained personnel, keeping wages relatively high and demonstrating the economic advantage of competitive over monopolistic tourism development for rural populations. Compared to local logging and agricultural employment, tourism jobs at Five Sisters still provide poor wages but good benefits and security for those fortunate enough to be a part of the year-round staff. An experienced guide can make US$4,000 per year, which is considerably less than a successful family farm might earn in the region. However, many local residents prefer tourism work as it is viewed as more skilled and more rewarding and it provides the possibility of upward social mobility within the industry. Much of the Five Sisters staff has experienced upward mobility, with some moving from waiter positions through guide work to high-level managerial positions. Loggers earn more money, but the work is difficult, dangerous, and insecure. For year-round staff, off-season employment is rotated on a 1 week on, 1 week off basis, which keeps the staff employed year-round but only part time. This arrangement helps to mitigate the problem of seasonality in employment, which is a common obstacle to the social sustainability of ecotourism.

The lodge provides housing and food for its employees, as is the norm for remote tourist facilities. Most employees are from San Ignacio, the largest town nearest the preserve, and most of the wages are spent in San Ignacio, contributing to the local economy. A smaller share of the wages is spent in San Antonio, a small village just outside of the preserve entrance. Local lodge operators view logging as the primary threat to their nature tourism investments and pressed the government for greater restrictions on logging as the disruption of forest ecosystems, erosion, fires, siltation, and degradation of scenic views reduce the quality of the nature tourism experience. Their concern is that nature consumers may choose to avoid working landscapes in favor of wilderness areas as the global competition to attract rain forest tourists has largely become a war of authenticity between tropical nations. The irony here is that logging provided the transportation infrastructure that made nature tourism possible in the Mountain Pine Ridge, and now the local tourism industry which logging inadvertently facilitated has become the primary force opposing the continuation of the logging industry. If logging is displaced by tourism, tourism will have to expand in order to provide enough employment to sustain local populations. That expansion of nature tourism would in turn present ecological threats of its own.

The government of Belize, in league with nature tourism investors, would like to create an elaborate network of jungle lodges in the Cayo using the Mayan ruins as focal points for development (a model pioneered by Chan Chich Lodge) as part of a five-nation regional tourism initiative. Such a system of lodges and trails would penetrate remote parts of Mayan country in the least developed region of Belize. Nature tourism development would then emerge as the primary threat to undeveloped jungle ecosystems as well as the subsistence economy of the Maya who inhabit them. The extension of roads, funded by World Bank loans, into remote jungle areas to make nature tourism possible simultaneously makes agricultural and logging development feasible by putting them closer to potential export markets, thus encouraging forest clearing. Such a development would therefore require the state to confer protected park and preserve status upon additional parcels of jungle to protect its investment in nature tourism.

THE PARADOXES AND TRADE-OFFS OF ECOTOURISM

The specifics regarding the case of Belize allow us to highlight some of the inherent questions of both ecotourism and sustainable development and to highlight some of the questions that serious attempts at sustainable development must address. For instance, who benefits? Whose economic growth is maximized? Which social groups make decisions about development? Do locals benefit? Does the state? How are benefits distributed? What's protected? At what cost? Recall that sustainable development, and ecotourism as an example of it, attempts to maximize economic, social, and ecological systems. Can ecotourism, as a form of sustainable development, really provide for sustained economic growth, sustained social equity, and sustained environmental protection?

We begin by highlighting the economic system and examining local employment. The cases demonstrate conflicts regarding who gets the best jobs as well as trade-offs between more employment and less environmental protection.

One of the best jobs in Belizean ecotourism is tour guide. In Belize, the state has developed a system of certification and regulation of nature tourism guides. With the assistance of a loan from the Inter-American Development Bank, the state contracted with northern academic and private sector tourism consultants to design a system to guarantee the quality and ability of tour guides. Through the Belize Tourism Board, the state established a series of mandatory courses leading to legal certification of nature tourism guides. Tour guides are required to pay a license fee in order to be legally employed in the industry. The licenses are available only to those who have completed the required courses. A steep fine has been established for those found engaged in guide work without appropriate certification and licensing.

This program of tour guide standardization and control has a big impact on who remains engaged in guide work and who is likely to enter guide work in the future. A key limiting factor is literacy and access to formal education. Belize is a nation where five different languages are spoken. Those with limited English reading and writing skills are less likely to pursue the required formal course work and to pass those courses if they try. The program therefore excludes many guides with extensive local environmental knowledge in favor of those with solid literacy but perhaps little local knowledge. In the rain forests of western Belize, literacy rates are lower but knowledge of rain forest ecology is obviously higher. The value of that indigenous knowledge has been decreased, while the value of formal academic skills has been increased.

As the program has been implemented, fewer rain forest dwellers have been employed as guides at the same time that more formally trained guides from coastal Belize now explain rain forest ecology to nature consumers. If a goal of nature tourism as sustainable development is to provide a way for indigenous environmental knowledge to be parlayed into a source of livelihood for local populations, such changes in the structure of the nature guide industry move away from sustainable development.

The number of people employed and "economically sustained" through ecotourism is often in direct relationship to the amount of environmental degradation caused by the enterprise. In other words, in terms of the scale of specific ecotourism development schemes, smaller-scale operations often employ fewer people and have fewer negative environmental impacts. The experience of Chan Chich Lodge shows that relatively small-scale operations can increase their employment capacity by providing more tourist amenities (pools, gardens, stables, etc.), but each of these comes at greater ecological costs. The concept of scale therefore relates not only to the size of the facility in terms of the number tourists accommodated but also to the number of built amenities and the level of luxury in which each individual nature consumer is accommodated. Larger-scale operations are likely to provide more jobs, even though the increases are likely to be greatest at the lowest level of employment (waiters, maids, grounds maintenance workers) rather than the higher levels (chefs, managers, accountants, guides, bartenders). However, those increases in the number of tourists or levels of luxury in order to boost the social sustainability of the enterprise clearly decrease the ecological sustainability of the enterprise in terms of level of natural resource demands and waste production.

This process can be seen at Five Sisters Lodge in the Cayo, where expanding occupancy requires additional clearing of riverine slopes and the construction of additional amenities (a new bar at the base of Five Sisters Falls) reduces the undisturbed quality of the local environment. As facilities expand and resource inputs and waste outputs increase, gains on the social side of sustainability become trade-offs with the ecological side. Without a careful and conscious balance, ecotourism development begins the slide into traditional tourism development, where ecologically low-impact tourism is abandoned in favor of ecologically higher-impact tourism of decreasingly intact ecosystems. While these kinds of changes in the ecological impact of nature tourism may not threaten local environments to the extent that all but the most discriminating nature consumers abandon the destination, the changes do mean that such a rural development scheme can decreasingly be defined as sustainable. As ecotourism becomes traditional tourism in a natural setting, social sustainability may increase (in terms of jobs) but ecological sustainability is lost, except in the relativistic sense that such development may still be more environmentally protective than resource extraction and export agriculture. The problems of maintaining appropriate scale, keeping ecological impacts minimal, and providing sufficient local employment while effectively competing with other potential uses of local ecosystems, notably resource extraction, lead us to the next paradox of ecotourism.

What is sustained by ecotourism? How does the environment fare? What are the ecosystemic costs? There are numerous ways that the environmental system is affected by ecotourism.

Although the "eco" in ecotourism often implies that tourism may be ecologically benign, even low-impact tourism brings new sets of ecological withdrawals and additions to intact ecosystems. Low-impact is not no-impact, and even the most responsible ecotourism operators must recognize that nature would be less disturbed without their operations in remote and ecologically sensitive parts of the globe. Hence, ecotourism development in untouched and unthreatened ecosystems is, in and of itself, an ecologically disruptive force. Such unnecessary intrusions upon nature, however mild, may be justified on the grounds that the exposure of nature consumers to these natural treasures increases their awareness of and dedication to the urgent need for environmental protection. As a consciousness-raising tool, low-impact ecotourism may generate more general environmental protection than local environmental destruction. Nevertheless, at the local level, ecotourism does represent a primary, and perhaps the singular, ecological threat to "wild" nature in many parts of the world. That is, low-impact ecotourism connects ecosystems to the global economy. In areas with no human populations or hosting indigenous subsistence-oriented economies, this can only bring ecological and/or social threat.

As noted, infrastructure expansion is one of the most obvious ways that ecotourism disturbs the environmental system. Ecotourism needs roads, dwellings, toilets, etc. Local roads are necessary to take tourists to remote regions. Typically, ecotourism either follows existing roads, which were built for extractive industries, or requires that new roads be built. In the case of the Mountain Pine Ridge, ecotourism occurs alongside logging and access to ecotourism lodges is ironically facilitated by the extractive industry. Ecotourism generates value from sustaining resources in place (scenic ecosystems) rather than removing elements of the ecosystem and sending them to distant markets. Here, ecotourism competes with extraction for policy protection from the Belizean government. By following a logging path, the state can generate short-term revenue for itself, private capital investors, and local populations. The ecotourism path generates less revenue, though ideally over a longer period of time. States that need to increase immediate capital flows for debt repayment are unlikely to prioritize more sustainable tourism development over less sustainable extraction development. This means that international debt is likely to cause governments to prioritize less sustainable fast moneymaking schemes over more sustainable options. Private landowners may have similar fast-money priorities as well. Recall that Chan Chich was created only in response to public outrage that the land would be sold for export-oriented development.

When ecotourism emerges independently of extractive industries, new roads may need to be built. Here, ecotourism is aimed at bringing economic development to remote regions with intact ecosystems that have yet to be integrated into the global economy. Then, new transportation infrastructure becomes the first requirement of ecotourism development. Even if infrastructure is intended to facilitate ecologically low-impact tourism rather than traditional luxury tourism, the new roads (and airports) constructed by states, funded by international financial institutions (IFIs), and promoted by private investors will represent the primary vectors of capital penetration into intact ecosystems. Ecotourism then becomes the vehicle of environmental disruption in otherwise undisturbed ecosystems, making it more difficult to view ecotourism as environmentally protective. This new infrastructure will make other potentially less sustainable economic activities (such as logging, mining, or agriculture) viable in previously inaccessible locations.

Finally, who decides? Who controls the process? What is the social system in which decisions and processes are developed? In Belize, two groups play key important roles: ecotourists and the government.

The ecotourist plays a large role in who decides. Like the definition of ecotourism, the definition of what constitutes an ecotourist varies widely. Nature tourists run the gamut from those using extensively modified nature (ski slopes, golf courses, etc.) to those using relatively undisturbed nature (all-terrain vehicle enthusiasts, jet skiers, etc.). Ecologically low-impact nature tourists tend to prefer lower-impact activities (hiking, canoeing, etc.) in relatively undisturbed nature. For this subgroup of nature consumers, the extent of the negative environmental impact of their nature-consuming activities is largely dependent on their proximity to the nature tourism destination and the total cost of their activity. The greater the distance they must travel to access ecotourism and the more money they spend to engage in ecotourism, the greater their negative impact on the global environment. Most ecotourism locations in the Global South are dependent on transnational ecotourists. These long-distance ecotourists may have the greatest negative environmental impacts despite their intention of engaging in ecologically low-impact forms of touring intact ecosystems and the value that they place on environmental protection. Despite their environmental awareness and concern, their global ecotourism endeavors require enormous levels of ecological withdrawal and addition.

What are the origins of the capital ecotourists need to tour? The paradox is that this need is likely generated from ecologically destructive economic activities and investments in such activities. The surplus wealth that allows for the emergence of a group of relatively affluent northern ecotourists who can be globally mobile is largely generated from the destruction of other ecosystems in other places, where other local populations pay the environmental, health, and cultural costs of production. Thus, even low-impact, environmentally conscious nature consumers seek to experience and protect some ecosystems by indirectly destroying other ecosystems, unless they fund their leisure travel from ecologically sustainable enterprises and investments.

The analysis brings us back to the paradox of transportation but here at the global level. Transnational ecotourism requires vast expenditures of finite energy resources for inessential activities. Most transnational travel is fueled by high-altitude combustion of nonrenewable fossil fuels in jet aircraft. Any human activity that depends on the increased use of nonrenewable resources for a completely nonessential luxury activity accessible to only a small minority at the top of the world's wealth stratification pyramid can hardly be considered a form of sustainable development. Transnational ecotourism may promote relatively sustainable development in a specific ecologically threatened location but clearly cannot be considered ecologically sustainable as a global enterprise. If we accept the premise that air travel itself is a significant threat to sustainability in terms of ecological withdrawals (fossil fuel depletion) and ecological additions (greenhouse gases, ozone layer destruction), then the booming transnational tourism industry and even its ecologically conscious subindustry, ecotourism, represent more of a threat to, than a promise of, a more sustainable global development path. For the most part, low-impact ecotourism requires that nature consumers think globally but tour locally.

Where ecotourism utilizes public lands protected by the state in parks, preserves, and refuges, the sustainability of ecotourism is dependent upon national development policy and orientation. That orientation will determine the extent to which public lands are managed in ways that are compatible with ecotourism and long-term ecological protection. As long as the state is dependent on ecotourism, public lands will be managed in ways that allow for that, even where other economic enterprises are permitted. Where ecotourism primarily uses privately owned land, the survival of ecotourism is wholly dependent on the economic choices of private landowners. In general, national development trajectories are less subject to rapid reorientation than private investment decisions, which may respond more immediately to shorter-term market opportunities.

The primary threats to state development orientation in terms of environmental protection and long-term management of public lands that is consistent with ecotourism development are the transnationally generated pressures originating from the IFIs. Structural adjustment policies promote the opening of national resource pools for TNCs in the interest of rapid national revenue generation to facilitate debt repayment. Debt crises and consequent structural adjustment policies therefore make national governments more likely to respond like private landowners to opportunities for quick profit and less likely to prioritize long-term sustainable development goals. Free trade reduces the authority of nations to set their own development priorities and agendas and undermines environmental protection initiatives necessary to promote sustainable ecotourism development. Ecotourism based on private land is primarily threatened by more lucrative short-term profit opportunities (as in the case of Chan Chich). Ecotourism based on public lands in nations with a large economic stake in tourism revenues is primarily threatened by the pressures of the IFIs to convert sustainable public land uses to rapid liquidation as a condition of further loans, entrance into free-trade blocs, or loan interest payment plans. The IFIs thus encourage states to prioritize short-term gain over long-term social and ecological goals. The IFIs have encouraged Belize to increase investments in agroexport production and extraction as a means by which to "stabilize" the national economy. However, agricultural and natural resource exports are subject to wide annual fluctuations in world market prices and have not historically been a source of economic stability for southern nations. And agroexport and extraction are the primary threats to ecotourism development. Within the context of the global political economy, ecotourism based on utilization of public protected lands probably has a greater chance of long-term social and ecological sustainability.

Sustainable development must ultimately be rooted in the relationship between specific human populations and specific ecosystems located in specific places. However, the main socioeconomic and political forces determining the relationships between human populations and natural systems are transnational and distinctly placeless. The TNCs and IFIs that increasingly determine the trajectory of natural resource utilization often operate with little regard for the specificities of places or the communities that inhabit them. Theoretically, ecotourism development can be designed and implemented in ways that meet both the ecological and social requirements of sustainable development in specific places. However, such local development does not occur within a macrostructural vacuum. In Belize, the impacts of the global political economy can be seen from the broad state reorientation toward unsustainable agroexport expansion down to the restructuring and redistribution of ecotourism guide employment. Therefore, if we are serious about pursuing sustainable development, we need to fully consider what is necessary to create the sociopolitical space in which communities may chart a sustainable development course in any specific place.

CONCLUSION

As you've now seen in both the global-level conflicts between the Global North and the Global South at the United Nation Conference on Environment and Development and the national- and local-level paradoxes involved in establishing ecotourism-based development, determining the appropriate balance and acceptable trade-offs between meeting human social and economic needs and protecting the environment from which those needs must be met is complicated. It is also clear that natural science can offer us guidance toward sustainable development in terms of what impacts ecosystems can bear but can't offer us much direction in terms of determining how socioeconomic trade-offs could or should be negotiated. Environmental sociologists can provide analyses of what, how, and why various social needs, goals, and groups compete or coalesce around different ways of operationalizing the sustainable development concept.

The three broad theoretical approaches to sustainable development can each be applied to the specific case of Belizean ecotourism as sustainable development. From a free-market environmentalism perspective, ecotourism could be made more sustainable with the creation of zero-emissions, renewable energy–based global transportation systems. With full knowledge of the ecological impacts of extractive, agroexport, and ecotourism industries, consumers in the Global North can choose to boycott products that compete with ecotourism development and to frequent ecotourism enterprises that provide the greatest local social and ecological benefits. From a policy/ reformist perspective, governments can choose to place limits on the scale of ecotourism enterprises and the enterprises that compete with them. They can also designate and enforce protected status on fragile ecosystems and make policy commitments to more ecologically benign development paths. Globally, they can establish debt relief policies that reduce the pressure on indebted countries to sell off their natural resources for short-term liquidity. From a critical structural perspective, free markets could be subjugated to social and ecological priorities, barring private landowners from acting in ways that produce environmentally and socially destructive outcomes and requiring governments to respond to the needs of their populations rather than international investors. Redistributive policies could be used to alleviate poverty without economic growth, so the need for southern communities to organize their economies and ecosystems around the interests of wealthy northern ecotourists would be diminished.

Ultimately, truly ecologically and socially sustainable development can be achieved only by making some tough collective decisions about what will be sustained and for whom and how social and ecological costs and benefits will be distributed. Such collective decisions are political; therefore, sustainable development is political. While sustainable development as a concept may have emerged as an effort to make an end run around conflicts between the economy, the environment, and distribution, sustainable development as a genuine enterprise will likely require that those conflicts be addressed directly. And it is the resolution of those conflicts that will prove to be the truly difficult work.

SOURCES

Buttel, Frederick. 1998. "Some Observations on States, World Orders, and the Politics of Sustainability." *Organization and Environment*. 11(3): 261–86.

Gould, Kenneth A. 1999. "Tactical Tourism: A Comparative Analysis of Rainforest Tourism in Ecuador and Belize." *Organization and Environment* 12(3):245–62.

Humphrey, Craig R., Tammy L. Lewis, and Frederick H. Buttel. 2002. *Environment, Energy, and Society: A New Synthesis*. Belmont, CA: Wadsworth.

McMichael, Philip. 2000. *Development and Social Change: A Global Perspective*. Thousand Oaks, CA: Pine Forge Press.

Meadows, Donella H., Dennis L. Meadows, Jorgen Randers, and William Behrens III, 1972. *The Limits to Growth*. New York: Universe Books.

Mol, Arthur P. J., and Gert Spaargaren. 2000. "Ecological Modernisation Theory in Debate: A Review." *Environmental Politics* 9(1):17–49.

Pattullo, Patty. 1996. "Green Crime, Green Redemption: The Environment and Ecotourism in the Caribbean. Pp. 178–86 in *Green Guerrillas: Environmental Conflicts* and Initiatives in Latin America and the Caribbean, edited by Helen Collinson. Nottingham, UK: Latin America Bureau Russell Press.

Rudel, Thomas K., and Bruce Horowitz. 1993. Tropical Deforestation: Small Farmers and Land Clearing in the Ecuadorian Amazon. New York: Columbia University Press.

Sunderlin, William. 1995. "Managerialism and the Conceptual Limits of Sustainable Development." Society and Natural Resources 8:481–92.

Sutherland, Anne. 1998. The Making of Belize: Globalization in the Margins. Westport, CT: Bergin and Garvey.

University of Vermont, Ministry of Agriculture and Fisheries, and Inter-American Institute for Cooperation on Agriculture. 1998. Belize: Citrus Production and Marketing Systems Profile. Burlington, VT: University of Vermont.

World Commission on Environment and Development. 1987. Our Common Future. Oxford, UK: Oxford University Press.

20

Conclusion

Unanswered Questions and the Future of Environmental Sociology

Kenneth A. Gould
Tammy L. Lewis

Throughout the preceding 19 lessons in environmental sociology, some interlinking themes emerged that coincide with the four parts of the book:

1. Historically, sociologists have separated social and ecological systems; however, environmental sociologists have sought to reintegrate these systems both theoretically and empirically.

2. Environmental problems are the result of human social organization, and as such, their solutions are not simply technical but require changing human social organization.

3. The negative effects of environmental problems are not equally distributed; less socially powerful groups suffer more than others.

4. There are varied responses to environmental changes; those that attempt to alter human social organization have a tall task and face resistance. There is no single or simple answer to solving environmental problems.

The preceding lessons in this book presented you with a broad overview of the kinds of questions environmental sociologists ask and the kinds of analyses they construct. Clearly, this book could not present *all* of the questions that environmental sociologists have asked or *all* of the analyses they have constructed. But even if it could, it would still not include all of the questions that environmental sociologists *could* or *should* ask or all of the analyses they *could* or *should* construct. And we do not pretend to be able to envision and list all of those here. What we can do with the few pages that remain is to suggest some of the questions that we believe most need to be addressed by environmental sociologists in the near future and to suggest the kinds of analyses that we see as most pressing for environmental sociologists to construct.

THE CITIZEN QUESTION—NO EASY ANSWERS

Throughout many semesters of teaching environmental sociology, students have confronted each other and us with the following question: What should we do to solve environmental problems? The lessons in this collection demonstrate how environmental problems are created by social arrangements and how the features of those social arrangements shape our collective responses to (or failures to respond to) environmental problems.

What can be done to address environmental problems? What can we do? How do we create social change? At what level should change be directed? Do we need to work simultaneously at changing individuals' opinions and actions and institutions' organization and practices? Where do we start? How do we begin to create a sustainable world?

The analysis inevitably leads to questions of our goals. What do we want? What's the desired end? What alternatives are available? How do we get outside the box? As sociologists, we understand that what seems "natural" and taken for granted is socially constructed and, thus, socially changeable. We encourage our students to reconstruct and envision new social arrangements. Some of their constructions and ours are utopian. However, given that they now also understand that power relationships are part of what keeps environmental problems problematic, we also think about how we can make pragmatic steps toward these utopias. We can analyze various strategies. Should we form a green army that storms capitalist headquarters? Work to elect leaders who prioritize environmental and social issues? Join labor movements? Become teachers? Move to the woods?

In the book *The Logic of Sufficiency*, Thomas Princen poses the following set of questions:

> What if modern society put a priority on the material security of its citizens and the ecological integrity of its resource base? What if it took ecological constraint as a given, not a hindrance but a source of long-term economic security? How would it organize itself, structure its industry, shape its consumption?

How we proceed will depend on what we value. We ask our students to define "the good life," "development," what they want for the future. Despite being bombarded with media messages, advertisements, and a dominant social paradigm of "more is better," our students (and hopefully you, too) now question these basic social assumptions. A higher gross national product per capita is typically not part of student responses to questions about their vision of the future. We hope you are also thinking about quality of life, not just quantity of stuff.

It would be nice if we could close this book by offering you "50 simple things" you could do to bring the social system–ecosystem interaction into better balance. Of course, by now you are familiar enough with the sociological perspective on environmental problems to understand that we think the solutions neither are simple nor rest solely on the changed behavior of individuals. More important than changing individuals is changing the relationships among them.

While it is nice to think that changing social institutions and social processes in ways that are more protective of the environment will ultimately be good for everyone, the lessons that have preceded this one illustrate that in social change the distribution of social and environmental costs and benefits can be, and often is, quite uneven. How the costs and benefits of proenvironmental changes are distributed is likely to have a substantial impact on who supports those changes and who opposes them.

A SOCIOLOGICAL ENVIRONMENTAL IMAGINATION

In looking to solutions to environmental problems, C. Wright Mills' classic piece on "the sociological imagination" in the book by the same name and the chapter titled "The Promise" presents a still useful analysis. Mills differentiates between "personal troubles" and "public issues." Troubles are within the scope of the individual and may be addressed by private strategies. The nature of social organizations creates public issues, which in turn affects individuals. Public issues must be addressed by public strategies. Individuals can change their "selves" but alone cannot change those institutions that create public issues and, thus, affect their lives. Public issues must by addressed collectively.

Environmental problems are "public issues," and as such, their solutions cannot be found in individual behavioral changes alone. The solutions to environmental problems will be found in changing social institutions and processes. One thing that we hope the preceding lessons have made clear is that environmental problems are not simply the result of greedy corporate executives, ill-informed consumers, or careless workers, whose bad individual behavior can be adjusted with better environmental (and perhaps moral) education. While we agree that greed, consumption, and work all play a part in the imbalance between social systems and ecosystems, the problems stem from the way these behaviors are woven into our existing social structures, norms, and roles. From a sociological perspective, it makes little sense to try to "fix" individuals if the roles they play and the decisions they make in regard to the environment are largely generated externally, from the social order they participate in.

Changing that social order to address environmental problems will be one of the great collective public issue challenges of our era. How, then, shall we proceed?

BACK TO THE CLASSICS

We know that our productive system and the ecological system are linked: Increased production creates increased environmental additions and withdrawals that lead to environmental problems; these environmental problems restrict further production. In his classic 1980 book *The Environment: From Surplus to Scarcity*, Allan Schnaiberg terms the tension between productive expansion and ecological limits the "socioenvironmental dialectic." He asks how the tension between the two can be reconciled.

He identifies three ways the dialectic has been synthesized historically: (1) the economic synthesis, (2) the managed scarcity synthesis, and (3) the ecological synthesis. These come about by the choices of social-political actors engaged in the treadmill of production. For each of these syntheses, he considers what would happen with production, the environment, and social inequality (see Lesson 3).

The *economic synthesis* continues with production expansion and accelerates the treadmill of production. The result is increased additions and withdrawals, as well as increased inequality, in part due to the use of high-energy technology and the displacement of workers. Politically, a great effort is required to deal with social welfare issues. Schnaiberg argues that under this scenario the social future will play out as "the rich rob the poor."

The *managed scarcity* synthesis involves reducing or altering production to some extent to protect the environment, largely through mild forms of state intervention. Socially, the protection costs are unevenly distributed, with the poor taking most of the burden. This constitutes "business as usual," at least in the United States.

The third synthesis, the *ecological synthesis*, reconciles the social and the ecological systems by decreasing both production and inequality. Here, we use Schnaiberg's words:

> If the ecological synthesis could be achieved, it would be the most durable of the three. Production organization, once set around the biospheric capacities and flows, would require only small adjustments over time to maintain a sustained material production....No eternal social peace is guaranteed by such a synthesis, though. Changes over time in the social and political structure could lead to increased pressures for production expansion. Capital accumulation could grow within certain groups, leading to constituencies favoring either managed scarcity or economic synthesis....The ecological synthesis is the most difficult to anticipate because it represents a major departure from managed scarcity....The transition from managed scarcity to ecological synthesis is likely to be a long and painful one, if it does take place.

Powerful growth coalition and treadmill actors make this path socially and politically difficult.

How do we create changes? How do we move toward an ecological synthesis? How can we change production to change the ecological and social systems? Schnaiberg argues that it would be tough to do this industry by industry or through the whole economy without causing social problems. A possible route is through state intervention. Again, Schnaiberg's words:

> The task is a monumental technical and political one. We must first estimate a biospherically and geopolitically feasible, sustainable production level for the society. And then we must decide how to allocate the production options and the fruits of such production.

Schnaiberg lays out "a socio-environmental program" with seven elements designed to shift us away from high-energy, low-labor styles of production to low-capital, high-labor forms. For example, it calls for taxation of new fixed capital (to shift to low capital) and employment tax credits (to encourage labor intensity). These goals are reformist in that they can take place within our current political–economic system. However, it is likely that those who benefit from the current conditions will resist them.

Another alternative—socialist restructuring—has potential in that social welfare is treated seriously in socialist systems; however, historically, Schnaiberg argues, there is variability in regard to how socialist approaches have interacted with the environment. For example, the Soviet Union destroyed many ecosystems, while China, in the middle part of the twentieth century, used a Maoist strategy which "involved careful husbanding of resources and intensive use of labor." In other words, socialism, on its own, is not the answer to reaching an ecological synthesis.

In the end, Schnaiberg's analysis of the treadmill of production suggests that the most fruitful path forward is in the formation of coalitions between social groups. He concludes his book by arguing as follows:

> The treadmill of political capitalism was not built overnight, nor will it disappear in the short term. Sustained efforts at consciousness-raising, commitment to political conflict and the development of coordination between environmentalist and social equity movements may serve to take it apart, strut by strut.

Interestingly, another important thinker in environmental sociology, Frederick H. Buttel, arrives at a similar conclusion in laying out alternative environmental futures. In one of his last publications, Buttel assesses four basic mechanisms of environmental improvement: (1) environmental activism/movements, (2) state environmental regulation, (3) ecological modernization, and (4) international environmental governance. (He also assesses green consumerism but largely dismisses it as a major source of reform.) He is concerned with understanding which is the most promising way forward for a "more socially secure and environmentally friendly arrangement."

> When all is said and done, the pressures for an environmentally problematic business as usual [Schnaiberg's managed scarcity synthesis]...have become so strong that citizen environmental mobilization is now the ultimate guarantor that public responsibility is taken to ensure environmental protection.

He sees the environmental movement and activism as the foundation of reform. Fundamental to this are the new coalitions that have been formed between environmental organizations and other groups. Some of these include coalitions with the anti-corporate globalization movement, the labor movement, the sustainable agriculture movement, the consumer movement, the antibiotechnology movement, the genetic resources conservation movement, and the human rights movement.

In sum, both of these founding thinkers in environmental sociology come to the conclusion that there needs to be coalitions of social movement organizations that come together to work both for ecological rationality and social equity.

A FUTURE FOR ENVIRONMENTAL SOCIOLOGY?

Environmental sociology has sought to integrate the natural environment into sociological analysis. What environmental sociology needs to do now is to take that integration and extend it into all aspects of sociology as a whole. Environmental sociology has largely remained a subdiscipline unto itself. The result has been that little of the analysis of the interplay between social systems and ecosystems has been infused into the other subdisciplines of sociology. If environmental problems are going to be solved in ways which enhance the general well-being of people, the relationship between social systems and ecosystems has to be an important consideration in analyses of the nature of work and labor, social institutions, science and technology, social movements, cities and communities, etc. That is, the promise of environmental sociology to fully integrate the relationship between human society and the natural world into the ways in which we think about what society is and how our goals for society can be achieved has yet to be fully realized. The ultimate goal for environmental sociology ought to be that there will no longer be such a thing as "environmental" sociology. Instead, sociology, the study of society, will, by definition, be fully inclusive of the ways that societies are shaped by and reshape the natural world.

Within such an environmentalized sociology, the study of labor and work would, by definition, include consideration of the environmental health of workers, the ways in which labor participates (or fails to) in natural resource decisions, the impacts of the distribution of remuneration from labor on the natural world, and the ways in which workplaces and the organization of work enhance or degrade environmental quality. The same would largely be true of the sociological study of institutions, culture, race, gender, law, religion, etc. Environmental sociology will be successful when it becomes unthinkable to attempt to analyze aspects of social life without consideration of, or reference to, the natural world that, ultimately, provides the context in which social life happens. To be a sociologist would then require an environmental analytical lens as part of the larger sociological lens. Without the relationship between social systems and ecosystems in the equation, the sociological imagination is only partial and ultimately flawed. In the end, we agree with Catton and Dunlap's call for a New Ecological Paradigm in sociology (see Lesson 1).

LOOKING SOUTH

We find some hope for a more fully environmentalized vision of sociology in the scholars and scholarship of the Global South. As you read in Lesson 17, most southern environmental movements and activists do not view environmental problems and development problems separately but rather as a cohesive matrix of production and distribution issues. Such a southern view resonates with the approaches suggested by Allan Schnaiberg and Frederick

Buttel. Therefore, one path for the social organization of environmental sociologists we see as promising is greater intellectual exchange with scholars in the Global South.

As we noted in Lesson 1, because of the way that sociologists have organized themselves professionally, there has been only limited organized intellectual exchange between U.S.-based environmental sociologists and our colleagues in other countries. Recently, there has been a concerted effort to foster greater interaction between U.S. and European environmental sociologists, and those exchanges have invigorated the subfield. Given that most of the environment, and most of society, is encompassed in the geographic and social space often referred to as the "Global South" and that the tendency in the South is to take a more holistic view of environment and development, we believe that a concerted and sustained effort at fostering similar intellectual exchange between northern and southern environmental sociologists is crucial to the future of the subfield. In other words, environmental sociologists need to consciously organize to change their patterns of social relationships too.

TWENTY QUESTIONS IN ENVIRONMENTAL SOCIOLOGY

The 20 lessons in environmental sociology have hopefully opened your eyes to new ways of seeing human-environmental relationships and have raised new questions about these relationships. To conclude, we leave you with 20 *questions* in environmental sociology that we have compiled from the 15 other contributors to this volume. We hope that you will join us in looking for the answers.

1. Our understanding of the environment is socially constructed, yet the consequences for our actions on the environment are real. What are the key channels through which we receive information from the "real" environment?

2. How do we create incentives for investors to prioritize investment in workers over production technology? Is this possible?

3. Will access to more information from a wider variety of sources enable us to better understand the structural causes of environmental degradation?

4. Will a democratization of research and development decision making result in a more environmentally sound and socially just technological trajectory? What parallel or preceding social changes might have to occur to make proenvironmental and proequity outcomes of a democratic research and development process more likely?

5. What types of changes to the industrialized agricultural system can maintain adequate food supplies while decreasing environmental degradation and social inequality?

6. What types of environmental change are associated with human migration? What are the impacts of migration (forced or voluntary) on environments in the sending and receiving areas?

7. At what point can lowering the global birth rate counterbalance growing consumption?

8. How do the structured interests of the medical establishment militate against addressing environmental health? How could those interests be restructured?

9. People have an interest in protecting both their economic well-being as well as their health and the health of their environment. But how do they prioritize those interests when trade-offs are necessary? What role do organizations, such as businesses, unions, and environmental organizations, play in shaping individual perceptions and priorities?

10. Can capitalism be "greened" to be an environmentally friendly system?

11. In addition to environmental movements, there are a number of other social movements in the United States, such as the labor, civil rights, and feminist movements. Which elements of the environmental movement are likely to engage in alliances with these other movements and why?

12. In what ways can the broad understanding of environmental movements in the Global South filter their way "up" to the narrower environmental discourses of the Global North? How might this impact the actions of U.S. environmental movements?

13. How do societies address the environmental needs of communities when those needs conflict with those of national economies or the global environment?

14. How can we realistically move toward living within the constraints of the climate system, while also addressing the requirement that the poorer countries develop in order to meet their basic needs?

15. What is the relationship between neoliberal governance reform and environmental inequality? Can neoliberalism be resolved with social and ecological sustainability?

16. How might anti-imperialist and antiracist political struggles be linked to environmental sustainability?

17. If social inequality is at the root of the global ecological crisis, what does that suggest about the ways in which we typically think about environmental sustainability?

18. Can the overall quality of life for individuals, families, and communities be improved while reducing the aggregate negative impacts of society on the natural environment? If so, how?

19. The scientific establishment has to some degree been corrupted by the influences of corporations and the military (among other powerful

interests). To what extent is there potential for the sociological establishment to be corrupted by similar influences?

20. How can environmental sociologists communicate their structural understandings of the causes of environmental change to a broader public and to key decision makers so that they can make a difference?

SOURCES

Buttel, Frederick. 2003. "Environmental Sociology and the Explanation of Environmental Reform." *Organization & Environment* 16:306–44.

Catton, William R. and Riley E. Dunlap. 1978. "Environmental Sociology: A New Paradigm." *American Sociologist* 13:41–49.

Mills, C. Wright. 1959. *The Sociological Imagination*. New York: Grove Press.

Princen, Thomas. 2005. *The Logic of Sufficiency*. Cambridge, MA: MIT Press.

Schnaiberg, Allan. 1980. *The Environment: From Surplus to Scarcity*. New York: Oxford University Press.